Courage & Grace | Yoseph Komem

Producer & International Distributor
eBookPro Publishing
www.ebook-pro.com

Courage & Grace
Yoseph Komem

Copyright © 2019 Yoseph Komem

All rights reserved; No parts of this book may be reproduced or transmitted in any form or by any means, electronic or mechanical, including photocopying, recording, taping, or by any information retrieval system, without the permission, in writing, of the author.

Translated from the Hebrew by Ira Moskowitz

Contact: jkomem@bezeqint.net
ISBN 9781072140993

Most profound acknowledgement and love are granted to all persons, alive and of blessed memory, who contributed to this study by their worthy actions and by testimonies.

To strive, to seek, to find and not to yield
(Alfred, Lord Tennyson: Ulysses)

He has told you, O man, what is good; and what does the Lord require of you: but to do justice, and to love grace, and to walk humbly with your God.
(Micha 6:8)

Courage & Grace

*Turbulent Journeys from Darkness to Light
In the Years 1936-1950 and Beyond*

YOSEPH KOMEM

TRANSLATED FROM THE HEBREW BY
IRA MOSKOWITZ

Contents

Family Trees 10
Introduction by Gabriel Moked 13

PART ONE Courage and Grace 19
   A. Introduction to Testimony Early Years 21
   B. Yoseph's Memoir Prior to Liberation 35
   C. Testimonies 99

PART TWO Freedom and Commitment 121
   A. Yoseph's Memories - Testimony after Liberation 123
   B. Personal Reflection Through the Lens of Time 205

PART THREE Moshe – Strength in Silence 223
   Moshe – Strength in Silence 225

PART FOUR The Kalisz 'Underground' in Warsaw 333
   A. Actions Taken by Mietek Kolski and His Family to
   Confront the Terror 335
   B. Stasia 387

Family Members and Others Mentioned in the Book 399

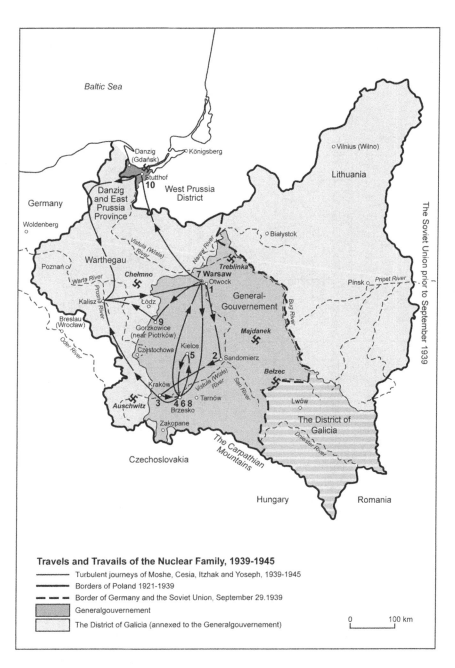

Travels and Travails of the Nuclear Family 1939-1945

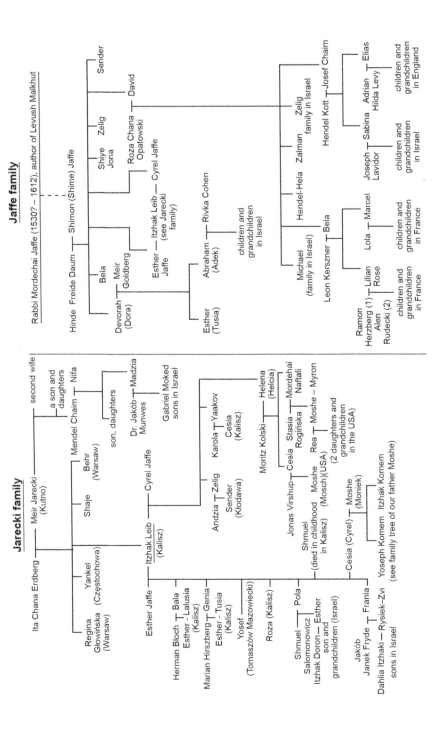

Family tree of Father Moshe

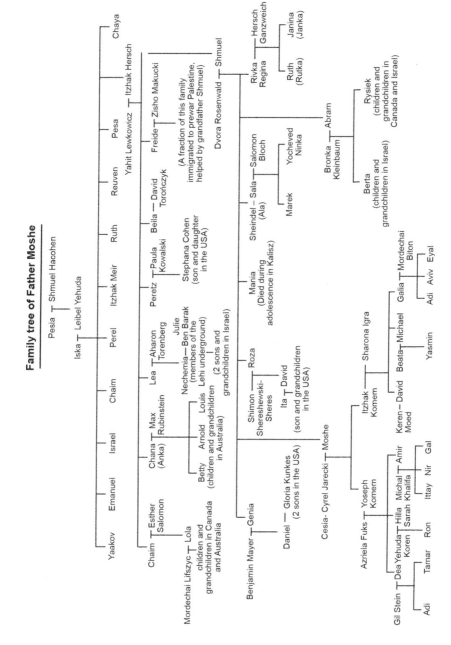

INTRODUCTION

By Gabriel Moked

The memories presented here of Yoseph Komem, which also draw from the testimony of his father and other members of the family including his brother Itzhak Komem, and which focus primarily on the Holocaust, constitute an amazing document – literary, historical, and biographical. First, there is something amazing in all of the memories from the Holocaust period. Despite all that has been told, and everything we know about that period and its horrors, we are astonished whenever we encounter the specific details of events that are unparalleled in human history – the creation of a human hell on earth (actually, an inhuman one), centered upon, or at least including, the planned murder of an entire people, of millions of its sons and daughters, by a mechanized bureaucratic-ideological leviathan in the form of the Third Reich. To be honest, this astonishment still grips even those who themselves were caught in the wheels of this machine of destruction, whether as adults or as children (and the writer of this introduction was one of the latter – a child in the midst of the Holocaust – who is still overwhelmed by those events).

However, the memories before us comprise a very special memoir even in this general amazing context of stories and records from the days of the Holocaust. Here it should be noted that the memories presented in this book don't focus on descriptions of the valley of death – the ghetto liquidations and the death camps. From this perspective, only the great Polish uprising of August 1944, its battles and many victims, and a number of other scenes describing the destruction and killing, stand out. The memories here primarily portray the broad scene of fleeing and hiding and rescuing under constant threat of death in the Polish "street," on the "Aryan side" (as it was called in that period). Thus, the power of these memories does not derive from descriptions of the genocide itself, as in testimonies, or in the books of K. Tzetnik, for example. Rather, it stems from that mix of everyday and nightmarish reality, of flashes of normal life and the hellish side of the Nazi regime, between the ghetto and escaping to the "Aryan side," and the struggle to survive within this reality.

And here, this book of memories-testimonies describes an extensive and colorful mosaic of daring, escape, hiding, and acts of valor, portraying – on a thin and cracked shell of the remnants of normality of semi-regular life on the "Aryan side" – the struggle for survival in the face of a giant mechanism driven by criminal ideology. And all this occurs on the rear lines of a war of Gog and Magog between the Wehrmacht and the Red Army. This visual mosaic is accompanied by a polyphony of voices. The mosaic of memories presented to the reader is not only a linear, multi-faceted, and fascinating description of the satanic kingdom that overran a cultured Europe and sprouted from within it. It is also a **polyphony** – a chorus of voices in a drama of tragedy and rescue.

On one side of this polyphony, we hear voices of memory about the rescue of the brothers Yoseph and Itzhak (or Marek and Marian, the Polish names they used). I will refer here to the written memories of both brothers, though Yoseph's memories are presented here in full, while only a summary of Itzhak's memories appears in the book. These are memories of children whose ages ranged from three to ten during the years 1939-1945. At first, they are in a good and safe situation, living with their family in their beautiful and ancient hometown of Kalisz. They were staying at a summer resort near Kalisz on September 1, 1939 as World War II broke out, and then in a villa outside of Warsaw. But later they live in ghettos, and after, with assumed Catholic identities, among Poles and in various hiding places until the savior arrives: the Russians, the Red Army, which ultimately crushes the Reich's giant machine of aggression and murder, and also saves the two children. The voices of the two brothers sometimes narrate separate life stories. Sometimes, however, their sound waves overlap and add an interferential dimension to the story line. At times, they begin recounting an incident in a single voice, only to diverge later into two different voices. And sometimes two streams of consciousness and two different sequences of memory reverberate, highlighting the differences in description and content. Thus, for example, the echoes of the memories of

Itzhak Komem, the older brother, tend more toward generalization, and satirical description, while the memories of Yoseph Komem, the younger brother, usually emphasize physical descriptions of the setting of the testimony, including the layout of buildings and detailed diagrams of hiding places. Among the particularly plastic and shocking "diagrams" of hiding places is a description of the top shelf where Itzhak is secreted as Gestapo agents discover the lower compartment of their hiding place and extract the other three hiders, including his younger brother, from just below Itzhak's feet.

Joining the voices of the two brothers in this polyphony is an important third voice – the father's. This third voice is absolutely amazing – first of all, from the perceptual, sensory, primary, and simple perspective. It is the voice of a deaf person, who lost his hearing due to an illness in early childhood, who conducts all of his contacts with his interlocutors in the rescue missions, in the heart of the murderous reality, by reading their lips. The deaf father, who co-owned a factory prior to the war, is an extraordinarily talented expert in sophisticated weaving and knitting machinery. With his blond looks, blue eyes and short, and solid frame, he perfectly fits the image of a Polish skilled worker. And as a deaf person who nonetheless speaks perfect Polish and German, his deafness, his expertise in lace curtains production and mechanics, and his ability to communicate in both languages, despite his deafness, draw the attention of those around him. His Polish and German interlocutors in the Nazi universe in which he lives during the war years rarely suspect that he is a Jew. He is accepted as a Polish expert craftsman who conducts conversations with the Germans in Kalisz in the Warthegau region annexed to Germany and in the streets of the Generalgouvernement[1] region of occupied Poland, from Warsaw to Kraków. He conducts himself in this way during those nightmarish years, with great daring, in the heart of the lion's den. This epopee or Odyssey of adventures – in the midst of the kingdom of Satan, with the deaf father managing to save the members of his nuclear family, who hide in different places in Poland (a unique mission that is almost unbelievable) – also features a salient economic dimension of saving the family's hidden treasures

---

1   The German occupation regime in Poland.

and using them for their very survival. One such prominent adventure involves risking his life to collect gold coins belonging to a third party, hidden in a basement, and in the woods. He also engages in smuggling special machine parts, worth a fortune – and in general, this "mechanical" and technological side is very evident in these memories, also against the backdrop of the murder of millions in factories of death. The father displays amazing resourcefulness throughout the years of the Nazi nightmare in finding various sources of livelihood, some of them among the Germans. The memories of the father, the sons, family members and others who recall him together create a legend of "the rescuer father." In any case, the memories of the father magnify and add a powerful dimension to the memories of the two brothers. The personality of the mother of the two brothers is also prominent in the memories. Yoseph lives with her for over a year on the "Aryan side," and at another point it is Itzhak's turn to be with their mother. Near the end of the war, she is taken, together with her sister and niece, from the prison camp of Warsaw Uprising refugees in Pruszków to the deadly Stutthof concentration camp, and miraculously survives, fleeing from the "death march" in the forest during the evacuation.

***

In addition to the Holocaust-era memories of Yoseph Komem, his brother, and the father of the family, there are also memories-testimonies of others, which amplify the polyphonic effect. Yoseph, his father, and his grandfather's written record also recount the family's history, dating back to the late nineteenth century in the provincial city of Kalisz. These introductory descriptions also illuminate the cataclysm in the context of Polish Jewry, adding a dimension of civic and traditional solidarity – primarily among the Jews, but also with a considerable number of Poles. The physical and emotional survival is also depicted in light of culture and tradition, in contrast to the Nazi barbarity.

The memories here conclude with the period of life after liberation: in the Polish People's Republic, in an orphanage in France, in a boarding school in England, and in the Land of Israel. It is noteworthy that this post-liberation period, which represents a return to a sort of normality, relieves the high tension of the memories and provides an interesting background for comparing extreme and less extreme situations. Undoubtedly, despite the emotional, and political pressures in Europe and in Palestine after 1945, everything seems open, and quite good actually, after the madness, and horror of the Third Reich. There is also the interesting story of how the two brothers, the father, the mother and the rest of the survivors in the family are received by the patriarchal national-religious grandfather, an owner of factories, and real estate, who had already immigrated to Palestine in the 1930s and avoided the Holocaust experience. At a time when pre-state Israel was beset by the tension of underground organizations, pioneering, and warfare, he repressed the great trauma of the Holocaust. For the Holocaust survivors, like the father, and the two brothers and their mother, he was a symbol of the healthy life that was not burned in the inferno.

***

This book of remembrances is also accompanied by the summarizing reflections of the brother Yoseph, voiced from a distance of sixty-five (!) years and more, which certainly gives a particular perspective to these things – if it is even possible to give them perspective. In my view, the most interesting aspects in reflexivity, in these summary thoughts, are on two levels: the Polish aspect in surviving the Holocaust and (less expectedly) the economic dimension of escaping the teeth of the Nazi machine of murder.

In all of these memories, the Poles don't fit the mold that is very accepted in Israel – that **all of them** are anti-Semites, ranging from the informers, and blackmailers, to the active participants in the Nazi acts of murder. It is true that these negative images of the Poles, hovering like a hawk over the remnants of a murdered minority, do appear in the memoir, but they certainly don't represent the majority. Alongside them are a considerable number of Poles who save Jews and are active in anti-Nazi underground activity. Many of these Poles (including the noble Kuropieska and Łoza-Nowak families) are humanists, secular, and Catholic. Among the Catholics, there is an interesting division between pathological anti-Semites and humanists who assist the Jews, and also between these, and others who refrain from participating in actions against the survivors. However, the further the public and political arc tends to the left (in the socialist and communist direction), the greater the willingness to help the destroyed Jewish minority. In any case, the two main families that help the Komems are Catholic-nationalists. But even from this perspective, the "record" of the left in Poland and in Europe as a whole is, without a doubt, incomparably superior to the "record" of the right. As a rule, the Polish intellectual class was relatively much less anti-Semitic than the peasants and residents of small towns. But here is also the place to note the heroism of the Polish underground in the fight against Nazi Germany.

The economic aspect, rather unexpected, is also very interesting, and figures prominently in this memoir. Not only did rescue throughout the period usually depend on the monetary resources of the people fleeing and hiding, but a financial shortfall meant almost immediate ruin; without a supply of funds, the rescued survivors could not have persevered. Thus, in these memories the economic struggle is very salient, precisely like the struggle to find a hiding place. This includes activities in the "black market" in the Generalgouvernement, selling off the family's hidden treasures and, in particular, the ability to improvise, and invent sources of employment that entail great risk. All of this continues even after financial assistance arrives from the Joint Distribution Committee, with support from the Polish Council to Aid Jews (Żegota); this assistance was a great help to the remnant that survived.

***

Finally, I must note a very specific facet that, in my view, must complement these memories, and is almost always present as a backdrop to them, but does not receive particular emphasis here. I am referring to the force that saved those of us who remained alive – the Soviet Union and the Red Army, under the brave, and determined leadership of Joseph Stalin and Marshall Zhukov – and the unbelievable heroism of the Russian people. Even the dark side of Stalinist dictatorship cannot efface the contribution of the Soviet Union to Hitler's defeat.

PART ONE
Courage and Grace

*Yoseph Komem's Memoir
and Complementary Testimonies*

A. INTRODUCTION TO TESTIMONY EARLY YEARS

1. Kalisz

Kalisz, where my parents were born, is an ancient city, which was part of western Poland at that time. It was built along the Prosna River, which often overflows its banks when the snows melt, and wide canals were dug long ago to protect from flooding and for transport. Remains of settlements dating from the Stone Age were discovered there, and the site is documented in the writings of the Roman historian Tacitus and of Ptolemy of Alexandria. It is described as being situated on the Amber Route leading from the Baltic Sea to the Adriatic Sea. A large and charming park is planted on the riverbanks. Kalisz was home to the oldest Jewish community in the Kingdom of Poland, and it was in Kalisz that the Prince of Greater Poland (*Wielkopolska*), Bolesław the Pious, granted the first charter of rights to Polish Jews in 1264. The charter was extended to the cities of the kingdom by Bolesław's grandson Casimir III the Great, and later was embodied in the freedoms of the Council of Four Lands. Kalisz featured a combination of urban charm, rich cultural life, and advanced industries. Prior to September 1939, there were about twenty-seven thousand Jews in Kalisz, accounting for about a third of the population. Over the generations, Jews left their mark on the city as minters of coins for kings in ancient times, as economic experts for princes, as innovative rabbis and, since the nineteenth century, as pioneers of advanced industries. Today there are no Jews in Kalisz or at least no one who identifies himself as such. The few Jewish visitors usually come as guests for a night or two.

2. Grandfather Shmuel Ben Itzhak Hersch

My grandfather Shmuel, the son of Itzhak Hersch and Yachit, wrote a fascinating memoir in his spare time in Israel. His writing project came to an end when he was seventy years old. The book begins, "I was born on Rosh Hodesh Iyar 5641 (1881) in the town of Działoszyn, Wieluń province,

Kalisz district, which is in the land of Poland." The story of his life with its many vicissitudes, hardships, success in commerce, and industry, as well as his principles, beliefs, and the conclusions he draws for the individual and the community is unfolded in detail over the course of hundreds of pages typed by his secretaries. He claimed that the book was linguistically edited, in part, by future Nobel Prize winner S. Y. Agnon himself, who was hired to do this, and who supposedly suggested that he Hebraize his last name to Shem-Shmuel. The slightly archaic Hebrew in these writings is much better than the Hebrew I heard him speak. Whether or not the descriptions of his success are absolutely true, they subtly suggest what seems to be a brilliant insightfulness. One might say he was pretentious and that he exaggerated, but the results of his activity in commerce and industry were indeed amazing. He candidly and unabashedly describes the stratagems he employed. His narrative also includes detailed references to the previous generation, his peers, the society, and the state in those days. However, he writes sparingly of his own children, mainly focusing on their compliance with his wishes.

His father, Itzhak Hersch, worked for his father-in-law as a peddler of scrap fabrics such as silk, tulle, and lace, which he purchased from local merchants. Later, as his business developed, he would also travel to buy scraps in Germany and Switzerland. The family grew and their poverty grew with it. My grandfather, Shmuel, the oldest son of young parents, was sent to the village of Sulmierzyce, a one-day journey by wagon from Działoszyn, to live, and study Torah and Talmud in the one-room apartment of his uncle, the *melamed* (teacher), where he shared a bed with one of the other youngsters studying there. Every day he would eat at the table of another generous poor person and would suffer from severe hunger and want, with only one kopek per week for his other expenses. Years later, he returned to his parents' home in Działoszyn, and studied Talmud with a tutor and later in the town's *beit midrash* (Jewish study hall). Based on his activity on behalf of his fellow students, he was appointed to a committee assigned to obtain and distribute food to the many penniless students who congregated in the *beit midrash*. In his spare moments, he also helped his maternal grandfather and learned the ins and outs of the trade in fabric scraps. My great-grandfather, Itzhak Hersch, was very successful in his business dealings and moved to the growing city of Łódz to expand his work as an importer and wholesaler. His family later joined him there. At age sixteen, my grandfather also joined the family in Łódz and worked in his father's business in the evenings after spending his days studying. He was quickly matched with a bride, engaged and married to my grandmother, Devorah, and at age eighteen was already sent to Germany to buy surplus fabrics and remnants for his father. On one of his purchasing trips, Shmuel stayed in the city of Basel, in Switzerland. While praying at a Jewish hotel, Rabbi Akiva Rabinowitz of Poltava, Russia invited him to join a delegation that was slated to meet two hours later with Dr. Herzl at his hotel and present ultra-Orthodox Jewry's complaints against the Zionist movement, prior to the convening of the Third Zionist Congress. My grandfather, who was then just nineteen, accepted the invitation. He was introduced to Herzl and spoke on behalf of the ultra-Orthodox youth of Russian Poland. The group later met with David Wolffsohn and participated in the three days of the congress as observers.

My grandfather decided to go into the scraps business on his own and even began to compete with his father in this field by importing goods to meet the growing demand in Łódz as the city continued to develop. According to his book, he received conditional permission to compete with his own father from the *Gur Rebbe*. My grandfather's father, Itzhak Hersch, relocated to London, initially by himself, in pursuit of livelihood and he was successful. He later (1907) returned as an importer-manufacturer with his wife, and built a modern lace factory in Kalisz, the first to run on electric power.Shmuel, my grandfather, also excelled in business. In the days of the 1905 revolution in Russia, he had already fulfilled his ambition of becoming a manufacturer by purchasing two lace factories in Kalisz. By 1910, he was also the owner and manager of a large, modern tulle factory he built from scratch (the likes of which could only be found in Moscow and Warsaw), and a modern factory for tulle embroidery, which he purchased from receivership. He then needed to train a cadre of workers for these industries in the city.

The outbreak of World War I turned everything upside down. Kalisz, a provincial town in the western part of the region annexed to Russia during the partition of Poland, was conquered, burned and mostly destroyed by the German Army, and the region changed hands. In the wake of the killing and terror by the German Army, many of its residents abandoned Kalisz. My grandfather Shmuel's family, including five children, fled on foot to the town of Turek to wait out the war. The family's property and merchandise in the factories were plundered. My grandfather was quick to get back on his feet: He took advantage of some old and new connections, and obtained licenses official and otherwise for travel and trade. He, along with my grandmother, traveled between Germany, Austria and the occupied territories in Poland, bringing food, and goods in wholesale quantities to places that severely lacked them, sometimes filling railcars, and sometimes in wagons. He would take financial and personal risks, even endangering his life, including money-changing deals. The situation that developed as the Great War continued the birth pangs of an independent Poland, whose occupied parts united during a tumultuous transition period, and the war of independent Poland against Soviet Russia was very good for the complex deals he orchestrated, which spanned periods of instability, borders, and dangerous front lines. By the time the situation and the currency in Poland stabilized, my grandfather was invested as a principal partner in two large flour mills: one in Kalisz and the other in the Danzig Corridor, together with Jewish partners. He also remained the owner of the tulle factories and land in Kalisz, and became a partner in his father's tulle factory in the city. He claims that he always closed his deals in cash, but only after carefully calculating the promised flow of income from production and commerce. This was in contrast to most of the Jewish industrialists and merchants, who became accustomed to relying on credit, and even usury. Later, he sold some of his properties and used his capital to build "Samuel F., The First Factory in Kalisz for Tulle, Curtains, and Lace, Ltd.," on 6 Fabryczna (Industry) Street. The company's logo was a red drawing of the earth, displaying the continents of the Old World and Australia. The factory was the most modern and important one of its type in Poland at the time, centered around six English machines for knitting lace curtains and lace, which produced high-quality merchandise, and handsome profits.

At the end of the 1920s, as he witnessed the global economic crisis that reached as far as Germany, bringing it to the brink of social upheaval, my grandfather decided to make a dramatic change in his life: to realize his dream of emigrating to the Land of Israel. At the end of an exhausting journey, he landed at the port of Haifa on the eve of the *Sukkot* holiday in 1931, and began to explore the country and its possibilities. The sights and the experience of praying beside the Western Wall and in Jerusalem synagogues are described with elation, leading to his decision which he announced to Rabbi A. I. Hacohen Kook to promptly come and settle in burgeoning Tel Aviv. Shmuel purchased and registered in his name two plots of land at 59 and 60 Rothschild Boulevard. Initial construction had already begun on two homes on this land, and he ordered the construction to continue in his absence. When he returned to Kalisz, he divided the positions in the factory among his two sons Abraham (Abram) and Moshe, and his two sons-in-law Salomon Bloch, husband of Sheindel-Shlomit (Ala), and Hersch Ganzweich, husband of Rivka-Regina. My parents married on January 15, 1933, and received my father's parents' apartment, which was part of the factory complex. Shmuel and Devorah and their unmarried daughters, Roza, and Genia, bid farewell to the family, the workers, and their acquaintances at a party held at the Kalisz train station, which concluded with the singing of *Hatikva*. They arrived in the Land of Israel (Mandatory Palestine at the time) after the *Purim* holiday in 1933. The financial control and management of the factory remained in Shmuel's hands via "remote control", through trustees, and in particular through Mr. Weiss, the accountant. Many German Jews sailed on their ship as tourists coming to explore the possibility of emigration after the recent takeover by the Nazi movement, led by Adolf Hitler. That same year, Shmuel bought an orchard of about twelve acres near Bnei Brak and started to build his two additional homes at 109 and 111 Rothschild Boulevard (in the Bauhaus style, designed by the architects Shlomo Gepstein and Pinchas Huett, respectively). Disagreements arose among the brothers and brothers-in-law, and especially between all of them and Shmuel, who practiced a policy of divide and conquer. My grandfather wrote that he wanted to force all of his children to invest their profits in Palestine prior to their imminent emigration. The children, all endowed with impressive abilities of their own, preferred to act independently in the field of business that opened before them, to develop, and invest in the factory and in other property. In late 1935, a serious fire broke out in the curtain factory, collapsing the building, and destroying most of the machines. My grandfather quickly arrived and spent a few months helping to restore the factory. Another building was added, and additional machines and parts were ordered from England. The work was done at a feverish pace, including the pouring of concrete foundations in freezing winter conditions. Years later, my father Moshe told me proudly and nostalgically about the period of rebuilding, which gave him an opportunity to express his technical aptitude and initiative.

3. Moshe

Our father, Moshe (Moniek), is the only one of his children to whom our grandfather devotes a chapter in his autobiographical manuscript. Apparently, in families of those times, with the many births, illnesses, and serious concerns about livelihood, fathers maintained a distant attitude toward their children. This was especially true in regard to my grandfather, who was occupied with business and travel, and who was extremely self-centered. Moshe's childhood and adolescence are described here in my grandfather's rather terse language, with quotes and corrections in parentheses; the following account is also based on what my father himself told me and on my research.

This is what my grandfather wrote about my father Moshe in his manuscript:

My son, Moshe, was born in 1911. When the previous world war erupted, he was about three years old. In 1916, in the midst of the war, the boy came down with a severe case of scarlet fever, with additional complications. We brought many doctors to examine him and loaded him with medication in order to raise him from his deathbed and heal him. The boy indeed recovered and regained his strength, but traces of the illness remained and damaged his auditory nerves. The boy became incurably deaf for the rest of his life. His ability to speak was not taken from him, but it was still a great tragedy for us.

Grandfather Shmuel and Grandmother Devorah and their children in the fruit garden of the factory in Kalisz. Standing (from right to left): Ala, Abram and Manya. Sitting: Shmuel, Devorah and Regina. Sitting on the ground (from right to left): Genia, Moshe and Roza.

What should we do? How can we prepare him for life with this defect and sweeten its bitterness a bit? After much consultation and careful consideration, we decided to send him to the city of Vienna, the capital of Austria, and that's what we did. I personally brought him to Vienna and placed him in a special school (established and operated by the Jewish community in Vienna) for children with such injuries, and he studied there and received a general education through the special methods used with such children. [I will add here that my father suffered there, together with his classmates, from a lack of food. This might be the reason he didn't grow taller than 1.62 meters, and was much shorter than his father, brother, and children.] The teachers discovered his special talent for drawing. I took note of this, and after he graduated from the school I enrolled him in a school for drawing and sketching, where he learned, and became expert in the various forms of that art. The young man spent ten years in Vienna and received diplomas from both of these schools.

Afterward, he returned home, a teenager, about sixteen years old. He had developed greatly in body and spirit, but he still lacked a profession. So, I enrolled him in a school for craftwork in Łódz. [Here my grandfather is mistaken: Moshe graduated from a Jewish secondary vocational school in Kalisz.] At this school, he became an expert in metalworking. The young man graduated from this school with a certificate of a mechanical locksmith.

That was the year I purchased the machines for curtains in Germany, in the city of Plauen. I decided to take advantage of my acquaintance with the manufacturer of the machines in order to place my son in his factory, so that he could become an expert in curtain weaving. I told him the history of the young man, about his defect, and that I was greatly concerned about training the poor fellow for life. The manufacturer, who suffered from the same defect himself, showed great empathy and agreed to accept him, and also promised to pay special attention to him. I made arrangements for the boy's life in Plauen so that he wouldn't lack anything. The youngster would visit the factory every day, watch and observe everything happening there, and he also engaged in real manual work and learned all of the ins and outs of curtain weaving. At the same time, he also entered the college of art in Plauen. To get the most out of this important school, I arranged for the youngster to live in the home of the professor, the principal of the school, who was also a member of the board of the factory where the young man worked. I also arranged for him to give private lessons to my son. The young man studied and became expert in all facets of this profession. He excelled in particular in drawing machines and their parts, and in calculating production costs and various expenses. The owner of the factory also involved my son in sports activities: He signed him up for soccer and boxing programs run by the local police. The youngster was smart, hardworking and agile, and everyone liked him.

His friends didn't know that he was from Poland or that he was a Jew. If they had known, they certainly wouldn't have welcomed him so readily, because both Jewishness and Polishness were unaccepted then. After two years, my son's friends at the college and at the factory began to suspect that he was not a pure German, but rather a foreigner. I myself was largely responsible for stirring this suspicion. I came to Plauen then to purchase two more machines from the factory where my son worked. And here, my son's friends saw that he was connected to me, which meant that he was a foreigner, and even worse: a Jew. They claimed that this profession contained many secrets that should only be revealed to 'the most modest of the homeland's sons,' and not, heaven forbid, to a foreigner and especially not to a Jew. In the end, my son was compelled to leave his patron, his work in Germany and the police sport association, and return to Kalisz.

My grandfather's description of the time my father spent in Plauen seems somewhat exaggerated. I remember hearing a different account when my father told me about this period of his life. My grandfather wrote that my father spent about three years in Plauen. I understood from my father that he stayed in Plauen for a shorter period, and that the important things he learned were to design, draw, and execute patterns for the Jacquard machines and its punched cards for lace curtains and for lace, based on a contract signed in advance to purchase machines. In any case, I learned and saw this with my own eyes that he had attained a high professional level, and had acquired a profound fluency in literary German. After returning to Kalisz, my father trained and boxed in the Jewish sports club (Żydowski Klub Sportowy, or ŻKS) and with Hakoach Kalisz, which became part of Maccabi Kalisz in 1936.

4. Cesia

The home of my mother Cesia's parents, "the Berliners," stood in the ancient Jewish Quarter of Kalisz, at the corner of Piskorzewska and Nadwodna streets. From the rough cobblestones of the street, there was a spectacular view of the old market square, today the city square, with the city hall building in its center and the clock tower rising from its roof. On both sides of the narrow street in the Jewish Quarter, two- and three-story buildings stood closely together, combining residential apartments and stores, entrances, and internal courtyards. It was said that my grandparents' apartment had seasonal flowers, including pansies, blooming in flower boxes on the balconies, which were adorned with stylish cast-iron railings. Opposite the home was a building that served in various periods as a hospital maintained by the Jewish community, with a *mikveh* (ritual bath) next to it. My mother Cesia's father, Itzhak Leib Jarecki, was born in

Piątek, a village near Kalisz, to a devout family with many children. His father, originating from Kutno, leased land in several villages and engaged in agriculture. Grandfather was remembered as a handsome man, modest, and mild-mannered. For his livelihood, he kept a store for upholstery fabric, curtains and carpets on 6th Sierpnia Street. He was an enlightened Hasid in his beliefs, and regularly traveled to spend time in his rebbe's court in Włocławek, or according to another version, in Aleksandrów. His wife, Cyrel, whose maiden name was Jaffe, gave birth to Helcia, Yaakov, and Zelig before dying in childbirth. Grandfather Itzhak Leib waited about two years (with his children's best interests in mind) until his first wife's sister, Esther, came of age, and then he married her. Grandmother Esther, a young, frail woman, gave birth to Bala, Genia, Yosek, Roza, Pola, Shmuelik (who died as a child), Cyrel (our mother, Cesia), and Frania. A few years after the birth of Frania, two years younger than our mother, she left them motherless. From a photograph of part of the inscription on the tombstone her husband Itzhak Leib erected, and later survived in Kalisz paving the the banks of the river, we learned that my grandmother Esther came from a famous dynasty of rabbis, led by HaGaon Rabbi Mordechai Jaffe, author of *Levush Malkhut* who was a pupil of Rabbi Moses Isserles and Rabbi Solomon Luria. Rabbi Mordechai Jaffe served as chief rabbi in a number of cities during the course of his life (1530-1612), including Prague, Lublin and Poznań, and was a leader of the Council of Four Lands. My grandmother's father, Shime Jaffe, and her brothers also served as rabbis.

Grandfather Itzhak Leib Jarecki.

Cesia was the most devoted of the children in the house and was her father's favorite. She helped in the store and looked after her father. She was bubbling with joie de vivre; it was said that she would pass in the street running, hopping, and skipping. After her father died, leaving the children parentless, the older sisters worked for a living and raised the younger children, using the revenues from a store that sold clothes and stylish upholstery fabric in the city. Cesia studied at the Jewish high school in Kalisz, where Hebrew was also taught, and she helped her sisters in the store. With an inclination for the arts, she focused on reading literature, drama, and Polish poetry, and could write well in that language. She was also active in the Hashomer Hatzair movement in her age group and in the *garin* (pioneering group) that formed in the city and prepared to emigrate to Palestine. When she announced her decision to marry a deaf man, the son of an industrialist, her devoted friends tried to dissuade her, and even held a noisy protest demonstration in the street under the windows of her home. Before long, our mother's Hashomer Hatzair *garin* departed for the Land of Israel. Her friends underwent a period of training in Poland and in Palestine, and participated in 1938 in establishing Kibbutz Mesilot in the Beit Shean Valley, as part of the "stockade and watchtower" missions. Cesia said that when the war broke out she barely knew how to make an omelet, and was not proficient in any housework. And now, from the beginning of September 1939, she faced one of the most difficult tasks of her tumultuous life.

Remnant of the tombstone of Grandmother Esther Jarecki (née Jaffe).
Pulled from the banks of the Prosna River in Kalisz.

Moshe-Moniek and Cesia on their honeymoon, January 1933

B. YOSEPH'S MEMOIR PRIOR TO LIBERATION

1. The 'tuning' of memory

My first memory, probably even prenatal, is of beats: ta-ta-tam, ta-ta-tam, at a steady rate of about sixty cycles per minute, loud beats that shook the building and made the floor of our apartment vibrate, along with everything in it. Was it really these beats that made me a persistent and precise person? Another memory, though two, or three years later, placed the first memory in a tangible context and gave it meaning: In the factory beneath our apartment, there were several gigantic looms, with weavers working to produce lace curtains. Each of the looms was controlled by a fan with thousands of thin strings sloping down from a Jacquard machine above it. From the top of the machine, a mysterious strip of countless punched cards streamed from a perforated polygonal drum. So much for my family's "work and craft" background, which had a strong impact on me ever since I was an infant. I also know-remember from the time of my infancy that people called me Jurek. I was named Yoseph after the father of my paternal grandmother, Devorah, in response to her fervent request, which reached us already from the Land of Israel. But everyone called me by my Polish name, Jurek.

A second early memory is of a physical detail a cast-iron triangular prism with a decorative carving-like pattern, coated with nickel, at the top of each of the four legs of my child's bed. I remember the iron bed was painted white and had a sliding rail guard. A third memory is of a burst of rocking and joy on the back of a portly wooden horse, wonderfully ornamented, and accessorized, in the children's room, with my big brother Ignaś in the background, who had finished his ride on the wooden horse and let me have a turn, and the radiant face of our nanny, Aniela, watching from above. A fourth memory is of grumbling about being left behind and longing for my parents, who traveled abroad to a resort. My wandering-searching for them in the family factory led me to the packaging room. Hela Lifshitz, my mother's dear friend, and Mietek (Naftali, or Nafcio)

Kolski, my mother's nephew, who worked in the warehouse, offered to pack me in a box and mail me to my parents. I immediately agreed and was happily packed in brown packing paper and string, but the package was never sent, much to my chagrin.

Itzhak and Yoseph in a park in Kalisz, 1938.

These are a few of the firm memories from our home in Kalisz before all hell broke loose, when I had yet to reach the age of three years and five months. These memories have stood the test of time and now that I'm committing them to writing, they can also now be cleared from my memory. I have kept these memories, and the ones that follow, for over six decades. They are not based on stories or photographs they are as alive and vivid as ever. But in the background, bits of stories, and many other names are also rustling. The full information on all of these was collected in part during testimony-meetings I conducted after writing these things, and is presented separately from the "direct memories" described above.

We spent the summer vacation of 1939 my mother, my brother, and I in a one-story farmhouse, one of the few homes in the small village of Krzyżówki (which apparently got its name from an intersection of dirt roads), about a dozen kilometers from our city, Kalisz. We had fun playing in the yard with the local children and, of course, found great pleasure in the crowing roosters, the squawking chickens that pecked at the plaster on the walls, their yellowish chicks scurrying in the yard, the geese, and ducks, the small rabbits, and the puppies and kittens. We also enjoyed lots of fresh food, based on eggs and dairy products: milk from the cow, cream and kefir and all sorts of fragrant white cheeses, fruits picked from the trees and vegetables from the garden, various types of baked goods and village dishes. We sometimes even grew tired of this bounty. Mother insisted on ordering these foods from the owner of the house, or on making them herself, and placing them on our table in great abundance, sometimes using methods that bordered on force-feeding. My father would often visit from the city of Kalisz on his motorcycle, and we would go on pleasure rides on the village paths, my brother, and I sitting on the gas tank and mother on the carrier in the back. We rode through harvested stubble-fields and forests. My parents also rode bicycles, giving us rides on them, too. And I remember them riding on a bicycle built for two, with Mother pedaling behind Father.

As time passed, without understanding what was happening, I could sense an atmosphere of discomfort and concern during conversations between my parents, their friends, and local adults. My parents would often consult and deliberate among themselves, sometimes heatedly, and I wondered what restrictions and prohibitions were about to be imposed on me because of my sinful behavior. One day, as evening fell, a black vehicle stopped on the dirt road in front of our house a taxi. We loaded its back trunk, roof carrier, and interior with objects prepared in advance. My brother, my mother and I, and another acquaintance, or two, squeezed inside. I remember feeling that it was an extraordinary event that would usher in a period of change. Unfamiliar words were spoken in a restrained tone due to the imperatives of the times, and I too became, seemingly all at once, an active partner in what was happening. The trip was long, on roads full of masses of people, carts, and cars too. I'm not sure whether we even passed via the house in Kalisz. If so, we stayed there only one night, or maybe even just one hour. It's etched in my memory that we stopped along the way at the apartment of uncles on my mother's side in the town of Kłodawa. I remember a gathering packed with conversations and loud and animated voices, in a tone expressing love and wholehearted devotion for the children, family unity and, finally, an emotional good-bye. The rest of the trip was by train. I don't remember whether my father made the whole trip with us or only part of it, or whether he just planned it and was not present at all. At the end of the journey, we reached Warsaw. There we met my father's older brother Abram with his wife, their son (my age), and their daughter (a few months old). We moved into temporary housing in an apartment in the resort town of Otwock, not far from Warsaw. We apparently arrived there before it became a battlefront. I can remember one or two instances of fleeing from the apartment and staying in the forest because of the bombings and sniping from the air by the Luftwaffe, the German Air Force. The experience of staying in the thick of the woods, amidst all sorts of greenery, the rain, the rays of light streaking through the foliage, is more deeply etched in my consciousness than the terrified talk of the adults, who scurried around in confusion, feeling helpless. The explosions sounded close, like they were inside the forest. This probably occurred at the time of the battle for Warsaw, because I remember that during the bombing in the forest there was talk about a precious box of sugar that remained hidden during the siege and a severe shortage of water and food in Warsaw.

2. Illnesses and a secret farewell

After living in Otwock for a while, we moved to Śródborów, a suburb tucked away in a forest, with small homes, and sanatoriums. Mother managed our lives while Father was away somewhere. He would send letters and secret messages, which we received with great excitement and whispers. Occasionally, he would suddenly appear for a short time. Relatives, who already lived in the area or had left Kalisz for Warsaw, came to visit, and we kept in touch with them.[2] My mother, with help from those around her, worked hard to overcome the shortage of money, goods, and services. In our small apartment, we lived a full life. I felt safe under the wing of my older brother, Ignaś. I remember a Great Dane we called "Dog" who stayed in our apartment for a while my father, a dog lover, apparently found him wandering around and brought him to us. I was in awe and a bit afraid of the creature, and I remember feeling a loss of status in my family.

We contracted infectious childhood illnesses, including whooping cough and chicken pox, and we might also have caught pneumonia. I remember this term mentioned by family members as a possibility, and perhaps also as a fact. The medical treatments I remember were administered by Mother and neighbors or family members, based on advice, and on medication they managed to obtain, such as gargling with boric acid and drinking *gogel mogel* (made from raw egg yolks) and chamomile tea. A particularly loathsome treatment was cupping placing scorching cups on the chest and back after burning off the oxygen inside them with an alcohol lamp. At the end of this procedure, the cups were painfully detached from the skin, making a loud "puck" sound. The cupping left blue and tender circles in the skin, which were treated with turpentine. I remember at one point there was great alarm when I was diagnosed with scarlet fever. This illness had

---

2   This included Abram, my father's older brother, until he was forced to leave, and his family: Aunt Bronka, Rysiek (a boy who was our age) and the infant Berta – who moved temporarily to Otwock; Helcia, my mother's older sister, and her husband Moritz Kolski and their children Mietek and Cesia; Frania, my mother's younger sister, and her husband Benek Wartsky; and my father's sisters: Regina-Rivka Ganzweich and her daughters Janka and Rutka, and Ala (Sheindel-Shlomit) Bloch and her children Ninka-Yocheved and Marek. In Warsaw, there were also my mother's cousins, the Munwes and Goldberg families. At the beginning of the occupation, Hela Lifshitz made a brief visit to look for her brother. I learned about my mother's other brother and sisters in Warsaw and in Otwock only later, from testimonies of Cesia Kolski-Virshup and my father.

special significance in our family, because my father lost his hearing due to complications from it when he was a boy of about five in Kalisz during World War I. I think that during this illness of mine, which lingered for some time, my father happened to come home, and a doctor's appointment was arranged. The magic word on everyone's lips was "sulfa." I'm not sure if this medication was indeed obtained and properly administered, or perhaps it only remained a wish. Based on the palpable anxiety around me, I sensed that I was in a very dangerous situation, and even somewhat accepted my imminent departure from the world of the living. However, I recuperated and also retained my hearing, unlike my father.

One time when I was in bed due to one of these illnesses, my brother was also ill, and lay in his bed across the room. His lungs were clogged and he had trouble breathing. Several times a day, my mother prepared steam inhalations for him, with camphor oil in a big pot of boiling water. One time, as Ignaś was inhaling steam, with our mother sitting in a chair beside his bed, he let out a bitter cry. The pot tipped over and my mother froze for a moment and then also shrieked in fright. The pot was lying on a towel on the bed, and soon the heat seared through the towel, seriously burning my brother's thigh. He jerked his leg away and the boiling water poured onto his leg and backside. The pain was awful, as was the self-blame that followed. His second-degree burns were treated at home. Here too the family feared for his life, or worried that he would be permanently disabled. I don't remember which treatments he received or whether they were correct. Ignaś suffered terrible agony and we all shared the pain and fears, but he pulled through. If it's true that every cloud has a silver lining, then we were lucky to overcome a series of illnesses in the conditions of Otwock and Śródborów. We became immune to a number of common childhood diseases, and my parents, my mother especially, managed to cope with situations of emergency and to safeguard the lives of her children.

One day, Father suddenly joined us, and I remember several changes in our situation. Every evening, when they thought we were asleep, I could hear hushed conversations, conducted in a serious tone of urgency and fear. Mother's written account indicates that one option they considered was for Father to travel to Lublin and check the possibility of sneaking across the border to the Soviet region, as his brother Abram had done.

But Mother emphatically refused to remain alone with the two of us. They immediately reviewed with me all of the prohibitions against talking with strangers and providing any personal information to anyone. This time the prohibitions included acquaintances and even relatives. Mother demanded that I act like a little boy, keep secrets and play innocent: to always say, "I don't know" and to change the subject to banal topics. Perhaps it was already during that period that I adopted, as a preemptive measure, the notion that I'm inclined to act carelessly, and even stupidly, unlike my wise, and level-headed brother. Meanwhile, my father would disappear and return, and my mother was busy preparing for the "fateful day." Within a few days, we packed, left Śródborów, and traveled by train to an "unknown" destination. [According to Father's recordings, we had already been confined in the Otwock Ghetto before fleeing to Sandomierz.]

< See testimony B2 in Chapter C: Hela tells about my father in occupied Kalisz >

3. Under occupation on 'Piaseczna Road'

We apparently arrived in Sandomierz in the fall of 1940. I remember the train ride as complicated, shrouded in danger. A squeaky horse-drawn carriage brought us to a white plastered house with a tiled roof sloping to the sides. The house stood at the outskirts of the city, on the border with the village of Gołębice, close to an intersection where two dirt roads met at an acute angle: Piaseczna (Sandy) Road and Sucha (Dry) Road. The entrance from Piaseczna Road led to the staircase of a first floor apartment, which was actually an empty wooden attic my parents rented for us. From Sucha Road, a gate, and path alongside a garden of fruit trees led to stairs to a ground floor apartment. There, below us, lived the Jewish owners of the house: Melech and his wife, their son Shlamek, and perhaps other children and adults I didn't notice. Fields of grain stretched beyond the two roads, leading to forested areas dotted with farming villages and fields. From our entrance, we would climb the stairs to a long hallway we used as a family room. At the end of the hallway was a door to a wooden porch, with a railing facing Piaseczna Road. Next to the wall of the porch, to the right, stood a broad, high heating stove covered with white ceramic tiles. Halfway down the hall on the right was a door to a small bedroom, and opposite it on the left was a door to the kitchen and the bathroom. From the porch, we could look across Piaseczna Road and see a large courtyard surrounded by a wall and planted with trees, with a two-story white plastered building jutting up from them German Army barracks. Behind us, on the other side of Sucha Road, facing the ground floor apartment, stood the wall of a cemetery. The wall was high and long, thick, and frightening, built of ancient stones. I later learned that it was a Jewish cemetery.

At first, my parents worked as peddlers in the surrounding villages. They would buy various goods they thought would be useful in a village, and try to sell them to farmers who were busy with their own affairs. Sometimes Father would work alone, and sometimes they would both get up early in the morning and head out together on foot, covering a distance of about ten kilometers, each shouldering a cumbersome backpack. We, the children, remained alone at home until they returned. It took courage and wisdom to evade robbers, schemers, and dogs. This type of trade was considered lowly and shameful, as well as a poor source of income. My parents tried not to emphasize our Jewish origin; however, it was easy to suspect they were Jews.

Father excitedly set out to furnish the apartment. I remember going with him to the market in the city, roaming among the stores together. He picked out a saw, a hand plane, files, a hammer, pliers, and other work tools. Later, he also bought some boards cut from light-colored wood smelling of resin, in calculated dimensions, and quantities. He hired a man with a horse-drawn cart and loaded the boards and tools onto it. We walked alongside the cart, and then unloaded it, and brought everything up to the apartment. First, Father built, and polished a large table and placed it in the hallway. Using the table as a workbench, he then built two long benches and placed one on each side of the table. The next project was two sets of bunk beds one for the parents and the other for the children. The remaining wood was used to build a chair and stools. We - the children, and Mother - helped with the sanding and other work, which I remember as a festive activity. I was awed by the result: an apartment with a plain wood floor became a cozy home in my eyes. Father sat next to us at the new table, and drew, for his pleasure, and ours, pictures of animals, people and situations. Father knew how to draw quite well and had a perceptive eye. In time, my brother also began drawing figures, and I did, too, but with less impressive results than our father.

We were allowed to play near the intersection of the two dirt roads, under strict conditions. We had no friends who came to visit our home. The children in the neighborhood rarely included my brother and me in their games outside, only when it was convenient for them. More often, they would taunt us to the point of verbal and even physical blows. I was the recipient of most of these blows. And my parents, who saw what was happening, would scold me for not wisely avoiding provocations, unlike my smart and restrained brother. I had to learn not to respond under any circumstances, to surrender and head home, in the spirit of the daily prayer, "Let my soul be silent to those who curse me." Father had already pegged me as obstinate, with a rebellious nature, to some extent, this was a case of the pot calling the kettle black. He tried to tame me. Ignaś, on the other hand, seemed similar to Mother in his quiet disposition. Usually, just the two of us played games that we invented, and we stayed close to the wall. In the background, we overheard talk of the persecution and murder of Jews, as a community and as individuals. Later, my mother's younger sister Frania fled Warsaw and arrived in Sandomierz together with her husband, Benek Wartsky, whom I remember as an impressive and pleasant young man. They were married in Kalisz shortly before the outbreak of the war. The couple rented a ground floor room further up Piaseczna Road in the nearby village of Gołębice. This occurred against the backdrop of conversations from which I learned that a ghetto had been created for Jews in Warsaw, and that my parents' sisters and their children were stuck inside the ghetto.

I later had a chance to occasionally watch from the side of the road or from the wooden porch facing Piaseczna Road columns of Russian captives being led on foot, under guard by German soldiers, who kept their guns aimed at the prisoners.[3] At first, this was exciting, and stirred my curiosity, but soon I was sorrowful and identified with the fate of the new enemies

---

3   After Adolf Hitler launched Operation Barbarossa on June 22, 1941, violating the Molotov- Ribbentrop pact.

of the German occupier. The faces of the foreigners, in tattered uniforms, some injured, disabled, and bandaged, leaning on crutches, or on their comrades, conveyed distress and despair. Sometimes they softly sang or hummed. Some of them were evacuated and led to the white house visible from the porch. I could look through the window in the door to our porch (I was already wary of standing outside) and see the ground floor of the large house. There was a sloped ceiling with a big black cross painted on it, and below it, a staircase leading to a basement torture chamber. Sometimes we could hear blood-curdling screams coming from the house. We could also occasionally hear an alarm, followed by the barking of orders and the roar of motorcycles. We knew that a prisoner had escaped. In most cases, a few hours later we would hear the noise of the motorcycles returning and the shouting resume, and sometimes the sounds of execution by firing squad.

My father spent a lot of time roaming the city and its environs, and also traveled by train to more distant destinations. His solid build, blue eyes, light hair, and complexion, the lines of his face, which could be Aryan, and perhaps also the seclusion of his deafness, imbued him with great confidence in his ability to initiate activities based on original ideas. His strength and energy radiated onto his surroundings and inspired faith in the ability to work things out. Over time, good relations developed with our neighbors at 1Sucha Road Mr. Stanisław Kowalski, his wife Marta, and their daughter Ryszarda, who was my age.

At some point, I heard talk about what was happening on the war fronts against the Allies, and the fear of aerial attacks by them. An order was issued to black out all lighting at night, so we taped black paper to the windows every evening. My father grew tired of this and developed a mechanism for blackout blinds constructed of wooden rolls, black paper, and twine. Father darkened our apartment with the blinds, which rolled up, and down and effectively blocked the light. He decided to try to pursue the idea and sell blinds of this type. Father partnered with David Lieberman, a young Jewish locksmith he knew from Kalisz, who also came to distant Sandomierz with his family. This collaboration was intended to solve Father's difficulties in communicating and selling. They installed a number of the blackout blinds in apartments and stores in the city for a handsome price. I remember how proud he was when summoned to install these blinds at the large store of the Czech shoe company Bata in Sandomierz. He drew and cut out the name "Bata" in the special logo of the brand and attached dark blue transparent cellophane to the cutout spaces. Another major project was to install blackout blinds at the military headquarters and Generalgouvernement offices in the city. Father made use of the perfect German he had acquired at the school for the deaf in Vienna. None of the Germans had any idea that the dedicated blackout contractors were two Jews from Kalisz. I don't know how my parents solved the problem of our family name and registration with the authorities, because my father was wanted by the Gestapo in his native city, and I was forbidden to use our original family name.

Ignaś was considered wise and intelligent, and at some point our parents decided that it was time for him to learn how to read and write. One day, a young woman teacher came to our home and began to regularly give lessons to my brother in Polish. I sat at the table across from them and followed along without attracting attention. I assume my parents saw importance in investing in education and language fluency, perhaps in anticipation of things to come. I don't know why or how they budgeted even a small sum for lessons, when my mother could have done this herself. But, as was her wont, she chose the very best. My mother believed, often correctly, that she had a "supernatural sense" for predicting the future. She ate sparingly and tried, as if driven by an internal demon of fear, to obtain resources, and to feed her children and husband the most nutritious food - whatever she could get her hands on to strengthen our resilience for times of scarcity. Ignaś was choosy about food and insisted on eating small portions and only what was tasty to him. I, on the other hand, eagerly seized this convenient opportunity to be obedient, to make my mother happy and to satisfy my hunger. During that period, we both contracted the mumps, but recovered with no complications.

I think it was the summer of 1941. Father returned from one of his secret trips to far-off places accompanied by a girl about ten years old, Janka, and said she would be staying with us. Janka and her little sister Rutka had lived enclosed within the walls of the Warsaw Ghetto with their mother, Regina, Father's older sister. Their father, Hersch Leib Ganzweich, disappeared at the beginning of the war. Father managed to get into the ghetto, smuggle in food, rescue Janka, and bring her to us to recuperate. Janka told us about her family and the extended family in the ghetto. She spoke casually about the severe hunger, the illnesses, and the corpses of children placed in the streets and covered with newspapers. The addition of Janka to our family was perhaps the most significant event in our lives on Piaseczna Road. The girl was talented, bursting with energy, and rode on the wings of imagination a real firecracker. She had visited Palestine with her parents at the age of three. The ghetto didn't break her spirit. Even in the ghetto, there were children who continued to dream and play. She easily and gracefully discarded the strict discipline imposed on us by my parents. She would sing, recite poems, and invent, and orchestrate games and plays, casting us in various, and exciting roles. She had a captivating personality that radiated warmth and good will. And several of the neighbors' children now began to come and join us in our games.

We wanted her to stay with us through the end of the war, and this was also what my parents planned. But after two months, Janka realized how much she missed her mother and her sister, who were far away in the ghetto. It was clear to her and to us that returning to the conditions in the ghetto would mean greater suffering than she had previously known, and almost certainly an ugly death. Everyone tried to convince her that it was impossible to bring her back to the ghetto, and that her mother wanted her to stay. Janka could no longer bear the anguish of her longings and concern. Her love for her mother and sister, and the connection between them, could not be severed. My father traveled with Janka by train, sneaked into the ghetto again, and returned her to her family. We later learned that, apparently, during the summer of 1942, in the face of unbearable suffering and with no hope remaining, Regina gathered Janka, and Rutka and turned on the cooking gas until the three of them died together.

I still remember a stanza from one of the songs Janka used in her performances. It's etched in my memory along with its tune, "Turkey, Turkey, Turkey, Turkey / He had gray sleeves and a green kaftan / And tarbushes embroidered with golden thread / *Oy aylala*, lamp of Aladdin / And tarbushes embroidered with golden thread." I was surprised to find four of the song's stanzas in a reference on the Internet. Janka improvised and created costumes for all of the actors she directed and choreographed. I also remember sections from a medley of songs from children's plays she organized in our apartment. As the actors chased, caught, fell to the ground, and so on, they would sing, "A circle of sides / With four corners / The circle broke / It cost us four cents / And we all *bentz* (fall down)!" Or the actors would make a bridge with pairs of hands, pass under it and recite, "Maple, maple / People of the maple tree / What are you doing? / Building bridges for Mister Starost /A thousand horses will pass over it / And one horse will stop: first one passes, second is saved, third is unneeded, fourth is halted!" Or later, "The old bear deeply sleeps / We're afraid of him / We walk on tiptoes / When he awakes he'll eat us / When he awakes he'll eat us / The first hour the bear sleeps / The second hour the bear snores / The third hour the bear ... catches!" Memory of the joy and pain remains. Janka indeed fell prey, but not to the claws of a bear.

In the winter of 1941-1942, the water froze in the well where we drew water for our needs. My father grabbed a yoke and two buckets and I joined him in plodding along a snow-covered path to bring water from another well, this one about a kilometer from our home. The load was heavy. Suddenly my father slipped on a frozen puddle and lost his balance, and the cold water spilled onto him and drenched his clothes. He was badly bruised and we barely made it home. My father came down with a terrible cold and felt severe pain in his hip and back. He developed sciatica, from which he suffered for the rest of his life. He lay in bed and later underwent many weeks of treatment. In addition to cupping and other remedies, my mother would fill bags of sand, heat them in the brick oven, and place them on the places that hurt him, with my father screaming in pain.

On April 20, 1942, I turned six years old. The main satisfaction I felt on my birthday was hearing the sounds of festivity coming from the big house across from the porch. It was as if the Germans were ardently celebrating my birthday, which fell on the birthday of their leader, Adolf Hitler.

One chilly morning in 1942, my young aunt, Frania, crept into our home, slumped over, exhausted, and in shock. My parents asked us to move aside and started tending to her and induced her to speak. A group of armed German soldiers had burst into their apartment in the early hours of the morning, and Frania, and Benek awoke in panic. The Germans said they knew that the couple were Jews and pulled Benek out of bed; they briefly and loudly interrogated him. The sound of gunfire immediately followed and Frania heard her husband's body fall to the floor. I didn't hear other details at the time. All this occurred a few houses away from us, up the street. According to registration data found in Kalisz, probably based on Frania's testimony submitted in 1946, Benek was murdered on March 31, 1942. This tragic event had an enormous impact on the refugees expelled to Sandomierz from Kalisz. Frania moved in with us, despite my father's frequent criticism of her actions, and despite the fact that all of us faced new danger in light of what happened.

The atmosphere became more and more oppressive. Rumors circulated about all sorts of frightening occurrences, and about orders to lock Jews in ghettos. Since I had faith in my parents' abilities, it seemed strange to me and wrong when they decided that we would obey the order and move into the Sandomierz Ghetto.[4]

< See testimony B3 in Chapter C: David Lieberman tells about installing blackout blinds >

4. In the Sandomierz Ghetto

The ghetto was formed in the ancient Jewish Quarter, on the hilltop of the fortified Old City of Sandomierz, overlooking a bend in the Vistula River. The main entrance to the ghetto was through the Opatowska Gate, which opened into a fortified Gothic tower. A turn to the right led to Jews Street and to the ancient synagogue, a community house adjacent to it, and the city's wall. The Jewish community and its merchants had been granted a charter of rights in the days of King Casimir III the Great, and the Jews knew periods of prosperity, as well as severe decrees, calamities, and persecution.

I recall our living arrangements. We were housed on the third or fourth floor of a stone building, and our small room faced a shared hallway. There

---

4   The Sandomierz Ghetto was created in June 1942 in the Old City, it was one of the last ghettos established under the Generalgouvernement. About 5,200 Jews from the city, from its environs, and deportees were held there. The ghetto was not bounded by a fence or a new wall.

were two wooden bunk beds in the room with our belongings stowed below them, a cupboard, and a small table. The window opposite the door and between the two beds faced the street. A number of strangers lived with us in the room. It was very crowded, with no privacy. In the courtyard there was a structure with a row of wooden toilet stalls. Through the foul-smelling holes in the wood, we could hear, and see the rats scurrying in the sewage ditch. We congregated and played with the children in the courtyard: hide and go seek, catch, and games with an improvised ball. In the rooms and hallways of the house, there was a constant bustle of people. Hushed conversations and poignant murmurs buzzed in the air all day. For the first time, I felt the taste of inferiority and general humiliation. Three years had passed since I lived in a Jewish milieu that was technologically and economically prominent, involved in its Polish surroundings, affluent, Zionist in part, and mainly secular-traditional. Later, I was part of an independent family unit that survived separately. Now, we were among a diverse Jewish public that included refugees from recent persecution. There was an oppressive atmosphere of poverty, detachment, and anxiety about the future.

I remember *Rosh Hashanah* and *Yom Kippur* in 1942. A place of prayer was organized in the attic, and twenty to thirty men wrapped in prayer shawls and women stood in the darkness among the sloping wooden beams. They prayed and swayed fervently and in a hushed tone of supplication to the Master of the Universe, despite the fear of deliberate harassment by the Germans during the holidays. I remember the expressions on the tormented faces, the atmosphere of fear, and uncertainty, pungent body odors, and old dust rising in the dim light. After the Yom Kippur fast, the topic of conversation was the upcoming *Sikkes* holiday (*Sukkot* in Yiddish), and issues of Jewish law related to building a *sukkah*. I heard discussion about strange words: *esrog* and *luilav*. Some people improvised well-hidden *sukkahs*. The whispered rumors continued. All of this commotion is etched in my memory as a grotesque spectacle, which I only fully understood years later. My parents were not among the worshippers. They had more urgent matters to tend to, and I was annoyed when they often spoke secretively. Our family converged under a veil of secrecy, fearing for its own private fate. Still, my parents interacted with people in the building and outside of it, and all of us became more acutely attuned to incidents, hints, and rumors.

The first *Aktion* took place in the early morning hours and woke me up. I can still see in my mind a picture of my father and his neighbor lying on the lower bunk bed, wearing long white underwear. Loud voices in German could be heard in the hallway. Suddenly, German officers and policemen appeared in the doorway, in shiny uniforms and visored caps, armed with pistols or clubs, and they said something to the adults, or asked them something. My father suddenly got up from the bunk bed, and one of the officers exclaimed in surprise: "*Also, Sie auch ein Jude sind, es ist ja unglaublich!*" ("So, you're also a Jew, it is unbelievable!") They conducted a short conversation in German, with my father reading lips and writing on a slip of paper. Father explained to us that he worked for this officer, installing blackout blinds in the German headquarters in the city, and that the officer was pleased with his work. [Note: My father remembered this incident differently, as described in his memoirs.] In this first *Aktion*, a number of people were taken for interrogation.

We prepared ourselves for the next *Aktion* in the ghetto, which was not long in coming. When signs of the roundup appeared, we went up to the large attic and hid deep under a big pile of objects that had accumulated over the years. We waited in dread for several long hours, listening to every sound, near, and far. Finally, when the voices grew silent, we very cautiously returned to the room, and my parents peeked out the window to the street. People, some we knew, were being led, carrying a few personal belongings in backpacks and suitcases. Suddenly my parents recognized my brother's teacher. I ran to the window to look and I saw the whole scene and the people. I wasn't able to recognize the faces of the teacher or of others; later, it turned out that I was near-sighted. Most of the people were young, and the rumor was that they were being taken to work for the war effort. The name of a camp was mentioned, which I don't remember.

On more than one occasion, my father disappeared for a few days during that period. I assumed he had sneaked out of the guarded ghetto and traveled on trains. The last time he returned, he smuggled in a bundle of Aryan certificates he had obtained or had forged with his own hands, each one a masterpiece. The connections he made for obtaining and producing the documents - a process he had initiated on earlier trips - reached fruition at a critical point in time. He told Mother, when only our family was within earshot, about the horrors he experienced in his travels, about life-threatening incidents during his stay in Częstochowa and in the ghetto there, and about meetings where he obtained the forms and prepared the certificates. They were stories of an entire Odyssey in a few days. It seemed to me then, and today too, that it was not just a matter of human wisdom. Father seemed to have supernatural senses and instincts, like a cat, tirelessly, and fearlessly prowling for food for her kittens hidden in the bushes. The certificates, which I still have today, appear completely authentic.

The first ones to be smuggled out of the Sandomierz Ghetto were Marian Dąbrowski (my brother Ignaś) and Ludmila, or Mila (Aunt Frania). My brother was dressed in the warm clothes of a city boy, with a fancy red beret on his cropped dark hair. The beret was purchased specifically for this occasion. They were accompanied by a deaf acquaintance, Mr. Mateusz Filipowski, that is, my father who held their certificates. The three of them slipped out of the house at night, heading to an unknown destination. I thought I would have to remain in the ghetto with Mother until the next *Aktion*, which was expected to occur soon. But after a few days, Father returned to the ghetto and informed us that he had found a temporary arrangement for the fugitives.

Meanwhile, we prepared for a more extensive *Aktion* than the previous one, and we searched for a safer hiding place. A rumor circulated among the children that during the last manhunt someone had hidden in the latrine, jumped inside, and drowned in the rat-infested muck. Together with a few other people, we found a large and dark attic. In its darkest corner, there was a narrow and high wooden ledge. It was possible to climb up to it, using a long wooden ladder. When the *Aktion* began, we rushed to the attic. Frantic arguments ensued. My mother and I, and a number of other people, struggled to climb up the ladder to the ledge. When we got to the top, we discovered a squeaky wooden trapdoor at one end of the ledge, leading to a hidden wooden alcove, built into the upper part of the attic. Its floor was covered with straw. With great effort, the heavy ladder was pulled up and laid across the floor of the ledge. Soon after hunkering down on the floor of the alcove, we heard the sounds of the search. The sounds drew closer and the people in the small room were terrified. At least this is what I felt: tightness in my chest and pressure in my gut. I plugged my mouth with a rag. Mother held me tightly so I wouldn't make a sound. The sounds of the search, including the barking of dogs, reached the wooden floor of the small room below us. Through the cracks in the trapdoor, I saw rays of light flickering on the wall of the ledge and heard the sounds of an argument in German. There was no one on the ledge, the ladder could not be seen from below, and it was impossible to detect our hiding place from there. The Germans decided to leave and didn't set the house on fire, as we had feared. After climbing down, I felt like we had been miraculously saved. This came after hours of imagining my departure into the next mysterious world. In those hours of intense fear, my memory froze and I don't remember clearly whether Father had returned and was with us, and if other children were in the small room. And perhaps there were no other children.

A week or two after the first operation, it was Marek Wojciech Łągiewski's turn to don a new red beret and warm clothes. The boy was accompanied by his mother, Mirosława Krystyna Łągiewska, née Langier, the daughter of a watchmaker from Pinsk. He was supplied with a copy of a certificate of birth and baptism at the Św. Jakuba Parish Church in Piotrków, adorned with a tax stamp and the seal of the Generalgouvernement there. His mother carried copies of her birth certificate from Pinsk and a certificate of her church wedding in Białystok to her husband, Zenon Wiktor Łągiewski. The boy received a detailed and strict briefing. He already knew the daily prayers by heart. He "forgot" everything he previously knew, especially the names. He never had a brother. His father was in a prisoner-of-war camp or lost in Germany. Mr. Mateusz Filipowski was his mother's cousin, and so on.

The two of us, together with Mr. Mateusz, left the house in the October cold, two, or three hours after midnight. There was snow mixed with mud on the ground. We sneaked between the houses and the courtyards, somehow crossed the border of the ghetto, and continued walking a long way until arriving at a place where a coachman awaited, wrapped in fur. A horse blowing steam from his nose was harnessed to a black carriage, whose roof was closed, and lanterns extinguished. There was a cold wind and snow fell. We snuggled in blankets on the seat, covered by the roof, and the carriage started to move. The sounds of the horseshoes beating against the cobblestones ("cats' heads" in Polish), in the still of night, terrified me. It was hard to know whether we would safely complete this journey. After already experiencing tests of horror in the past, the child in me learned to also enjoy the adventure of traveling and the sense of fear, and of course the fresh air and the freedom outside of the ghetto. Everything was supposed to be different, and new responsibilities and roles awaited me. We traveled the length of one train station or more toward the city of Kraków, in order to catch the early train there. Purchasing the tickets at the station, the short wait, settling into our seats on the train, and the travel intensified the feeling of tension.

Copy made by a registration clerk of the "original" marriage certificate of Zenon Wiktor Łągiewski and Mirosława Krystyna Langier on August 2, 1934, issued by authority of the Catholic Church in Białystok.

Certificate of birth (November 16, 1936) and baptism (December 25, 1936) of Marek Wojciech Łągiewski in Piotrków Trybunalny. Certification (July 9, 1941) of the original document of the Św. Jakuba Parish Church from 1936.

The train was then like a frontier region, a breached front, teeming with surprises. Inspections were conducted on the train by the Gestapo and the Polish blue police, which still remained intact under the occupation regime. The passengers included Wehrmacht soldiers, informers, and people who turned in Jews, black market smugglers, and criminals. I was warned against all of them. I learned and memorized presenting my new identity in fluent Polish, in a natural way, and self-confidently. If asked anything other than what I had practiced answering, I was supposed to take on the look of a regular boy of my age and politely apologize "but I don't know." The trip lasted until nearly sunrise, and I don't remember if anything unusual happened besides the parade of various characters on the train. I was apparently focused inward, imagining meetings and interrogations: questions and answers, and the arrests that would follow. Before arriving at our destination, I was gripped with intense fear. We got off at the crowded main station in Kraków, site of the dreaded General-gouvernement headed by Hans Frank. We rode in a carriage and I saw trolley cars for the first time, or maybe we rode in a trolley car and I saw carriages. The gray streets were full of mud, the sky was gray, and it was snowing. We came to the neat urban apartment of Roman and Julia Jaworski, a deaf Christian couple who were friends with Father's acquaintance Oskar Wassermann and his wife, a deaf Jewish couple, residents of Kraków. The Jaworskis knowingly endangered their lives out of solidarity with other deaf people, driven by a human commitment to save the lives of others, and as an act of resistance to the occupier. The escape route of Marian and Mila also passed through this apartment, and we even met there for a short time. We stayed in this apartment for a few days until my father confirmed that a new arrangement in life for my mother and me was ready: a complete and indisputable transition to Aryan identity. According to family tradition, our flight occurred two, or three weeks prior to the liquidation of the ghetto in Sandomierz. I'm not sure which of the liquidations.[5]

5. Brzesko 159

My father took my mother and me back to the main train station in Kraków, to the tracks leading east toward the city of Tarnów. This time I was more relaxed and curious. I was interested in observing the scenery and stations we passed, and I particularly remember the signs for the stations of Wieliczka and Bochnia, towns known for their ancient salt mines deep in the earth. The train stopped for a moment at a small station in the forest, where the sign read "Słotwina-Brzesko." We transferred to a carriage, or maybe we just walked with our light baggage for a few kilometers, traipsing

---

5 Almost all of the residents of the Sandomierz Ghetto were murdered in the Bełżec extermination camp in October 1942. Those remaining were joined by other Jews from the area and also from the German Reich. The ghetto was completely liquidated in January 1943. About one thousand Jews were shot to death in a number of incidents, some of them in the cemetery on Sucha Road, and their bodies were burned. About one thousand people capable of working were sent to the Skarżysko-Kamienna work camp. The rest were sent to the Treblinka death camp and murdered there.

along forest paths, and snow-covered fields. We later came to the main street of the town, Bocheńska Road, part of the intercity route connecting Kraków and Tarnów. We moved into the basement of a small house on the outskirts of town; the address was 159 Bocheńska Road and it was on the right side of the road heading toward Bochnia. We rented it with the help of Antoni Herbert, a deaf neighbor, and a friend of Mr. Roman Jaworski from Kraków. Did my parents know and consider at the time that the approximately six thousand Jewish residents of Brzesko and its environs had been murderously evacuated in September and October of 1942 from the ghetto established in Brzesko, and that most of them had been sent in cattle cars to death camps on the same railway track? In any case, my parents had few options. During my first visit to Brzesko as an adult in 1992, I was surprised to come across the old stone wall of a large cemetery containing hundreds of tombstones with Hebrew inscriptions. Some of the tombstones stood erect and others were about to collapse. I realized that many Jews had lived in this area, practicing their faith, and customs.[6]

Our cover story was that the husband, Zenon Łągiewski, was drafted into the Polish Army for the September campaign, fell prisoner to the Germans, and disappeared. The woman, Mirosława Krystyna (Krzysia), together with their only child, Marek, was forced to flee their home in a town in eastern Poland, in an area previously occupied by the Soviets,

---

6   There was a Jewish presence in Brzesko and its environs for hundreds of years. In the 1930s, Jews accounted for over half of the town's population. The Jewish residents actively participated in the life of the town, in its economy and in the municipal government. Prominent Jews included rabbinical sages from the Teitelbaum and Lifshitz families, and the Brandstadter family of Hebrew and Polish writers. The discriminatory edicts already began in 1939, with an order to wear an arm band with a Jewish star. The Judenrat was established in November 1939 and the Jews were required to work in public forced-labor projects. In the spring of 1941, a ghetto was established and about six thousand local Jews were fenced in. The expulsion of Jews began in the summer of 1942. They were sent in cattle cars toward Tarnów (Bełżec) and Kraków (Auschwitz?). At the same time, hundreds of Jews – and perhaps more – were shot to death in the ghetto and in the Jewish cemetery. The ghetto was liquidated on September 17-18, 1942; about two hundred Jews who remained were killed a month later, on October 17.

because their apartment was requisitioned by the Germans and because of the harassment they suffered at their hands. She became an indigent refugee and wound up in Brzesko, where she found inexpensive lodgings. Her cousin Mateusz and his family lived in Warsaw, where the cost of living was high, and they were providing her with a bit of support until she found some work. In those days, this story sounded plausible, but there was the danger of someone coming to Brzesko who knew the people of our supposed "hometown" in eastern Poland, or that some other suspicion might arise. I feared the anticipated departure of my father, but I also looked forward to receiving my mother's full attention and felt proud of the role I would play at her side.

It was a one-story house and faced the street. The basement windows were at sidewalk level, while the windows of the more spacious home above the basement offered a view of the street, the yard, and a large garden in the back. The residents included Mrs. Feliksa Gardzielowa, her nineteen-year-old daughter Janina-Janka, and her twelve-year-old son Julian-Julek. Mrs. Gardzielowa was the widow of Jan Gardziel, who taught Latin and geography at the high school and conducted choirs and orchestras at the school and in the town. When teaching was prohibited in high schools, he continued to teach clandestinely. In May 1941, he was arrested by the Gestapo for his alleged subversive activity against the government. He was taken for questioning and a long period of imprisonment in Tarnów, and from there was sent to Auschwitz. In March 1942, word came of his death there.

Mrs. Gardzielowa rented the basement to my mother to help boost the family's meager livelihood a bit. In the yard, rabbits were raised, and reproduced in cages; a few hens provided eggs and a pig or two fattened in a small pen. During the months of the short summer, the garden produced vegetables for the family's needs: potatoes, tomatoes, cucumbers, pumpkins, beets, cabbage, beans, peas, and more. Fruit trees were also cultivated there, providing nuts, apples, pears, cherries, peaches, and plums; there were also bushes: raspberries, currants, gooseberries, and strawberries. Everything was nurtured by the family without outside assistance, only with the blessing of Mother Earth. Mrs. Gardzielowa's noble and elegant comportment befitted a widow in dark clothing, a woman of the educated ranks. Except for polite neighborliness and social ties with a few of the town's educated people, the family's life strictly and even piously followed the calendar of festivals and holy days, in accordance with local customs and the rituals of the Catholic Church. The daughter Janina spent long hours practicing the piano, which stood in the guest room. She may have also occasionally earned money from giving private lessons to children and from other odd jobs. The son Julek was a friendly boy, energetic, and very mischievous. The mother was busy with housework and the garden, and the children assisted her.

In the basement, there were two attached rooms: a living room and a storeroom connected by a hallway. The windows, long, and low, were installed under the ceiling and faced the road at sidewalk level. To look out the window, I had to climb onto the table and onto a chair placed on it. In the main room where we lived, there was a single bed, a table, and one or two chairs, a stand and basin for washing, and a stove with a cast-iron chimney, fired with wood, or coal. The room was dark during the day, lit by a weak electric bulb in the evening, and had a musty odor. The second room was used by the owner to store potatoes, wood and coal, and other things, and was not inhabitable. Nonetheless, a folding bed was set up there. Next to the house, facing the road, was a well. I sometimes drew a bucket of water from it, using a crank, and a rope wound around a cylindrical wooden beam. The water level in the well was only a few meters below ground. The outhouse was in the garden, in a wooden structure with a pit. From then on, 159 became my lucky number and good luck charm of my childhood years.

Mateusz stayed with us for a few days. Then they secretively whispered to me that "Marian" and his aunt "Mila" were renting an apartment with people in Słotwina, a village just outside of Brzesko, in dangerously close proximity to us. Complete separation was an inviolable condition, and required Mateusz, the breadwinner, and contact person, to exercise extreme caution.

Mateusz quickly formed a close friendship with Mr. Antoni Herbert, a deaf man about thirty-five years old, who was married to Marta, a woman who was not deaf. They lived on our street, a few houses away from the Gardziel family, toward the center of town. Herbert, who worked as a bookbinder, was *Volksdeutscher*, the son of an Austrian general from World War I, who married, and settled in Poland when it won its independence. Brzesko previously belonged to Galicia under Austrian occupation.

Mateusz made several trips and traveled as far as Warsaw. Perhaps he kept some gold coins and a few pieces of jewelry with him from Kalisz. Perhaps he engaged in dangerous smuggling and in selling luxury and forbidden goods. He had a few contacts he trusted. One of them was Mr. Stanisław (Staszek) Kowalski, our neighbor from Sucha Road in Sandomierz. Some of them were Jews and even family members living on the Aryan side, including Mieczysław (Mietek/Nafcio) Kolski, the son of my mother's oldest sister. He was the same age as my parents and made his way from Kalisz to Warsaw. Kolski was able to avoid being caught in the Warsaw Ghetto and lived on the Aryan side of the city under his real last name, camouflaged by his blue eyes and the blond hair framing his shiny bald pate. Mateusz also took the risk of keeping in contact with his sisters, who lived with their children in the Warsaw Ghetto, and with his sister-in-law Bronka, Abram's wife, and her children there. His goal was to secure a regular source of income that would enable the dispersed family to survive. One objective was to find a suitable arrangement for Marian and Mila that would be far from Brzesko. We all regarded this absolute commitment to the immediate and extended family as something obvious, and never questioned it.

The question of how much you could trust someone was a matter of life or death. You were dependent on others and others depended on you. Your fate might depend on the wisdom of their actions, on their moral backbone, and on their ability to keep a secret in conditions of severe physical and emotional duress. A growing number of fathers fled or disappeared for various reasons. There was no trace of Regina's husband, who had already disappeared at the beginning of the war. He probably fled and was killed. My father's brother, Abram, who was an enterprising industrialist and trader, was taken hostage by the Germans as a representative of the Jewish community in Warsaw. Under threat of death, he fled Warsaw, leaving behind his five-year-old son Rysiek and infant Berta with his wife Bronka, who was unwilling to endanger their children by fleeing together via the new border to the Soviet Union. Abram eventually made it to

Palestine. My mother believed in Mateusz's commitment to us and in his abilities, and she encouraged him, and contributed her wisdom to analyzing scenarios, options, and risks. Both were courageous and dynamic, and they thought alike in many cases. My mother believed that Mateusz had a better chance of surviving because of his strikingly Aryan appearance; his deafness, which he was able to use as a guise; his technical talents and abilities; and, no less importantly, because of his keen senses and intuition. Mateusz carefully maintained a network of personal connections, keeping each contact discrete. Each person could be an asset or a disaster. Like many deaf people, he was extremely suspicious. More than others, he was also a natural actor. He believed in his ability to judge a person's character, and had a talent for winning people's trust and for eliciting a desire to help him. People he met were fascinated by his knowledge, talents, and abilities, which he was quick to demonstrate with a captivating innocence. People didn't expect this from a deaf person, and no one had the slightest suspicion that he was also a Jew. This is also how I saw him in those days, together with the concealed relations of father and son, and the sense of fateful dependence. In his travels, he would wear a wide yellow armband on his jacket with three black circles arranged in a triangle with the words "deaf-mute" in bold Gothic letters in German and in Polish: **Taubstumm Głuchoniemy**. This was intended to prevent the various police forces from shouting commands ("Stop!") and shooting him when he failed to respond to commands he couldn't hear.

At the beginning of the period in Brzesko, we lived in complete austerity. Mother starved herself in order to feed me whatever she could find that she considered nutritious and healthy. In her eyes, she was young, and healthy; but I had to grow, become strong, and also store up reserves for "a dark hour" though no one knew when this hour would come or how long it would last. I argued with her and claimed that I was full, and I tried to persuade her to eat. But she would insist, falsely, that she had already eaten, even when she felt hunger. During the summer, we sometimes were able to pick the blossoms of linden trees (*lipa*) for tea, and Mother, on rare occasions, obtained some chicory as a festive coffee substitute. These were a few of the alternatives to the real thing, substitutes referred to in German as *Ersatz*. I hazily recall how once or perhaps even twice in the past, back in Sandomierz, or even earlier, my parents obtained an orange can of Ovomaltina for preparing a "wonderfully delicious and healthy" beverage, invented in Switzerland.

One day, the mailman knocked at the door and we were terrified. He delivered a notification that a package had arrived for us. Collecting the package at the post office required identity documents and entailed the danger of interrogation and informers. In such cases, Mother went by herself in order to avoid adding the sin of my dark complexion and the risk of me blurting out something incriminating, to the sin of her straight black hair and brown eyes, as dark as mine. We learned that the package, sent from a fictitious address in Warsaw, contained large-format books of Christian prayer and theology for the fervently religious. One of the books contained an innocent-looking letter intended for those who could read between the lines and understand that banknotes were masterfully hidden within the book covers to provide for our livelihood. From time to time, the collection of sacred books grew. We also received two or three packages of clothing that included brushes for clothes and shoes. The flawless polish of the wooden handles gave no indication that money was hidden in the hollowed space of the brushes. The packages were not enough for our needs, but they showed that Mateusz was able to get by and to provide some money for our livelihood, and apparently for Marian's needs, too. Letters to Mateusz, written in code language, and kept to a minimum, were addressed to Poste Restante in Warsaw. I soon learned that Mateusz had arranged for Maryś and Mila to move to Warsaw, outside the ghetto walls. I had to erase their existence from my consciousness.

Through Herbert, Mateusz met a local deaf person, Eugeniusz (Geniek) Łoza, a twenty-two-year-old bachelor, a tailor by profession, who lived in the suburb of Słotwina. Geniek was a pleasant and good-hearted fellow. He worked with an old tailor and it was said that he sewed the suit jackets, while his employer only sewed the pants. There was not a lot of work, so he also did alterations. Geniek loved to visit us in the basement, and my mother spoke with him very patiently; he read her lips or she scribbled words on a paper. He loved sports and was an excellent skier, and he did gymnastics exercises with me to improve my meager athletic ability. When Mateusz came, they would meet at Herbert's home and conduct lively conversions in sign language that went on for many hours. The communication with hand motions, body language, and facial expressions drew them closer to each other. Mateusz used the standard, formal sign language he had learned during his studies in Vienna. But here he tried to use more informal language when conversing with his friends, who had also received special education for the deaf. Geniek also invited Mateusz to meet his family, and he had a number of enjoyable visits there.

The town's main church was on our side of Bocheńska Road, a few minutes by foot from the center of town. During the occupation, the church, and its parish comprised a spiritual center and focus of identification especially for those suffering at the hands of the German government. The masses and prayers were conducted in Latin, a language that was not spoken by the worshippers, who lacked a high school education; it was certainly a foreign tongue for the children.

The children were involved in the religious life of the community. During the Mass, youngsters served as altar boys, dressed in white robes, carried candles, and incense, and held the cup of wine and the wafers (*opłatek*); older ones even served as ministrants (assistants) to the priest during the communion rite at the altar and during the procession among the worshippers and collection of donations. The priest conducted religious lessons for boys and girls. For young children, a series of lessons were offered in preparation for the First Communion ceremony, following the first confession. Since I was still too young, I didn't have to participate in this ceremony. I just had to regularly attend church on Sundays and holidays, make sure to uncover my head in church, make the sign of the cross with a hand dipped in holy water, and kneel at the correct time. I listened attentively to the Mass ritual in Latin, and was impressed by the priest's homiletics in Polish delivered from the podium. His preaching was usually based on the Gospels or Psalms, which were beyond my comprehension. The older children let out their frustration by secretively telling forbidden jokes. I'm embarrassed to say that the only text I remember from my many visits to that church is riddled with sacrilegious flippancy, with Polish words inserted in rhyme with the Latin liturgy: Dominus vobiscum (*dostaniesz po pysku*). Et cum spiritu tuo. Sursum corda (*aż ci spuchnie morda*). Habemus ad Dominum. (The Lord be with you [may you be punched in the face]. And with your spirit. Lift up your hearts [until your big mouth is swollen]. We lift them up unto the Lord.)

As required at the time, I memorized the daily prayers in comprehensible Polish: the Lord's Prayer (*Pater Noster*), Ave Maria (*Zdrowaś Maryjo*), the Credo of the Catholic Church, the Guardian Angel prayer, and the Ten Commandments. My mother, who had a beautiful voice and loved to sing, made sure that I knew the Christmas carols and hymns for New Year's Day, and we could sometimes be heard singing from the depths of the basement and also in the yard, "Christ is born this evening, let us go rejoicing! Though the night so gloomy, day will soon be dawning! Angels from on high are singing, to the One who comes from heaven: *Gloria, Gloria, Gloria in Excelsis Deo* (Glory to God in the highest)." The same was true for Easter, and so on.

The first holiday we celebrated was Easter 1943. Weeks in advance, my mother turned a large pot and bowl upside down, covered them with coarse, wet linen, and thickly spread seeds of bittercress (*rzeżucha*) on the top and sides. She kept the seeds moist and they sprouted, producing two wonderful mounds of bright green. At the church, she purchased postcards and statuettes of the Lamb of God (*Agnus Dei*), made of fine sugar and holding the flag of the church, and she baked traditional cakes and cookies in the landlady's oven. Mateusz also came by for a few days. With the masterful hands of a lace curtain designer, he decorated eggshells with colorful, splendid drawings. We drew and painted imaginative decorations and invited the landlords and neighbors to join us. They praised our knowledge and talent, and particularly our devotion to the tradition and religious faith. The barriers of foreignness were removed thanks to my mother's pleasant personality, her positive and endearing disposition during times of daily hardships, and her natural willingness to help and give.

Julek Gardziel, his friend Michael Damaszewicz, Marian, and Lusia Herbert were all a few years older than me, went to school, and didn't pay much attention to me. Fortunately for us, I was still too young to go to school. I became friendly with a girl who was about my age. She lived alone with her mother, who was also a foreigner in town, in a one-room apartment on the ground floor across the road. I don't remember what we played; perhaps we were bored in each other's company, but we had a need to belong. She didn't show great imagination, and I was afraid to take initiative and expose secrets. After months of this type of acquaintance, I remember her squatting down in front of me and peeing into the snow, as if it were the most natural thing to do. I recoiled, aware of the danger of inadvertently revealing my identity.

I went a few times to the local Sokół sports club, which included a gymnasium with ladders, and equipment for gymnastics, and scouting. I probably went with children from the neighborhood and perhaps with Geniek. This was not long after the place had been used to collect the possessions of the town's Jews, who were murdered, or expelled. It was still being used by the Wehrmacht, but we could sneak in when no one was there.

I spent most of the time with Mother. She would teach me Christian prayer and holiday traditions and customs. She told fables from memory, some of which she made up herself. She recited and sometimes sang verses of well-known children's songs from memory and from books she found somewhere. When I turned seven, she decided to teach me the multiplication table, and I knew it by heart up to 100, perhaps to show when needed that I had acquired the knowledge taught at school.

Occasionally, Mother would sing. She loved to sing. Mother had a good ear and pleasant voice, with a wide and very expressive range. She apparently inherited this talent from the Jaffe side of the family, which produced an outstanding cantor (*hazan*) who was appointed in 1862 to lead prayers at the Great Synagogue of Kalisz. Mother sang hymns by herself after learning the words and melodies perfectly at church. She sang Polish folk-songs, also poignant and joyful romantic "*Schlagers*" from operettas, plays, and movies from before the war. She refrained from singing tunes that were really sad. Years later, when I was studying the poems Julian Tuwim wrote during the interwar period (some of which were put to song), I came across the words to three of the songs she sang. When she sang them, I understood the words in the context of my world. I remember her combing my hair with a fine-tooth comb to catch lice, while singing a popular song with these lyrics, "It's the last Sunday, already tomorrow our paths will separate; tomorrow we'll leave each other forever." If someone outside heard her singing, they would have assumed she was pining for her missing husband. I understood the lyrics literally that is, I thought they described what might happen one day to me and her. My mother loved to sing romantic songs, and this time she didn't give much thought to the words.

After the snow melted, when it was warmer, we would hike in the many fields and forests around us. Nature and the sights outdoors left an indelible impression on me. Near the train station and in the thick of the forests, we discovered isolated graves, or small clusters of graves with rotting wooden crosses and the details of the deceased. They had died in the cholera epidemic that raged in this area during World War I, and also many years earlier. We were amazed by the many types and shapes of trees and greenery. Further off, among the patches of forest, we sometimes came across farms with a tall swing beam for drawing well water. Horses and cows stood and grazed. In open spaces in the forest, we found natural pools with small fish, crabs, frogs, and toads, with butterflies hovering over them and dragonflies buzzing, their rich colors glittering in the rays of the sun. On the far side of one of the forests was a place we especially loved: a series of three artificial rectangular pools, where people would come to fish. Ducks floated in the pools, and swans too; you could find turtles and even deer near them. The weeds and wildflowers were knee-high. We sat, ate a bit, and wove wreaths from clovers and daisies. In the summer and fall, we picked berries in the thick of the woods and among the ferns: blueberries, cranberries, strawberries, and raspberries. We cut pine mushrooms and other types of edible mushrooms with a jackknife, and I learned to avoid poisonous mushrooms. This was a welcome addition to the menu. In the summer, it was spectacular to watch the golden grain swaying in the wind on their tall stalks, having turned yellow from what originally looked like green grass. Red poppies and blue cornflowers blossomed in the fields of rye, wheat and barley, and we picked the flowers and brought them to our home in the dark basement. There was a constant danger of dogs and strangers everywhere, but the need for space and freedom was stronger. On these long outings I was free to talk with Mother about anything, without the fear of being overheard. We spoke about the mysteries of life and the world outside. We almost never spoke about our situation; there was nothing new to discuss. The connection with nature became the tonic of life for me. Nature's wonders reflected what was real and worthy of trust.

I'm not sure where the new proposal to earn money arose. If it was proposed by Mrs. Gardzielowa, it was unreasonable to reject. If it was proposed by my mother, this indicated that the help from Mateusz was not enough, or that Mother wanted an independent source of income in the event that something happened to him if he was uncovered or lost his sources of income. Mateusz came infrequently now. Our landlady and my mother started a sort of partnership. Mrs. Gardzielowa would use the tiled stove in her kitchen and bake various types or rolls, round, and crescent-shaped, coated with poppy seeds or cumin; she also specialized in different types of cookies. Mother paid the cost of the materials for the first batch from money Mateusz had provided. Her main job would be to sell the baked goods in Brzesko and the surrounding area: at snack bars, grocery shops and stores where the Germans bought their goods; in the local restaurant, and the few cafés where a small number of local residents sat, along with German soldiers from the garrison and from units that passed through the town; and to individual customers in homes and institutions. Mother sold and distributed the baked goods in the late afternoon and evening, fresh from the oven. She would put on a jacket and matching headscarf and set out with a basket or two full of baked goods produced that day. She sometimes encountered problematic customers. There was also the danger posed by curious passersby and gossipers in the small town. She needed great tact and courage, too. My mother always planned for the worst-case scenario. She asked me if she could entrust me with Mateusz's secret address in case she didn't return. I didn't have a clear answer. My mother told me an address in Warsaw, and I memorized it. At night in bed, before I fell asleep, I would imagine Mother being caught by the Gestapo, and the Gestapo coming to our basement and taking me for interrogation. After discovering that I was circumcised, they would torture me to get information about my relatives. I resolved to continue to claim that I didn't know my father's address, despite the excruciating pain. I had nightmares about not being able to endure the pains of torture. I wouldn't go to sleep until Mother returned. Even today, I clearly remember the pain of anxiety and impatience, waiting for her to finally return. I would climb onto the table and then onto a chair I placed on it, and look for hours through the window at the feet of the people passing by, hoping to recognize my mother's shoes.

Before I fell asleep, Mother would sit at the edge of the bed we shared and tell or read fables and children's poems, most of which she knew by heart. She defined herself as a "Polonist" by natural inclination. One of the poems I loved was *Lokomotywa* (The Locomotive) by Julian Tuwim. In her wonderful understanding and sensitivity, Mother tried to keep my spirits up by reading stories and poems about the heroism, hope, and devotion of children (such as the story of the boy Marco "From the Apennines to the Andes" in the children's novel *Heart* by Edmondo De Amicis), or lives of hardship (as in *Uncle Tom's Cabin* by Harriet Beecher Stowe). One of the poems that became a source of identification and prayer for me was Adam Mickiewicz's ballad "Father's Return" (*Powrót taty*), part of which I knew by heart. The ballad opens with a woman asking her children to go together to the hill outside of town, to kneel before the miraculous icon and make a "fervent" prayer because, "Father is not returning, morning and evening, in tears, and anxiety I await him. The rivers swell, wild animals abound, and the roads are full of bandits." The leader of a gang of bandits, lying in ambush for the rich merchant's caravan, hears the children's prayers. When the gang is about to murder the merchant, ignoring his plea that his wife and children are awaiting his return, the gang leader steps in and frees the merchant. The children's prayers have softened his heart, he explains. He also has a wife and young boy waiting for him at home. The gang leader asks the children to pray for his soul. Faith in God could have been a natural and obvious source of strength for me in Brzesko, and my soul longed to pray for the lives and well-being of my loved ones. However, in those days, my mother did not deem it appropriate to dwell on this complex subject, except for diligently practicing, and keeping up the appearance of Christian worship. When my mother returned from her sales trek in the evening, she would share with me what she had experienced that day.

We were accepted in our close environment, and even participated in a group photograph in the landlords' garden. In the rare photograph, we appear dressed in our "Sunday best": Mrs. Gardzielowa linking arms with my mother in the center; Janka with a friend; Julek, Mateusz, Marta and Antoni Herbert and their children Marian and Lusia, and me; the youngest of the children. My appearance is not flattering: a shaved head, a restless expression, a chubby face, and paunchy body, wearing knee-length shorts, held up by suspenders. It was the first photograph taken of me since the outbreak of the war (or at least the earliest one that remains). Another picture was taken in the basement and includes Geniek Łoza, who apparently was the one who took the photograph in the garden.

Some of my mother's compensation for her work in the baking partnership was paid in produce. In the summer, there were fresh fruits and vegetables, and sometimes they were cooked, pickled, preserved, and served in other concoctions by my mother, who learned to be a talented cook. We also always received a few eggs. Sometimes on holidays, or when Mateusz came from Warsaw, we were given a live rabbit or hen. My mother would slaughter the hen with a knife, pluck its feathers, place it over the fire, clean, and cook it. She would hold the quivering rabbit by its long ears in her left hand, kill it with a mighty blow with her right hand on the neck, and skin the fur with a knife, with my help. The rest of the preparation was similar to that of the chicken. On at least one occasion, I was assigned to kill a rabbit with my own hands, in the presence of the neighborhood children. My mother and I were really disgusted by this act of slaughtering the animals, with the streams of blood, the work of dismembering them, and the subsequent preparation. Mother used the fur to sew a hat with earmuffs for the winter, rough mittens, or a muff. Apparently, my mother didn't really earn money, or only a very little; but her share of the proceeds from the partnership were also probably credited toward our rent payment for the basement apartment. The collaboration between my mother and Mrs. Gardzielowa was conducted in a spirit of friendship. I remember at least once spending an evening in the well-heated guest room in the upstairs apartment. I also recall one time when Mrs. Gardzielowa flinched in surprise upon hearing Julek talking in his sleep in the next room, perhaps about a forbidden game with his friends, "Michael, bring the cards here already."

In the garden of the Gardziel family (from right to left): Marek, Antoni and Marta Herbert, Mateusz, Janina Gardziel, Tadeusz Palej, Feliksa Gardziel, Krystyna, Lusia Herbert, Julian Gardziel and Marian Herbert. Easter 1943.

Our parents hosting guests in the basement of 159 Bocheńska Road in Brzesko. Standing: Julian Gardziel and Geniek Łoza. Sitting (from right to left): Michał Palej, Krystyna, Mateusz, Marek, Feliksa Gardziel, Marta Herbert, Tadeusz Palej and Janina Gardziel.

One day, Mother returned home late, and I could see right away that she was distressed. In response to my pleas, she confided in me that she saw a Polish man she knew from Kalisz while delivering her baked goods near the town square. He also noticed her, and she had the feeling he recognized her. This was a serious situation. Would he turn her in? Would he gossip? Perhaps he would act normally, continue on his way, and disappear. The next day, Mother sent a secret message to Mateusz. We continued to act as if nothing happened, and Mother continued to sell the baked goods as usual. But then things got complicated. Mother became a victim of ongoing extortion by the man, who apparently lived in the region or passed through it periodically. I don't remember exactly when all this began or how long it went on. I think the person Mateusz turned to for help was Mr. Staszek Kowalski, his confidante from Sandomierz. Apparently, Staszek came to Brzesko, met with the stranger and my mother, and straightened things out. Staszek was an impressive and handsome man of about thirty-two, tall, sturdy, blond, and blue-eyed. He knew the facts and rules of life from various sides and directions. Years later, I learned that he was involved in the Home Army (*Armia Krajowa-AK*) national underground. It seems that a deal was made, accompanied by an implicit threat. The man would receive a considerable sum in hush money if he maintained complete secrecy. The ground began to burn under our feet and we had to make decisions.

6. Mysteries of Kielce

One day in the summer of 1943, I was suddenly told that I had to leave my mother and move in with the family of a train worker in the city of Kielce. I immediately realized that this was an imperative I could not oppose. My trip was portrayed to outsiders as a vacation with relatives in the countryside. The Kielce period is foggy in my memory. The shock of separation from my mother and from what was already familiar, and the transition to the unknown, in those circumstances, led me to repress identifying details. It seems logical to assume that this occurred as my mother was being extorted by the man from Kalisz, but there were also other reasons that were not disclosed to me. I was not privy to all of the information, calculations, and uncertainties, and I developed a mechanism of deliberately forgetting incriminating details. I set off on my journey, switching trains at Kraków, accompanied by a man - an acquaintance or perhaps someone I had never met before. I was scared stiff, feeling despair, and fear for my family, and for myself.

My guardians lived in a modest apartment in the heart of the city of Kielce. They had two children, a girl and a boy who were older than me, and perhaps also a younger child. I served as a source of additional income for them in tough times, and perhaps more than that. An appropriate cover story was spun for me about a tragedy that struck their relatives in this or that town, which ended with my being sent to live with them. They treated me in a natural and decent way, and the children, who never doubted my Christian identity, included me in their games at home and in the neighborhood.

I have clear memories of the garden where we played in Kielce, and can picture its vegetables and the ripe fruit on its deciduous trees. I also vividly recall the flowerbeds of big hollyhocks protruding from their erect stalks, with bees buzzing around their stamens, while I watched them from below.

One evening, the neighborhood children told me I had to pass an entry test for their secret society. My suspicions and fears soared, and I felt faint. I was led in the dark through a series of connected basements among the houses, with my eyes blindfolded. The children whispered incomprehensibly, in a severe and frightening tone, with intermittent shouting. Suddenly, the blindfolds were removed, and I was led along a dark corridor into a dim room. A figure draped in white robes was seated on a high chair in the center of the room, holding a powerful flashlight by his belly and shining it into my eyes. The participants were wrapped in white sheets and danced around, shrieking in excitement. The figure spoke to me in a firm girl's voice about what would be done to me if I deviated from the rules and directives of the leaders. They made a cut in my middle finger and read the text of the oath. I declared "I swear" and signed with my blood. I found it hard to believe that I made it back to the open air of the yard alive, without exposing my identity.

I remember a Sunday trip with the family to Karczówka Hill, a forested area outside the city, where an ancient monastery sits on a hilltop covered with weeds and wildflowers. The father told the children with restrained excitement about the uprising of January 1863 against the Russian occupation, and that this church played a central role in the revolt in the Kielce area. In the grass on the slopes, we found bullet shells, and bits of shrapnels. We picked them up and examined them with reverence.

One day, the mother of the family calmly approached me and told me to get ready to have my picture taken. This stirred suspicion and resistance in me. I said to myself, "They've betrayed me and are going to hand me over to the Gestapo." I innocently believed that the photograph was somehow intended for this purpose. They gave me a haircut and dressed me in a festive white shirt with a blue and white sailor's collar that reached down my back. The shirt was pulled out of the bottom of one of the closets, or borrowed from the neighbors, starched, and ironed. A professional photographer came with his equipment, and they sat me in a chair to be photographed. A few days later, I was ordered to write a letter, for the first time in my life. On the back of the picture, I wrote with a pen and ink, and with a hesitant hand, "Dear Grandma and Grandpa! This is how I look, really – I'm big already. Please don't forget about us – Jurek." The words were dictated to me and the picture was sent somewhere. Somehow, it made its way to 111 Rothschild Boulevard in Tel Aviv. The photograph is now in my possession, with eight needle holes along the left edge and coarse white thread for attaching it to a letter or form that was lost at some point.

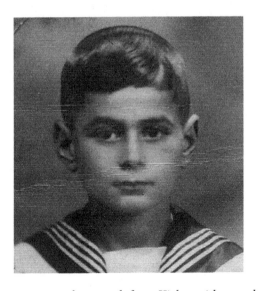

Marek in a mysterious photograph from Kielce, with strands of thread connected to a letter form from a POW camp (summer 1943).

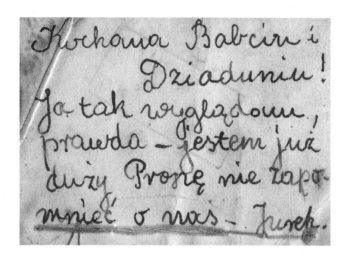

Letter from Marek to the grandparents in Palestine he had never met before, on the back of the photograph.

There was an incident that shocked the family and neighbors: the execution by firing squad of a group of hostages or members of the underground. We heard the shots from the direction of the nearby square. The next day, I sneaked with the children to look at the whitish-gray traces of brains sprayed against the wall of a building in the square. I probably stayed in Kielce for two to four months before returning to my mother, to the house on 159 Bocheńska Road in Brzesko. Perhaps I was sent back to my mother because the family in Kielce became more fearful after the execution and its repercussions. The names of the family members who hosted me and the location of their home in Kielce are erased from my memory, so I cannot thank them.

In the summer of 2003, during my second trip to Poland, I visited Kielce, which had grown enormously, in an effort to trace the past and stir memories. But this effort was futile. At the spacious information office in the ancient municipality building, a well-educated, and friendly secretary, about forty years old, knew nothing about the execution incident. She immediately put me in touch by telephone with a retired judge, in his eighties, a former member of a regional committee that investigated Nazi war crimes. On the spot, the man told me about two group executions of fighters from the many underground groups in the region and of civilian hostages, carried out at two different locations in the city on the same day November 18, 1943. Ten people were executed near the St. Wojciech community parish, and ten others in the neighborhood adjacent to the train station. The winter came late that year, he recalled. The areas around the two memorial monuments didn't spark any memories, but helped me to establish the timeline of the Kielce period. Perhaps the family of the train employee agreed to host me as a response to the train transports[7] to the death camps?

< See testimony B6 in Chapter C: Testimony of Ryszarda Kowalski-Kamys >

7. Circumcision test

I returned to Brzesko more mature and experienced. I resumed the routine and attended church. My mother didn't send me to school to start first grade. She found some pretext to keep a seven-year-old boy home during wartime. I was known as a shy boy, inclined to keep to himself, but not a simpleton. Thanks to my mother's personal charm and the affection people felt toward her, adults suppressed their doubts. But not the children. I was occasionally interrogated by older children with clever and embarrassing questions that I answered as best I could. The children were influenced by the words and bits of rumors they overheard when adults conversed. Did word of my mother's exposure and the ensuing extortion also leak and spread to some extent?

Once, when the snow was melting in the spring, the neighborhood boys played in the puddles and streams of water by the house. I was assertively invited to join their games. Suddenly, they decided to ceremoniously pee

---

7   A Judenrat was established in Kielce shortly after German occupation, and the ghetto was created in Kielce on March 31, 1941, and about twenty-seven thousand Jews from the city and its vicinity were concentrated in it. Within a few days (August 20-24, 1942), three transports with a total of some twenty-one thousand people were sent in trains to the Treblinka death camp. There were also mass murders in the ghetto itself, including shootings and forced injections of poison. Kielce then became nearly *Judenrein*.

into a puddle, and pleaded with me to join the line of urinating boys. I refused, claiming that I had nothing to pee, and later argued that it was not polite and that I was embarrassed and wouldn't act this way. The children grabbed me by my arms and said they would now move on to a game of tickling. I was wearing knee-length shorts and the children started to lay me down in the weeds and tickle my right thigh. I ran out of excuses and was not strong enough to free myself. I felt my fate was sealed, like a fish that made the critical mistake of swallowing a hook – and it was not that I did this willingly. I was unaware that my mother and Mateusz, who happened to arrive in Brzesko, saw what was happening through the wooden fence of the house. My mother shouted, "Marek, come home immediately!" Mateusz also raised his voice, the grating voice of a deaf person, calling me to come home. The children were frightened and relaxed their hold on me for a moment, and I immediately obeyed my parents' command. I broke free and ran home. My mother and Mateusz might have simply thought that the bigger children were hitting me, but I felt in my heart that the die was cast. Mateusz set off on his travels. I continued to act as if it was all a joke and that the matter was forgotten. My mother continued on her rounds of selling baked goods every day.

I try to remember and assess what type of boy I was then, and what led me during those years to persevere in playing the game of disguises and hiding. I don't remember receiving praise for my good qualities. My brother was considered wise, intelligent, and easy, while I was scolded for being frivolous and for a lack of self-restraint. I was considered to be as stubborn as a mule, despite my efforts to disprove this. So, I convinced myself that I really was not very wise and had to watch my step. I was not happy to hear Mateusz's occasional comments about me being cross-eyed, a condition that went untreated, but this was much less troubling than the color of my brown eyes and dark hair. I didn't have the conditions to develop pleasantness. But I sometimes suppressed sparks of anger. I was not endowed with an innate quality of being popular among other children, and I lacked the confidence to develop and acquire this quality in such conditions of alienation. I think it's correct to say that I sometimes suffered from seclusion and despondency, if not depression. Adults who didn't know me interpreted this as restraint, and attributed it to the outstanding education

I received from my mother. I think it weighed on my conscience that my loved ones were risking their lives to invest endless efforts in me. I had the advantage of not knowing a different life; if I had been older, I would have had memories and visions of better times. My mother's boundless and unconditional love and devotion cushioned my attitude toward external reality and toward my precarious existence, infusing me with emotional strength and the will to live. My mother invested her all in me, but didn't let me become overly dependent on her. It was clearly explained to me that I might be left to cope on my own. I only dreaded torture, which I was determined to bravely endure. I accepted the fact that information was withheld from me so that I could not be tricked or tortured into divulging it. I lived the moment without any horizon or illusions, and I found consolation in the folk saying, "The goat only dies once." I developed an ability to react quickly and a discerning view of reality. My love and devotion were directed toward my family, reflecting my parents' attitude, and conduct. I felt surprise whenever strangers showed affection toward me.

One spring day, Mateusz came to take me. I felt both relief and apprehension about leaving an environment swarming with tangible dangers and moving to an unfamiliar place that might prove to be even more dangerous. It was hard for me to say good-bye to my mother. I knew that I would really miss her guidance and support. It frightened and pained me to think of what could happen to her in Brzesko, alone in the musty basement. I bid farewell to the Gardziels and the Herbert family, before heading off to "the village of my mother's relatives," where I would get stronger by eating butter, cream, and meat from the farm at no cost, the wish of every devoted mother in such difficult times.

< See testimony B7 in Chapter C: Meetings with Janina Irzabek and Julian Gardziel >

8. The courage of the officer's wife

I remember. The three of us walking on sodden paths to the train station in the forest. A horn sounded. A stabbing sensation in my gut. Farewell hugs and kisses with Mother. Fearful awareness that this might be the last time. The huge, black train approached, blowing steam, and came to a halt. We entered the passenger car, took a good look around, and settled into our compartment. The train slowed and sped up at the stations (which grew familiar), and various people boarded. We switched trains at the Kraków station after what seemed like an endless wait in the lion's den. No one told me exactly where I was headed or whom I would meet. Judging by the platform and the announcements, I realized we were traveling toward Warsaw. I refrained from questioning Mateusz. Thoughts raced through my mind. Were we traveling to the Warsaw region or to the city itself? I was excited and impatient, expecting to perhaps meet Marian I had not seen him for about a year and a half. We disembarked at the Warsaw train station as a cold day was dawning. We hurried through the crowd and Mateusz signaled with his hand for a vacant rickshaw, a common means of transportation for two passengers safer because of the lack of other passengers (except for the pedaling driver). The rickshaw squeezed between the trams, vehicles, and passersby. Mateusz stopped the rickshaw at a safe distance from the destination: the Mokotów district, 45 Aleja Niepodległości (Independence Avenue).

After entering the building, we went up one floor from street level and Mateusz knocked on the door to the right of the stairway landing. After a long wait, the door was opened by the owner of the home, Mrs. Leopolda Kuropieska. I was led through a narrow entrance to a bedroom, and from there, via a short hallway, to the spacious kitchen, which also served as a dining room and living room. And then I saw Marian, named Maryś here, wearing wool knit slippers, with closely cropped hair, studying me with a pair of dark brown eyes. We greeted each other with a quiet "Serwus" ("Hello"). Maryś had been hiding in the apartment for a long time already. He knew the conditions and rules of the place; I was his little brother, a greenhorn who arrived at the hideout in circumstances of duress. The atmosphere was not appropriate for displays of joy. Mateusz, now openly identified as our father, stayed for a short while and left.

As forewarned, everyone vigorously signaled me to keep quiet. I was not allowed to speak loudly. I could only whisper quietly in someone's ear, and only when there was a good reason for doing so. I also had to walk slowly, tiptoeing in bare feet. It was forbidden to move chairs or heavy objects. I could not be near the window curtains during the day, and certainly not at night without checking first that the shutters were shut tight. There were also rules for flushing the toilet as silently and sparingly as possible. At that time, there were also two adult Jewish sisters hiding in the apartment. We lived in silence alongside the official family, invisible from outside the apartment, like bats in a cave. The precautions we took seemed the little we could do. Coming to live here was extremely difficult, complex, and dangerous. In the living area, there was a wide window facing the backyard and an open field beyond it. Opposite the windowsill, on the other side of the room, stood a large rectangular wooden table, where I would spend most of my time. On the perpendicular wall to the right of the window was a wooden door painted with white varnish. Behind the door was a small closet room of plastered brick. Inside the room, on the right, was our hiding place. It was a narrow space separated from the closet room by a wooden partition with a trapdoor of matching wood, which turned inward on its hinges. Bluish wallpaper with a floral pattern was skillfully pasted on the four walls of the truncated closet room. The internal hiding space had been secretly constructed about a year and a half earlier by Mrs. Leopolda's father, who was a professional carpenter. About six metal poles were installed along the wooden partition in the closet; hangers bearing jackets, suits and dresses were hung densely from the poles to conceal the trapdoor to the hiding place and make it harder to access. On the right side of the entrance hallway, another door led to the study reserved for the father of the family. The room contained a rich library with many volumes on history and military strategy. I never received permission to enter there. Of those hiding in the apartment, only Maryś was allowed to sit and study the books.

The husband and father, Captain Józef Kuropieska was in the Woldenberg prison camp for officers (*Oflag*) in Germany, where Polish officers were held after being captured during Germany's invasion of Poland in September 1939. Leopolda raised her daughter Barbara (Basia), who was about twelve years old, and her son Wojciech (Wojtek), who was about a year younger than his sister. They were the two most important keepers of the secret. Anyone withholding information on Jews in hiding was at risk of immediate death, not to speak of those who actually hid Jews in their home. Even if their mother went through the motions of asking the children's opinion, they were placed in a perilous situation that posed dilemmas for them every day: the crowdedness, the constraints on their behavior in the apartment, the siblings' relations with each other and with the mother, relations with one foreign child and another one, who received some of the limited resources of maternal attention, relations with the two older women, and so on. Outside of the circle of life at home, Basia, and Wojtek were vivacious and intelligent children who went to elementary school, played outside and had friends at school, in the apartment building, on the street, and in the neighborhood. The mother, who also filled the father's role, was authoritative, and set down clear rules. It's also true that a state of emergency existed and their patriotic resistance to the occupier was a duty and source of pride. In addition, their heroic father was wasting away in captivity, far away in enemy territory. But I was already familiar with the anti-Semitic and xenophobic atmosphere in the street. The clever and mocking contempt and invective for Jews, heard in the street from both children and adults, rang in my ears. Basia was a devoted, responsible, and loving girl. Wojtek was a decisive, assertive and vulnerable youth who didn't tolerate insult and wouldn't refrain from responding with words and perhaps also with his fists. I immediately understood that the situation was very complicated, full of contradictions, and far from stable. And I knew that I was in Warsaw, while my mother was still in Brzesko. I had to rely on the adults. I played the role of the little boy, innocent, and passive. I carefully guarded my tongue and walked on tiptoes.

There was a patriotic atmosphere of solidarity and mutual support in the apartment. From time to time, Mrs. Leopolda would furtively bring her husband's officer's saber (*szabla*) from the basement and polish it. Once a month, a letter on a printed form would arrive from the Woldenberg camp, along with a response card with space to write a few sentences in pencil. Here, part of the puzzle of my photograph in Kielce was solved. My uncle, Samek Bloch, the husband of my father's sister Ala, was also a prisoner in Woldenberg. The photograph apparently was sent to him somehow. It was here that I also heard the first snippets of information about the Jewish armed uprising in the city's ghetto, and how it was snuffed out, and about the burnt, and abandoned ruins visible from afar.

Mrs. Leopolda was a nice woman, down-to-earth, direct, and

pure-hearted. She was courageous, trusting and determined in a way that immediately won my admiration, and also made me wonder: How was she able to do it? She didn't hesitate to harshly scold her children sometimes, and even more. She was a seamstress by occupation, and I understood that her main work was tailoring women's clothing or other occasional sewing jobs on the side. The rattle of the sewing machine was a frequent background noise in the apartment. A well-operating sewing machine is a valuable asset in times of war, and Mateusz made sure the machine was in good working condition. Mrs. Leopolda managed the relations with the customers, receiving orders and taking measurements, usually at the customer's home. It seemed to me that most of the sewing work was done by the sisters; I imagined them to be outstanding seamstresses. Perhaps the noise of the machine served as camouflage. The hideout demanded no less meticulous coordination and discipline than the work itself. There was a set code for ringing or knocking at the door. The apartment was always sparkling and tidy to avoid any indication of the four additional residents in the event of a sudden visit, when the shadow residents would disappear, locking themselves in the closet hideaway. We ate our meals hastily, allocated portions, of whatever could be afforded.

Mrs. Leopolda was openly fond of Maryś. She would explicitly praise his wisdom, obedience, and self-control. I still had a lot to learn from him. He spent a lot of time reading. Sometimes Maryś drew pictures of events involving numerous people. He was good at drawing galloping horses and their riders in complex war scenes. There were many wooden boxes in the apartment containing sorted units of lead soldiers, infantry and cavalry, in battle-dress of various colors, armed with an assortment of weaponry, in movement, or in battle position. There were also batteries of several models of cannons, blocks of wood, and whatever was available. Maryś would conduct imaginary battles on the table, or historical ones based on descriptions in Captain Kuropieska's books. Wojtek sometimes joined in the war games, and occasionally I was also invited to play and try to show my skill. A popular game was a naval battle conducted on graph paper, with submarines trying to sink the enemy's warships. We played all these games mutely, as required. I began to become accustomed to the routine in the apartment. There were not many visits that required us to hide in the dark hideout, and we didn't usually have to stay there for more than half an hour. At that stage, I was more concerned about my mother than about our situation in the apartment.

One morning, after ten or more weeks as a "guest" of the Kuropieska family, there was a mishap in identifying knocks on the door and we didn't have enough time to lock ourselves in the interior hideout. The four of us huddled in the closet room, hiding among the hanging clothes, with only a wooden door separating us from the dining room, where the visitors sat, conversing in loud voices. The visit continued for a long time, and we stood without budging, trying to breathe quietly, and slowly. I had a bit of a cold and was also affected by the mothballs, and I felt an uncontrollable sneeze coming on. After a desperate struggle, I grabbed several dresses and pressed them tightly against my face to muffle the sound as I let out a controlled sneeze, and another shorter one. I thought I had succeeded. But when we came out of the closet room, I saw in Mrs. Leopolda's face that she was worried. She asked what that muffled noise was, and expressed hope that the guests had not noticed, or that at least the incident would pass without a reaction. Otherwise, nothing changed in the rules of the apartment, except for a scolding I received from my father, Mateusz, when he heard about it. How could I do this to those who looked after me and loved me?

About two weeks passed. Early in the morning, there was stronger-than-usual knocking at the outside door. I immediately threw some clothes over my nightshirt, and Mrs. Leopolda commanded, "Hide quickly." I entered the dark hideout after the two sisters, stood behind the secret trapdoor and latched the lock. I was breathless. Loud voices could be heard in the dining room. Mrs. Leopolda claimed innocence, but aggressive male voices ordered her to open the door of the closet room. The door opened, the clothes were pushed aside and we could hear dull knocks moving along the wallpapered brick wall, until they soon changed to booming knocks against the wallpaper covering the wooden partition of our hideout. My racing heartbeats and the throbbing pulse in my temples muffled the knocking sounds. "Open!" the voices commanded. I was determined not to open, no matter what. Mrs. Leopolda herself asked us to open because there was no longer any point in hiding. I still silently refused until the sisters signaled with mute and impatient hand motions for me to comply. I opened the latch and the trapdoor, and we emerged, shamefaced. There was a heated discussion between Mrs. Leopolda and a policeman in a blue uniform, accompanied by a man in civilian dress. They ranted about the *Żydzi* and the unforgivable crime of hiding them. Mrs. Leopolda answered with a firm voice and even threatened them: If they harm one hair on the head of anyone in her home, the Polish underground will come and kill them both. The tone changed to one of businesslike negotiation between the two sides, whose bargaining power was unequal. From my corner on the big bed in the bedroom, I didn't understand what was happening.

A long time passed after the police left before Mrs. Leopolda let Maryś down from the high and dark shelf below the ceiling of the hideout. He was placed there first, and sat enfolded in such silence that I didn't even imagine he was with us. Mrs. Leopolda handed Basia one secret address or more, and sent the girl to deliver a message to my father, and perhaps also to the sisters' contact persons, if there were any. My father arrived, looking distressed, and helpless. He was able to give Mrs. Leopolda an appropriate sum for the ransom demanded by the potential informers (*szmalcownicy*), who were persuaded by Mrs. Leopolda to be content with extortion. She said that the two even assured her that she could continue to host us without any worries. Mrs. Leopolda decided that she didn't believe them and was unwilling to continue to be blackmailed. However, she also decided that Maryś could continue to hide in her home, by himself, since he had not been discovered in the search. Her illogical decision reflected her great love for Maryś and her enormous courage.

I later saw the two sisters leaving in secret. I felt deep despair and remorse. I felt that I had taken the last shelter from these women and sent them to their death. This thought continued to haunt me. In my eyes, I had sentenced myself to eternal disgrace. It was only many years later that I was relieved to learn from Mrs. Leopolda that the sisters had managed to survive and settled in Australia. They were seen in Warsaw after the liberation; however, they never contacted Mrs. Leopolda.

I've sometimes wondered whether the neighbors and children tried to trick Basia and Wojtek into spilling their guts. If so, were they able to resist and evade such efforts? After all, it's not hard to imagine one of the two children feeling a momentary urge to take revenge for something, or against one of us, and not catch himself in time. In the absence of any evidence that this actually happened, it only remains to admire their maturity and devotion, children of the war.

I sometimes took cold comfort in thinking that because I refused and delayed opening the trapdoor, the searchers became impatient, and didn't bother to look up at the shelf where Maryś was hiding. The fateful mishap was entirely my responsibility look what my carelessness caused! It was a fatal mistake that should not have occurred under any circumstances, and for which there was no atonement. In normal times, this could have been explained by my propensity to catch colds. Sometimes my colds developed into bronchitis. In time, I was diagnosed with a severe allergy to various sorts of dust and feathers. But in this case, only the test of results counts, and I completely failed this test and foiled a herculean effort. I was ready to even accept the death penalty with understanding. There is no doubt that this lesson affected the way I looked at things going forward that is, I learned that the tiniest fault could lead to disastrous consequences, and that it's necessary to always calculate and plan things with full responsibility, down to the smallest details. The next day, I parted from the Kuropieska family and from my brother in utter humiliation, and went down the stairs to the avenue with Basia.

At a designated corner of a side street near the avenue, I was handed to Stasia, a young and friendly woman, with blond hair, and blue eyes. I didn't know who she was; they only told me that she would lead me to a new hiding place. We traveled in a tram, or maybe two. Then we entered a garden gate and followed a path that ran along a wing built onto the main building; then we turned left into the building and went up to the hideout apartment.

Three people were sitting in the inner room. An older man sat in a chair by the wall to the right of the door, looking sideways out a large curtain-covered window toward the path from which we entered the building. Two women, a mother, and her daughter sat on the edge of a wide double bed, wearing soft slippers, and slowly rose when Stasia and I entered. I was not sure if I had ever seen them before. Their faces radiated kindness and restrained affection, as if welcoming a beloved son. The older, gray-haired woman, Maria, embraced me and whispered warmly, "Here, it is Jurek, you've grown so much!" I immediately corrected her, telling her than my name is Marek. The daughter, Cesia, looked about my mother's age, similar to her in build and in the colors of her hair and eyes. Stasia left, with the older woman in her wake. They explained the rules of conduct in the room, which I was forbidden to leave. The room was equipped with a chamber pot, and a tin wash-basin full of water was brought in every morning and promptly returned to the kitchen. Inside the room, a narrow rectangular opening was cut horizontally into the wall near the entry door. The opening, nearly at floor level, was precisely fitted with a brick trapdoor that silently turned on internal hinges. It was possible to crawl through the opening and stand in a narrow hiding space in a niche in the wall. The four walls of the room were covered with bluish wallpaper with little flowers, which also covered the trapdoor to the hideout. After entering the hiding space, someone had to quickly and expertly paste the edges of the wallpaper to the wall, aligning it with the pattern, and move a couch to cover the opening. I was instructed how to enter the hiding place and stand in crowded conditions. I practiced this with my companions a number of times. A lookout person was stationed by the window, day and night, with a changing of the guard every few hours. Cesia went to the kitchen two or three times a day to bring food. I remember them bringing me a rather festive first meal, including a special gesture of a boiled egg in a cup with a bit of melted butter, together with two slices of bread with jam, and a mug of hot cocoa. They made general conversation with me, but refrained from mentioning details about any particular person. I knew that my stay there was temporary, only until another solution was found if indeed one could be found. I felt in my heart that my stay there was dangerous and endangered everyone I was a curse and brought bad luck. About a week later, Stasia came back to sneak me out of the apartment. The farewell was warm and businesslike, with each person silently immersed in their own thoughts. Stasia took me to Mateusz, meeting him at an apparently predetermined street corner. After the liberation, I was told that Maria was my aunt Helena (Helcia, née Jarecki), my mother's eldest sister. Her husband Moritz Kolski and her daughter Cesia, who had a Semitic appearance, were hidden in the apartment of Mrs. Zofja Kałuszko and her son Jan at

19 Ciepła Street, at the initiative of the son and brother Mieczysław-Mietek Kolski and Stasia, a young woman from a Polish Catholic family who married Mietek about two years earlier. (I also remember Mietek from the shipping room in Kalisz as Nafcio/Naftali.)

Mateusz looked tired and very tense. He explained to me, to my surprise, that I was going to the home of Geniek Łoza's family in Słotwina, a suburb of Brzesko. I understood from what he said that Mother had already left or was about to leave Brzesko for Warsaw. As in my previous travels in similarly dire circumstances, I was in a state of bewilderment, trying to digest the new situation, observe and analyze scenarios of danger, and have thus forgotten the details of this trip. Who accompanied me? I have three different images in my memory: Mateusz, Geniek Łoza, and Stanisław Kowalski from Sandomierz. In an interview with Stasia when she was ninety years old, she described a tall man she met in Warsaw in regard to my trip. According to this description, my escort may well have been Kowalski. On the other hand, according to the testimony of Helena Łoza-Skrobotowicz, it was her brother Geniek who brought me to their home; and, indeed, Mother's written testimony relates that she persuaded Mateusz to take Geniek with him on this trip from Słotwina to Warsaw. It could be that all three were involved, with each accompanying me on parts of the journey. Kowalski may have also met us in Kraków and accompanied us to Brzesko.

My father brought me to the train station in Warsaw at night. We blended into the crowd and walked to the platform where the train would depart for Kraków. I was nervous and frightened standing on the platform swarming with strangers. The atmosphere was foreign and alienating. Meanwhile, we were joined by the man who would accompany me. The announcements, mainly in German, were foreign, and threatening, giving me the chills and making my stomach cramp. From time to time, the loudspeakers cried, *"Achtung, Achtung, Personenzug!"* ("Attention, attention passenger train!"), which was followed by a quick list of the train's main destinations and travel regulations. The tone of the voice and the words still ring in my ears today, even if I first understood their simple meaning only ten years later. A minute or two later, a steaming locomotive would approach in a fury, pulling a long line of cars, and then slow down, and stop beyond my field of vision. Finally, the loudspeakers barked, *"Achtung, Achtung, Personenzug!*

... *nach Krakau!"* In panic and suspicion, I saw the arrival of the gigantic black train we boarded. What remains in my memory from this trip is the part when I was already looking out at the familiar train stops on the Kraków-Brzesko line.

< See testimony B8 in Chapter C: The house on 45 Independence Avenue, from the testimony of Wojtek Kuropieska >

9. In the Łoza-Nowak family's home in Słotwina

It was a time of agonizing pressure and desperation for Mateusz. He had to find credible excuses to gracefully extricate himself from the routine relations with the managers and skilled workers at the Többens plant in Warsaw, where he provided maintenance services on a regular basis. He also was worried that my mother had stayed too long in the basement of the Gardziel family in Brzesko, at the risk of exposure by the extortionist from Kalisz. He had been trying for some time to move her to a rented room in Warsaw in the guise of Krystyna Łągiewska, the Catholic woman whose soldier-husband was missing in action. However, the main problem, a seemingly hopeless one, was to urgently find a hiding place for me. Mateusz did something that seems unreasonable and illogical, an act of desperation by a man whose back was to the wall. He wagered on his extraordinary ability to read human beings, and once he fully convinced himself to try, his self-assurance radiated strength. He traveled to Brzesko and met Geniek Łoza. Mateusz confided in him that he was my father and Krystyna's husband, and that we were Jews living under assumed identities, with the threat of death hovering over us. He asked Geniek if he and his family would be willing to risk taking me under their wing. Geniek expressed willingness and immediately arranged a meeting with his family in Słotwina. At the meeting, Mateusz tearfully explained the hopeless situation and dilemmas he faced. He begged for the family's help and cooperation in rescuing me. The participants in the meeting included the mother (Mrs. Stefania Łoza) and her three children living with her: Irena Nowak, who was older, Geniek, and the young daughter Helena. The four conducted an exhaustive discussion and reached an affirmative decision: They would take me into their home. And what did I think about the new arrangement? I had already demonstrated to everyone that I was a risk and bad luck; my presence didn't bring anything good to anybody. Therefore, I was ready to submissively accept anything they did with me. I don't remember having a burning will to survive during that period of my childhood, but I do remember being afraid.

The Łoza-Nowak family lived on Szczepanowska Street in a small brick house with a tiled roof. The house was divided into two ground level apartments, connected by their spacious kitchens. The kitchens were used as family rooms, and their windows faced a small vegetable garden in the front and the broad dirt road. From the internal wall of each kitchen, opposite these windows, a door led to a separate, large bedroom. Light streamed into the room through a glass door and big windows looking out toward a spacious rear garden. The rectangular garden was as wide as the two apartments plus the paths on the side of the house, and it was twice as long as it was wide. The garden was hidden from the neighbors and the dirt road by a tall wooden fence. On the left side of the garden was an area paved with stones, and in the center of this area was a well that served all of the water needs of the home. A table-high wall of bricks surrounded the well, which was covered by a thick wooden board with an opening in the center for a pail and rope wound on a round beam, with a hand crank to raise and lower the pail. Wooden benches were placed next to the well, and everything was shaded by the thick branches of a walnut tree and a mulberry tree. Stretching back into the yard was a well-tended orchard of fruit-bearing trees and bushes and several cultivated garden beds. At the far end of the garden, along the back fence, a deep trench ran across the yard in which to take cover from aerial attacks. There were storage units attached to the house, and under the tiled roof was a sizable attic with a staircase. A long path behind the apartment on the right led to the outhouse, a wooden structure built over a dung pit.

The apartment on the right was managed by Mrs. Stefania, and she slept there with young Geniek and Helena. The apartment on the left was the domain of her daughter Irena Nowak, who was not yet thirty years old and already a widow. Her husband, Antoni, secretary of the Brzesko town council, died of tuberculosis about a year before I joined the family. The bedroom was used by Irena's small children: Adam-Adaś (six years old), Bogumiła-Bogusia (four years old) and Barbara-Basia (two years old). The three slept in a broad double bed. In this children's room, to the left of the door and against the wall to the kitchen, a child's bed was set up for me. To the left of our bedroom, a door led to Mrs. Irena's room. This room was sublet, even before my arrival, to none other than Stanisław Kowalski from Sandomierz. Kowalski had fled from his city (for reasons that remained unspoken) and he peddled luxury foodstuffs, selling some of his wares to the Germans, too. The leader of the house was the elderly mother, Mrs. Stefania Łoza, about fifty-five years old, widowed by the death of her husband Bazyli. At the beginning of September 1939, the train station in Słotwina was suddenly attacked by German dive bombers. There were trains full of refugees from the west at the station, and hundreds of civilians were killed and injured. Some family members fled east toward Tarnów and reached the retreating Polish Army's line of resistance. Bazyli Łoza died of a sudden heart attack when the heavy cannons began to thunder and flash around him. It was a devastating blow for the family. The esteemed father was an educated man who had worked as a police secretary since the days of the Austro-Hungarian Empire. Stefania and Bazyli had six children, including a physician, an artist-painter, and an engineer. Another blow struck the family when the young Antoni Nowak became ill and died.

Stefania Łoza, Geniek Łoza and Irena Nowak working in the garden behind their home in Słotwina-Brzesko during the Nazi occupation.

From the first day, I saw the members of the household as a cohesive and harmonious family, with everyone devoted to each other. Despite the natural disparity between adults and children, an atmosphere of family unity prevailed in the home, together with deep-rooted religious faith that required proper behavior as a way of life and internal choice. This faith was bound together with loyalty to the Polish homeland, which was trampled by the German occupiers so soon after achieving its long-awaited independence.

Now, after about fifteen months in Brzesko, where I could be seen in the street, in church, and in the fields, the extended Łoza-Nowak family was willing to take me into their home on the outskirts of town. I was free to roam the house and back garden, but not the street. Indeed, the local residents tended to keep to themselves during those days, and didn't often visit acquaintances and neighbors in their homes.

In an effort to integrate into the extended Łoza family, I tried even harder to control myself and act obediently. My hair was cropped short, washed occasionally by Mr. Kowalski with a bleach solution to lighten its color, and combed daily with a fine-toothed comb to catch lice. When I woke in the morning and before going to bed at night, I knelt and fervently recited my prayers: the Lord's Prayer (*Pater Noster*), Ave Maria (*Zdrowaś Maryjo*), the Guardian Angel prayer, and the Credo of the Roman Catholic Church. Everyone expected me to help out with Mrs. Irena's small children and to set a good example for them. My most enjoyable pastime was playing in the sprawling, and manicured garden in back of the house. The branches of the trees were still full of plums, apples, pears, mulberries, and walnuts. There were bushes laden with raspberries, currants, and gooseberries. In the tidy vegetable beds, bean plants and garden peas in plump pods climbed up wooden supports, growing alongside rows of tomatoes, cucumbers, cabbage, lettuce, cauliflower, potatoes, beets, rhubarb, strawberries, and more. We picked and tasted whatever was ripe. I experienced a conscious illusion of freedom and security behind the planks of the fence, concealing everything, a conditional gift of God. I was always shadowed by a feeling that I would eventually be recognized and uncovered. We ate in the kitchen whatever was prepared from the food rations, enriched with produce from the garden. Preparation of the traditional rye flour, mushrooms and potato borscht (żur) seasoned with, dill and pickles, and, on rare occasions, even slices of salami signified a festive event. I remember two or three times at the end of the summer going out early in the morning with Aunt Helena and Adaś to walk in the forests. We picked mushrooms and berries to supplement the menu at home. We almost never met anyone. I was scared that someone would recognize me and I was afraid to tell this to Helena, who was too nonchalant in my view. I loved to walk with them in the thick of the dark forest.

Mateusz managed to come from Warsaw for a short visit once, or perhaps twice. He brought a refurbished German Pfaff sewing machine head and installed it on an old Singer machine table in Mrs. Irena's room. Then he left, and I received no sign of life from him for many weeks and months. I figured I would never see him again, or my mother, or my brother. I felt deep sadness and immense distress. I felt like the last Jew in the world; I had to conceal my secret, become absorbed into my new family, and do everything to please them. My parents didn't impart concepts of faith to me; they never spoke about God watching over me not even an angel in heaven or a star in the sky. I received unlimited and unconditional love directly from my mother, and from my father in the background. When I lost them, I found consolation in the merciful, tormented Jesus, and in Mary, the compassionate mother. The Holy Ghost was something abstract and impenetrable, like a white dove as fierce as an eagle, while God the Father was a frightening essence in the heavens; it was best to not even think of Him so as not to draw His stern attention to the fact that I was a Jew. As protection and as a personal prayer, I would sometimes earnestly sing, silently, or aloud, a psalm-prayer I learned at church, "Father in heaven, hiding under Your wing / A handful of your children, their fate we bring. / Save us in time of need, grant us Your blessings / And protect us from destruction when disaster looms. / In the quiet of the ocean depths or in the thunder of your waves / As Your children take shelter under your wings / We lift up a prayer today to glorify You. / You are our shield, our Father, God." I daydreamed a lot, too, trying to unravel the web of troubling questions that remained unanswered. At the home of the Łoza-Nowak family, as I despaired of surviving another day and harbored no hopes for the future, it was the family routine that gave me a little strength, enabling me to function despite the pervasive gloom. To a great extent, the morning, and bedtime prayers kept me going. The routine of prayer, the submission and attribution of what happens to me to an all-powerful entity with a bit of personal divine Providence this all provided some support and kept me from collapsing. I eagerly added to the Morning Prayer the verses of praise, "As dawn breaks in the morn / The land, the sea / To You all creation sings / Praise to You, Almighty God."

Helena, the young aunt, invested special attention in the children's education. She had the ability to give generously and with awareness. She was willing to take the time to devote attention and convey empathy. At the age of eight and a half, I was able to respond to her messages in a more intelligent way than the others, and this was also evident in my progress in reading and desire to listen. Unfortunately, the first children's book that fell into my hands included a long story about *Bazyliszek* (basilisk), a dragon with a rooster's head. I imagined him as a monstrous and evil bird or a huge flying lizard, whose glare and breath were deadly, and which hid among the ruins of an ancient building in Warsaw. Thus, in addition to my real fears, horrors from the book's supernatural world filled my imagination. My mind was fertile ground for religious and patriotic education in line with Helena's spirited conceptual and emotional worldview. From the depths of my helplessness, the conversations with her raised me to the level of the Łoza family's beliefs and perspective on everyday reality. The divine Providence of God in heaven over every personal action and omission, for good, or bad, the dialogue with Him, and the slight chance of Him answering my prayers these became articles of faith that I readily adopted.

Helena boosted my spirits even more by sharing with me, unwittingly, her patriotic sentiments, which only grew stronger after her father was killed. She showed me a thick book illustrated with photographs portraying the battles of liberation waged by the legions of Józef Piłsudski against the Austrian and Russian armies of occupation. The captivating pathos of the text helped me learn to read. The transition in consciousness to a new identity - a Polish patriot - accelerated through old and new songs that young Helena sang in a soft and pleasant voice. From these songs, I learned the ways of the people and their homeland, as in the words of the anthem-oath (*Rota*) from the beginning of the twentieth century, written by Maria Konopnicka, a resident of the Kalisz region, "We will not forsake the homeland of our people, we will not allow our language to be buried. We are the Polish nation, the Polish people, from the royal line of Piast. We will not allow the enemy to Germanize us. So help us God!" Or the soldiers' songs, "We are the brigade / Of Grandfather Piłsudski / To the stake / We've pledged our lives / To the stake, to the stake." Or other forbidden songs, "Axe, hoe, moonshine, glass, air raids and manhunts, day and night … Axe, hoe, cable, wire / Mr. Painter [Hitler] is already kaput …"

The forbidden songs were a way of communicating sentiments and messages in the absence of a newspaper, radio, or gatherings. They were an ancient tradition in an oft-conquered land and took on a special character when sung together while raising glasses of vodka at holiday events. It was easier to identify with the heroes of these songs and their thematic melodies than with a persecuted people, whom I knew nothing about at that time and from whom I had to disassociate. I had to deny my Jewish identity even to myself. Once in a while, I heard incidental remarks disparaging "Jewish conduct," such as slovenliness, disorder, weak discipline, and a lack of self-respect.

As we, the children, lay in bed after saying our prayers, I was sometimes disturbed by the friendly relations between Mrs. Irena and Mr. Stanisław, who had rented the adjacent room. She would pass through our room in the evenings on the way to his room, where they would conduct long conversations in whispers and make toast on the electric heater. I was barely five years old when I lost the last of my childhood innocence regarding human nature. However, when it came to relations between the sexes, I was innocent of any knowledge or even the slightest notion, despite the very crowded conditions in which we lived during the two Sandomierz periods. I'm not sure whether the adults around me were particularly modest in their intimate relations or refrained from intimacy during these hard times. I remember feeling jealous of the attention my new "mother" showered upon a stranger. It never occurred to me that adults also have a need for human contact and an understanding of their distress. Meanwhile, Brzesko had apparently been cut off from Sandomierz by the battlefront. And there were also important and secret aspects of my guardians' behavior as I learned years later.

One day, there was a change in the makeup of the home's residents. Parallel to my bed, on the other side of the kitchen wall, another bed was set up for a German corporal named Walther. He was a Wehrmacht soldier, an older soldier in his thirties, who was stationed at the nearby headquarters and billeted in the home of the Łoza-Nowak family. The enemy's presence in the home shook me to the core. Moreover, I had to put on a friendly and pleasant face. He was a simple man, with a family in Germany, who spoke broken Polish, and tried not to make things harder than necessary for us. In fact, the first time I remember the taste of chocolate was when the soldier received a package from home and gave some to the children. Nonetheless, when going to sleep, and waking up, I had to overcome fears of a new sort, and offered up my prayers with even greater passion. A few weeks later, a bed was installed in another corner of the kitchen for a second Wehrmacht soldier, younger, and taller, with a ruddy complexion. There were now coarse and grating sounds of German, incomprehensible and intimidating, in the kitchen, the center of our daily life. My level of anxiety and tension rose. Mrs. Irena's children loved to hang around the soldiers and this frightened me even more. Part of my fear stemmed from the awareness that I was placing the lives of the entire Łoza-Nowak family at dire risk, and that it would have been reasonable for them to banish me from the home. But the family members were able to conduct correct and even respectful relations with the uninvited tenants. Did the occupation pay a symbolic sum for these "hospitality" expenses or were they an additional burden for the family? Another guest began to occasionally appear in the yard, in a shabby uniform, and bearing a wooden yoke and pair of tin pails on his back. He was a captured Russian soldier or perhaps a deserter, who worked at the nearby German headquarters and was occasionally sent to bring water from our well in the garden behind the house. He had such a sad countenance, and he was so despondent, that I even felt sorry for him. He would sit and brood for many long minutes on a bench next to the well, under the mulberry tree, or the walnut tree. Sometimes he would come with a mandolin that somehow fell into his hands, and would play, and sing folk songs and melancholy soldiers' tunes in Russian. I was able to understand that one of the songs was about the fierce bombing or shelling of the city of Kiev by the Germans, sung to the tune of "The Little Blue

Kerchief" (*Sinii Platochek*).

As I recall, the raid occurred before the first snowfall of winter. I think it started early in the morning, before I woke up. Through the kitchen wall, I heard several male voices speaking in gruff German and in broken Polish, countered by the voices of the women of the house, pleading, and denying. Then Helena entered and helped me to quickly get dressed. She told me there were Gestapo men in the house and that I had to stand aside with the children. I was suddenly swept with a paralyzing fear. *Here, it's happening I'm now in their hands.* Frantic thoughts raced through my mind: *What will happen to everyone after I'm discovered? After all, I myself am as good as dead.* The situation was incomparably worse than when we were discovered at Mrs. Kuropieska's home. All I could do was to try to hang on, keep silent, and be as inconspicuous as possible. I saw them pass by in their uniforms, with their weapons and symbols in the kitchen, in the rooms, and in the garden. The tension was visible in the faces of the members of the household. They tried to keep calm, even when aggressively interrogated by the *Gestapowcy*, and also when they spoke in a soft voice with the soldiers billeted in the house. The Gestapo soldiers conducted a thorough search in all of the rooms of the home: in the closets, beds, ovens, cupboards, and outside of the house too. Some of them left afterward; others remained in the kitchen and in Stefania Łoza's part of the house. The young women and Geniek sat, spoke, and even played with them. After sunset, I saw the old mother slip away from the house into the garden. I have a picture in my memory from later that evening: Mrs. Stefania moving furtively, stooped a bit, her hands clutching the sides of an apron containing a handful of kindling wood, feeding the sticks into the big wood-burning stove in the kitchen, which was coated with white tiles. The next morning, many soldiers filled the house again, in Gestapo uniforms, and in Wehrmacht uniforms. I stood outside next to the well. I saw a platoon with about twenty to thirty soldiers standing in a line against the wall of the house, with military folding shovels in their hands. The line stretched across the entire width of the garden. The soldiers advanced, digging from one end of the garden to the other, making rectangular holes about two shovel blades deep. The soil was saturated from rain and the platoon made quick progress. When they reached the air raid trench at the far end of the garden, they continued to dig there, and in the sides of the trench. They found nothing. The Gestapo personnel remained in the house, waiting in ambush. This method of entrapment was known as *kocioł* (cauldron) in Polish. They interrogated, snooped around a bit, and slept in the house for a week or more. The adults were confined to the house and the children were not involved in what was happening. I don't remember if they asked me any questions, as the oldest child. I understood that the raid was conducted because of suspicions about a cache of weapons and contacts with underground partisans in the forest. Afterward, they left, and we remained with only the two soldiers billeted with us. I cannot reconstruct any other memories from this traumatic episode. The adults displayed courage, wisdom, and wonderful self-control during the raid. I think Mr. Kowalski was staying in the house at that time.

During the following weeks of cold and snow, our routine life continued under the strong impression of the cauldron experience and increasing rumors that the Red Army and battlefront were drawing near. There was an atmosphere of fear vis-à-vis the Germans' actions, the battles anticipated in Brzesko, and the behavior of the Russian soldiers - a transition from a dreadful reality to a dauntingly uncertain future.

After Christmas and New Year, celebrated with a decorated fir tree, gifts, and vodka, the faint sounds of cannon fire could already be heard in the distance, growing louder as they approached. The German soldiers left and the command headquarters was evacuated. The day of my liberation arrived on January 19, 1945.

Soon afterward, the house suddenly filled with excited and sweaty Red Army soldiers. A group of male and female officers moved into the house, their uniforms adorned with wide epaulettes replete with stripes and stars. Upon hearing them addressed by their ranks major and colonel (*polkovnik*) I regarded them with awe and respect. They also took over the two kitchens and cooked their food from their meager supplies and plunder. They offered us loaves of bread, which were scarce, as well as food they cooked in a field pot on the stove. We crowded into the apartment of Mrs. Stefania and made short forays into the kitchen. The officers acted in a friendly and familial way, without putting on airs. Their facial expressions and body language expressed the range of their emotions. Words and signs of affection were heaped upon the children, who were not accustomed to this. The outhouse at the end of the garden was usually occupied; it often got filthy, and we had to scrub it.

Amidst all this, Mateusz appeared, with a small suitcase in hand. For me, this was a vision of the resurrection of the dead a miracle. Mateusz looked very tense and also exhausted. He didn't know whether he would even find me there. After seeing me safe and sound, and acting normally, he was relieved. We exchanged bits of information. I heard for the first time about the great uprising in Warsaw that had severed the connection between us, and about the hardships, and mortal dangers the three of them experienced during the uprising. I learned that Ignaś had survived and was living in a village in central Poland, and that Mother had been sent to a concentration camp and that nothing was heard from her. We all sat around the kitchen table for a filling meal, starting with traditional rye flour borscht with pieces of meat and potato. We told Mateusz about the incidents at the house. It was hard for him to believe that these things actually happened and ended as they did during the period of our separation. His entire body and face expressed gratitude and release of tension. Around the table, there was an atmosphere of relief, compassion, and fraternity. I felt mixed emotions and was confused by trying to digest the flood of heartening and disheartening details. How would I find myself in the new situation? I didn't really believe what I was told about Mother and Ignaś. I suspected that both had been killed and that Father was just trying to sweeten the bitter reality. He came from Kalisz and said there would be suitable conditions for me there; however, he had to first go back alone and get things ready for my return. The extended Łoza-Nowak family immediately recognized his right to take this course of action and didn't try to dissuade him. Together with the joy of my lost father's return, I secretly expected them to express a strong wish for me to remain with them. I was afraid of returning to the unknown. After about two weeks, my father returned to take me with him.

The trip to Kalisz both excited and terrified me. The constant state of fear of being caught already gave way to the stress of uncertainty: What really happened to Mother and Ignaś? What awaited me in my life after liberation, in the foreign Kalisz, as the land was awash with Soviet armies and ongoing fighting? How would I manage alone with Father? How would

I maintain the ties with the Łoza and Nowak families?

I have bad memories of the train trips. The pent-up tension of my father and my other escorts, the strict demands for discipline, the fear, the vigilance, and the acceptance of my fate (along the lines of "the goat only dies once") made me forget many details about these journeys. From this particular trip, I especially remember the huge open and paved concourse in front of the Kraków train station. It was an impressive stone building with one floor above the entrance level, featuring styled openings through which I passed several times. There were bustling lines of people at the ticket counters in the passenger terminal, and crowded waiting rooms. Personnel in various uniforms walked around the offices between the waiting rooms; some of them carried guns, including *pe-pe-sha* submachine guns, ready to fire. They were also present at the exit to the station's main platform, which led to rows of intermediate platforms and tracks laid on wooden ties and a coarse gravel floor. When we heard an announcement that a train had arrived at a particular platform, at the Kraków station and at stops along the way, we would leap with our luggage into the crowd on wooden walkways or cross through parked trains, sometimes dangerously climbing on the bumpers between the cars or crawling under them. My father usually carried a suitcase in his hand, and also a cloth backpack on his shoulder. When he had a free hand, he always held my hand, or turned toward me every few steps, fearing I might slip away from him and get lost without him noticing. This was hard for him due to his deafness and the severe back pains he suffered since falling on the ice in Sandomierz.

The trip to Kalisz took at least three days. There were no regular timetables then, and we had to ask unreliable sources about the chances of a particular train heading in the general direction of our destination. I served as an interpreter, translating questions and answers from spoken language to lip reading, and vice versa. A train could arrive or a locomotive could connect to standing cars without advance notice. Most of our travel was in crowded freight cars that had been adapted slightly to accommodate passengers. As during the occupation, I saw people riding on the roofs of the cars and on the bumpers between them. We saw many trains for transporting troops, heavy weaponry, and military, or government supplies. We suspected that some of the passengers were pickpockets or even ruthless bandits during these times of deprivation and dubious opportunity, and in the absence of a functioning police force. We had to remain vigilant during our travels, including the long waits for the train to arrive or start moving, and especially when we succumbed to sleep. In Łódz, we walked a great distance with the load we carried from the central train station to the Kalisz station. We finally arrived in Kalisz. Upon leaving the train station, in the northwestern part of the city, my father hired a horse-drawn wagon that took us a few kilometers to the center of the city, to 28 Pułaskiego Street. In an impressive stone building at this address, on the second floor, the authorities allotted an official three-room apartment to my father and his brother-in-law, who had returned from German captivity.

<See testimony B9 in Chapter C: The Gestapo's "Cauldron" >

C. TESTIMONIES

The testimonies in this chapter refer to the memories in Chapter B of Part 1.

B2. Hela tells about my father in occupied Kalisz

Hela Lifshitz, a close friend of my mother's since childhood, when they were neighbors on Piskorzewska Street in Kalisz, was a generous and very loving person, blessed with wisdom and a remarkable memory; she remembered every detail from the time she lived in her parents' home to her final days in Givatayim, where she died at age ninety-three. In her waning years, it was hard for her to tell me everything I wanted to know about my father's life in the early days of the occupation of Kalisz, because she was suffering from heart disease and became very emotional when recounting that period. Thus, it took three meetings (from 2000 to 2003) to collect her testimony.

According to Hela, she came with my father Moshe (Moniek) on his motorcycle to visit us, her parents, and her younger sister Mitka, who were vacationing with us in Krzyżówki. It was a time of great apprehension about the impending war, which indeed erupted about a week later. My father and Hela returned to Kalisz by motorcycle, while her mother and sister went back with us in a taxi. The taxi waited for less than a day in Kalisz and continued on to Kłodawa, to Mother's brother Zelig, who worked there as a sales agent for the factory in Kalisz. Hela didn't know our destination at the time. On September 1, 1939, the day the war broke out Moniek sent a horse-drawn carriage from the factory to bring Hela's father, Yehiel Meir Lifshitz, back to Kalisz. He had remained in Krzyżówki to guard the belongings of the two families. It was Friday, and when the carriage had still not arrived, Moniek hopped on his motorcycle and sped to Krzyżówki to bring her father back before the onset of the Jewish Sabbath. On the same day, Moniek, and his brother-in-law, Hersch Ganzweich, buried all of the ledgers, including records of customer debt, in the basements, and in hiding spaces in the ground. All of the finished textiles had already been sent to the customers, under Hela's management. On September 4, the day Kalisz fell, no member of the family remained in the factory. The sisters Regina Ganzweich and Ala Bloch and their children left for Warsaw before the outbreak of war. Salomon Bloch was conscripted into the Army and fought against the Germans. On the day the war erupted, Hersch Ganzweich sank into depression and urged everyone to flee; he disappeared without a trace, never to be seen again. Moniek went to take care of his family, and then returned alone. Moniek, the accountant Weiss, Mietek Kolski, and Hela operated the factory, using the existing stock of thread to provide emergency pay for the dozens of Polish workers. Only three older weavers remained who were not conscripted into the Polish Army. Soon German workers came to the factory, along with an expert from the Baltic region, asking many questions about the production processes. Mietek secretly left for Warsaw. Hela continued to work until Christmas. She didn't want to flee, and stayed to look after her sick mother in "the open ghetto," which shrank rapidly due to the liquidations, expulsions and transports to the east.[8] Moniek and Hela were able to obtain transit permits to enter and leave the ghetto. In the spring of 1940, the remnants of the prewar Jewish population of about thirty thousand in Kalisz and its vicinity were placed in a section of houses that constituted the ghetto, together with the community hospital.

Moniek, an expert in his profession, was permitted by the Nazi government to remain in the city and work at the factory during the day. In the evenings, he would sometimes bribe the watchdog with slices of salami and abscond with merchandise, mainly lace, in a backpack, bringing it to Hela's father's home in the ghetto. He found ways to sell the goods outside of Kalisz to provide a livelihood for his family, and he may have also smuggled them to Warsaw. He managed to obtain a permit from the German *Gendarmerie* to travel across the "green border," enabling him passage from Warthegau (the region in western Poland directly incorporated into the German Reich) to the Generalgouvernement (regions in central and southern Poland under German administration). He found a German police officer who had a deaf sister and convinced the policeman (speaking

---

8   Occupied Kalisz was annexed to Germany as part of the Warthegau (or Wartheland) region. The persecution of the Jews and edicts against them began immediately after the entry of the Wehrmacht units. On October 10, 1939, H. Marggraf, the *Landrat* (civilian administrator) of Kalisz, ordered the formation of a council of elders, comprising twenty five of the notables of the Jewish community, headed by Gershon Hahn. The plan was for Kalisz to become *judenrein* by February 1940. Starting on November 20, Jews were concentrated in subhuman conditions in the Szrajer brothers' hall in the Rynek Dekerta camp, fenced in with barbed wire. The incarcerated Jews included members of the council of elders who had not fled the city. Mass expulsions departed from there to the *Generalgouvernement* in cattle cars, in subhuman conditions. Some of the Kalisz Jews were sent to labor camps and some were shot to death in the forests or killed in gas trucks. In the spring of 1940, only about six hundred Jews remained in Kalisz, working in the factories and municipal services. They were concentrated in a ghetto of three homes on Złota Street and in an active Jewish hospital; it was absolutely forbidden to leave the ghetto and enter the city. The liquidation of the ghetto took place during July 4-8, 1942. The Jews who were still alive (about 150) were transferred to the Łódz Ghetto.

with him in fluent German) to permit him to travel to "his deaf son" in order to support him.

During that period, there was a Polish man who spoke fluent Yiddish and roamed around Kalisz, going in, and out of the ghetto. He would mingle with the Jews, buy items, sell food, and trade dollars, and valuables. One day, after Father traveled to his family with the permit he received, the man came to Hela and said she should inform Moniek that the Nazis had apprehended two or three Poles who had apparently conducted business with Moniek at the factory or at the border crossing. He said that the chairman of the depleted Jewish community council had instructed him to go to Hela Lifshitz with the message, "The woman should tell Moniek to stop traveling across the border he should flee!" This meant the Nazis were looking for him. Hela wrote a letter in Polish using code names, addressed to Otwock, apparently to a public mailbox (poste restante), "Hela is very sorry that the father of Itzhak and Yoseph is in poor health and needs a change of air." Even before this, when Moniek's transit permit expired, Hela had advised him to stop crossing the "green border", and now he had slipped off to Otwock for the last time. He was in contact with guides who were experts in stealing across the border. Years later, already in Israel, Hela heard from Moniek's sister-in-law, Bronka, that detectives came and searched for him in Otwock. Hela also noted that the appointed community council wasn't fond of Moniek because he didn't cooperate and mobilize to help meet the community's needs.

Hela also recounted two incidents. Once, Moniek arrived at her home with a bloodied face and a backpack full of lace. He was unaware of the blood. Upstairs at the factory was a finishing room and he fainted from the chlorine fumes. When he awoke in the evening, he tried to flee, and was hurt, perhaps bitten by a dog. Afterward, Hela gently asked him to stop storing merchandise in their apartment. She firmly reiterated this after the "triumvirate" came to her father's one-room apartment one day: the chairman of the council; a Jew from the underworld nicknamed "the Black Hand," who served as the chairman's bodyguard; and a German Jew from the border area, who was a manufacturer prior to the war and knew Hela and Moniek well. They said they knew Moniek was bringing merchandise to her apartment, and demanded that she hand it over to them. Hela feigned innocence and said they could take any merchandise they found. The manufacturer responded, "We'll leave that honor to the chairman." But the latter stood up, and everyone left the apartment, nodding respectfully to Hela. The merchandise was indeed close at hand, stored under the bed.

In early July 1942, Hela and her father (her mother had died in the meantime) were transferred to the Łódz Ghetto with the last of the Jews in Kalisz, about 150 in number. Her sister Mitka was previously sent to do forced labor in the neighboring area, later to Germany, and from there to Auschwitz, where she died. In the Łódz Ghetto, Hela married David Kushel. In 1942, Sander, the sixteen-year-old son of Zelig (my mother's brother) and Andzia Jarecki from Kłodawa, came to the Łódz Ghetto to work as a butcher. He would meet with them in the ghetto. One time, he told her that he was on the list to be transported to Częstochowa. She never saw him again. On August 24, 1944, they were evacuated in a train to Auschwitz, and underwent a "selection" conducted by Josef Mengele. The father and husband were put to death. Hela was kept alive and spent time in both Auschwitz and Birkenau, where she organized a group of five women, who slept together in the top bunk and supported each other. Hela saved the lives of two of the women, including Rosa Fuchs, the sister-in-law of my future father-in-law. Rosa, in despair, was determined to commit suicide by throwing herself against the electric fence. Four of the five women made it through five more selections by Mengele and were sent to work in a factory producing casings for anti-aircraft shells near Chemnitz. Hela sabotaged many shell casings. She was evacuated to Theresienstadt, released when she was already very ill on May 5, 1945, and returned to Kalisz on July 9. In Israel, she married Zyga Schönbach, a survivor who had lost his entire family, and together they started a modest clothing business and rebuilt their lives. Hela was very close to her sister Kazia, who survived on the Aryan side. Hela was regarded as a second mother by her niece, Ilana.

B3. David Lieberman tells about installing blackout blinds

In June 2006, I met with Mr. David Lieberman at his home in Tel Aviv. David was writing his memoirs at the time. He said that in November or December of 1939, the Germans expelled by train a "transport" of Jews, including his parents and brother, from the detention camp in Dekert's Market (*Rynek Dekerta*) in Kalisz to Sandomierz. Later, David (then about twenty years old) and his sister also joined the family in the Old City of Sandomierz, and he began working as a peddler and occasionally engaged in trading in the villages of the area. My father and David met in Sandomierz. At the end of 1941, the hours of curfew grew longer and the Jews were ordered to black out their homes. Father and David saw in this an opportunity for a joint venture of installing rolling blackout blinds, which Father developed in his house. Many Jews in Sandomierz, who didn't want to be caught violating the order, or who didn't want others to see them lighting Sabbath candles, asked them to install the blinds in their homes and in their places of work. Their reputation spread. Later, a German officer came to their point of sale and hired them to black out the windows of his home. The business partnership and relations between David and the deaf Moshe were excellent, based on trust, and mutual appreciation. Their enterprise developed and continued for some months, until the ghetto was formed. David's father was murdered in the ghetto in October 1942, together with all of the others who were hiding with him. A month later, the ghetto was reduced to a single street and tightly closed. His mother died earlier, in 1940, and was buried in Sandomierz. David, his brother, and his sister survived under false identities, managing to find work in various places. He worked as a lathe operator in an aircraft factory in Będzin. When we met in 2006, many years after the chaos, David (then eighty-eight years old) and I could not reconstruct how the rolling blackout blinds operated.

B6. The testimony of Ryszarda Kowalski-Kamys

In 2005, after the Passover *seder*, I flew with my son Amir and his son Gal, my grandson, to learn more about the family's past. It was my third such journey to Poland. In Sandomierz, standing in front of the house where we lived on Piaseczna Road, Mrs. Ryszarda Kamys, the daughter of the late Stanisław and Marta Kowalski, shared a few of her memories with her family and us. She illuminated and tied together some of the loose ends of my memories. When she was about six years old, the Germans brought Jews, some dead, and some alive, to the Jewish cemetery across from their home, poured oil on them, and incinerated them. The stench was awful. This was apparently after the liquidation of the remnants of the ghetto in the city in January 1943. The Germans borrowed buckets from the neighboring homes. Most of the residents of Sucha Street were evacuated from their homes, but the Kowalski family was not.

Her father, Stanisław-Staszek, was a member of the underground army, the AK (*Armia Krajowa*, or Home Army the leading Polish underground organization, which was tied to the Polish government-in-exile in London). The Gestapo discovered this and he had to go into hiding. At first, he fled to a village. One day, he was homesick, sneaked back to his home in the dark with his face disguised, and hid in the attic. The neighbor M. recognized his silhouette. M. was a *Volksdeutscher* and a known informer who lived with his family next to our house on Piaseczna Road. He informed, as usual. Ryszarda vividly remembers the search the Gestapo conducted in their home, with the help of bloodhounds. Even after a dog was given the fugitive's clothes to smell and began to climb the ladder to the roof, the mother, Marta, continued to deny that her husband was hiding, and the Gestapo agents left. One day, the informer was caught by the partisans, sentenced to death, and executed. Kowalski went to Kraków and continued his underground activity there. Later, or during the same period, he rented a room (upon Mateusz's advice) in the Łoza-Nowak family's home in Brzesko.

Marta earned a livelihood by selling goods that were in short supply. In her travels to her husband in Kraków, she sometimes served as a courier for the AK. Once when she was traveling on the train to Sandomierz, there was an inspection. Marta was conveying two large packages of yeast. One of the packages was stuffed with pistols, forged identity documents and underground pamphlets. She had taken that package with her into the passenger compartment and left the other in the baggage car. The first package, with the contraband, was confiscated. However, train employees who knew her were able to switch the two packages in time, and Marta safely completed her mission.

Ryszarda's stories raised questions, which she clarified in a letter she wrote with her younger brother, Marek Wojciech Kowalski:

- "We are certain that our father participated in the meeting with the extortionist and your mother in Brzesko."
- "Apparently, it was our father who took you from Brzesko to Kielce, and brought you back."
- [See Part Three, Chap. 4. Between Brzesko and Warsaw, a testimony recorded by Moshe (Mateusz).]

It's possible that Stanislaw Kowalski in person, or trustworthy train employees on his behalf were responsible for transporting me. I have no recollection at all. It's almost certainly thanks to Staszek Kowalski that a family of railway employees in Kielce agreed to take me in at great risk to themselves. Who other than Kowalski could have made this contact? My parents, who were then very anxious and at their wits' ends, gave their consent for this arrangement.

B7. Meetings with Janina Irzabek and Julian Gardziel

In August 1992, I visited Brzesko for the first time in forty-six years and easily identified the house at (what was then) 159 Bocheńska Road. My wife Azriela and I were received warmly and cheerfully, despite the lack of advance notice. Julian (Julek) Gardziel and his wife Maria had just started to renovate the basement apartment we had rented. I went down to see the debris in the room and the high window facing the street. There were many new buildings in the neighborhood and most of the garden had been expropriated and filled with apartment blocks. The water well now had a hand pump. Julek remembered escorting my mother to the train station in May 1944, when the lilacs were in bloom.

A few days later, together with Barbara Nowak, we also visited the stylish wooden house of Mrs. Janina (Janka) Irzabek (née Gardziel) in Niepołomice, deep in the forested hunting grounds of the ancient kings of Poland. We waited with her husband Mr. Tadeusz Irzabek, a chief forester, and a charming man for her to return from Sunday prayers in church. When she arrived, slender and youthful, in festive, and tasteful attire, we spoke at length about our late parents. She sadly showed pictures of her father, Jan, who died in Auschwitz, and her mother, Feliksa. Janka spoke fondly and even a bit longingly of "Mrs. Krzysia" (Krystyna, my mother), noting that "she left Brzesko in May or June of 1944, when the forget-me-not flowers were blooming in the fields. We organized a family farewell party for Mrs. Krzysia. I wove a wreath of forget-me-not flowers, and we escorted her to the Słotwina station, where we said good-bye to her." My mother bid farewell and left Brzesko pleasantly and without burning bridges; she set out from there alone, with an assumed Christian identity.

During a second visit to Niepołomice in June 2003, I met with Janka and her daughter and son-in-law, and with Maria, and Julek Gardziel, who came from Brzesko. I joined them in attending a Mass where Janka prayed for the soul of her husband, who had died about a year earlier. The warm welcome I received in the homes of the brother and sister was emotionally moving, delightful, and endearing. They confirmed what I remembered, and also provided some new details.

According to them, it was indeed Antoni Herbert who brought my father to their home, upon the recommendation of Jaworski, his deaf friend. They also said that in the winter of 1942-43, they saw Mila-Frania walking in the street in Słotwina in mourning clothes. According to them, the people whispered that the *Volksdeutsch* in charge of the flour mill in Słotwina (the *Trauhänder*) was pressuring or extorting her because he suspected that she was a Jew or a convert to Christianity, and that Marian was a Jewish child; there were later rumors that Mila was my mother's sister, apparently because of Marian's appearance. Janka explained that when we were living in their home, they didn't concern themselves with suspicions that we might be Jews. If we were discovered as Jews, they could have claimed that they had checked that we had valid identity cards (*Kennkarten*) and food coupons from the authorities, so they could have emerged blameless.

Mrs. Feliksa had a ceramic-tiled brick oven in the kitchen. She and Mother prepared and sold about thirty to fifty rolls per day, made from flour, yeast, and water, sprinkled with poppy seeds, cumin or salt, and in various designs. My mother paid for the initial materials and afterward they split the costs. Krystyna distributed the rolls in the evening to grocery shops, restaurants, the pharmacist, the physician, and also to the Germans. Julek sometimes helped her.

Janka met Staszek Kowalski after Geniek Łoza came to their home and introduced him. Later, Kowalski also introduced them to S. B., a member of the AK underground from Sandomierz, and convinced Feliksa Gardziel to let him stay temporarily in their home. S. B. would come occasionally to sleep there; once or twice he came with two pistols, which he hid in the bathroom. The AK underground had positions in the forests in the area. One time, they held a trial in their home and convicted a man of collaborating with the Germans; he was later executed by shooting. Janka also knew that during the cauldron operation in the Łoza-Nowak home another underground fighter named K. S. was living in the room with Kowalski.

Jan Bolesław Gardziel taught Latin and geography at Brzesko's high school from 1918 until the outbreak of World War II. In addition, he directed the school's drama club, choir activities, string ensembles and symphony. He was a central figure in the cultural and civic life in Brzesko. After the Nazi occupiers shut down the high school, Gardziel organized teachers to provide underground instruction and directed an amateur choir for men. He realized he was in danger, but refused to flee he didn't believe that German culture would permit the occupiers to carry out the criminal actions that occurred. In May 1941, he was arrested by the Gestapo, with the assistance of the "blue" police. He was charged with "subversive activity against the Reich" and was imprisoned in the nearby city of Tarnów for seven months, then transferred to Auschwitz. On March 20, 1942, the family received a message that he had died of gangrene in an injured foot. Janina believed that he suffered from arthritis and was taken to the gas chambers, or perhaps died earlier from a heart attack. Mrs. Feliksa and her children were fully aware of Jan's activities, and even continued to participate in some of them, but in such a modest way that I had no inkling of the family's status in the city. In May 2005, I visited Julek, and Maria Gardziel with my son Amir and my grandson Gal. Janka was already ill, and she passed away a few months later.

B8. The house on 45 Independence Avenue, from the testimony of Wojciech Kuropieska

Wojciech-Wojtek, a mechanical engineer, was endowed with the Kuropieska family's qualities of excellence: profound intelligence, awareness, and knowledge, as well as an astonishing memory. He visited our home in Ramat Gan for the first time in November 2003, and spoke about the period of chaos.

His mother Leopolda was born in Warsaw in November 1906 to Walentyna and Józef Jabłoński. In her parent's home, Polish anti-Semitism did not exist. At the age of fourteen, she applied to a Jewish company and was accepted as a tailoring apprentice. During the years 1921-1939, she worked in Jewish companies, and also did piecework for them from her home. She was sent by a Jewish company to an advanced tailoring course for women and received a certificate of master tailor. Her father had Jewish friends and would tell his eight-year-old grandson Wojtek about the customs of the Jews. Her mother was a "fundamentalist" Catholic who believed it was a duty to help the Jews. Leopolda's father Józef, a retired railroad carpenter, built the hiding place in his daughter's apartment with the help of his son Michael, Leopolda's brother. Michael, an officer in the Polish Army, went into hiding with an assumed identity after fleeing from captivity. Upon Leopolda's request, the parents hid Herman Bloch for over two years in their home in Bródno, a neighborhood in Warsaw, at 5 Myszyniecka Street. According to Wojtek, Bloch was a Jewish policemen in "one of the ghettos." [Note: It was in the Otwock Ghetto; Bloch was the husband of my mother's sister Bala, who was almost certainly murdered there earlier, together with their daughter Esther-Lalusia.] All traces of Herman Bloch were lost during the August uprising in Warsaw. The parents of the captured father, Captain Józef Kuropieska, lived in Warsaw in the apartment of their daughter Janina (Józef's sister) and her husband Mieczysław Wolski, a former communist. The Wolski family was recognized by Yad Vashem as "Righteous Among the Nations" in 1989 for their contribution to saving Jews.

Until 1942, Leopolda received some assistance from the Red Cross as the wife of a prisoner of war. Later, she would travel between the

Generalgouvernement, where there was a food shortage, and the Warthegau, bringing food products to sell. Her father took care of the children in her absence. In late 1942, the Germans tightened border control and Leopolda stopped making these trips. She also did sewing jobs for neighbors; they would come to be measured in the apartment. But this work did not provide a sufficient livelihood, so in late 1942 she decided to sublet parts of her apartment and stopped doing sewing jobs. That was also when her adventures with the Jews began. First, the Kaplicki couple came for a month or two, but then they left, and disappeared. They had apparently come under suspicion; *szmalcownicy* (extortionists) came to the apartment when painters were working there and expelled the couple. Later, another man came to live in the apartment for several months. According to Mrs. Leopolda, my mother told her that his name was Kedushin. The man returned to the apartment, destitute, after the outbreak of the Warsaw Uprising, and Mrs. Leopolda gave him her husband's clothes to wear. He survived and immigrated to Israel after the war.

Around the time of the Warsaw Ghetto Uprising, Mila, and Marian Dąbrowski appeared in response to a newspaper advertisement for an apartment rental. They moved in and lived openly there. Leopolda recognized from the first glance that Marian was a Jewish boy. Mateusz would come to visit on Sundays. When Marian was identified by the children in the yard as a Jewish boy, the hiding place was built and Marian went underground. Mila rented an apartment on Sandomierska Street, about twenty minutes by foot from their apartment. For a period of time, Maria Tomaszewska (Helena–Helcia Kolski) also lived in their apartment. Later, the sisters Maya Orenstein, and Paula Blum-Kodre came to live there clandestinely. The husband of one of the sisters was murdered in the Częstochowa Ghetto. There were two sewing machines in the apartment, and I remember having the impression that the sisters did sewing work. During our meeting, Wojtek denied this, and claimed that the sisters were wealthy and did not engage in sewing.

Stasia Kolski told me by phone about a Jew, perhaps the Kedushin fellow, who lived in Leopolda's apartment; his wife, who had an Aryan appearance and spoke fluent Polish, lived in relative safety on the Polish side of Warsaw. One day, the woman decided to travel to the Lwów area in the east and to bring her child from there. She was identified as a Jew by a Ukrainian woman, handed over to the Germans, and sent to Auschwitz. A piece of paper with Leopolda's name and address was found in her clothes. Leopolda was summoned to the Gestapo headquarters on Szucha Avenue, and asked why her address appeared in the notes of a Jewish woman. Leopold explained that she makes her living by tailoring women's clothing in her home and does not interrogate her various customers especially when they look and act like that particular woman. There was no reason to suspect that she was not a Catholic Pole, she added. Leopolda was convincing and was released from the intimidating headquarters. While she was being questioned, Stasia Kolski sat outside the entrance of the headquarters, watching the people entering and exiting, until Leopolda finally emerged from the building.

Wojtek's initial impression of me was that I behaved naturally, without the restraint required in conditions of hiding, and that I spoke and even laughed too loudly. "You didn't take anyone into account," he said. Mrs. Leopolda scolded me about making noise. When the extortionists pulled me out of hiding, I went into bed, and didn't look scared, as if I didn't understand the danger I was in. Apparently, I was either "acting" or was convinced that the game was already over. When the extortionist dressed in civilian clothes entered the bedroom, he said I looked like a "real messiah" (*prawdziwy mesiasz*), and I burst into laughter. Wojtek was still lying in our shared bed. This was in contrast to the two sisters, who scurried around the room, wept and argued, and even offered hush money on the spot. As far as he remembered, the incident occurred in late May or in early June 1944. Wojtek happened to meet both of the sisters in Warsaw after the war; they didn't contact Mrs. Leopolda before emigrating to Australia.

Wojtek recalled that Michael, Leopolda's brother (the officer in hiding), spoke favorably of the Warsaw Ghetto uprising. In his conversations with Leopolda, Michael said he hoped that as many German soldiers as possible would be killed, and cried, "Kill them!" ("*Zakatrupić!*"). Perhaps the ghetto uprising influenced Leopolda; perhaps someone she knew died there. It's also possible that the Germans' brutal treatment of the Jews stirred a feeling of resistance in her. Leopolda was the wife of a captured Polish officer in an army that lost in war, and perhaps she wanted to express resistance to the occupier. The imprisoned father also expected her to do this. Her half-brother, a career officer, was murdered in Katyń, and the murder was attributed to the Germans at the time.

Wojtek was sure that his mother was in contact with one of the underground organizations. As the wife of a career officer, she could clearly be trusted. She would perform errands and help people. It's very likely that she carried out secret missions such as delivering documents, permits, perhaps money and Wojtek accompanied her. She always took Wojtek on these errands because a woman with a child at her side was safer, and Basia had difficulties walking. However, this didn't happen often because she was occupied with the problems of everyday existence. Leopolda went to the city to arrange the affairs of other Jews, not only those hiding in her home (Kolski, Mateusz, Mila) perhaps people she knew before the war.

Friends of Basia and Wojtek didn't come to play in their apartment. A number of excuses were used to keep them away the apartment was too small, and so on. Likewise, Wojtek, and Basia rarely visited the homes of their friends. A police curfew was already in force at 8:00 p.m. It was forbidden to go outside. German patrols roamed the streets and checked people. It was not customary to visit in other homes. Conversations about the situation were not held in the presence of the children so that they would know as little as possible, to prevent them from talking and disclosing things to others. Consequently, Wojtek didn't know where Mateusz and Kolski lived. Leopolda sent Wojtek to Mila on some matter even before I arrived. All in all, he went to Sandomierska Street on family matters only twice. Both times, he brought an important and urgent message to Mila - perhaps money, or a letter. Leopolda was very independent and charismatic. She did what she believed was right and didn't consult with anyone.

In Wojtek's opinion, the neighbors surmised that Jews were staying in their apartment (No. 5) and could hear sounds from it. He said, "At that time, we were unaware that the neighbors in apartment No. 6, the Kościnscy family, were sheltering a Jew, and we feared they might inform on us. The Jew, who was an intellectual, and a reserve officer in the prewar Polish Army, hid in their apartment for several months before leaving to join the Warsaw Uprising. Wiska, the daughter of the building's caretaker, Mrs. Schmidt, harassed Marian when he went down to the yard, and he eventually stopped going there because of her. Mrs. Schmidt surely knew that Leopolda was hiding Jews. If she had informed, they would have known that she was the informer."

Wojtek also told me the following story, "One Sunday, apparently in July 1944, soon after Marian left the apartment accompanied by Mila, three uniformed Polish policemen came to search for Jews. But there were no longer any Jews there. I remember my mother walking out of the room with one of the policemen to the kitchen. And she later told me that the policeman disclosed to her the identity of the person who had informed the police and the *szmalcownicy* that she was hiding Jews. It was supposedly our neighbor on 36 Independence Avenue, Mrs. W., a naturalized Polish citizen of German extraction."

B9. The Gestapo's cauldron maneuver

Excerpts from a conversation recorded at the home of Helena Łoza-Skrobotowicz (Brzesko, August 1992).

In attendance: Helena and her husband, Józef Skrobotowicz, Barbara (Basia) Nowak, Azriela and Yoseph (Marek) Komem.

Helena: In the children's room were Basia, Bogusia, Adam and you, and we had to keep everything secret. It was very dangerous, and a German soldier lived with us, Walhter.
Marek: And later a second soldier arrived.
Helena: If so, you remember everything very well.
Marek: What was the name of the second soldier?
Helena: I don't remember.

Helena: I know, all of your family survived through luck.
Marek: Through luck, but not only luck. Through luck, too.
Helena: The most energetic was the mother, Mrs. Krystyna, She was full of energy.
Marek: Yes, she was full of energy, so was Father.
Helena: He seemed like a very energetic man. Very ... He was a very level-headed man, quiet. Very balanced.

Marek: He had self-confidence.
Helena: Yes. I remember his face. I really remember the way he looked. He would come to us most often because of Geniek. Geniek would bring Mr. Mateusz and that was the beginning. The beginning of the relations. Yes, the relations because Geniek connected with Herbert.

Marek (to Helena):
Now, I'd like you to concentrate on the months when I stayed with you. You certainly remember this better than I do.

Helena: So, you do remember a lot! Really, there are things that stick in one's memory.
Marek: Yes, I remember a lot. I remember that two German soldiers stayed with you in the "mobilized apartment." And later I remember the raid by the Gestapo. In 1944.
Helena: Yes, I confirm. Yes, you indeed remember. It was in 1943, perhaps in 1944, yes, but it was in the month of September. September.
Marek: Maybe later?
Helena: No! So you remember. In 1944. It was nighttime. At night, the Gestapo raided. It was related to the partisans.
Marek: What was there? What did they hope to find? How did they find out? Who? What?
Helena: Look, my friend from school, Kazik, was with the partisans. He was older than me, perhaps by a year. He knew a lot of the partisans. And there was one man who commanded a unit of partisans who had no place to live. And it was suggested that Mr. Kowalski, who rented a room from my sister (Irena), would take another man in with him.
Marek: Was he (Kowalski) a member of the AK?
Helena: Kowalski didn't say anything about this. But even if he didn't belong, he had a lot in common with them … You know, we sort of had protection when there was a man. There were children, and the sisters, and Mother and there was no man in the home. [She didn't count the deaf brother, Geniek.]
Marek: Were Germans already living with you then?
Helena: Not yet. There was a constant turnover. Since the headquarters

of one of the units was not far from here, they had to billet a number of people in the homes in the neighborhood, even in inferior conditions. Our apartment was on their list. When these soldiers left, others from the Wehrmacht arrived.

Helena: Regarding that guest [the other tenant, the commander in the partisans], the sister expressed willingness to also take him in. You know, to save a human being.

Marek: Also, considering the fact that your father fell during an aerial bombardment by the Germans during the war.

Helena: Yes, that was also a factor. But Mother was a great patriot. A very great patriot. And so we accepted the second gentleman. He lived in a regular way. [This second man's name was not mentioned during the conversation.]

Kazik, my friend, apparently liked to drink a bit. I knew him, but he never drank in my presence. He carried out an action (*akcja*) against a German in Jasień, about four kilometers from Brzesko. That is, he shot a German, and killed him. And his mother lived in the neighborhood here. He lived with her, he was the youngest brother. His oldest brother was in hiding. Another brother was in German captivity somewhere. We told him, and our tenant also said, "Kazik, go to another district, and disappear." But he roamed around this area. Maybe he didn't have time it's impossible to know. One time, our mother went with Irena to the city to do some shopping or something, it was a Saturday, I was home. The two men lived in the house then: the tenant and Kowalski. And just imagine, the Germans identified that Kazik who killed the German.

Marek: That means there were witnesses? Maybe someone informed?

Helena: There had to be witnesses, because they searched for him here and it [the shooting] didn't take place in Brzesko. He didn't put enough thought into it. It was not planned. And so the Gestapo caught him.

Marek: And your mother found out about it?

Helena: Yes. The Gestapo headquarters was at the old high school, near the main street. They dragged him there and started to beat him. They beat him so he would reveal where he kept the weapon which was a very serious crime. He said he had a weapon stashed in his family's home. They brought him to the house. His mother saw that he was under arrest, in handcuffs,

and beaten. "He's not guilty," she cried. "It's not his weapon. It belongs to so and so, who lives in this place and that …"
Marek: And they killed him?
Helena: No. They took him to Tarnów, where he was interrogated. And later in Montelupich prison in Kraków. And there they finished him off.
Marek: They killed him? Did he talk?
Helena: They killed him. Yes. In the end, he talked.
Helena: When they caught him, Mother and the sister (Irena) found out. Mother came home and said they had arrested Kazik. Then we started to clear out everything. Because we had partisans in the house.
Basia: The one who lived with us?
Helena: Yes, and there were weapons.
Marek: There were weapons inside the trench in the garden.
Helena: There were weapons, there were papers, and there were identity documents. There were all sorts of … So we started to clear everything out… When we cleared things out, we did it in a foolish way, because one of the new partisans brought a suitcase and shoved it under the bed where I slept. Yes, there was this "genius" who left a suitcase behind. And they searched for photographs of his. So, imagine we cleared out everything possible. One man fled to a particular house and hid there in the attic. And Mother had to give him a signal to indicate whether they were coming to look for him. If the Germans were at our home he would flee.
The Gestapo came at night. They surrounded the house, the entire garden. They aimed floodlights toward the house and inside it. Yes.
Marek: And they entered the apartment.
Helena: Yes. But first they rang at the door. The German tenants opened [she laughs] and said, "But there is a very respectable family living here." They were very surprised by the visit. So, there were very "hot" days. Very.
Marek: And it continued for about a week.
Helena: Yes, it went on for about ten days, starting on Saturday. It was a cauldron (kocioł) maneuver, an ambush. In this method, they pulled everyone inside, and then arrested them. They wanted to draw in as many people as possible. In addition, you know, it was 1944. Since the front was approaching, they transferred some of the handing of our affairs to the Army. The Army [the Wehrmacht] was a bit more refined, because the

Gestapo was going to execute us by shooting.

Marek: But those who entered, I remember them searching the entire home.

Helena: Yes, they sat in the house.

Marek: I don't remember exactly. There was a break when your mother went out to the garden and dug. I remember that scene. She returned with weapons inside her apron.

Helena: And we played chess with the Germans. I played and the sister, too. Kowalski didn't play he walked around the apartment between the windows from one window to the next. Mother took a bucket. You know, there was Grandfather's wooden crate from the time of World War I. They [the partisans] had wrapped the weapons in paper, tied them with a rope and buried it in the trench in the garden, inside the crate. Mother was able to dig out the crate in daylight. A light rain fell. And we played. Kowalski winked to us that the crate of weapons was already in her hands. And then she went to a sort of small wooden shed. Ahh. There were rabbits there, and maybe a pig, too. She stashed the weapons there under the hay. On the other hand, she took the papers, placed coal and wood on them, and burned them. All of the papers, because there was a second box buried near the drainpipe, and she also dug that one out.

Marek: [feigning innocence, to elicit more details from Helena] She also burned the weapons?

Helena: No. Because there were two crates, one near the drainpipe and one near the wall [at the end of the garden]. The documents and the *Kennkarten* were in one crate and the weapons in the other crate in the trench by the wall.

Marek: So the Germans were inside the apartment and she dug out the weapons, and you played. This was at night?

Helena: It was during the day, between eleven o'clock a.m. and twelve noon. Because they guarded us closely. There were always two guards watching us. And then she went again to take these weapons and hid them inside the chimney (*komin*), in the ash dump. Only after everything quieted down, we contacted the partisans. And mother removed the weapons, hid them inside a jug of milk, covered them with bread and sausages and took them back to the woods.

Marek: Wasn't the Gestapo still in the house then?

Helena: They were in the house the whole time. But why was it necessary to dig out the weapons? Because they said at the outset that they would dig up the whole garden with a sort of rod, down deep.
Marek: But I remember, I remember that the day after your mother hid the weapons in the oven, the company, or platoon came, about thirty soldiers.
Helena: And they drove rods into the soil.
Marek: They dug. They had military shovels. They stood in a row and dug across the entire garden, from the house to the air raid trench.
Helena: Do you remember?
Basia: Maybe they dug with rods where the gasoline was? [Note: I didn't remember the story of the gasoline.]
Helena: The partisan (the tenant) fled. Why did Mother have to give a signal? Because they came suddenly at night. They conducted a search and shook everyone. They definitely wanted to find photographs. They pulled out the suitcase from under my bed. They found it. But there were no photographs in it. They harassed me on this matter. Later, they left us alone, but they stayed in the house.
Marek: I remember that when the Gestapo arrived, they moved me to your mother's and your room for the entire time. Usually, I slept in the children's room by the kitchen wall. They didn't find anything in the end?
Helena: No. They didn't find any documents.
Marek: Despite everything that she [the mother of imprisoned Kazik] said, they didn't believe her?!
Helena [agitated]: That woman, from the home where the partisan slept, came in the morning to clarify something. But before she managed to say a word, Mother grabbed a pot, handed it to her and said, "Look, ma'am, we have some guests. Please bring us a little milk." She saw the Germans herself and then told that fellow, and he fled to Szczepanów on an old bicycle with no air in its tires. I don't know, Maybe someone brought him a bicycle. I don't remember exactly.
We sat and everyone who came, lots of people came in, the partisan also sent a few, came to ask if we have an apartment to rent. They came to get an idea of what our situation was, to see whether we had been harmed. It was unpleasant. It was a very dangerous situation.
Marek: And I was the last thing you needed there, right?

Helena: A very dangerous situation. They wanted to expel us. First, they wanted to execute us. Later they said they would expel us [to a death camp or forced labor in Germany]. There were terribly severe punishments then. For possession of weapons, for … [she was too polite to explicitly say "for sheltering Jews"], or for lesser infractions. What's more, they brought that Kazik to us at night to my sister's apartment and he said, "Mrs. Irena, tell them the truth!"

Marek: He was fighting for his life then.

Helena: He was in handcuffs, beaten, and after torture; it was impossible to even recognize him.

Marek: So what did Mrs. Irena say? She didn't confess to anything?

Helena: No! Of course not! He had to talk that way. So, I saw him for the last time. His father didn't survive the war and died earlier in Auschwitz. And he himself was gone. But the mother survived. She was sent to the Ravensbrück camp and survived.

PART TWO
Freedom and Commitment

Yoseph's Memories-testimony After Liberation,
Additional Testimonies, Personal Reflection

A. YOSEPH'S MEMORIES-TESTIMONY AFTER LIBERATION AND ADDITIONAL TESTIMONIES

1. The wake-up - Kalisz

My father was temporarily appointed manager of the old family factory for lace, curtains, and tulle in Kalisz. The Germans expropriated the factory in September 1939 and partly converted it for war purposes. Now, after the Germans were gone, it was placed under the authority of the Polish government. The Daub family had been living in the apartment before it was allocated to my father. Mr. Gustav Daub, a German, managed the factory during the period of occupation. He had been working in Kalisz prior to the invasion and my father knew him then. They had worked in forced cooperation during the occupation, when my father remained alone in the city.

The Daub family had left the three-room apartment in haste and no one had broken into it. In the pantry room adjacent to the kitchen, there were shelves neatly arranged with jars of jam, canned goods, sausages, wine, and a bounty of foodstuffs and accessories of a well-ordered home. Handsome oil paintings in carved frames hung in the guest room and living room, and stylish chandeliers dangled from the ceilings of the three rooms. A heavy wooden bookcase stood in the guest room, with many books arranged behind glass doors. The books featured elegant covers stamped with German words, most in Gothic lettering, and there were also a few books in Polish. What immediately fascinated me was a detailed wooden model of Columbus' ship, the *Santa Maria*, displayed on a shelf in the library, with all of its masts and beams, transparent, and decorated parchment sails, systems of ropes and ladders made from tendons, a "crow's nest," bronze cannons, and a picture of Mary and baby Jesus painted on the stern above the helm. I was barely able to drag one of the two deep leather armchairs to the big window overlooking the backyard and the wide Rypinkowski Canal branching out from the Prosna River; I adopted this as a lookout and reading spot. From the bedroom, which had two solid wooden beds where my father and I slept, we could go out onto the balcony, which faced Pułaskiego Street.

I cannot recall whether Uncle Samek (Salomon Bloch) was already there when I came to the apartment, or whether he joined us a few days later. Uncle Samek fled the evacuation march from the Oflag II-C Woldenberg prisoner-of-war camp for Polish officers in Germany. Following the defeat of Poland's Army, nearly ninety Jewish officers were crowded into a single barrack and showcased for representatives of the Red Cross in Geneva. When Samek returned, my father gave him the job of general manager of the factory, and he himself remained its technical manager and chief "Meister". Samek was about forty years old, tall, and thin, with black hair, and a receding hairline. He was an economist, level-headed and precise, and he spoke decisively. He declared that he was vigilant about speaking truthfully and acting according to the code of conduct of a Polish officer. Samek, from our first meeting, addressed me in his deep voice with affection, respect, and concern for my welfare. I loved and respected him. His relationship with my father at work and in our shared residence was harmonious. They each were very fond and respectful of each other. Samek was the husband of Ala, my father's sister, who perished with their daughter Ninka-Yocheved and son Marek in the Warsaw Ghetto or in a death camp, during the ghetto uprising. I remember him as "an officer and a gentleman" in his principles and conduct, sensitive, and considerate of others, a professional, and determined in his work. He never forgave all those he held responsible for bringing tragedy upon the Jewish people and upon the family he lost. He died in Melbourne, Australia, after many years of sorrow.

I was employed in various houseworks: errands, shopping, and frying omelets. I wandered around the city's squares and park. I loved to roam the factory's production facilities, which were quickly restored to their original purpose by the veteran weavers and other workers. On warm days, I loved to spend time in "our" small orchard at the factory, with its deciduous fruit trees. The entrance to the factory was from Fabryczna Street, very close to our apartment.

I was promptly registered for the nearby school, which had just started to operate. There was also "Pioneers" activity for young pupils. As long as the fighting continued, and afterward, too, I continued to use my assumed name (Marek) with the children, and I was determined not to mention my Jewish origin; and if it was mentioned, I immediately attributed it to the past.

On May 9, 1945, the armed conflict on European soil came to an end. The official and private expressions of joy, which we shared, did not lighten the heavy mood in our home due to the losses and fears for my mother's fate. With each passing day, our hopes of Mother still being alive diminished. I convinced myself that it was best to assume that Ignaś was also not among the living. I didn't believe my father's stories about visiting him on some of his trips. I was not resolute enough to demand a convincing sign of life.

It was early on a Sunday morning in May or early June. I was sleeping with my father in the inner bedroom, and I thought I heard some muffled sounds coming from the direction of the staircase. Uncle Samek, who slept on the coach in the middle room, went to open the door to the apartment. He quickly returned and appeared at the entrance to our bedroom, and instructed us to come with him right away. I got up and followed him and there was Mother standing in the doorway, gaunt, and dressed in a motley assortment of clothes she had found along the way. Her face, exhausted from the hardships of her journey, expressed restrained excitement, and tension. Father took her bulging backpack, and my mother walked inside. When the door closed, we hugged, and kissed, without uttering a word. We sat down in the kitchen and then Mother told us that she had arrived in the city before dawn on the train. She waited for sunrise and then walked several kilometers on the empty road, from the station to the city, a suppressed fear gnawing at her heart would she find someone from the family here? As she approached Fabryczna Street, deserted at that hour, she saw a man sweeping the sidewalk by an entrance to his house and recognized him as Mr. Markiewicz, one of the veteran weavers in the factory. Mr. Markiewicz told her that Moniek and Salomon Bloch had returned to the city, and that Moniek's son was with them in their apartment. He noted that he couldn't say whether the boy was the older or younger son.

Father immediately reassured Mother that Ignaś was safe and that he would now go to bring him. Mother took off her coat and removed her worn-out work shoes. She pulled out some sought-after commodities, including a large loaf of country bread, dry salami and a complete ham, and gave them to Father and Samek. Then she pulled out the striped suit of a concentration camp prisoner, placed it on the edge of the table, and told us about the hardships of her journey to Kalisz. As the Red Army's offensive in eastern Prussia advanced, Mother was evacuated in January from the Stutthof death camp in a death march [*Todesmarsch*]. The column of evacuated women marched toward Lebork (in Pomerania), accompanied by armed German soldiers and dogs. The prisoners, in their tattered clothing, feeble from hunger, and illness, some of them infected with typhus, had difficulty keeping up the brisk pace in the freezing cold, in the snow, hungry, and thirsty. Many of those who faltered and fell by the wayside were put to death by a bullet in the back of the neck or by a rifle butt shattering their skull. Today I know that the column marched about twenty kilometers a day, and sometimes at night. Rest stops were occasionally improvised in barns and abandoned farms. At some stops, the prisoners on the death march were ordered by the retreating German Army to dig antitank ditches in the frozen ground. In this situation, Mother and a Polish prisoner she had befriended at the camp decided to try to flee together if an opportunity arose. At one point, when the march entered a forest path, the two started running with the last of their strength, their feet plodding through the snow and stubbing into whatever was buried below it. The soldiers shot at them, but missed, and the fugitives were able to vanish in the thicket of trees. There was apparently a commotion in the column, and the soldiers decided not to split up and chase after them. In the evening, Mother and her friend sneaked into a farm they had observed as abandoned and found some scraps of food and items of clothing. They stuffed the striped prison camp uniforms into old backpacks they found and took them with them. They waited and advanced cautiously toward the front lines, passing a motley stream of refugees and soldiers retreating in the opposite direction. Finally, they reached a unit of the Red Army. I remember my mother speaking angrily about the disappointing encounter with the liberators. Together with many other refugees and liberated people, predominantly women, they were forced at gunpoint to do construction work on wooden bridges over rivers or canals for the Red Army, sometimes while under fire by the German Army. The forced mobilization of exhausted camp prisoners and refugees continued for two to three weeks. From there, the two continued by foot, on carts, and by sneaking onto freight trains traveling to the south and east, until separating, each woman heading to her city of origin, into the chilling unknown.

The next day, my father set off, as promised, and returned about two days later with my brother Ignaś. While we were waiting for them, Mother told Uncle Samek, and me how, after suppressing the uprising of the Polish underground in Warsaw, the Germans gathered the local population in groups at the temporary camp in Pruszków, and from there, after selection, they were sent to concentration camps or to work in Germany. When Krystyna, Mateusz and Marian arrived and stood in line before the German selection officer, he gave them a choice - one of the parents could stay with the child, while the other would be sent in a transport. Krystyna decided that Mateusz had a better chance than her of surviving on the Aryan side and said that she preferred to be sent. Her sister Maria Tomaszewska (Helena Kolski) and niece Cesia also were sent to the Stutthof concentration camp and survived there until Mother was evacuated.

We also learned that Mother received a food package or even two at the concentration camp. Samek would occasionally receive a package at the prisoner-of-war camp from a woman in Warsaw, a volunteer in a group organized to support Polish POWs in Germany. Somehow, Mateusz was able to send the prisoner Second Lieutenant Salomon Bloch a message that Krystyna Łągiewska was incarcerated at the Stutthof camp. Samek decided to inform the volunteer in Warsaw that the food supply had recently improved in his camp and asked that she instead send her packages to Mother in Stutthof. And the volunteer indeed did this, and Mother received a package that helped to sustain her.

Besides Helcia and Cesia, who were missing, Frania was the only one who survived from among my mother's brothers and sisters, including their children. Frania arrived in Kalisz, a young woman, bitter, and withdrawn; the times had completely changed her. For some reason, the relations between her and my father were distant and antagonistic, and my mother tried to reconcile them and help.

Our lives entered a more orderly routine. Mother registered as a returnee with the council of the small Jewish community. She was listed as No. 107 in this Jewish community, the most ancient in Poland, which numbered about twenty-seven-thousand before the war. With the condescending heartlessness of a child, I was disgusted by the sight of the solitary people crowding frantically in the council's corridors, restless, with nowhere to turn, or sitting at the simple wooden table for meals at the soup kitchen. After a short period of time, Uncle Samek left, unfortunately, for separate quarters.

Survivors from the family who returned to Kalisz. At the right: Samek-Salomon Bloch.

I also developed a close friendship with two children my age, who had survived and returned to Kalisz from wherever they had been with their parents. One was Rysiek, who lived down our street, the son of the head of the provisional Jewish community council. The second was Janek, who lived near the city hall, the son of an attorney who had converted to Christianity. Usually, we met, and played quietly inside the apartments or in the yard. Janek was the only one with the chutzpah to engage in mischief. One time, I was dumbstruck when he tried to call his mother from our home via the post office operator, was annoyed by her response, and dared to call her "stupid" and "cuckoo." We never spoke about the past.[9] I went first with one of them, and later with Ignaś to one of the two cinemas that opened. We usually saw Russian films about the war of heroism against the Nazi Army, such as *Rainbow*, based on the war novel by Wanda Wasilewska, or *Zoya*, the heroic story of the self-sacrifice of a partisan under the occupation, and we also saw films of the concentration and death camps, revealing their horrors. However, we also saw *The Thief of Bagdad*, which was filmed in the West.

Mother was a different person than the one who had left Kalisz. As if to soothe the pain of losing most of her family and the wasted years, she surged with independence, and a hunger for action. First, she organized the household, and routine of family life. Next, she opened a shop for selling and sewing curtains, tulle, and lace, as well as upholstery produced at the factory or from other renewed facilities. On Śródmiejska (City Center) Street, inside the show window, I could see, to my great chagrin, the model of the *Santa Maria* ship. And through the curtains, the silhouette of my mother was visible. I would have preferred to see her at home. When she was home, I would sometimes hear her beautiful voice in song. I still remember a section from a melancholy tango hit that was on the lips of many people, expressing their emotions, "Golden chrysanthemums / In a crystal vase / Standing on the piano / Relieving sadness and complaint / ... / Nothing will cheer me today / Because the dreams have vanished. / Who will heal my heart / Wipe tears from my eyes?"

---

9   Janek completed his studies in agricultural mechanical engineering at age twenty. He became a famous jazz percussionist and promoter, organizing performances on a national scale. He served one term in the Polish Sejm and appears in the list of honorary citizens of the city of Kalisz. Rysiek and Janek already completed their high school matriculation at age sixteen. Rysiek excelled in his medical studies in Poland, married a Christian woman and died at a young age, about thirty years old.

Certificate from the district Jewish community council in Kalisz, affirming that our mother had returned from the Stutthof concentration camp and registered with the council. Her registration number was 107.

In the bookcase, I found *Tristan and Isolde* and *Don Quixote of La Mancha* in Polish, and thus began to learn the ways of the world through reading books. However, it was only several years later that I understood why the king sprinkled talc powder at night on the floor of the palace in order to track Tristan's path to the bed of the queen-designate. Only then did I perceive the meaning of the sad denouement of these lovers. My brother and I learned geography from a scientific globe that spun on a splendid wooden base, with borders that had changed beyond recognition. After he left for London (see below), I continued to learn geography from a stamp album I received from Hela Lifshitz for my tenth birthday. A handsome chess set encouraged us to learn the rules of the game. After reading a number of books that began to appear in the stores, on topics such as the Wild West, pirates, and Greek mythology, Mother registered me at the public library, where I visited religiously. At school, in third grade, I was a below-average pupil, especially in arithmetic. They moved me up to the second row, but I still didn't understand the concepts of decimal fractions. In the end, I had to consent to wearing eyeglasses to correct nearsightedness. My brother, on the other hand, was an outstanding pupil in everything, and his compositions won praise from the teachers. I excelled in catechism lessons taught by the priest. In fact, the mother of a classmate, a God-fearing Catholic, asked me to help tutor her son at home with religious lessons, and so I did.

Meanwhile, we learned that Aunt Helena-Helcia and her daughter Cesia had survived the evacuation by sea from Stutthof. They remained in the camp among the exhausted and ill, and were finally evacuated in April and placed in motorless barges that were left to the mercy of the waves, sea currents, and aerial assaults by Allied warplanes. After severe hardships, those who remained alive landed near the city of Malmö in Sweden. Helcia's son, Mietek Kolski, and his wife Stasia survived the Warsaw Uprising and occupation without being sent to the camps, and moved to the city of Łódz. We traveled to visit them at their home after the birth of their son Maryś, from a pregnancy that began around the time of the Warsaw Uprising. Later, Hela Lifshitz returned, after surviving the liquidations in Kalisz, the Łódz Ghetto, the Auschwitz death camp, and forced labor in Germany. Her husband, David Kushel, whom she married in the Łódz Ghetto, perished in Auschwitz.

My parents invited our recent protectors to visit, and we tried to repay them as best we could. The visit I particularly enjoyed was of Geniek Łoza, who came with his brother, Dr. Emil Łoza, a military doctor, and lecturer at the University of Łódz. Their sister, Helena, who had moved to Łódz, may have also visited with them. Geniek, a natural athlete, sat me on the frame of a bicycle and rode with me on the sides of streets and dirt roads for tens of kilometers in the beautiful rural surroundings of Kalisz. We passed farms, windmills, churches, and towns, eating and drinking from a basket Mother prepared. Geniek and I were very fond of each other. Another visit was by the Kuropieska family. Józef Kuropieska, who was promoted to the rank of lieutenant colonel, arrived in an official car with Mrs. Leopolda and their son Wojtek. It was a particularly emotional meeting between the two mothers and also between the two friends from Oflag Woldenberg. The children were full participants in the happenings and in the meal, except, of course, for the festive drinking. Father and Samek proudly showed the visitors the factory, which they had restored to full production in record time compared to government factories in liberated Poland. We showered the visitors with gifts, including some for those who were unable to come with them. We felt that this was just a drop in the ocean of what we wanted to give them. Stanisław Kowalski became a sales agent for the factory's products in a large territory around Sandomierz. He brought packages of curtains from the factory and fabric to the Łoza and Nowak families in Słotwina and also to the Gardziel family in Brzesko. One time, father traveled himself to the area in order to testify in court on behalf of his deaf friend Antoni Herbert. The authorities sought to imprison him after he was falsely accused of collaborating with the occupation forces as a *Volksdeutsch*. Conniving neighbors not only coveted the homes of Jews who had disappeared.

At the beginning of fourth grade, most of the pupils in the class began preparing for their First Communion. My parents didn't get involved at all. Once a week, I would go with my friends in the afternoon to the priest's office in one of the churches or ancient monasteries of Kalisz for lessons on religion and faith, and later we practiced for the ceremony. They didn't check whether I was baptized, or perhaps I lied, and said I was. A day before the ceremony, ready, and willing, I suddenly was swept with a wave of strong emotions and thoughts. I had not anticipated this and didn't know where this came from. I decided I wouldn't go for communion and my parents told the school that I was sick. Soon afterward, I stopped going to school and my mother hired a private teacher, who lived in the apartment below us, to teach me languages: Polish and English. My parents sensed an anti-Semitic atmosphere and were concerned for my safety.

I loved to roam the streets of Kalisz. It's an ancient city, built on the site of a prehistoric settlement, on the Amber Route, and which was mentioned in Roman writings. The city is situated on a number of waterways: the Prosna River, its tributaries, and canals the "Venice of the East." From the stone bridge, on the way to the old market square around the city hall, my father would angrily point to the tombstones the Germans had uprooted from the ancient Jewish cemetery to reinforce the steep banks of the Prosna Rypinkowski Canal and block the spring flooding. There were bookshops and exciting game stores in the city center. The Jewish Quarter stretched to the west of the old market. My mother pointed out the family's home on Piskorzewska Street, a picturesque alleyway of stone buildings, which afforded a beautiful view of the city hall and the square clock tower above it. My mother also showed me the site of the store her older sisters had managed after the death of their parents. The signs of destruction and neglect were very evident here. My father spoke proudly of the charter of rights, the first in Poland, which Prince Bolesław the Pious granted to the Kalisz Jews in the thirteenth century and which his grandson, King Casimir III the Great, extended to all of the cities in the kingdom a century later. My father, who loved drawing, and graphics, also noted that the text of the Kalisz Statute was published in magnificent print by the eminent artist Arthur Szyk. At the time, I didn't want to hear the story of the expulsion and liquidation of the Jews of the city and its environs under the Nazi occupation. There were whispered stories about executions by shooting in the city and in the forests outside the city, about the use of exhaust fumes from black vehicles to kill Jews, about transports to the Generalgouvernement and to the Chełmno extermination camp, and about the expulsion of the city's surviving Jews to the Łódz Ghetto. On the other hand, my brother and I were particularly intrigued by the churches and the ancient, dark, and fortified monasteries of the Franciscans, Jesuits, and other orders.

From the center of Kalisz and our neighborhood, it was easy to get to the city park, the pride of the city and its showcase. The well-tended park encompassed the branches of the city's waterways and featured many different types of trees. I remember chestnut trees, ancient thick-trunked oaks, and towering birches. On the sides of the trails, a variety of ornamental shrubs grew, with broad lawns between them. The park included artificial lakes, and in the center of one lake an island was planted with trees and greenery. The lake froze in the winter and one could walk over to the island and explore it. During the summer, swans and ducks floated on the lake, and in the winter people ice-skated on it. By a dock on the banks of the Prosna, kayaks, and rowboats were anchored for team competitions. A large wooden building there served as a boathouse for an active rowing club. The park also accommodated two soccer stadiums. Inside one of them was a running track encircled by a concrete track with variable gradients for bicycle racing. I remember the pleasurable sensation of flying while racing my friends on these tracks (which my parents forbade). My father played soccer for Maccabi Kalisz in one of the two stadiums.

The cemetery in the park for Red Army soldiers who fell in the battle for Kalisz left a strong impression on me. Along with the desire to honor and express gratitude for the many who fell in battle, I was also angry that the subject of death took over the most beautiful part of this park, a jewel of culture. Next to the concrete pathways and graves, field cannons were placed as monuments, with their barrels pointed upward, as if ready to fire a gun salute. I deciphered the Cyrillic script with my brother, and we read the names and ranks of the soldiers. The inscriptions on tombstones of the small communal graves for simple soldiers indicated a large number of unknown soldiers. On these tombstones, and on the more personal ones for officers, including those of high rank, we could identify quite a few conspicuously Jewish names. Their mobilization and sacrifice had a profound emotional impact on me.

My strongest memory of the Prosna River is of walking one summer day with my father and Ignaś to the outskirts of the city to splash around in the river. We found bathing shorts in the apartment. They were brown, made of cotton, and had a *Hitlerjugend* (Hitler Youth) badge sewn onto them. I wore them defiantly. The river flowed slowly and we entered the water at a bend in the river. After a while, my father went out, and sat on the riverbank. The water was shallow, only up to my waist. I slowly ventured further out, to the middle of the river, and the water still only reached my chest. I walked another two or three steps, expecting the river to become shallower again, enabling me to cross to the other side. However, I started to sink in the mud and the water reached my nose, and I was unable to retrace my steps. At the last moment, my father saw what was happening, swam toward me with his slow strokes and pulled me to the riverbank. This was decisive proof of my foolishness, even beyond a lack of good judgment. I later attributed my actions in the river also to qualities of inquisitiveness and determination. Many years later, every time I encountered the Coriolis acceleration effect in my studies and work, I recalled the bend in the meandering Prosna River.

Exempt from studies at school, I spent a large part of the day at home reading, sunk in the leather armchair by the window of the guest room. Besides a weekly magazine for youth and a satirical publication, *Szpilki* (Pins), I spent most of the hours of the day reading books and adventure series by authors such as Thomas Mayne Reid, Karl May, James Fenimore Cooper, Jack London, and Jules Verne. The librarian guided me toward patriotic-historical reading, including books by Józef Ignacy Kraszewski and Henryk Sienkiewicz. I remember struggling with the mystical vision in *Forefathers' Eve* (*Dziady*) by Adam Mickiewicz. Through this reading, I reconnected with the national Polish identity instilled in me when I lived in Słotwina.

When my parents suddenly and secretly informed me that they planned to leave Poland, I regarded this as a betrayal of the homeland. Meanwhile, the work of my father and Samek at the factory was successful. The factory's rehabilitation and production won praise from the government's office in Łódz. Father marched at the head of the factory's workers in the Workers' Day parade on the first of May, holding one end of a giant banner. The employees received generous bonuses packages of goods under the table. However, the grip of the communist regime tightened, and the legal efforts of Uncle Samek to restore the family's property were summarily rejected, down to the last item. The loss of families and the alienation tortured them. My brother and I overheard in conversations, and were also told explicitly by our parents, that they didn't survive the deathblows of the war in order to continue to live in servitude under an arbitrary communist regime. They expressed confidence in their ability to start over in a different country. My mother had strong faith in my father's ability to succeed beyond tending to the basic needs of the family. From the outset, they rejected the possibility of trying to reach Palestine to join my father's parents, Shmuel, and Devorah, who were very wealthy; his brother Abram; his sisters, Roza and Genia; and my mother's sister Pola. Palestine seemed harsh and unsafe in the present and future, and both of my parents harbored bitter feelings from their relationship with my grandmother and grandfather in the past. My father apparently felt deep resentment toward his parents for not making concrete efforts to rescue family members during the war period. My mother voiced fears about an imminent takeover of the Near East by Soviet communism. The pogrom against the Jews of Kielce and frequent murder of Jews in Poland, primarily by members of ultra-nationalist remnants of the AK underground (mainly the *Narodowe Siły Zbrojne*, or NSZ faction), accelerated my parents' decision-making process. At the time, it was relatively easy to obtain immigration visas to countries in South and Central America, and my father received a visa for Colombia and my mother received one from Venezuela. However, restrictions on leaving Poland went into effect.

I again wrestled with a crisis of identity. I began to pay greater attention to disturbing expressions of overt and implicit anti-Semitism that I had previously ignored. The final straw was a derogatory song in rhyme that was popular in my surroundings and which infuriated me. In loose translation, the lyrics were:

> "Who are you? A little Jew boy. / What is your emblem? A piece of challah. /
> Where do you live? In Palestine. / And what do you do there? I am a swineherd."

And this was a paraphrase of a patriotic song of identity of a proud Polish child,

> "Who are you? A little Pole. / What is your symbol? A white eagle. /
> Where do you live? Among my compatriots. / In what country? In Poland, my land…"

I thought to myself in simple terms: *If they don't want us because we are Jews, and also don't allow us to assimilate, let's develop our own country, as an alternative to Poland, even if it's a barren desert, dry and hot; at least there we will be masters of our fate. It would indeed be worthy to devote years of one's life to such a cause.* I decisively informed my parents that if we were to leave Poland, I would only agree to go to Palestine, and that I had no interest in Latin America or any other country. To my surprise, they seemed to take my opinion seriously this time, and said they would see how things worked out.

The 10th birthday party of Yoseph-Jurek in Kalisz, 28 Pułaskiego Street, 1946. Standing: Mietek, Stasia, Moshe-Moniek and Yoseph. Sitting (right to left): Dr. Michael Stier, Hela Lifshitz, Frania, Cesia, a friend, Nagórski (chairman of the Jewish Committee) and his son, Rysiek, Samek and Halina.

Ignaś was the first to depart. He flew to London with the Kuropieska family, who were willing to take him into their home. Lieutenant Colonel Józef Kuropieska was appointed as Poland's military attaché in England. A fascinating exchange of letters began between us, the two brothers.

During this period, Uncle Samek married Halina, who had lost her husband (a physician) and family in the Nazi onslaught. Years later, Halina told me, with great fondness, that my mother was the one who persuaded each of them separately to find a spouse, helped them overcome their personal traumas, and "matched" them at a party she made in her honor. Each of them eventually learned all of the details about the other's lost family members.

My Aunt Frania also soon married Jakub - Janek Fryde, a friend she met in prewar Kalisz. Janek returned with the Red Army, demobilized as a lieutenant, and didn't find any members of his family alive. An accountant by profession, he was a dedicated employee of the Polish Ministry of

Public Security, which was hated by the citizenry. He remained a devout communist for most of his life. Frania could not have imagined a more dedicated husband.

We started preparing for our departure. Mr. Stanisław Kowalski came on business and offered to take me by train to Słotwina-Brzesko on a farewell journey. My parents were very worried about this trip, because there had been quite a few cases of armed men stopping trains or covertly boarding them and executing Jews by shooting. Kowalski assured them that even if such an incident occurred, I would be safe because he himself was a member of the AK underground and he would say I was his son. My parents acquiesced. During the long trip I felt a familiar fear. At first, we arrived in Kraków, where we toured Planty Park, the gardens of this old capital. We climbed up Wawel Hill, where Poland's kings once lived, and then walked down to the lair of a legendary dragon. From Kraków, we traveled to Sandomierz. I met and ate dinner with Mrs. Marta and her daughters, Ryszarda, who was my age, and her younger sister Alicia, at their home on 1 Sucha Road. Mr. Stanisław took Ryszarda and me on a walk through the streets of the Old City, and we reached the slopes of the Vistula River and bathed. Here again I had some bad luck I fell into a "horse pit" and began to sink, until Mr. Kowalski managed to pull me out. Later, we traveled to Brzesko. We bid farewell to Stefania and Geniek Łoza and to Mrs. Irena Nowak and her children. The young Helena had already moved temporarily to Łódz. I also met with the Gardziel family. From Brzesko, we returned to Kalisz by train.

We again split up. I was supposed to fly to Paris with my father, who planned to look for further opportunities from there. My mother was supposed to remain alone, to clear our debts, and try to transport as many of our household belongings as possible by land. I also bid a personal farewell. Prior to leaving, I bought with my own savings a silver ring crowned with an eagle, the symbol of Poland, against the backdrop of the red and white flag. I thought, *Good-bye Kalisz our city, a city with no Jews. Farewell Poland, host country-homeland, saturated with death, and torment. A future of new beginnings and mysterious adventure awaits.*

We traveled to Warsaw, still entirely a city of ruins, and from there to its small airport. In September 1946, we walked up a narrow ramp to a Dakota plane from LOT Polish Airlines. I felt great satisfaction during the flight in the military aircraft. The seats consisted of aluminum benches facing each other, designed with concave spaces for soldiers to sit before parachuting from the door through which we entered. The long flight and the vibrations of the plane above the clouds as it flew over occupied Germany infused me with a sense of liberating pride and stirred my imagination. After a refueling stop in Germany, the long flight ended at the airport in Paris. Except for Frania, all of the members of our family and its few close Jewish friends left Poland on their own initiative by the middle of 1947, heading to Sweden, or France. From there, they would continue on to the places they would make their home.

Stanisław Kowalski, his daughter Ryszarda, and Yoseph-Marek in Sandomierz, autumn 1946.

2. The wood palace between Paris and Versailles

I loved her. Paris, the huge city, fascinated me from the moment I arrived. The sounds of the foreign language, the boulevards, the squares, the streets with stands of neatly arranged fruits and vegetables, the stone houses and, of course, the Metro system all left me spellbound. I loved the taste of the roasted chestnuts peddled in the streets, the taste of the house wine I was allowed to drink at lunch in the bistro, even the smell of the exhaust fumes from the cars. Most of all, I enjoyed driving electric cars on the tin floors set up in main squares, maneuvering among the other drivers and their peppy girlfriends.

My father tried to make things easy for me, but he himself was very troubled by the uncertainty of our situation as refugees, with the family scattered in three different countries. We lived in a dim room with a basin and jug for washing, in a modest hotel in the ninth arrondissement.

My father had the addresses of local relatives. First, we contacted Grisha, and Flora, the brother, and sister of Sima-Shimon, who was married to Roza, my father's sister. Shimon and Roza lived with their son, David, in Palestine. Grisha was a bachelor who fought in the French Army against the German invasion, and Flora was a divorcee. They had studied in Riga and immigrated to Paris in their youth. The two siblings survived the Nazi occupation in a rural area under assumed identities, with Grisha working as a gardener. They welcomed us graciously and with aristocratic manners into their small apartment (one room, or perhaps slightly more) in an ancient building near the Place de la Madeleine. It was a symbolic address: 24 Rue des Martyrs. They and their discourse, in Russian, and in German, reminded me of some taxi drivers I had met in the city white immigrants of elite backgrounds, Russian speakers, completely different from the simple Red Army soldiers I had known. We also traveled on the Metro to meet relatives on my mother's side: Bela, the daughter of my mother's uncle David Jaffe, her husband Leon, and their six-year-old son Marcel. Bela emigrated from Poland to France before the war and married Leon (Aharon Leib) Kerszner. I later learned that their young son had hidden in the home of French Christian farmers, Denis and Louise Arsene, from the summer of 1942 until the liberation of France. The Arsene family was recognized by Yad Vashem as "Righteous Among the Nations." The boy's parents survived, wandering from place to place, without knowing the language well, and with assumed identities, thanks to the outstanding underground activity of Leon (under the name of Thomas Marcel) in the French Resistance in the city of Châtillon, from November 1942 through the end of the Nazi occupation. In their apartment on 90 Voltaire Boulevard, I met another relative, Elias Jaffe, Bela's nephew. He was a young man, cheerful and fond of children, and wore the uniform of the Royal Air Force (RAF) of Britain. In July 1939, when he was not yet fifteen years old, Elias was sent by ship from the Free City of Danzig (Gdańsk) to England in the *Kindertransport*, prior to the Nazi conquest of the city. He volunteered for the Royal Air Force (RAF) at age eighteen and, thanks to his talents, and personality, successfully completed training as a bomber pilot. Among his exploits, he flew a four-engine Short Stirling, with an air crew of seven or eight, in the battles of the Rhine River crossing (March 1945), towing heavy gliders manned with parachutists and dropping equipment and supplies. When I met him, he was serving in Germany in an intelligence role as a technical-scientific translator of German, and he came to his aunt's home on vacation. While he was serving in the RAF, his sister Sabina and their mother Hendel (née Kott), from Kalisz, spent the war years in a British detention camp on the island of Mauritius after being expelled from Palestine by the British Mandate authorities. This followed their attempt to flee from Poland to Palestine in 1941 on board the *Atlantic* clandestine immigration ship, after no space was found for them on the *Patria* expulsion ship that sank in Haifa Bay. Their father, Yosef Haim Jaffe, was hung as a political prisoner at the beginning of the war in the nearby Stutthof death camp, where my mother was sent about four years later.

At the entrance to our hotel and in the elevator, I also met Madzia Munwes the daughter of Mendel Chaim Jaretzki, my mother's uncle. Madzia, a well-groomed, and educated woman, told me that her son Gabriel (Moked) had just celebrated his bar mitzvah in Palestine, and that she was on her way there from Poland. She and her son had managed to flee from the ghetto in Warsaw, and they survived the war by hiding in the city and using false Aryan identities. Her husband, Dr. Jakub Munwes, a well-known hematologist, and a public figure, was murdered in the ghetto after refusing to abandon his patients and join his loved ones on the Aryan side.

I went at least once with my father to visit the Louvre. My father revered, and spoke often about the great masters of the Renaissance from Italy and Germany and the Baroque artists from the Low Countries. His knowledge was complemented by his natural intuition for painting and forms, as well as a fertile imagination that drew from practical wisdom and working with his hands. Climbing with him and Grisha to the heights of the Eiffel Tower and the Cathedral of Notre Dame, and standing at the tomb of Napoleon (then a hero of mine) at Les Invalides are etched in my memory as thrilling childhood experiences.

One day, my grandfather Shmuel from Palestine appeared at our hotel. About sixty-five years old, he was erect, and thin, with a skullcap perched on light-colored hair that was now predominantly gray. A pointy goatee covered his chin. His eyes were watery blue and his parched complexion had a foul odor from using '*Mishi*' shaving gel, applied with a wooden stick to singe facial hair. He walked and moved briskly, and spoke broken Polish with a mix of Yiddish and English words. He didn't curry favor and acted as if bound by the lofty ideas he tried to promote and fulfill. My grandfather had a vision of building a Jacquard lace curtain factory, like the one he had built in Kalisz between the two world wars, and which had recently been nationalized. He started to construct a large industrial building on his citrus land in Bnei Brak, purchased two huge Jacquard knitting machines in Nottingham, and was in advanced negotiations to buy spinning machines and other equipment in France. My grandfather proposed that my father manage the technical aspects of setting up and running the factory and promised him the moon. At first, my father seemed hesitant about my grandfather's visit and his ideas. In the end, however, he agreed to work with his father. My mother warned in her letters from Kalisz that she was completely opposed to this collaboration and to the notion of traveling to Palestine in such times; she was concerned about the family's future there. Perhaps my father's decision was also influenced by the offer to send him for training in knitting and spinning technologies at the textile center in the city of Mulhouse-Mülhausen, at my grandfather's expense. The training was indeed arranged, with Mr. Grisha, friendly as always, conducting the correspondence, and telephone conversations in French.

One Friday evening, I was asked to accompany my grandfather to the elegant synagogue nearby for the evening service the first time in my life. When it was decided that my father would be heading to the Land of Israel, my grandfather and Mr. Grisha also found a solution for me, with my father's consent. The solution was to place me in a new Jewish orphanage in the town of Bellevue, directed by Mrs. Lena Küchler. No one asked my opinion about this idea. From the outset, I was not privy to the plan, and it was stitched together behind my back. Bits of conversations and hushed whispers stirred melancholy fears in me. I was not at all pleased by this decision suddenly imposed on me. It seemed completely unfair to me. I felt betrayed and angry.

To get to the orphanage, we took the electric train from Montparnasse in Paris to Versailles, exited at the Bellevue station, and continued about twenty minutes by foot to 2 Rue de la Tour. (At the time, we thought the street was named for Gustave Eiffel, a native of Bellevue, who designed *la tour Eiffel*. But the street name actually derives from the round turret in the ancient royal garden there.) The orphanage was housed in an ancient and stylish three-story wooden structure, built above a tall entrance floor with a staircase and a well-lit basement. The multi-sloped roof featured sharp vaults, with numerous rooms bulging from the attic, large windows, and balconies. The building was primarily constructed of wood: beams and panels outside and floors and squeaky stairs inside. The building was once the palace of an aristocratic family. A large garden was planted around the house with ornamental trees, as well as fruit trees and vegetable plots.

The time I spent at the institution as an external child, about five months, was difficult for me at the time and wonderful in retrospect. The ages of the children ranged from kindergarten to about sixteen. Besides the Hebrew teacher's son, I was the only one who knew at the time that he had even a single parent or relative alive. I was also the only one whose expenses were paid for privately, a distinction that didn't add to my popularity. The children, teachers, and small staff had coalesced into an extended alternative family. Together they had traveled the tortuous road from their home in Zakopane, in the Tatra Mountains in Poland, which they had defended with guns against hooligans; they had stolen across borders to Czechoslovakia and elsewhere, and had wandered within France itself, as described in books, and films. Each child had his own complicated story of losing his family and traumatically escaping death: by finding refuge in a monastery, by surviving with an assumed identity, or by joining partisan units in the forests and fighting the enemy. The children were divided into several groups by age and personal suitability, with each group living in one of the spacious rooms in the house.

The wooden mansion in Bellevue.

Lena, the director and "mother," focused on rehabilitation and education from wake-up untill lights-out. We studied in groups in the entrance hall, sitting on wooden benches at a long table. There was an emphasis on learning Hebrew and French, and I had a long way to catch up. I started to receive private lessons in Hebrew and Bible stories in the teacher's living room, apparently under the terms of an agreement made with my grandfather from the outset. If I recall correctly, the arithmetic lessons were still in Polish. The older children imposed an atmosphere of opposition to anything connected to their country of origin, seeking to erase the traumatic past. The goal was to succeed and somehow reach a land of their own one day. In the evenings and at parties, they sat, and sang Land of Israel songs, or danced the *hora*. The children also sang during chores of peeling potatoes, washing dishes and pans in the basement kitchen, or sweeping the wooden floors. I learned the words and melodies of the songs, but didn't participate in the dancing. My Hebrew and my French improved, but remained very limited. I came to love the traditional *Oneg Shabbat* celebration in an extended family atmosphere after the Friday night meal, which included a slightly upgraded menu. We were also assigned gardening and home maintenance chores. During the warmer periods, we worked the soil of the garden, digging, and raking flowerbeds, and planting, plowing, and harvesting potatoes. Some children received acting and dance lessons, but everyone was included in the plays and skits, which were performed at every opportunity. I remember participating in a play on a wooden stage in a small theater in Paris; the audience was mostly composed of the orphanage residents, with a few guests. Occasionally, the older boys and girls would be asked to accompany younger children on the train to see a play or visit a museum in Paris. In this way, I toured the Musée de l'Homme near the Place du Trocadéro, the colorful museum of the French colonies at that time, and other museums. I remember twice, on cold winter days, slogging through the snow in groups to a public bath, a walk of over twenty minutes from where we lived.

I was placed in the room of older boys, who were all at least one year older than me. They treated me with respect and courtesy at first to please Lena, the venerated director, and mother, who wanted to help me. I innocently empathized and identified with the orphaned teenagers. Soon, after the lessons, I was interrogated at length by members of the group, and I responded truthfully. I felt that finally I no longer had to be cautious, conceal information, and lie. From their stories, I learned a bit about the travails of their families, about what the boys did when left to fend on their own, and about their worldviews. They expressed hatred and anger about the utterly hostile and threatening Polish surroundings with the Germans in the background. My stories, told in a sentence or two, about the Poles who saved me were received with skepticism and hostility, as was my fluency in proper Polish the only language I knew. One morning, while washing, I took off my silver ring with the eagle and white-red background and placed it by the sink. I went back to the room for a moment to bring a toothbrush and toothpaste I had forgotten among my things under the bed. When I returned, my beloved ring was gone. My vehement questioning led nowhere and elicited strange looks. I'm sure no one wanted it and that it was thrown away. One week, after a Saturday visit by my father, a tough twelve-year-old, whom I had considered my friend, raised the subject of my family status. In his view, it was not fitting that I was the only one in the group, and in the whole orphanage, who had parents. I felt my world collapsing and started to weep. I tried to appease him by saying that his father and mother had indeed been murdered, but until then they could hear. My father, on the other hand, would be deaf for the rest of his life.

Soon afterward, my father came to take me to Paris for a weekend vacation, and my mother arrived. It was an emotional reunion: Mother managed to leave Poland and even safely passed the threatening border checks when crossing between Poland and Czechoslovakia, and from there to Germany and to France. The journey by train, undertaken with her childhood friend Hela Lifshitz, took two, or three days. Mother was able to organize and bring in her baggage a handsome collection of household items. Together with Mother and Hela, we met French relatives, including Bela.

One Saturday, Mother came to see me at the orphanage for the first time, together with Father. When I was told they were coming, I became very stressed, and uneasy. I ran to Lena's room and then my world went black. My mother looked wonderful, dressed in fine clothes, and a coat adorned with silver fox fur. After my mother made acquaintance with Lena, we went to see my room and I could sense the looming disaster. Later, as we headed out the gate, I vented my anger at Mother for wearing splendid clothes when visiting me at the institution for impoverished orphans. My mother responded that she was not dressed any finer than Lena the director, who wore elegant clothes. This was not completely accurate, and I also felt that what was permissible for the esteemed director was not allowed for my mother when visiting. I told her I never wanted her to come visit me there again. Soon afterward, so I assume, Lena met with representatives of my room; I was asked to move down one floor to the large sleeping quarters of the intermediate age group children up to the age of ten. I felt a stinging personal failure and social humiliation. I had no interest in this age group of children. I remember that one of them, the son of the Hebrew teacher and his wife, apparently was afraid at night and crawled into my bed on more than one occasion so he could fall asleep.

The orphanage operated like a kibbutz. Both the older and younger children served on committees in various fields. One time, I was called to the nurses' clinic for a developmental checkup by an external physician. They prescribed injections for me that I feared. I watched a boy and a girl about fifteen or sixteen years old huddle together in the clinic. From the way they conversed, they seemed to me to be a mature couple who had been together for some time. I was embarrassed and enchanted by their degree of intimacy, understanding, and mutual dependence. I didn't know whether they were a couple or a brother and sister, but it was clear to me that each of them had experienced things that were worse than death. I envied them. I didn't have a single friend in that orphanage. I was alone. Reading in the language I knew was frowned upon, and much of what I had absorbed during the past two years was deemed contemptible here. It seemed to me that my parents and brother, who returned from the devastation, were also regarded in the same way. Each of my peers had a story of loss and a terrifying story of survival. Some were injured physically, and all were emotionally scarred, without showing it or even being cognizant of it. Each wrestled with his past by himself and contended with a foggy future that offered only struggles. But the orphanage was the domain of these children and of Lena, a mother to all of them. They developed a way of facing life together during the short and stormy past they shared, and a joint responsibility for maintaining the home, and for the young and weak among them.

One afternoon, I went to Paris with my parents for the weekend. I expected to spend an evening alone with them, perhaps to recharge my batteries. However, my parents informed me that we were invited that evening to the home of Grisha and Flora, and that they were waiting for us. I said I didn't want to go there, and that they could go without me. My parents got angry, I insisted, and an argument ensued. My father promised that after dinner, we would go to Place Pigalle and that I could drive the electric cars there. I consented. The dinner dragged on and when we finally left it was already late. I insisted on going to Place Pigalle as promised. My father decided that this was now out of the question. Perhaps he had his reasons, and perhaps he had also received a negative report on Place Pigalle from the hosts. I argued in vain that they must keep their promise. In a crosswalk on one of the streets, I broke into a sprint and disappeared from view. I went down the first set of Metro stairs, studied the train lines, turning on the small lights on the station map, and chose a route. I had enough money for tickets, and after changing trains once, I arrived at Place Pigalle. I don't remember if there were indeed electric cars there. If there were, I didn't drive one. Instead, I hurried back to Pigalle station and returned via the two trains to the hotel. My mother was in a panic. She said that Father had returned to Grisha and together they went to the police to seek help in searching for me. Mother took off my clothes and ordered me to go straight to bed and to pretend that I was sleeping, because otherwise I could expect a severe beating for what I did and for embarrassing us in front of Grisha, Flora, and the French police, and the latter could make trouble for us. Around three o'clock in the morning, I heard Father and Grisha enter the hotel room in a rage, and Mother trying to calm their anger. The morning passed peacefully. My father spoke again about silly stubbornness and childishness, and found it hard to believe that I was able to navigate my way in the Metro. I felt that it was perhaps the first time in my life that I allowed myself to act according to my own judgment and understanding. During the next free weekend, on a beautiful spring day, we took Hela, and little Marcel with us and spent a whole day visiting the palace and gardens of Versailles. Besides little Marcel, I had no connection with any native-born

French person during the months of my stay in France.

We read and heard a lot in the news about underground activity against the British in Palestine. At that time, none of us could foresee the elusive web of complex equations with countless variables that would continue to rattle our lives from the day we stepped into the longed-for safe haven. The news that I would soon immigrate to the Land of Israel elicited respect from the children my age and real envy from the older ones. The first group from among the eldest adolescents in Bellevue, the "partisans," would suddenly set sail about ten weeks later from the port of Sète on the *SS Exodus* 1947.

Mrs. Lena Küchler at her home in Rehovot. Azriela and Yoseph visiting with their daughters Hilla (left) and Dea.

3. Providence

Visas to Palestine were issued for the three of us at the British Embassy on April 23, 1947, with the help of the Joint Distribution Committee in France, and I understood there was some question about their validity. Perhaps my grandfather sent a letter declaring that my father was an expert needed for the factory he was building in Palestine, and a house of cards was built upon this. The name of our passenger ship, *Providence*, inspired optimism. It anchored at the port of Marseilles, three giant black smokestacks shooting up toward the sky, and sailed under a French flag in conditions immeasurably better than those of the clandestine immigrant ships. Our tickets were for a third-class cabin with bunk beds of two or three levels; the cabin's round portholes were close to water level. Steerage-class passengers were allowed to sleep on the floor or on easy chairs with wooden slats. I also tried this option in order to escape the stale air in the cabin. I became friends with Rysiek, a boy in our cabin, blond, and blue-eyed, smart, and opinionated. He was sailing to the Land of Israel with his Jewish, Slavic-looking father who had a pleasant and friendly Polish wife. Rysiek's Jewish mother didn't survive the war.

My first encounter with the sea and the atmosphere on the ship sailing toward Palestine filled me with a sense of inner freedom unlike anything I had experienced before - the freedom to imagine. I recalled stories and characters from books I had read, and I imagined that I was experiencing the maritime exploits of these heroes. I wandered among the decks open to our passenger class. I sat on a pile of thick rope on the deck, looking at the Mediterranean Sea, the scene of so many tales, and read *The Count of Monte Cristo* by Alexandre Dumas in Polish. With Rysiek, I also sneaked into the decks of more expensive passenger classes, the crew's quarters and the bridge, and peeked into the control and navigation room. A more frightening adventure was sneaking into the belly of the ship, to the boiling hot, dark space of the steam boilers, fired by piles of coal, with giant piston engines shaking the enormous sailing vessel. Black human figures shuffled among them. When sailing in the open sea, I looked through old binoculars of the type used by German officers in World War I, which Father bought for me on my tenth birthday. With my binoculars, I watched as we sailed past Corsica, Elba, and Monte Cristo, and saw each of these islands disappear in the fog. These places excited me because of the characters associated with them. The next day, Sicily came into view, the Strait of Messina, and the city of Messina. A trail of gray smoke billowed from the mouth of Mount Etna, an active volcano.

My excitement grew: *Would we manage to enter, or would they arrest us?* I brimmed with longing and warmth for the mysterious land, which I considered mine by right. I also felt fear and curiosity after hearing stories of the dangers - the British, the savages in the desert, the poisonous creepy-crawlies. There was talk about the difficult climate, the hardships of making a living, and even the need to hide again this time from the British police. I imagined how I would be accepted with open arms as a lost son returning from a tortuous journey to his awaiting people and family. I felt confident in regard to the store of knowledge and life experience I ostensibly carried with me. I also felt regret about disconnecting from the identity I had fostered during the bad past (which, of course, I didn't define as a bad past – it was the only reality I knew).

When the ship anchored at the port of Alexandria, I was immediately exposed to the diverse and colorful East. Sailboats and large rowboats loaded with leather products and fresh exotic fruits quickly surrounded the *Providence*. On the decks of these boats, tens of meters below our deck, were sturdy, dark-skinned people scurrying in white *galabiyas* and pants with an internal sack that hung down below their knees, which inspired outbursts of laughter and jokes. Ropes were tossed from our deck, pulleys were installed, and commerce commenced, at surprisingly low prices. A large bunch of bananas was pulled up for my parents. I thought this taste was only for the wealthy, but I was accorded a generous portion.

Yoseph looking toward the coast of Haifa from the deck of the Providence, with British destroyers in the background, May 6, 1947.

As we approached Haifa, I spied the British corvettes and destroyers through my binoculars. These ships surrounded the Providence to ensure that no one could slip on or off it. A boat approached with a group of policemen and civilians, who climbed up a gangplank to one of the decks. We remained for many hours at anchor, outside the port. Together with my parents and all of the passengers, we looked toward the city of Haifa from afar and toward the green slopes of the Carmel Mountains. My binoculars were passed from hand to hand. Early in the morning on May 6, 1947, after my patience was about to expire, the *Providence* started to follow the guide boat to the wharf in Haifa Port. We hurried with our baggage in hand down the gangplank and, behold, our feet touched upon the shores of Palestine the Land of Israel.

I stood with my parents while our documents were being checked, dressed in a wool suit and tie in order to make a good and respectable impression. Behind me were British policemen, and in front were policemen and officials seated behind long wooden tables. Most of them were wearing short pants, short-sleeve shirts, and khaki-colored wool socks pulled up to their knees, talking, and perspiring. Small trucks entered and exited the gates of the port, but I also saw convoys of camels and donkeys loaded with sacks and led by Arabs. We passed the border check, entered Palestine, and quickly went underground: We were not recognized by the Mandate authorities as valid immigrants, despite the British visas stamped in my parents' passports.

4. The first day in Palestine

They came to welcome us. From Tel Aviv, my mother's sister Pola Salomonowicz came with her daughter Esther. Pola was slightly older than my mother, and her daughter was a tall teenager, assertive, and overflowing with warmth. Genia Mayer, my father's younger sister, and her husband Benjamin (Benya), who lived in Haifa, were also waiting at the port. It was an emotional reunion with Pola, and the two sisters were very excited. We also received a warm reception from Genia and her husband, though in this case both sides maintained a cultured restraint.

We all traveled in two taxis to Aviv Street on Mount Carmel to a small hotel owned by Benya's parents. We introduced each other, conversed, and we all ate lunch with Benya's parents and with Danny, the pleasant five-year-old son of Genia and Benya. Everyone conducted themselves in a meticulous manner, as required in the presence of educated German émigrés. For me, there was something new and interesting here, embarrassing, and also mysterious, because it was quietly hinted, with an air of importance, that Benya was a commander in an underground movement (the Haganah). The hosts showed general interest in our voyage at sea and in our family's history during the years of incommunicado. The family in Tel Aviv was mentioned, and the conversation quickly turned to the complex situation with the British government and with the Arab population. There were also subtle references to attacks and gunfire by Arab organizations against Jewish settlements and public transportation.

We didn't stay for long, because we wanted to arrive in Tel Aviv before dark. We rode in a big taxi, with Aunt Pola and Esther, to the central bus station in the Hadar section of Haifa, and continued by *Egged* bus to Tel Aviv. After traveling for a while, a tense atmosphere pervaded the bus, apparently when we were south of Atlit. The slopes of the Carmel Mountains, the green Jewish settlements, and the Arab villages we passed along the way were now far behind us, and the landscape was dominated by pristine sand dunes with rippled patterns created by the wind. The sand reached the road and even covered its shoulders. In this arid, desert-like landscape, I excitedly observed the sparse scattering of black tents, camels, donkeys, and herds of goats and sheep. Apprehensively, I imagined moustached Bedouin riders suddenly charging forth from the sand dunes, wrapped in white robes, on swift horses from noble Arab stock, firing at our bus with Winchester rifles, as in the stories of Karl May. I wondered who among the diverse group of passengers, dressed in summer clothing, and including several Arabs, was packing a well-concealed weapon.

From the central bus station in Tel Aviv, we traveled to the apartment of my father's parents. It was in a new and modern-looking house at 111 Rothschild Boulevard, across the boulevard from the home of the mayor, Israel Rokach. My grandfather, whom I met in France, and my grandmother Devorah, whom I was meeting for the first time, welcomed us at the entrance and led us to the dining room. At the dinner table sat Ignaś, my brother, with his back to the boulevard, a white embroidered skullcap on his head. He ate vegetable salad with a fork and knife and a soft-boiled egg with a teaspoon. I remember the occasion as one of profoundly mixed and restrained emotions. My grandfather's conduct immediately established a religious patriarchal atmosphere, and he made it clear that the Hebrew language was superior to our Polish tongue. As I soon discovered, he was not fluent in modern Hebrew and had forgotten most of his broken Polish, so he inserted phrases in Yiddish, which I didn't understand at all. My first impression of my grandmother was that she was inarticulate and that her opinions were not particularly valued. I was quite surprised by what I perceived to be the reserved "British" behavior of Ignaś at least until our future became clearer. He was now called Itzhak. My grandparents' apartment, on the first floor above the high ground floor, was spacious and awash with sunlight during the daytime. It had rounded balconies with blossoming flower boxes cast onto the railings. One balcony overlooked the green boulevard, and the other the path to the entrance of the home. The interior was furnished with heavy veneer furniture, crystal chandeliers, and cabinets with glass doors, that displayed silver religious ritual items and tableware and lots of fine china, and cabinets with books in leather and cloth bindings with gold-colored Hebrew words imprinted on them. My father's older sister Roza, who had immigrated with her father when she was still single, emerged from the door of the apartment opposite my grandparents' home and joined us, together with her husband Sima (Shimon) the brother of Grisha and Flora in Paris and their son David, who was a year younger than me. Again, the joy was not effusive. Apparently the loss of the two older sisters and their children in the Warsaw Ghetto cast a pall over this reunion. I immediately felt the underlying tension in the relations of my father's family in Palestine, which derived from excessive dependence on my grandfather and from his domineering nature.

At the end of this long and jam-packed first day in the Land of Israel, my parents received the first real shock of their immigration. My grandfather led my parents and me to the house next door, 109 Rothschild Boulevard, which he also owned, and took us into the apartment where we would live. It was on the ground floor, a few steps above the level of the sidewalk. The apartment had three and a half rooms, connected by a narrow and dim corridor leading to a bathroom, toilet, and small kitchen. Tenants were living in two of the rooms a family in one room and a newlywed couple in the other. My grandfather had cleared out one and a half rooms for us a room and a niche, with no partition between them, with an exit to the balcony. My brother continued to sleep in our grandparents' home upstairs, until our parents settled in, purchased two folding couches, a cupboard, a table and chairs. At the end of the corridor, before the entrance to the kitchen, two Primus stoves were on, making a whistling noise, and two grimy kerosene stoves stood on the kitchen counter, where the three women would take turns cooking. For each of my parents, it was the reawakening of immense frustration, perhaps foreseeable, which would only grow deeper in the future. The insult they felt stemmed from the huge gap between the economic wherewithal of my grandfather, one of the city's wealthiest residents, and his unwillingness to help properly absorb his son's family a surviving remnant of the extended family. I also remember later hearing angry complaints about Father's failure to save his two sisters and their families a clear case of the pot calling the kettle black. My grandfather took pride in his generosity and contributions to the national-religious community. His arrogance and attitude toward my father and mother - he seemed to regard Father as someone dependent on him, who could be treated disrespectfully and exploited because of his deafness, and Mother as a modest, weak, and inferior creature stirred profound sadness and resentment in me, since I knew my parents' true strength. I felt the same way toward my grandmother, who was ostensibly submissive, and silent, yet also justified her husband's approach. In my eyes, then, and now, there was no justification, or atonement for these wrongs. However, in order to preserve peace in the family and for reasons of dependence and good upbringing, my parents instructed me to keep my opinions to myself.

5. A new reality in the Land of Israel

I entered the new reality in the Land of Israel as someone foreign and inferior, in need of repair, together with parents who were trying to find their way in the thicket of daily hardships and to function under emotional pressures that I could now witness up close. My parents acted with determination and courage, without showing any inclination toward self-pity, as if mortgaging the rest of their lives and health. They seemed to be forcibly propelled toward an uncertain future, in a tumultuous present, with the traumas of the recent past still simmering inside them. Each of us tried to deny and disown the past in his own way. Starting in early summer, we would escape the suffocating heat of the room and niche to sit for a light meal by the door leading from the kitchen to the narrow balcony, facing west toward the sea breeze. A fire escape with an iron staircase led from the balcony to the yard at the basement level. The yard bordered a large lot on Ahad Ha'am Street with a one-story home that was empty at the time; a sparse grove of pine trees surrounded the house. Children played in this space, and it was used on Fridays and on Saturday evenings for youth movement activities, including singing, and dancing. I tried to understand some incomprehensible words from afar. For example, I heard them singing "David, King of Israel lives and ..." and thought they were senselessly saying *nikayon* (cleaning) instead of *v'kayaam* (exists) a word I had yet to learn.

The present was demanding, with waves of challenges before me. The Yishuv (the pre-state Jewish community) was engaged in bloody disputes with the Mandate government. While still at the orphanage in Bellevue and during our voyage on the *Providence*, we had already heard about such incidents as the Irgun underground organization's raid on the Ramat Gan police station, and the trial and execution of Dov Gruner and his comrades. On the very day our ship approached the shores of Haifa, the Irgun broke into the Acre prison, and we learned of the daring escape of the Irgun fighters and prisoners. These episodes fired my imagination and instilled identity and pride. However, the controversy and pain that followed each violent incident also left me confused about the different underground factions and gave me a sense of aversion. On the walls of the boulevard, and even in the stairway of our home, stealthy teenagers pasted bulletins and posters (*Hahoma* and *Hama'as*, for example) in the dead of night. The presence of British soldiers and policemen in armored cars patrolling the streets, as well as the sight of "Bevingrad," surrounded by barbed wire, from the window of the *Hamekasher* bus in Jerusalem sparked immediate patriotic opposition. But I could not allow myself to stand out or get into trouble. The cry of *Hebrew state! Free immigration!* seemed to unify the Hebrew Yishuv, but the first part raised doubts and anxieties. My mother expressed her "proven prophetic senses": Soviet imperialism and communism would take over the entire Middle East and would soon conquer the rest of the Balkans. The power of the declining British Empire still served as a dam, temporarily keeping the Arab sea from flooding the homes of the Jewish settlements. After all, she knew from Poland what it was like when a conquering army flooded a country.

I immersed myself in three years of the most focused learning activity of my life. During this period, I no longer kept up my habit of reading literature every day. The last novel I read before taking this recess was *Quo Vadis*, by Henryk Sienkiewicz, which I read in the original Polish. My grandfather immediately registered me at the Bilu religious school for boys; my brother Itzhak and my cousins Rysiek and David were already pupils there. There was an element of coercion in this, but also a challenge and opportunity, and I responded to them. I was accepted toward the end of fourth grade, a year behind the other boys my age. My grandfather hired a tutor to help me with Hebrew and Jewish studies. Grandfather was one of the main contributors to the school and the magnificent synagogue attached to it. He planned and dictated our educational paths as Jews in the Land of Israel, and his word was law. This was in coordination with Rabbi Haim Mishori, the school's mythological principal. I made sure to cross the boulevard in the morning wearing my *tzitzit* (a fringed garment worn by Orthodox Jews), with a brown beret on my head. I went down to the yard, and on my way up to the classroom, I would take from my bag a thick *siddur* (prayer book) for pupils, a special edition published for the school, and begin the day of lessons with morning prayers led by the head teacher. Starting from third grade, all of the teachers were men, and they were supposed to be strict in all matters, large, and small. I felt a sense of competition among the pupils; there was even sleuthing after those who deviated from the codes of behavior, which were foreign to me. I was again a bit afraid of possible informers, and there were indeed a few of those. The older boys treated me with contempt, and I was teased openly and implicitly about being foreign, alone and different, and thus inferior, and weak. On more than one occasion, I benefited from the fact that my brother and cousins were there to protect me in the schoolyard. On the other hand, my teachers were willing to sometimes overlook my behavior which was flawed compared to what was considered acceptable there, and my very deficient knowledge of religious customs. I tried to meet expectations, to fit in, and to make things easier for my parents. As a secular child, I was curious about the religious demands and willingly adopted them at school and in the street. I was happy that for the first time I had the opportunity to begin an orderly path of education, with special emphasis on the sources of my people's culture. My grandfather reserved seats for his grandsons in the synagogue for Bilu pupils, where he prayed on the Jewish Sabbath and holidays, so that we would come to pray at least on Friday evenings and holidays. The seats were by the eastern wall, near the prayer leader and pupils' choir. I received a monthly allowance for all of the times I came to my grandfather's home for *kiddush* or *havdalah* (prayers marking the beginning and end of the Sabbath, respectively). I put all my efforts into learning. During the daytime, I studied on the open balcony facing the bustling boulevard, and in the evening I would read and write while lying on the fold-out couch in the living room niche allocated to my brother and me in the three-family apartment. In keeping with what I felt were the expectations of the street and of my friends, I ignored my mother and refused to answer whenever she addressed me in public in Polish; and she was forced to speak to me in the broken Hebrew she remembered, which never really improved. More than once, I refrained from going out to the street with my father so that no one would hear him or see him reading my lips and in Polish!

I was, in fact, very willing to adjust and acclimate. However, in addition to inherent traits, such as stubbornness and persistence, that characterized my behavior for better and worse, I had unconsciously assimilated values that could be traced to my experience under Nazi occupation. As a reaction to the need to lie and adopt a false identity, I felt strong revulsion toward lying and pretending to the point that I was unable to shield myself with white lies. This trait sometimes put me, and others, too, in situations of weakness, and embarrassment. My criteria for responsible and moral conduct were much more demanding than those I discerned in most of my friends, and that was because I knew that reckless acts by an individual and a group could lead to disaster. Thus, it was not surprising that I was sometimes considered problematic in the company of my *sabra* peers, and sometimes I was not good at getting along even in the eyes of my parents. I started far behind in most of the learning material, and I lacked skills, and perhaps the talent for easy camaraderie in my peer group. On the other hand, I surpassed all of them in knowledge and in general outlook, and I was mentally mature, with an unconscious tendency to brood about disasters and frightening situations.

The first summer vacation introduced us to the charms of the sea. Itzhak and I would walk from our home to Aunt Pola, who lived on 132 Ben Yehuda Street, and from there, under the supervision of Esther, to the sea. We loved the sand, the salty air, and jumping and diving into the rising waves as they rolled and crashed into the foam at the edge of the shore. We also loved the warm-hearted welcome from Pola, who offered us fresh-squeezed orange juice and a shower. I tried to teach myself to swim. One time, Mother came with us. I swam and the undertow pulled me out to sea, by the end of the pier. Mother called the life-guard. I learned to beware of the sea's undercurrents and also to swim in an undefined style. At first, Itzhak and I played a little at home or outside, primarily with Rysiek, the boy our age from the *Providence*. Later, we also played soccer and other games with our cousin Rysiek (the son of Uncle Abram and Bronka), in our neighborhood or his. Cousin Rysiek and my brother were bigger and stronger than me physically. At first, Aunt Roza kept David at home, in their apartment across from our grandparents. Perhaps she was concerned about our new and "foreign" influence in the family, and perhaps also because he was prone to asthma attacks.

Just before starting fifth grade, we expanded to the second room, adjacent to the kitchen. The additional room became a dining room and place to study. I don't know who paid the "key money" in place of the family that left. The young couple, the Meisel family, continued to live in the third room. The husband, Shlomo, was from Warsaw, in his late thirties, and worked as a plasterer. After a strenuous workday, after washing the remnants of cement from his dry skin, he took on the character of an autodidact intellectual at home. He considered the fact that he was a manual laborer a supreme value. I would later turn to him when I needed the assessment of someone who was an authority in my eyes on questions of logic in writing and language. While he spoke, he would pull out Hebrew books from his shelves and sometimes lecture me, the ignoramus, about Baruch Spinoza, Moses Mendelssohn, or Solomon Maimon, or he would show me with great pleasure one of the two black volumes, printed in Warsaw, of the Yehoyesh translation of the Bible into Yiddish, a language that was foreign to me. In his conversations, he would insert Yiddish or Polish sayings and jokes in Warsaw street slang that was not free of an accent betraying his origins. His amiable wife, Atara, from a Lithuanian family, was younger than him by about a decade and clearly preferred restraint and institutionalized education. She was proud of her brother, a brilliant student of mathematics at Hebrew University. When I started my high school studies, her brother (then already a lecturer at the Technion) helped me out of a mental block, explaining to me the meaning of an algebraic expression. After about three years of living as neighbors, they brought in a bed for their infant Eli, the apple of their eyes. I was saddened by their move to a housing project in the Yad Eliyahu neighborhood when Eli was about a year old, even though my brother and I gained another room for ourselves.

The national-religious school was run imperiously and with an all-discerning eye by its founder, Rabbi Haim Mishori, who had an orderly set of ideas about education, culture, and Jewish lifestyle. Another source of his pride was the large and magnificent synagogue for pupils, with a choir of cantors conducted by Rabbi Shlomo Ravitz, who arranged, and composed many liturgical melodies. A wide staircase led from the front of the synagogue to an exedra and to the synagogue hall, which featured a series of large windows offering a view of the boulevard to the west. The rest of this modern and spacious building was devoted to the twenty-four classrooms, a gymnasium, a kitchen and lunch-room operated by the pupils, and more. The school year began and the standards in fifth grade were strict. At 7:15 in the morning, the pupils in the four highest grades took their places by classrooms (twelve of them) for morning prayers in the synagogue. The prayers were led by trained and enthusiastic pupils, who also read the Torah on Mondays and Thursdays. We had classes in all of the usual subjects of study, with extra lessons in religious studies. In Bible classes, the teacher Israel Sobol started with memorizing the first eleven chapters of Jeremiah, in parallel to studying Exodus and Kings. I would pace the vacated room in our apartment and memorize about ten verses each day in the evening, before going to sleep, and when I awoke. As I worked to memorize the verses, I would come to understand them. I identified with and liked the personality and admonitions of the prophet of wrath and champion of social justice, and I also liked the teacher, who was a respectable person in my eyes.

About a month after the school year began, my parents suddenly informed us that they were no longer willing to submit to the demands of our grandfather and that they had registered us at a mixed secular school the Ahad Ha'am School about a ten-minute walk from our home. The new school was much more liberal and relaxed than the previous one, and I began to acclimate myself again. However, about two months later, I was transferred back to the bustling turmoil of the Bilu School. At the end of the first trimester, I received a regular report card with the grade of "sufficient" in Hebrew and religious studies. In the meantime, subjects were added to our program of study that seemed strange to me and also aroused resistance, based on my prejudice: Torah cantillation instead of music, Talmud, and Jewish law, which we didn't observe at home. On the other hand, the book of Exodus, and its laws, with commentary by Rashi; the history of the kings of Israel and Judea; and the poetry and power of Jeremiah's prophecy were for me a revelation and challenge, to which I wholeheartedly responded. Unknowingly, I swelled with pride, and satisfaction about belonging to a people with such an ancient culture and historical impact, rich in myths, and stories that are still exciting in their biblical language. The binding of Isaac and the story's denouement, which was repeatedly discussed on various occasions, symbolized for me a giant step forward, breaking away from rituals of human sacrifice that were prevalent in the ancient world, eventually converting to values of compassion and charity. This was in complete contrast to the attitude of disdain for everything Jewish by many of my classmates and playmates in Kalisz an attitude I also sometimes heard adults express when I was pretending to be Catholic. I often compared the ancient, one Hebrew God (though I had yet to be convinced to believe in Him) to the Holy Trinity of the Catholic Credo in the daily prayers. I identified with Jeremiah's prophecy: the passion of the pursuit of justice; the expressions of people's suffering; the love for the poor; and the poetry in Jeremiah's flowery language. I filled with pride. Ecstatically, and with a sense of joy and relief, I memorized Jeremiah's prophecy of redemption in chapter 31, wondering if the ancient words of prophecy, uttered about six hundred years before the birth of Jesus, might soon be fulfilled in my lifetime, "O Lord, save Your people, the remnant of Israel. I will bring them in from the northland, gather them from the ends of the earth … In a vast throng they shall return here … For the Lord will ransom Jacob, redeem him from one too strong for him … A cry is heard in Ramah wailing, bitter weeping Rachel weeping for her children, she refuses to be comforted for her children who are gone." These words expressed emotions I had suppressed in the past, and the atmosphere of tension and anticipation I now felt in the air. I preferred to relegate Jeremiah's prophecies of wrath to the oblivion of ancient history. My storehouse of Polish language, which I had decided to shut down, was now being covered by a mixture of flowery biblical Hebrew and street lingo. But I could not fluently express myself in either Polish or Hebrew. I learned to discuss the material we studied, but found it hard to formulate and express my ideas orally or in writing because of internal barriers: I didn't want to be exposed or fail in something that was said incorrectly or not absolutely accurate. The lessons in English, arithmetic, and nature provided me a comfort zone.

In retrospect, it turned out that I fell into a classroom of outstanding human talent. In a period of national unity and blurring of social disparities, there were representatives of various social classes and ethnic groups in the class, from the center of the city and from its southern neighborhoods. The distinctions between the children were expressed more in their affinity for the different resistance movements than in their parents' status, which was not taken into consideration. A refugee from the siege on Jerusalem joined us in fifth grade. The weaker pupils secretly admired the brilliant ones, but the greatest admiration was reserved for those who excelled in the games in gym class, and in recess in the yard, or in the sixty-meter run. I was still chubby then, the result of compulsive feeding by my mother, and this made me too cumbersome to succeed in the ball games. My mother succeeded in fattening me even during the period of strict food rationing. The most popular teacher was Reuven Grisman, the gym teacher, a young and energetic *yekke* (immigrant from Germany), who was a commander in the Haganah. When Tel Aviv was attacked from the air or from Jaffa, or during lulls in the fighting, he would sometimes enter our classroom or the improvised bomb shelter in the sunken ground level, whose doors and windows were blocked with protective silicate bricks, play the mandolin, and tell us about his exploits and those of his comrades. Among the pupils in my class, there were many future careers: professors, including a president of the Hebrew University of Jerusalem; a district court judge; R&D engineers; journalists; industrialists; and merchants. There were also those who would fight and fall defending the country. David, my cousin, was also in the same class. In fifth grade, I became friends with a boy my age, Dov Hartblei, who skipped to our classroom. He and his mother survived in Warsaw under an assumed identity.

There was not much joy in my parents' home. They felt they were in their prime years in terms of their strengths and abilities, yet they were deprived, and exploited. They radiated confidence in their good judgment, knowing that they had successfully met countless practical challenges in their lives, some of them incredibly difficult. Now, they sought an outlet of activity and recognition of their abilities.

In the meantime, the Solel Boneh Company was building an impressive industrial structure on my grandfather's citrus land near the Zichron Meir neighborhood of Bnei Brak, close to the residence of the famous rabbi known as the Chazon Ish. Shipments of various machines arrived at the port of Haifa, and Father traveled every morning to Bnei Brak to assemble and calibrate the machines for efficient production. Nearly all of the machines purchased by my grandfather were used and came disassembled; some of them were of early twentieth century vintage. The pioneering factory for producing lace curtains was built in an area of few industrial services or skilled workers, and was self-financed with British Mandate currency. The production process began with the problematic spinning of thread from long-fiber imported cotton, and ended with the artistic repair of flaws, laundering, finishing, stretching, packing, and shipping. Two gigantic lace curtain machines, which came disassembled, comprised the heart of the operation. An English engineer from the manufacturer of the machines in Nottingham was commissioned to help assemble them. The machine's warp threads came from thousands of spools rotating on two or three layered surfaces. Thousands of woof threads, each leading from a thin and split disc-bobbin made of brass; in their jerking movement, about one round per second, each bobbin either created or was kept from creating a single lace knot with the corresponding warp thread, in accordance with the commands of the Jacquard mechanism. The Jacquard was, in essence, an early digital mechanical computer, reading the pattern of the curtain from a series of punched cardboard cards, which rolled on a polygonal perforated drum in complete synchronization with the movement of the thin woof bobbins. The machines were each powered by a single electric motor. All of the movements of the lace curtain machine's parts were synchronized with the Jacquard's rotations via a chain of toothed transmission wheels, rods, and camshafts with very precise tuning. The performance or non-performance of tying, according to the curtain pattern, was controlled by thousands of strings transmitting information (the presence or absence of a hole) from the punched cards. If the weaver detected a tear or weakness in even a single thread in the curtain, he would stop the machine and perform a repair.

My father was an expert designer of patterns for lace curtains and a gifted mechanic. Much to his chagrin, he was made subordinate to the English engineer and his father's other assistants, most of them bootlickers dependent on him for their livelihood. At one point he rebelled, and it was then that Father also transferred us to the secular Ahad Ha'am School. Weeks and months went by and neither of the two machines produced satisfactory curtains. The English engineer returned to his country, claiming that the conditions in Palestine made it impossible to operate the machines. When my grandfather sensed that the enterprise of his later life was about to fail, he turned to my father as a last resort. The son accepted the father's offer, but set certain conditions, which were approved. My father spent day and night with the machines, made adjustments, and succeeded in producing some initial meters. However, new malfunctions frequently occurred. He reached the conclusion that the new mishaps occurred primarily when there were small changes in the air humidity, which affected the tension of the Jacquard strings. My father overcame this problem by flooding the floor on arid days, raising the humidity in the factory to the appropriate level for optimal production; this was before central air conditioning was introduced in the country. Finally, the machines operated efficiently, as in Kalisz. My father was a workaholic, laboring nonstop, instructing workers, and training curtain weavers. He had brought a great treasure with him from Kalisz: an illustrated and annotated book of patterns, containing the secrets of German Meisters. Years later, this book unfortunately disappeared. During this period, my mother requested and received from her father-in-law a high-quality *His Master's Voice* radio with seven tubes. We could listen to the quizzes and music, and no longer had to go into the Meisel couple's room to hear the news.

When he was not working (due to disputes with his father), my father sought an outlet for his energy and frustration, and fellowship, too. He found and was drawn to meetings and activity in the deaf community, which operated a members' club and association committee in homes and in a café, and later also in a gymnasium that was rented twice a week at a school on 5 Kalischer Street. There he would pour out his heart, telling his life story mostly focusing on his exploits during the Nazi occupation in Poland. In time, a number of deaf survivors also joined the meetings. My father was a compulsive raconteur and could go on and on, speaking about that period in particular, if only he found a listener. In his memories and dreams, he would recall, and imagine people, situations, and circumstances that happened, or that could have happened. In contrast, my mother kept her history inside her, like many survivors of the death camps. She didn't want to sully our lives. She would secretly delve into the pain of the loss of her family, her memories and her nightmares, and express only the final conclusions she reached, with acute insight, wisdom, and exceptional inductive ability. With the exception of her sister Pola and her friend Regina, who lived far away in Kibbutz Mesilot and later in Kibbutz Ma'abarot, my mother didn't have anyone for heart-to-heart conversations. She didn't seek friendship with members of the Kalisz immigrants association, and she was embarrassed to invite guests to her home, which fell below her expectations. My brother and I likewise refrained from inviting friends.

The barrier of language and culture was apparent: Mother revived the remnants of Hebrew from high school by ear, and Father was able to read from the prayer book in the synagogue on holidays based on what he remembered from the *heder* when he was five or six, before he became deaf. He didn't always understand the meaning of the words, however, and his efforts to learn Hebrew were not successful. This difficulty was compounded by the barrier of Father's deafness. He got involved in the deaf society, where he became an influential leader. Father sometimes invited people to our two separate rooms, and I was charmed by their innocent and warm-hearted attitude. They would sit politely with a cup of tea and conduct lively conversations in sign language, with vigorous hand motions, and bits of spoken syllables. I fondly remember from that period Hofshi Ben-Ami, Edmond Padida, and Haim Apter, who have all passed away, and others who are still active, who were leading figures in the organized deaf community in Tel Aviv from its early days. The short visits of Emanuel Marom left a particularly strong impression on me. He was a young deaf man who knew Polish, had a doctorate in chemistry, and worked in research at the Weizmann Institute. Marom was also active in the Haganah's underground industry, and was injured conducting an experiment for the Haganah. Mother received the guests warmly, but didn't find real interest in their company. She and Father also didn't find a circle of educated friends who were not deaf, despite the fact that my father was an interesting person, able to communicate, well-respected, and appreciated. Those who knew him said he was intelligent and talented to the point of genius in technical and other areas. At the time, this depiction of my father seemed exaggerated to me and easy to refute, and I sometimes viewed his conduct as playacting, as an attempt to make an impression. My parents did not make new mutual friends and would not in the future, except for Hela Lifshitz, after she immigrated to Israel. Frania would also later arrive with her husband Janek Fryde and their only child, Rysiek-Zvi. Most of Mother's attention was focused on helping and fostering her nuclear family, but it also turned to the extended family, of course. In retrospect, the feelings of family cohesion in my parents' generation and in their milieu seem incredibly strong.

Repressed urges and sensations lodged in our subconscious minds and dictated patterns of behavior, pretending to reflect our true desires and what was required of us. Hidden feelings of guilt that we failed to recognize grew stronger with age and time; they would awaken at times and torture us day and night. I wondered why I had survived while others my age, like Janka, had died in agony, in strange deaths. Why had such phenomenal efforts been invested in saving me by many unfamiliar people, at great risk to their lives? And what moral obligation did this impose on me? My mother mourned from the depths of her soul for her brother and sisters, their children, their spouses, and others. They were lost without leaving a trace, and I never got to know them at all. My father was burdened with enormous guilt and anger over the loss of his sisters Regina and Ala and their children in the Warsaw Ghetto. I also never got to know them, except for Janka. I think he also blamed himself for the fact that he made great efforts to save Frania, my mother's sister, yet failed to save even one member of his sisters' families. In Israel, he turned his frustration on Abram's wife Bronka, in whose large apartment the sisters had stayed in the ghetto. Bronka, together with her small son and daughter, managed to survive in the Bergen-Belsen camp as hostages for German citizens imprisoned in

Palestine. My father's near ostracism of Bronka clouded the family relations and harmed our absorption in Israel. Her family admired her for surviving – rightfully so, in my opinion. Later, after meeting quite a few survivors from Poland and being hurt by the behavior of some of them, I set a rule of reference for myself: *A Jew who survived the Nazi occupation there has the right to behave in peculiar and unconventional ways.* One can be wary of being hurt by them, but usually there is no point in holding a grudge against them. They earned this right through unfathomable suffering.

The tension of impending changes could be felt in the air. On the evening of November 29, 1947, my brother, and I crowded into the large mob of people waiting in front of the Mograbi Cinema. My heart skipped a beat at every uproar from those around me. Finally, with radio sets turned on full volume, and perhaps also loudspeakers, the crowd listened as the voting regarding approval of the United Nations Partition Plan for Palestine at the UN General Assembly in Lake Success was announced country by country, in alphabetical order. Upon learning the final result of the voting, I nearly burst with happiness and relief. It was an once-in-a-lifetime experience.

The attacks on the roads immediately intensified. Once I was invited to visit the home of Yoram Ben Porat, one of the best pupils in the class, who lived at what was then the northern edge of the city. As darkness fell, we watched, in a field near Sharona a convoy of supply trucks and armored vehicles secretly preparing to go up to Jerusalem. I remember a sense of anxiety and sadness about those riding in the convoy and protecting it, and the thought that some of them might die or be injured in breaking through the siege to Jerusalem. The fighting reached the outskirts of Tel-Aviv and I was warned about sniping from Jaffa. Even earlier, a protective wall of silicate bricks was built opposite the window of our room, by the spacious entrance to my grandfather's home on 111 Rothschild Boulevard. Soon afterward, I was astonished to find a large family of refugees from the Yemenite Quarter squatting in the stairway of the entrance. As I entered the house, I saw the father, a Yemenite with curly earlocks, sitting Eastern style and rapidly transcribing Hebrew verses on parchment for *mezuzot* and *tefillin*, and other sacred writings. The mother was cooking on a Primus stove and taking care of the young children. Both of them were affable, good-spirited, and noble, making do with very little for many months.

Our family also faced a shortage of food, but we attributed little importance to this. However, the atmosphere of uncertainty also lingered in our home after May 15, 1948, the establishment date of Israel, and even after we excitedly watched the first Israel Defence Forces (IDF) parade in the summer of that year. When the sirens sounded on the roof of the adjacent Bilu School, we usually didn't leave our beds to go down to the basement. On the contrary, when the sirens went off in the daytime, we would hurry to the roof of the house to watch through my binoculars the Egyptian aircraft attacking and the machine gun fire from the ground - once even a dogfight. Nonetheless, the reports I read in *Al Hamishmar*, Shlomo Meisel's newspaper, about the Egyptian column advancing toward Tel Aviv, filled me with fear. I found it hard to believe the reports that the defense forces had indeed managed to block the threatening column, and had even used planes in this battle. From the start of the first truce, we continued to go to the sea, and I even swam, and climbed onto the deck of the *Altalena*, feeling amazed, and shocked. The ship, organized by the Irgun, with its cache of weapons, was burned, and tipped against a sandbank. I didn't understand what could possibly justify destroying such a big load of weapons that were so badly needed in the war for survival. I also heard a rumor about one or more Jewish fatalities on the deck of the ship shelled by the IDF.

I continued to study diligently during the war, and the gaps in my knowledge steadily narrowed. A year after our immigration, I was diagnosed by the school physician, Dr. Philip Friedländer, with bronchial asthma. I was later referred to medical experts who were unable to clearly identify the causes of this illness or effective methods of treatment. For me, the asthma was a natural continuation in a series of colds and bronchitis that regularly bothered me, bringing to mind my sneeze in the closet room while neighbors were visiting in Mrs. Kuropieska's kitchen. Besides, I had always been accustomed to coping with difficult limitations. My mother saw this in a different light and perspective. She made a big deal of the asthma and decided to send me to a dry and high-altitude environment to help me recuperate. At the end of fifth grade, the battles in Jerusalem, and its vicinity were still being waged, so instead we went to Safed at the beginning of summer vacation. The city had just been liberated after stubborn fighting, and its Arab population had fled in panic. I traveled with my mother and brother in an *Egged* bus, passing through Afula, and Tiberias, a route that was still considered dangerous at the time. The battles in the Upper Galilee had recently ended. I recalled from conversations and radio broadcasts the names of kibbutzim that clung to the land: Manara and Misgav Am, and the fierce battles of Malkia. We rented a room in the apartment of Safed's police chief. The encounter with the beauty of the Upper Galilee and the sense of freedom there was intoxicating and imbued me with a feeling of transcendence. We roamed through gardens, bunkers, communication trenches, and abandoned Arab homes, despite the danger of mines, traps, and unexpected encounters. We hiked Mount Canaan a number of times, headed north to Ein Zeitim, and sneaked into the Biria fortress. In the abandoned orchards, we filled our bellies with grapes, figs, and walnuts. In the Arab Quarter, Itzhak, a lover of books, collected a trove of books in English for reading and study, and I helped him, driven by curiosity, and a sense of adventure. Later, when studying English in high school, I made extensive use of this booty from Safed, including an English dictionary compiled by M. West; an annotated copy of Shakespeare's *Macbeth*, with notes in Arabic written in pencil; and an English translation of Balzac's *The Wild Ass's Skin*. Judging by the things the wealthy families left behind, especially the Christian families, they impressed us as educated enemies. The residents of Safed had already plundered the household items and furniture in the abandoned Arab homes, but there was apparently no demand for the many books that remained. We felt some affinity toward the population of the fearsome enemy defeated here, but also relief, and hope for a possible future for the newly declared state that had come under attack. On the way back to Tel Aviv, we visited the home of Aunt Genia on the Carmel. Her husband, Benya, a math teacher at the Hebrew Reali School of Haifa and a commander in the Haganah, was then in charge of forming a secret heavy mortar unit.

In sixth grade, Mr. Yehuda Aryeh Glick was assigned to be our head teacher. A regular at the Bilu synagogue on Sabbaths, he taught religious studies, and ruled the class high-handedly. We started to learn with him the *Baba Metzia* tractate of the Talmud from its beginning, with the Rashi, and Tosafot commentaries. Before Passover, in light of my academic progress, it was decided that I should also study for an examination to skip to eighth grade and catch up to my age group. This entailed memorizing and being tested on Numbers and Deuteronomy with Rashi's commentary; Ezekiel; part of the Twelve Prophets; and about twenty pages of the *Baba Kama* tractate. I was left to fend for my own in the secular subjects.

At the same time, I was in the final stages of preparing for my bar mitzvah ceremony. I would need to step out of my shell for the first time in order to appear in front of a large and unfamiliar crowd and go up before the Holy Ark for the priestly blessing. I enjoyed the content of the moving and lofty *haftarah* from Malachi, chapter 3. In particular, I liked the sentence, "And all the nations shall account you happy, for you shall be the most desired of lands." On the big day, I went up to the podium as the second of three bar mitzvah boys. I succeeded in completing the mission reciting the blessings and chanting the *maftir* from the Torah scroll my grandfather had donated to the synagogue, and then chanting the *haftarah* and its blessings. After the sermons and blessings for the bar mitzvah boys, the participants were invited to a *kiddush* celebration. My grandfather's assistants had set up numerous tables brimming with refreshments in the corridor surrounding the classrooms and overlooking the yard. Later that day, my mother set up tables in our crowded apartment for about thirty-five invited guests. The china and silverware my mother had schlepped with her on the trek from Kalisz to Tel Aviv were arranged on linen tablecloths. My mother worked for many hours preparing delicacies, including meats, applying all of her culinary skills and circumventing the limitations of the rationing regime. I felt tense and uncomfortable when suddenly my grandfather and grandmother, accompanied by the school principal, Mr. Mishori, and his wife, joined the other relatives and friends at the table. It apparently never occurred to them to doubt that the festive meal would be strictly kosher. The disaster struck when the dessert was served strawberries with whipped cream [Note: this violates the prohibition against serving meat and milk products at the same meal]. A commotion arose. The shocked principal and his wife, together with my grandparents, got up, and hastily fled the home of the *goyim* in protest. I was devastated; I felt so humiliated and frightened that I just wanted to dig a hole and disappear. I could never understand how my wise and tolerant mother, whose father was a Hasid, could make such a mistake. I really doubt it was a flagrant act of rebellion against the tyranny of her in-laws. Perhaps the arrival of the elders had only been arranged at the last moment? How could my mother have put me in such an embarrassing situation in front of the fearsome principal?

The school year ended. The road to a divided Jerusalem was open, and armistice talks were underway. My mother registered me for a summer camp, sponsored by the Tel Aviv municipality, for children suffering from respiratory problems and allergies, in the hilly climate of Jerusalem's Beit Hakerem neighborhood. I adjusted relatively easily and had scant interest in my fellow campers from the city, most of them secular. I also found little interest in the counselors and the daily routine. During the rest periods in the afternoons and evenings, I would study the pages of the *Baba Kama* tractate, the Torah, and the Book of Ezekiel. I must have looked strange to my peers, since I didn't tell them about the plan to skip grades - I didn't expect to succeed. After camp was over, I stayed with my mother and brother in a modest guest-house in Beit Hakerem, where I studied for the exam and also was able to watch the convoy bringing the remains of Benjamin Ze'ev Herzl to his gravesite on the mountain. The test at school was conducted orally by Rabbi H. Cohen a teacher with a thick black beard, whom I didn't know. The rabbi didn't seek to trip me up, and I transferred to the eighth grade, the last year of elementary school.

With this, I parted from my private tutor for religious studies, Yehudah Mishori, who had also prepared me for the bar mitzvah. He was a secular Jew whose educational approach and deep-rooted knowledge from his own religious upbringing helped to connect me to my Jewish heritage, and I'm grateful to him for this. I saw many immigrants from Eastern Europe of my generation who remained detached and alienated from the sources of this culture. And many of them, older than me, ended up rejecting all forms of institutionalized education, and became, in my view, the lost generation of learning. The few who broke through the barriers and excelled usually had received support from surviving family members or from older supporters in their surroundings, in addition to having innate talents.

My integration into the eighth grade went smoothly. I was assigned, with two classmates, to correct the dictation tests given at the beginning of each English lesson, taught by the popular teacher Shimon Meisel. We also had an intelligent history teacher, Mr. Sapir, who would often give us independent assignments in public libraries. I gradually returned to my habit of reading literature, now in Hebrew. In eighth grade, I was absent quite often because of my asthma. It also kept me awake many nights, so I was permitted to pray at home and come to school straight to the first lesson. A series of pedantic final exams awaited at the end of the school year, covering all of the subject material in religious studies. We had to demonstrate extensive knowledge in all of the Pentateuch with Rashi's commentaries, in the early and later prophets, and in the pages of the three *Baba* tractates we learned in the Talmud. I was angry and disgusted when some of my classmates managed to steal many of the questions from the principal's office or teachers' room and read them secretly to the entire classroom. At the beginning of each final exam, I would suffer strong and uncontrollable anxiety attacks. I felt paralyzed by the fear of failure, and I had to invent mental and physical tactics to relax and concentrate on the work of writing. Just before I graduated, my teacher registered me, without my knowledge, at two religious institutions, the Kfar HaRoeh Yeshiva, and the Midrashiyat Noam in Pardes Hana, saying that I could choose between them. Later, I was also registered at the religious municipal high school in Tel Aviv. However, upon my mother's initiative, I ended up at the Ironi Aleph secular high school in the city. She ignored my explicit request to study a technical profession, which would allow me to move ahead and free myself from my dependence on my parents. The atmosphere at home was difficult and tense. The relations with my grandfather were on the verge of collapse after he had stripped my father of basic authorities in his work. My father went through periods of unemployment, and he searched for, and found other jobs. First, he worked assembling complex textile machines, and later became a partner in a flour mill, working far from home and in a difficult environment full with dust. His voluntary activity in the deaf community became a dominant part of his life; his vision and organizational ideas led to the formation of local branches in various cities and to the establishment of a National Association of the Deaf in Israel. In 1951, he was elected chairman of the Tel Aviv branch. With his friends, he later founded the Helen Keller House in Tel Aviv's Yad Eliyahu neighborhood and secured its funding, and was elected to serve as the organization's chairman on a voluntary basis.

Helen Keller and her companion Polly Thomson with Moshe on a visit to the Helen Keller House in Tel Aviv. In the background are members of the Association of the Deaf in Israel.

I spent part of the summer vacation between elementary school and secondary school with my brother and my cousin, Rysiek in a stone house in the farming community of Metula, which was situated at high altitude, and had relatively low humidity. We became friendly with the charming old farmers and their sabra children and friends. They took interest in us as representatives of the big city. We wandered through the fields and strolled along the Ayun stream and its falls, in Abel Beth Maachah, in Tel Hai and in Kfar Giladi. Our hosts often let me ride and gallop on their mare, and reap green corn with a scythe for animal feed. During this vacation, I began to see myself as a son of the land, a real sabra. However, this was not to be, and in time the models of identification would change.

6. Echoes of the Warsaw Ghetto

For about forty years, I kept a wall in my consciousness, shielding me from the traumatic residue of memories from that chaotic period, in an effort to live as a free human being. Whenever these memories breached the wall, I quickly suppressed them, keeping them hidden from myself and others. Now, in attempting to document that period, I needed to uncover the history of my family in Warsaw, and I lacked many details about it. When Kalisz was annexed to the Warthegau region in the Third Reich, which launched its campaign to make the city *Judenrein*, many of its Jewish residents fled or were expelled to Warsaw. My father's sisters, Regina Ganzweich, and Ala Bloch, moved with their children at the outbreak of the war to the apartment of their brother Abram and his wife Bronka on 38 Nalewki Street. When the ghetto was decreed in October 1940, their home fell within the confines of the ghetto.

6.1 Uncle Abram and his family

Abram, who was about ten years older than my father, had a great talent for business. At a young age, he accumulated many assets in Poland through wide-ranging commercial and industrial activity, even surpassing his father, and receiving no assistance from him. After my grandfather immigrated to Palestine, Abram was appointed general manager of the family's lace curtain factory in Kalisz and also worked in Warsaw and Łódz. He became one of the richest Jews in Warsaw and, as such, the Germans took him as a hostage when they occupied the city. After fleeing during those days of uncertainty and arriving alone in the Land of Israel during the war, he turned again to commercial activity, starting from scratch, and built a successful factory and store for top-quality wool weaves. My grandfather, in accordance with "his principles," didn't help him, but Abram treated his parents with respect. In addition to being a tough businessman and strict father, Abram had great personal charm and was a gregarious person. On more than one occasion, he assumed the role of the eldest brother. When Genia, the youngest sister, decided to study life sciences at Hebrew University in Jerusalem, her father didn't approve. She left the home against his will and without his support, and Abram supported her. Pola, my mother's sister, married the son of a wealthy family of industrialists in Kalisz, the only one in his family infected by the bug of Zionism. They immigrated to Palestine with their toddler, Esther, and were saved. After they divorced, Abram supported my Aunt Pola and her daughter, and might have married her if not for his hope that his family might have miraculously survived. Abram also helped my mother and employed her during the two-year absence of my father, who went to work in the United States. Later, when Abram was already ill, he agreed to enter into a problematic partnership with my father to start a factory for weaving wool fabrics. The enterprise was aimed at allowing my father to return to Israel and establish himself economically within the family. Abram was also solicitous of the welfare of Mr. David Domb and the family he built in Israel. Mr. Domb saved Abram's family in the Warsaw Ghetto and was their guardian at the Bergen-Belsen concentration camp.

Rysiek's story

In August 2003, Rysiek, the son of Abram, and Bronka, told me that he was smuggled out of the Warsaw Ghetto by Mr. David Domb, who had a permit to work on the Aryan side. Mr. Domb worked as an exterminator of rats and other pests for the Poles and also for the German occupation authorities. When Rysiek came down with whooping cough in the ghetto, Mr. Domb invited German soldiers for drinks on the Aryan side. They got a bit drunk, and he told them about a Polish boy named Rysiek who had entered the ghetto to be examined by his Jewish doctor and was now stuck there. Soon afterward, he asked the same soldiers to help bring Rysiek, the Polish boy, back from the ghetto. Domb and the soldiers, including an officer, arrived in a command card with an open roof, and thus Rysiek was transported by the Germans out of the ghetto. Rysiek lived in his maternal grandfather's villa in Otwock, where they had a Polish housekeeper. There was a group of Jews who worked for the Germans in Otwock at that time, and the grandfather was allowed to stay in his home. The area was fenced. When they began liquidating the Jews in Otwock, the Polish housekeeper sneaked Rysiek out of the local ghetto to her home. One time, a group of

Poles accosted them in the street, claiming that Rysiek was a Jewish boy. They denied this, but the Poles forcibly stripped him to see if he was circumcised. The house agent bribed them with a sum of cash and they went to bring someone else, who also received money. They fled, and Rysiek continued to hide in her home. The grandfather was also whisked out of the ghetto by the house agent and hid in the same apartment. After Rysiek, his younger sister Berta was also taken out of the ghetto by Mr. Domb, thanks to his transit permit. It was winter and he hid her under his long coat, and she walked between his legs. Berta was taken to a different hiding place. Bronka was the last to leave the ghetto, escaping via the sewer pipes. The three had authentic papers from the British Mandate government, because before the war broke out they were planning to depart soon for Palestine. Thanks to these papers, they were assigned to a special group in Bergen-Belsen. After much debate, they decided to report as ordered for the transport to Bergen-Belsen, which left from Hotel Polski. The grandfather and Mr. Domb came with them, apparently with forged documents they had purchased. They joined a group of about two hundred people who were not required to work at the camp. My brother Itzhak's future wife Sharona Igra, then still a child, and her parents were also part of this group. There were transports to Auschwitz from Bergen-Belsen, under the pretext of sending people to the destinations cited on their "documents." The members of the group who were not sent and were unaware of the real destination of these transports envied those who were actually being sent to their death. The grandfather died of natural causes at the camp at age seventy-five. Prior to the liberation, they were evacuated from the camp by train, which was bombed en route. In the Warsaw area there was an industry of forging documents of very high quality. The Germans usually didn't detect that they were fake. Uruguayan, Paraguayan, and other documents were produced; forged Palestinian documents were the least expensive. This was apparently the type of documents that Bronka offered Mateusz. Rysiek claims that their group was held because negotiations were being conducted on the Allies' sale of trucks to the Germans in exchange for Jews, and they were needed as bargaining chips. The real reason was apparently the presence of German hostages, residents of Palestine, in the hands of the British. Many of those German hostages, including many of the Templer settlers, were supporters of the Nazi regime.

Earlier, Rysiek, and his family lived in the ghetto in their spacious apartment on Nalewki Street. Regina and her daughters and Ala and her children lived in the living room of their apartment. The living room was divided into two areas by a line that was drawn, and it was agreed that each of the two families would stay on its side of the line. Rysiek remembers arguments between the two sisters. He doesn't know how my father managed to get Janka out of the ghetto and then back inside, and notes that there were various methods for entering and exiting the ghetto. Ala's son Marek was one year older than Rysiek and they were good friends, spending a lot of time playing together. Rysiek only vaguely remembers his older sister Ninka and has almost no recollection of Regina's daughters Janka and Rutka. He remembers Moniek, my father, visiting the apartment on more than one occasion, and recalls how Moniek repaired a broken pipe in the kitchen. In response to my question, he said that there was cooking gas in the apartment, as well as electricity, and coal for heating. I raised this question in order to check whether it might be true that Regina Ganzweich and her daughters put an end to their bitter lives by inhaling cooking gas, as in the stories I remembered.

Rysiek told how at the beginning of the war the Germans had taken Poles and Jews from Warsaw as hostages and forced them to dig graves for themselves, but then conditionally released them. It was then that Abram decided to flee to Russia via the front lines. Bronka didn't want to subject Berta, then only a few months old, to the perils of this journey and preferred to remain in Warsaw. Abram left money, jewelry, and goods with her that were well hidden. These enabled the family to live under better conditions in the ghetto and even to help Bronka's two sisters-in-law and their children. In conditions of great uncertainty, Bronka's primary concern was for the well-being of her small children, and she acted according to the best of her understanding.

6.2 Mute testimony – letters to captivity Uncle Samek and his family

More than twenty years after the events, Samek Bloch left me an inheritance of family history that included photocopies of a series of fifteen letters (written in Polish) he received while in German captivity. Below are excerpts from some of the short letters, translated from the Polish originals. Second Lieutenant Salomon Bloch, an officer in the reserves, was stationed with the 25th Light Artillery Battalion of Kalisz's Lands (*Ziemia Kaliska*). He was mobilized on August 18, 1939, as tensions mounted; he fell captive on September 20, 1939, near Warsaw. Samek was the husband of Ala (Sheindel - Shlomit / Sala), my father's sister, who was murdered by the Nazis. After the war, Samek married Halina, a survivor, whose family had perished, including her husband, a physician. Without any living descendants, he wanted to pass on information to me, perhaps in hope that I would make it known to the family and to the public in Israel. Samek was a man of strict ethical codes. He would periodically receive a package of basic commodities from a Polish woman who lived in Warsaw and was mobilized to assist the prisoners of war. When it became clear to him that his family had perished in the ghetto or in a death camp, and he somehow learned from my father that my mother was in the Stutthof camp, he asked the woman to send the packages to my mother in his stead. I know that my mother received at least one package from the Polish woman at the camp. Samek was a close friend of my father; he greatly admired Father's virtues and forgave his faults. He also tried to offer my father various pieces of advice, in long letters from Melbourne, Australia, and during his visits in Israel. Samek and Halina, who were often of the same mind, exuded deep affection for my mother and credited her with the "gift of matchmaking" that brought them together in Kalisz.

Letter 1: April 16, 1940

Sender: Ninka Blochówna, Warschau (Polen), Nalewki 38
Adderessee: Bloch Salomon, p.pr. Oflag XVIIIC L.W.B.

Happy birthday wishes from Ninka and from Marek. On April 16, 1940, Ninka-Yocheved Bloch, a girl of nine years and three months, from 38 Nalewki Street in Warsaw, wrote a letter to her father, Second Lieutenant Salomon Bloch, addressed to the prisoner-of-war camp for officers (Oflag) in Germany. The letter was written in verse, in pencil, for his birthday, on a postcard form they were allowed to send once a month:

> For my dear Daddy on Your birthday.
> I'm letting you know
> That today is your birthday
> And therefore I'm sending good wishes in your honor.
> May you live a long life and enjoy good health!
> Until you return to us again, my father.
> And when we live again without lacking a thing
> I'll want to be a pilot, free as a bird.
> I'll fly above the forests; I'll fly above the mountain
> And I'll see you through a wonderful cloud.
> Ninka
> Marek sends his regards and kisses

Within three years, Ninka saw her father from the heavens, and perhaps she also became a cloud herself in Treblinka, together with her brother Marek and her mother Ala. I read this poem at my retirement party from the Space Technologies Administration at Israel Aerospace Industries, and also during a visit to Auschwitz-Birkenau with an Arab-Jewish group led by Father Emil Shoufani from Nazareth, next to what remains of the production line of extermination.

A birthday poem by Ninka-Yocheved Bloch from 38 Nalewki Street in Warsaw to her father, Salomon Bloch, at the POW camp in Germany (April 16, 1940).

Letter 3: July 13, 1942

Sender: Bloch Ala, Warschau, Nalewki 38I, Gen. Gouvernement.
Addressee: Bloch Salomon, p.por., Gefangenennummer: 45/XVIIIC, Baracke 12a, Kriegsgef. – Offizierlager IIC, Woldenberg / Nm., Deutschland

My beloved,
Mrs. Braun sent a package to you. Moritz [Note: my father, Mateusz] wrote to me that he would be sending you a package for the sticker from June 18. There was a time when there was a lot of talk about traveling to the parents [to Palestine], but that pertained to those such as Bronka and the young children. Now it has become quiet again. I received forty marks from you, and Mania also received. I'll write to Mr. Emil and again to Mr. Julius.

I think they'll pay greater attention to a letter from you. You can write Kowalski [Józef Kowalski from Kalisz imprisoned in the same barrack] as the sender and inside the letter your [name]. I'm very happy that finally you'll send me a sticker. Kissing you affectionately, yours, Ala.

Letter 4: October 8, 1942

Sender: Bloch Ala, Warschau, Siegesstr 25 w. 5, Gen. Gouvernement
Addressee: Bloch Salomon, Baracke 12a; Woldenberg

Dear Mr. Kowalski, I ask you please to deliver this letter to pp.Bloch and thank you in advance. I live at 38/1 Nalewki.

My dearest. Thank God, we are healthy and sound. I'm surprised that I haven't received a letter from you for so long, when other women were still receiving [letters]. I personally took a great risk to receive them. At my request, the letter carrier went through complete piles of letters [and searched] in vain. How do you feel, my love? I complained a lot to my acquaintances when thinking about you. Now a great many of them envy me. So it turns out that I'm no longer together with Bronka and Regina. The apartment of Adaś [Abram] is being used by the main office of the company I work for. I'm very satisfied. Ninka and Marek have become gaunt because they've also gone through a lot. I hope to God the situation will improve. I suffer terribly from not knowing what is happening with those most dear to me. That's the way it is. Because of Nina and Marek, I can't take risks. A great many have traveled to where our two sisters and mother are [Note: Roza, Genia and their mother Devorah in the Land of Israel], or it seems to us that we will meet. I would really like to send you the cigarettes [*papierosy* – a code name for documents, photographs] that we wrote so much about, but how? I implore you to write to me forthwith at the address of our honorable manager – and I will receive it: Pan Leo Kowal, Warschau, Siegesstr 25 w. 5, Gen. Gouvernement. Be well, I kiss you heartily, your Ala. (in Marek's handwriting): Beloved Father! We are all well and sound, kissing you.

Signed: Nina and Marek[10]

Letter 5: January 20, 1943

Sender: Władysław Günther, Warschau, Ulica Hoża 39 m12, Gen. Gouvernement
Addressee: Bloch Salomon, Baracke 12a; Woldenberg

My beloved. I thank you also for the postcard from January 6. I'll also share with you my pain from the loss of Regina and her children. This was expressed in a fatal way since she fell ill. I'll describe this in detail for you in a letter. Thinking about her troubles me to no end, though they assure me that perhaps we'll yet see each other. I'm just with Nina and Marek. Only unfamiliar faces. I'm working as a waitress-house agent. Bronka's cousin is living with us, and I've become quite connected to her. Bronka received a certificate from Adaś [Abram], perhaps she'll be saved. We send our cordial wishes to you. Yours Ala, Nina, Marek.

Letter 6: March 5, 1943

Sender: Władysław Günther, Warschau, Ulica Hoża 39 m12, Gen. Gouvernement
Addressee: Bloch Salomon, Baracke 12a; Woldenberg

This letter includes mostly personal family matters. Ala comments about Bronka coming to visit her at the apartment on 38/1 Nalewki Street.

---

10   September 11, 1942 marked the end of the *Grossaktion Warschau* in the Warsaw Ghetto, during which about 315,000 Jews were dispatched in cattle cars from the *Umschlagplatz* to the Treblinka extermination camp. Perhaps "to meet" meant in their code to meet in the afterlife. It's possible that at the time Ala wrote this, she suspected that the promised transport was a pretext by the Germans and that those "traveling to Palestine," including Bronka and her children, were traveling to their deaths, since they lost all contact with them. Regina and her daughters and Bronka and her children were no longer living in the apartment.

Passport photos: Ninka-Yocheved and Marek Bloch, made in the Warsaw Ghetto

Letter 7: April 1, 1943

Sender: Bloch Ala, Warschau, Nalewki 38/1, Gen. Gouvernement. Addressee: Bloch Salomon, Baracke 12a; Woldenberg

The postcard is addressed to Salomon Bloch from the address of Ala Bloch on 38/1 Nalewki Street and was written on "her" form by her friends Leonek and Jadzia to Bolek [Note: I'm not familiar with them]. Ala Bloch added just one single significant line:

My beloved. The date of birth of Szejndel-Sala – April 15, 1907, of Janina – January 25, 1931 and of Marek – April 11, 1934. Hearty embraces, Ala.

Letter 8: April 2, 1943

Sender: Władysław Günther, Warschau, Ulica Hoża 39 m12, Gen. Gouvernement
Addressee: Bloch Salomon, Baracke 12a; Woldenberg

This is also a letter from Leonek and Jadzia to Bolek with an additional line from Ala. The postmark is only one day after her previous letter!

April 4, 1943. Dear Bolek! I already wrote to you a few days ago, also attached to a letter to Samek, that everything is fine here. I'm working at a flour mill and would like very much to send you a package. There's a very important addition below. My address is 38 Zamenhof, apartment 92. We are well and wish you good fortune on your birthday. We kiss you, Leonek and Jadzia.

[From Ala] We discussed this with Mr. Leonek because it was necessary and urgent, if you could arrange for us, so we wouldn't be forced to travel from here; you are the only ones in the world we have. Kisses, Ala.

Letter 9: April 15, 1943

Sender: Władysław Günther, Warschau, Ulica Hoża 39 m12, Gen. Gouvernement
Addressee: P.porucznik Kowalski Józef, Gefangenennummer: 2000/IIA, Baracke 12a, Kriegsgef. – Offizierlager IIC, Woldenberg / Nm. Deutschland

[Note: Second Lieutenant Józef Kowalski serves as the addressee here, too, because the series of letters exceeds the permitted monthly quota].

My beloved. I wrote to you because I thought that by turning to those in charge you could do something for us. A letter written directly from you would be futile because no one decides locally. A decision can only come from the capital city, and it's only possible to submit a request via a very influential personage. But if this is not possible for you, don't feel bad.

Somehow, God willing, we'll find a way. Try if possible. I send regards to all of you, Leonek and Jadzia. I'm waiting for word from our beloved Bolek [these are regards from Leonek and Jadzia that are "smuggled" between the lines]. I haven't heard from Arek in a long time. It's now possible to see him. Let Arek contact Dr. Saul Wajngot in Montreaux, 29 Belmonte, Switzerland. D. Torończyk made this possible for us and for the family. Arek's parents are apparently no longer alive. Afterward, Eda and her young daughter traveled to Michael, and had to move again from there. I heard this from a distant relative of hers – (I'm attaching pictures of the uncle, who sends you regards and all good wishes) – but I cannot absorb the terrible news that Eda died from a heart defect. The child (*dziecko*) is with her brother Michael. I'm repeating what I heard, there's no certainty of one-hundred percent. Hala is now where Mateusz is. Moritz [Note: probably, Mateusz, my father] was with me, looks very exhausted and nervous. He cannot forgive me for recklessly giving Bronka what belonged to me, and if it were not for me, everything would have gone to the river. Bronka still has complaints because I'm doing fine, and despite my "foolishness." I send you regards and kisses, your Ala, Nina, Marek. Arek's last address from August 20, 1942: M. Nowak, Matzingen, Thurgau Canton, Switzerland.

It turns out that Mateusz, my father, "visited" the ghetto soon before this letter was written, and Bronka also was still there, or "visited" then. Additional details can be found in the testimony of Mateusz-"Moritz" below. I'm not familiar with the other names, and perhaps some of them are codes.

This is the last correspondence that Samek Bloch gave me, written just prior to the liquidation of the remnants of the ghetto and the uprising. It indicates the presence of censorship and the use of a simple code language that was completely understood only by the correspondents themselves. Despite the horrendous situation in the ghetto, the correspondence reflects the tenderness, love, and support that prevailed from afar between Ala (and the children) and Samek. Regina, who committed suicide with gas or poison together with her children, Janka and Ruth, and Ala, and her children, whose deaths are not documented, refused to surrender their humanity, despite the physical and emotional distress we know they experienced in the Warsaw Ghetto. Samek conducted a lively correspondence, albeit a limited one, via the Red Cross in Geneva, with: his brother Kazik in Ireland, friends in Switzerland, his in-laws Shmuel and Devorah in Palestine, Anka Rubinstein in Elizabethville in the Belgian Congo, and others. Anka Rubinstein, the youngest sister of his father-in-law Shmuel, had fled with her husband and three children to Elizabethville from Belgium via Portugal. All this correspondence was aimed at informing them of Samek's existence and at rescuing his family from the Warsaw Ghetto. He was left with the passport pictures of Ninka and Marek, which were taken in the ghetto and sent to him for this purpose - in vain.

Letter 12: Traces of the photograph from Kielce

I was particularly interested in the two sides of a form for correspondence with prisoners of war in Germany (*Kriegsgefangenenpost*), approved with the stamps of the British censor T.1 in Palestine and the stamp *Geprüft* of the Woldenberg camp's censor. The letter was addressed to Second Lieutenant Salomon Bloch, prisoner number 45/XVIIIC, in Barrack 12a of Jewish prisoners of war. It was written and sent to him on January 10, 1944 by his father-in-law Shmuel from 111 Rothschild Boulevard, Tel Aviv, Palestine, and took about six weeks to arrive. Samek apparently received the letter only in November 1944. It was written, according to the rules, succinctly and in pencil, in Polish:

Dear Salomon,
We received your letter with the photographs. We sent packages of food and clothing for you, and for my friends Captain Kuropieska and Lieutenant Kowalski. We don't have any more vouchers for basic goods. Please send some to us as soon as possible. Write in your next letter about your state of health. All of us, thank God, are in good health, only worried, and depressed about the fate of our Regina's children and others, those who are dearest to us. We only have one consolation from Mateusz and his family. We know who is responsible for this kindness. In anticipation of your next letters, and the vouchers for sending basic goods, we sign with our regards.
(Signed) Samuel F.

So, the photograph from Kielce arrived at its destination. I discovered it in my grandparents' album together with the threads with which it was sewn and attached to the letter. In my view, the response was written with wanton recklessness and was extremely dangerous due to the connection it made with Kuropieska and Mateusz. It expressed a bad conscience, confusion, and helplessness. I assume that the correct Polish wording and some of the content came from my Aunt Roza. I don't think that my know-it-all grandfather bothered to consult with his son Abram, a wise and thoughtful man, who was more familiar with the situation.

The envelope side of a letter from Grandfather Shmuel in Palestine to his son-in-law, Second Lieutenant Salomon Bloch, in Oflag IIC, Woldenberg. Written in Tel Aviv on January 10, 1944; it reached its destination via the International Committee of the Red Cross in Geneva in November 1944.

Two testimonies of Samek from captivity

The first testimony pertains to remarks made by one or more officers from the Polish underground (AK) who were captured during the Warsaw Uprising and brought to the Woldenberg officers' camp after the uprising was suppressed. In letters to my father, and in conversations with me, Samek repeatedly cited the remarks of a colonel who delivered lectures to the captive officers about the Jewish uprising in the Warsaw Ghetto. The colonel, whose name he didn't remember, had served on the staff of General Bor Komorowski, the commander of the Polish uprising in Warsaw:

> The Jewish uprising in the ghetto is an invention of your "kikes" in the camp (*żydków obozowych*). It's not true that there was supposedly some sort of uprising in the Jewish ghetto in Warsaw. On the other hand, the truth is that the Jews in the ghetto stored weapons with the aim of turning them against the Poles, in order to take revenge on them for allowing the Jews to be confined within the ghetto.

After the liberation and back in Warsaw, Samek sent two witnesses ("seconds") to the colonel to challenge him to a pistol duel for causing insult with his lies. Two other liberated officers (Salzenstein and Lev) did likewise, each separately. The colonel refused to respond to their challenges.

A second testimony came in a letter sent from Melbourne to my father, dated April 19, 1984. Samek sent this written testimony about General Józef Kuropieska prior to the latter's visit to Israel and Yad Vashem:

> [Józef Kuropieska] showed me [at the prisoner-of-war camp] pictures of children together with members of his family, which he received from his wife in Warsaw. In response to the question of whether they were my children, I told him during the course of our ongoing conversation that they were the children of my wife's brother. We had a long conversation on general subjects and I told him that we are "patriotic Jews," [despite the fact] that the grandparents of these children emigrated to Palestine before

the war and so on. At the end of our conversation, he placed his hand on my shoulder and said, "Don't worry, sir, my wife will take care of the children."

Later, he again read a letter to me from his wife in which she wrote that she and her children were under danger of "infection" from Ignaś' disease. I think it was then that Ignaś was discovered by Polish children she clearly led him to understand that she was asking his advice, whether "to deliver these children to the hospital" or something like that. Kuropieska [then a captain] asked me, "What do you think about this?" After giving this some thought, I responded that I cannot give him an answer, because this must be his own decision and responsibility, since it entailed risking the life of his entire family. He didn't reply, but just asked me for a form from the camp for a letter, and casually and immediately wrote a letter to his wife, and gave it to me to read. I'll never forget the ending of this letter "When Bloch and I went to war, there was no guarantee that we would return. We could fall or survive. In this, we weren't doing a favor for anyone, just fulfilling our civic duty. Now it's your turn. Now you must do what is your duty. And remember, I will return." Underlining in the original.[11]

---

11   Sources on the history of the Jewish officers' barrack:
   1. Rafael Łoc, Looking Down from the Third Bunk, Moreshet Publishing, Mordechai Anielevich Memorial Holocaust Study and Research Center and Sifriyat Poalim, 1976. (Hebrew)
   2. Wyprawa do Oflagu, Marian Brandys, PIW, W - wa 1955 r.
   3. Obozowe refleksje Oflag IIC, Józef Kuropieska, Wydawnictwo Ministerstwa Obrony Narodowej, W-wa, 1974.

7. Grandfather Shmuel Ben Itzhak Hersch in the Yishuv and in the State of Israel

In April 1936, a law was enacted in Poland prohibiting the transfer of money out of the country. Before the legislation entered effect, my grandfather turned his remaining property in Kalisz into a company whose shares were divided between his children in Kalisz and in Tel Aviv. Not all of my grandfather's wishes were honored, including his wish that everyone would immigrate to Palestine. A tone of anger remained. My grandfather's memoirs end one year before the outbreak of World War II. He concludes his story by saying:

I decided to punish them for this. They were antagonistic toward me, so I will be antagonistic toward them.[12] In the presence of my son-in-law Bloch [who was visiting in Palestine], I wrote a will [pertaining] to all of my property in this country. In my will, I dedicated one of my four houses in Tel Aviv to feeding the yeshiva children [that is, the Bilu School] for twenty-five years ... a large part of my property will not be for them to enjoy [the members of my family!]. My conscience was definitely clean. In nearly all of my demands from them, I had their best interests at heart, and they in their foolishness and arrogance didn't realize this. Now they will recognize and know that there is no reward for the sinner.

The thought that these words were written during or after the war leaves me speechless and exhausted. No less so, if they were written before the war and were not subsequently erased without anyone seeing.

After the war broke out, all traces of Herman (Hersch) Ganzweich were lost. Salomon Bloch was called into active service, fought, and survived in captivity. The brothers and sisters, children of Shmuel and Devorah, and their families were mobilized in the fatal war of survival in Poland, as recounted. These concluding words of my grandfather and his shortcomings symbolize for me the conduct of the entire leadership of the Yishuv: obtuseness, provincial narrow-mindedness, lack of decisiveness, and perhaps even some implicit self-righteousness vis-à-vis the tragedy in the Diaspora. In light of what is known today, it's impossible to claim

---

12   A reference to Leviticus 26:27-28

that they were unaware of the facts of what was happening; the leadership of the Yishuv knew almost in real time. The general public in the Yishuv, however, was not well-informed or properly briefed. The parachuting of a handful of bold emissaries near the end of the devastation was, relative to the enormous needs, like a futile sin offering, late, and unnecessary. No resounding cry for assistance came from the Yishuv. It didn't explore ways to collect and send contributions to save Jews in hiding the type of action performed by the Polish Council to Aid Jews (Żegota), the Joint Distribution Committee and veterans of the Bund organization in the US, and by the Polish government-in-exile in London. My grandfather knew, and he could have contributed a house or apartments to saving Jews, though there was no fundraising campaign to solicit from him. He preferred to win praise for donating an expensive Torah scroll that was festively brought into the Great Synagogue in Tel Aviv during that period.

My grandfather named the curtain factory he built in Bnei Brak "Tova." I later realized that Tova was actually the Hebrew translation of the name Gitel, the childhood nickname in Yiddish of my Aunt Genia. That is the way he found to express his love for her and to ask for forgiveness and reconciliation after opposing her decision to study microbiology at the Hebrew University of Jerusalem. She succeeded in her studies and marriage on her own, despite his refusal to support her studies in Jerusalem.

Since his youth, my grandfather was decisive and determined, industrious and unrelenting: rose, fell, and got up again. He envisioned and executed. He harbored no doubts about the correctness of his ways. He was prepared to firmly confront partners and competitors and to trample them as mercifully as he deemed appropriate. In different periods of his life, he was able to interpret stormy waves of political and economic upheaval, which enabled him to generate large profits during the relatively short periods of transition and stability. However, when he was already old and ill, he experienced failure in the emerging reality of the State of Israel, which was his heart's desire since his youth. In his industrial activity in Bnei Brak, he applied the same patterns of activity that had proved successful in Poland, purchasing everything himself, without seeking funding from the government. In fact, he donated about a third of his remaining real estate to *Keren Kayemet* (the Jewish National Fund). In 1953, with great fanfare, and in the presence of ministers and dignitaries, a cornerstone was laid for a secondary school for textile engineering on his citrus land, near the factory. The factory subsequently failed and underwent a process of voluntary liquidation. On the one hand, he caused pain, and sorrow to his closest family, who survived the Nazi chaos by the skin of their teeth. On the other hand, he supported the immigration of more distant relatives prior to the World War, as well as immigrants from my grandmother Devorah's family who fled to the Soviet Union. Throughout his life, he longed for the public's respect and appreciation, but his contribution to the establishment of the Jewish state and to the religious community is not recognized today.

When he was in his seventies, and perhaps beginning in his sixties, my grandfather would go to the rabbi's class at the Bilu synagogue every evening. He spoke with me enthusiastically about what he learned and about the value of "spirituality." When his illness made it difficult for him to climb the stairs to the Bilu synagogue to join a *minyan* [prayer quorum], he would stubbornly shuffle down the sidewalk, one small step at a time, to the nearby synagogue affiliated with the Mizrahi movement, hiding in his clothing the catheter he needed due to prostate problems. During this period, his physical frailty was exploited by Mizrahi functionaries encouraging him to use his remaining assets to create charity funds, such as the Shem-Shmuel Fund. Much of this was used for their own benefit, and perhaps a little also went to needy orphans and widows. I kept his typewritten, yellowing memoir for about fifty years, from the time my grandfather gave it to me as a spiritual inheritance until I gathered the strength to read it in astonishment and to investigate the events that occurred.

8. Itzhak, a missing voice and other voices

The voice of my brother, Itzhak Komem, is missing. His complete memoirs were supposed to be added to this book, but we disagreed in principle about including some details. The absence of these details does not detract from the story itself. Missing from this book are parts of Itzhak's childhood memories and his personal perspectives as a high school teacher of history and civics, and as someone who participated in the momentous events described here. This loss spares the reader some of the burden of details of this rather complex story. A summary of situations and events according to Itzhak is presented below to fill in some of the missing parts.

After fleeing from the Sandomierz Ghetto, my mother's sister Frania (under the name of Ludmila, or Mila) rented a room in Słotwina and lived during the freezing winter with Itzhak (under the name of Marian Dąbrowski, or Maryś, her "son"), in conditions of cold and want. Itzhak remembers that he rarely went outside. One day, there were knocks on the door, and a man of medium age, stature and presence entered the room. He was a *szmalcownik* and he started to speak of blackmail that is, saying that he was aware of their Jewish identity. Mila denied this, but the extortionist insisted, and hinted about examining the boy to confirm his Jewishness. Then Mila unleashed a torrent of curses in juicy and flawless Polish vernacular. The man was shocked, apologized that "perhaps the lady really isn't a Jew," and went away. However, he apparently had no doubt about the identity of the silent Marian, and this fright led to the urgent departure of Mila and Marian in a train to Warsaw.

Mila (Frania) and Marian (Itzhak) arrived at Father's rented room, or at a hotel room in Warsaw. The adults looked in the newspaper advertisements for rooms to rent. One such advertisement led Mila to the apartment of Leopolda Kuropieska, who agreed to rent them a room in her apartment under their assumed identity, though at first glance she already identified Marian as a Jewish boy, based on his dark and fearful eyes. She assumed that Mateusz (Father) and Mila were a Polish couple who were trying to save a Jewish boy. She later explained that if she had closed her door to them, she would have felt like a murderer, and that was out the question. Marian would go out to yard and play with the children, including Wojtek and Basia, Mrs. Leopolda's children. In time, she came to understand how Marian, Mateusz, and Mila were actually related.

Soon the situation began to change for the worse. The neighbors began to suspect him. Leopolda's father, with the help of his son Michael, built a hiding place inside a wall closet a sort of interior closet. Marian was supposed to go inside it and stand in complete silence if they heard a knock on the door, or when a guest was expected to visit one of the children or Leopolda - and there were quite a few guests. They told the neighbors that Marian had left the apartment. Mila moved to a different apartment.

Marian was forbidden to make any noise, since the apartment was supposed to be empty, especially during the morning hours. He could not go out onto the balcony, peek through the window, or even come close to the window. Sometimes Marian would stay in the hiding place for hours of strict silence. Since there was no electric light in the closet, his mind was the only means of entertainment. Marian called Mrs. Leopolda, at her request, "Aunt" or "Aunt Leopolda." She was a warm-hearted woman, who treated him as a mother would, just as she treated her own children. She loved him dearly and allowed him to read in her husband's rich professional library. Marian and Wojtek monitored the course of the Allies' war against the Germans on a wall map with colored pins.

Marian was not discovered during the extortion-visit by the man in a Polish "blue police" uniform and a civilian, who came to the hideout based on information provided by a neighbor. Marian sat in darkness on a high shelf in the closet. During their search, they discovered me (I had come to the apartment about ten weeks earlier) and two Jewish women whom Leopolda had hosted for a while. The three of us managed to leave the apartment after sending the extortionists off with a bribe. Leopolda continued to hide Marian alone.

Wojtek and Basia Kuropieska and Marian Dąbrowski (on the left) at the Kuropieska family's home on 45 Independence Avenue.

Itzhak describes an additional episode of blackmail. Leopolda showed him a letter written in ink. A man was inviting her to meet in a café on a discreet matter that could endanger her. She explained to Marian that she was sure this had something to do with him. When Leopolda sensed my brother's despair, she promised him that she knew what to do and that everything would be okay. The next day, she showed Marian a typed letter with the symbol of the Polish eagle at the bottom and the stamp of the Polish underground. The short letter declared that Mrs. Kuropieska was the wife of an officer held captive by the enemy, and that anyone who harmed even a single hair on her head would risk severe punishment by the underground. That same day or the next, Leopolda set off for the meeting with the blackmailer. She returned with rosy cheeks, happy, and good-hearted. "I placed the letter from the underground in front of him," she told Marian. "He read it, grew pale, got up, mumbled a good-bye, and left. We won't hear from him again." And that was indeed the case.

On a June morning in 1944, when Marian was still in Leopolda's apartment and the children were in school, a knock was heard at the door. Leopolda opened the door and an unfamiliar man was there, who said that he knew with certainty that she was hiding a Jewish boy in her apartment. If he had expected her to begin negotiating, he suffered a disappointment. She invited him to come in and find the nonexistent boy. He indeed conducted a search and opened the wall closet, but did not find the hiding place. Leopolda demonstrated admirable composure, and did not budge from where she was sitting on the bed. Marian lay all the time under the blanket on which Leopolda was sitting motionlessly, and he heard everything.

Captain Józef Kuropieska before outbreak of World War II

Following this incident, Marian parted from Mrs. Kuropieska after living with her for nearly a year and a half. Aunt Mila, who had not appeared at the apartment for a long time, came, and took him to Mietek and Stasia Kolski. After Father completed the arrangements, Marian moved into a rented room. Meanwhile, Mother arrived in Warsaw after the extortion episode in Brzesko. Later, Marian lived for about two months with Mother, in a room in Mr. Krzyczkowski's home, and did not venture out of the apartment.

On August 1, 1944, Marian and our parents found themselves in the heart of the Polish uprising against the German Army in Warsaw for many weeks. They fled to the tunnels of the underground power plant of Warsaw's tram system, crossing through a battlefield amidst shelling, machine gun fire, explosives, and firebombing from the air. They hid in those tunnels together with the extended Kolski family, most of them Jews, among the many Aryan tram employees and their families. Itzhak's description of the events is nearly identical to the description in Father's recorded memoirs, but from the perspective of a child, without any expression of emotion except for feelings of fear, as well as boredom from spending hours among adults. He expressed his fear of the bullets fired at them, of the grenades the Germans tossed into the tunnels where they were hiding, and of being exposed as a Jew by the tram workers, the German soldiers, and the Ukrainians who served them. The separation of the family in the selection at Pruszków, and our mother's departure in a freight train, are reported in a matter-of-fact way.

Father and Marian, together with Stasia's cousin Hela and her infant Wiesio, whose father Michał had been burned and shot to death, were expelled far from Warsaw to a distant village near Piotrków Trybunalski, named Gorzkowice. The four of them lived in a room that once served as a bakery, with the family of a farmer who built coffins. At first, Marian had some degree of independence: He played with the farmers' children, and tried to help tend to the chickens and farm animals, and took part in cleaning chores in the small yard with the strength of an unskilled child. Father would disappear occasionally in his search for a livelihood, and Marian was sometimes assigned to babysit for the infant. It wasn't long before suspicions began to arise about Marian's Jewish origins because of his appearance. Hela decided to dye his hair, and after it took on a strange shade of pink, she shaved it all off. However, the dye had also colored his scalp pink, so he wore a cap that also aroused suspicion. He no longer played in the yard. Marian seldom went outside, remaining cloistered in the room with Hela and the baby. In order to minimize suspicions, Marian began going to church on Sundays for the first time in his life, trying to mimic the conduct of the worshippers. He tried to fill the hours of the day by reading anything he could get his hands on, including German propaganda newspapers in Polish. The villagers suffered from a shortage of food and basic commodities, and Marian had to even steal boards from wooden fences in order to heat the cold room and protect the baby's health. He also began to wander alone in the snowy forest in search of branches to use for heating. On January 15, 1945, the village was liberated in an extensive counterattack by the Red Army; it was his tenth birthday.

Since the start of the German occupation, Itzhak had not been in close touch with nature. Years later, he remembered his amazement at the avenues of chestnut trees in Planty Park in Kraków. He also wrote that, during his wanderings in the snowy forest outside of Gorzkowice he was enchanted by the beauty and splendor of the forest scenes in winter: trees laden with snow, puddles, pools and streams that froze - even a rabbit scurrying by. After the liberation of the village, he was also exposed to the sight of bodies of German soldiers, left lying in the snow, and Russian troops stampeding westward. Besides a pencil for drawing or a pen for writing, he had no tools to use to work with his hands. The world spoke to him through sights and events, and to a large extent through books and listening to bits of the conversations of people around him. Some of the chapters of his life in those abnormal situations were lost in the far depths of his memory. For example, Itzhak could not remember the period of months from the liberation in the village until his return to Kalisz in May or June of 1945, only after Mother returned to Kalisz from Stutthof. During that period, Marian lived in the basement of the Władysław family. Today we know nothing about that family except for a short reference in Father's memoirs. Itzhak remembers that he sat and read a lot of books and booklets there.

It was a shock, a positive one, to be living again with family members who had survived and reunited, in comfortable conditions, in a spacious apartment in the modern city of Kalisz. It was apparently easy to adjust to this situation after the awful wartime period. When he went to school for the first time, his reading and language skills, and the knowledge he had acquired on his own, made Itzhak a good pupil in the fourth and fifth grades; he only had to catch up in arithmetic. Some of the ancient sections of the city, including churches and the city walls, remained largely intact. He could take walks in the city and in the park famous for its beauty, and obtain and read books, and even purchase attractive titles in bookstores. Nonetheless, the new conditions of freedom were far from normality. There were explicit and implicit expressions of anti-Semitism, including curses, and fistfights. We continued to use our assumed names and Catholic identities. Our busy parents, who had yet to digest what they had experienced and could not imagine what awaited them in the future, did not have an opportunity to learn how to take care of us; they did this instinctively, providing for our basic needs, but apparently leaving some of these needs unfilled. And we, aware of their contribution to the family's survival and the many difficulties they faced in the present, tried not to burden them with demands of our own. They decided to emigrate from Poland. On January 15, 1946, Itzhak turned eleven. After living in Kalisz for about a year, another significant turning point in his life occurred in May 1946: He soon found himself in London, "adopted" by the Kuropieska family. Colonel Józef Kuropieska, who was appointed military attaché of the new Poland in Britain, and the devoted, and loving Leopolda, took care of the diplomatic "adoption" documents and flew Itzhak to their home, with a status similar to that of their own children, Basia, and Wojtek. Itzhak tells about the exciting flight to London in the Dakota plane with Leopolda, with a stopover in Potsdam. There he found some release for his urge for revenge, which had been stirred by the sight of the destruction in Berlin, though the Potsdam damage was still less than what he had witnessed in Warsaw.

Itzhak settled into the life of the military attaché's family, in their magnificent apartment near Hyde Park in London, and he made pleasant and interesting acquaintance with Józef Kuropieska for the first time. Itzhak also had the opportunity to spend a little time in the company of officers of the Polish Army in exile. Basia and Wojtek were then at a distant boarding school, and Leopolda was pregnant with her youngest child, Jędrzej. Itzhak was allowed to wander the streets and parks of the city on his own and even to ride on the famous London Underground. Before the children returned from boarding schools for summer vacation, Itzhak was sent "to learn English" in a guesthouse for foreigners, in a town near the southern coast, not far from the historic town of Hastings. He studied and spent time with the sisters who ran the guesthouse in a traditional and enjoyable English lifestyle, and then was summoned back to London to meet Grandfather Shmuel. Grandfather came from Palestine to purchase machines for the lace curtain factory he was building, and to meet his oldest living grandchild. Itzhak spent time with Grandfather and accompanied him on his trip to Nottingham, where he bought two huge Jacquard looms for lace curtains, and where it was agreed that an engineer would come to Palestine to assemble them. Grandfather, who was religiously observant, was shocked that his grandson was being educated under the tutelage of non-Jews and that he ate things that were absolutely prohibited. After exhausting negotiations with our parents in Poland and with the Kuropieska family, it was agreed that Itzhak would be educated in a Jewish boarding school for boys in Brighton. Perhaps Grandfather footed the bill for this.

The boarding school imposed rules of order, cleanliness, and discipline, including corporal punishment, in accordance with the British boarding school tradition of the time. There was a variety of team and individual sports activities, including boxing, and croquet competitions. The lessons were conducted entirely in English, so Itzhak was dropped to the fourth grade. However, after making a great effort, he was able to read books in this rich language. The pupils also studied French, Latin, and Hebrew (second year - he received an exemption) as foreign languages. At the end of the first trimester, Itzhak finished fourth in his class of twelve pupils. As a foreign boy from Poland, he made few friendships with the boys his age in Brighton, and the relations with the teachers were distant and lacking in empathy. He sometimes fell into melancholy moods, to the point of tears. Itzhak suffered from being severed from the family, which had moved from Kalisz to France, and he was also separated from Leopolda in London, except for her letters in the mail. Occasionally, Grandfather sent messages in Polish via Aunt Roza, praising the Land of Israel. Itzhak was not pleased by our parents' decision to travel to the Land of Israel, which he imagined (based on the newspapers in England) to be a land of strife and terror. A letter from our parents informing him that he would move again, this time to the home of Grandfather and Grandmother in Tel Aviv, did not ease his anxiety. Itzhak bid farewell to England at a party in the office of the principal, who craved publicity, with the faculty in attendance and with the principal noting that Itzhak was setting off for the Land of Israel. Years passed before Itzhak was able to digest and recall some enjoyable aspects of his stay at the boarding school. He landed in Lod on January 22, 1947, accompanied by the English engineer, who came to assemble the Nottingham looms for curtains. I remember hearing rumors that Grandfather had deviously "snatched" him from the hands of the Kuropieska family.

Itzhak became accustomed to living in the home of our grandparents, with their national-religious lifestyle. Our grandparents did not ask him about his experiences or about their daughters and grandchildren who perished in the Warsaw Ghetto. Our Aunt Roza also did not inquire about her sisters and their children. He started learning Hebrew with a personal tutor, Mr. Yehudah Mishori, and entered fifth grade at the Bilu School for boys (affiliated with the Mizrahi stream) under the directive of Grandfather and the principal, Mr. Haim Mishori. Shortly after my parents and I arrived in Palestine, he moved in with us in the apartment we shared now with "only" one family on 109 Rothschild Boulevard, in the house next to our grandparents' home. At the end of sixth grade, Itzhak was already able to skip to eighth grade, joining boys his own age with the assistance of the tutor Mishori, of course. Itzhak was not drawn to the subject of religion beyond a cultural and intellectual interest. He wrote favorably about studying Jewish history, which was something new and fulfilling for him, and he also enjoyed learning the Talmud in eighth grade. He found less satisfaction in studying the Five Books of Moses with Rashi's commentaries, the Prophets and Writings, and the Mishnah. Itzhak mentions the charismatic teacher A. D. Adereth in a positive light; I remember being terrified of him when he scolded me on two occasions for walking on the Jewish Sabbath without a hat on Mazeh Street, on the way to my cousin Rysiek's home. Itzhak's bar mitzvah (the *Bo* Torah portion) in 1948 filled him with a sense of pride and satisfaction. He did not comply with Grandfather's demand to only use Hebrew, and because of the availability of books in Polish and in English, he only began reading primarily in Hebrew when he was in the ninth grade.

Itzhak intensely experienced the events of the declaration and founding of the State of Israel and the 1948 war. He was apparently very affected, as I was, by the years of war in Poland and the ensuing changes, without recognizing the inevitable impact these early conditions would have on our conduct in the present. Itzhak developed a critical and intellectual personality, urban in essence, without a connection to public activity, or the task of building and producing. His creative work was expressed in teaching and educating generations of high school students in history, civics and English literature, in addition to translating, and editing fiction, non-fiction and poetry in Hebrew, English, and Polish, as a natural continuation of his love for reading during childhood. It seems to me, though it's difficult to judge, that he made a point of avoiding the complications entailed in far-reaching initiatives, which require strong, and persistent internal motivation. In its extreme form, our mother called this type of approach "walking the path of least resistance." He expressed an aspiration for normality in a land that is abnormal. In my eyes (and perhaps also in my brother's eyes), this is a land that requires you to heroically give your body and soul primarily to give; not taking from the land and from the weak, but instead working to strengthen them. All of this with the aim of maintaining a Jewish culture of four thousand years, which is supposed to carry lofty messages, ancient, and modern, for us, and for non-Jews - a culture that should be worthy of its victims in the march of the generations and, in particular, in the generation of the Holocaust and revival.

Itzhak is married to Sharona. Her childhood was in occupied Lwów, where the extermination was conducted in full force. Her parents, who could have obtained Aryan documents, decided to take a chance; they reported to the Gestapo headquarters, offering to serve as "exchange Jews", who were permitted to live outside of the ghetto. The Gestapo "conditionally" registered them as Jewish "citizens of Palestine," who were slated for possible exchange with the descendants of the Templer colonists and other Germans in the Holy Land, who were then thought by the German Reich to be in danger under British Mandate rule. The family was sent from occupied Lwów to Bergen-Belsen. They stayed at the camp in the group of Jews with Palestinian documents a group that included Bronka, Rysiek, and Berta. They survived the hardships of the camp and the evacuation on the train that was bombed from the air, and they finally made it to Palestine.

I'm married to Azriela. When her mother was pregnant, she took Ora, her eighteen-month-old daughter, who was born in Beilinson Hospital in Petah Tikva, and traveled to her parents in Łódz, where she could give birth and care for her newborn in better conditions than in Holon, which had just been built in the sand dunes. The baby was born in June 1939 in Łódz, which was conquered by the Germans in early September. Her father, Alexander Fuks, an expert in knitting machines who moved to Holon to build the Lodzia knitting factory, was able to add the name of the newborn to their certificate, which miraculously found its way to occupied Łódz. The mother, Esther, decided, against her parents' protests, to set off for the Land of Israel, not knowing exactly how she would make this journey. After about ten weeks of wanderings, hardships, and illness on a chaotic route, she arrived with her two young girls at the port of Trieste. There they boarded a Jewish Agency ship that waited for refugees and returned home to Holon. Soon afterward, Shlamek, the twenty-year-old brother of Alexander Fuks, fled eastward from Łódz on his own; his parents refused to allow his younger sister Yehudit to go with him. He spent the war years fighting in the woods with a group of Jewish partisans.

B. PERSONAL REFLECTION THROUGH THE LENS OF TIME

1. Not just a game of luck

Imagine simultaneously tossing two polyhedral dice that have many more faces than regular cubic dice, with each face of each die representing the likelihood of survival during the entire period of Nazi occupation of Poland. Each of these two dice represent the fate of one of two small circumcised children with dark eyes and hair; let another such die's faces represent the chances of a circumcised deaf man, and let still another die express such chances of a young woman with dark appearance - all of them Jews. The slight chance of tossing four such dice at the same time and each of them landing on the single particular face that signifies "alive and well", this slight chance expresses the scant likelihood of survival of our entire nuclear family. Our parents mobilized all of their personal resources to boost this likelihood. We, the children, were too young to compare the world of the Holocaust to the previous world into which we were born, and we accepted the Nazi world as natural.

2. Our parents

Our parents were blessed with abilities that helped to save us, and they also acquired further abilities during their lifetimes: fluency in Polish, without a foreign accent; Father's mastery of German; good health; Jewish values of family cohesion and mutual assistance; cultivation of professional skills and work habits; and the ability to communicate with others.

In times of crisis and in moments of terror, they showed remarkable personal traits: the discipline of composure, courage, and resourcefulness. In conditions of uncertainty, they were able to read extreme situations, using logic, and intuition without giving in to despair, and against all odds. Every evening and morning for five and a half years, they watched, examined, and devised their steps for the coming days, while never losing sight of a more distant future. From the outset, they instinctively decided not to rely on the organized Jewish community. And indeed, the Nazi occupiers, almost from the outset, ordered that Jewish councils be formed to facilitate their control over the fate of the Jews. Still, my father maintained very dangerous connections with family members in the Warsaw Ghetto. My parents were also able to take advantage of rare flashes of luck when they occurred. I have no doubt that my father's external appearance, his deafness, and his confident demeanor led people to like him and identify with him. He trusted his understanding of reality, and was confident in the bold actions and risks he took. It seems that my father also drew upon qualities he had acquired in his life as a deaf person: a dramatic flair and an ability to read lips, control of body, and facial expressions, sensitivity to shocks and vibrations, and suspiciousness about what was being said behind his back. My mother attributed to herself, justifiably, an outstanding ability to see the big picture and anticipate events, but she also had complete faith in her husband's ability to carry out their plans. Their collaboration and like-mindedness during this period of chaos was nearly perfect.

3. The extended family – a struggle for life and human dignity

The story of my parents' families entails a struggle waged by each nuclear family and each individual against the monster of destruction. All belonged to the urban middle class. Some participated in the fight against the Nazi occupiers by taking up arms or engaging in underground activity. The others struggled, with determination, and guile, for the lives of their families and children in the face of the regime's atrocities. Miraculously, their courage paid off in many cases; in other cases, they were led to their deaths or even took their own lives. It's noteworthy that the family's Jewish underground in Warsaw on the Aryan side and in the ghetto comprised people expelled from Kalisz. Mietek and Stasia Kolski served as a unifying axis for them.

4. The saviors

Our family's saviors deeply and emotionally identified with the Polish people and its struggle for freedom in its homeland. Most of them were involved, actively or emotionally, in the underground struggle against the Nazi German occupation. They included the Łoza-Nowak family and Mrs. Feliksa Gardziel's family in Brzesko, Mrs. Leopolda Kuropieska and her family, Mrs. Zofja, and Jan Kałuszko and Stasia Kolski in Warsaw, Stanisław, and Marta Kowalski from Sandomierz, Roman, and Julia Jaworski in Kraków, the anonymous train employee and his wife in Kielce, and others. Some of them acted in accordance with their Catholic faith and its basic human values; others sought to defend civic ideals. Their supreme courage and readiness for self-sacrifice was driven by a sense of compassion and love of others as human beings, which took precedence over any prejudice. They had little concern for the negligible compensation they received, which sometimes did not even cover our living expenses. We didn't know any of them before the war and were lucky to have crossed paths with them. Eight of them were recognized by Yad Vashem as Righteous Among the Nations. We maintain a close multi-generational connection with most of these families.

Leopolda Kuropieska in Yad Vashem's memorial hall in Jerusalem at the ceremony awarding her Righteous Among the Nations recognition (1967). Standing (right to left): representative of Yad Vashem, Moshe, Cesia, Mrs. Leopolda Kuropieska, Itzhak and Sharona Komem.

Mrs. Irena Nowak planting a tree on the Avenue of the Righteous Among the Nations at Yad Vashem on behalf of the Łoza and Nowak families. From right to left: Amir Komem, his father Yoseph and Mrs. Irena Nowak (April 1984).

Certificate of tree planting on the Righteous Among the Nations Boulevard in the name of Irena Nowak, Eugeniusz Łoza and Stefania Łoza on March 22, 1984.

5. Preserving the memory

Over the years, I became increasingly aware of the great importance of documenting the history of my extended family destruction and rescue, struggle and compassion. However, I had to overcome an inclination to procrastinate. We indeed owe this to the dead, the living, and the future generations. I repressed my wartime memories until 1982, when it became possible to reestablish contact with the Łoza and Nowak families in Brzesko in communist Poland. My application to recognize them as Righteous Among the Nations required me to write testimony about their actions, and essentially about my history since the outbreak of World War II. I reviewed in my memory the key events and sketched a precise and detailed timeline. My family learned the story of how we were saved when Mrs. Irena Nowak and her daughter Basia, an engineer, were guests in our home for about two months in early 1984. The two women were honored at a memorial ceremony, received a medal, certificates, and planted a tree for their family on the Avenue of the Righteous Among the Nations at Yad Vashem. My family also learned more of our history when General Józef Kuropieska and his youngest son Jędrzej were our guests in May 1984. The elderly general was eager to see the sights, and insisted that we take him to see a kibbutz, battlefields on the Golan Heights, and the "Good Fence" on the border with Lebanon. I had always kept letters and documents in drawers; in the late 1980s, I asked my father to record his testimony, and he did this flawlessly and independently, despite being unable to hear himself speak. In the summer of 1989, I recorded three interviews with Cesia Kolski-Virshup when she stayed at our home. In 1992, I returned to Poland for the first time, accompanied by my wife Azriela. We visited the scenes of my past and met acquaintances who were still alive and their families. A few years prior to my retirement (in March 1994), I began meticulously reconstructing my memories and spilling them onto the computer in a chronological record. I had not discussed these events in the past and refrained from reading and being influenced by the testimonies of others. As I finished documenting my memories, I recognized the need to fill in some details. I was not aware of everything that occurred and not everything was explained to me at the time. While I remembered many details, I still feared that my memory could betray and mislead me. I documented, in writing and in recordings, the testimony of important witnesses to the events in order to complement and verify my memories. Most of these witnesses amazed me with their precise ability to remember, even in very old age. Thus, I was able to successfully cross-check my memories with the accounts of these witnesses in some cases, even correcting their testimony. Naturally, there were some insignificant contradictions.

My father's testimony focused on describing the events and their impact on him, without strict attention to chronological order. He recalled his actions under the occupation, and recounted them to his deaf friends in particular. So perhaps he embellished here and there and took some credit that should have gone to Mother, especially in his second testimony, which was recorded in his later years and was intended for his children and grandchildren. I have no doubt whatsoever that the amazing events he described actually happened. By nature, he saw himself in the center, unlike my modest mother, who often faced very difficult and awkward missions. The complementary testimonies took on the role of the chorus in a Greek tragedy, adding the backdrop for the events.

6. Three trips

My wartime memories were fixed in writing and in my mind (and separate from the testimonies I collected) before I ever returned to visit the scenes of the events. I later made three trips to Poland.

My first trip, with my wife Azriela, was a two-week journey in the summer of 1992. We boarded a night train to Danzig and continued on to the Stutthof death camp. I took in the reality of the three-level bunk beds in the women's barracks. Wrapped in a prayer shawl and donning *tefillin*, I recited the *kaddish* prayer for the dead next to the Jewish star erected by the gas chambers and crematorium. We discussed memories with Basia Kuropieska-Kuczmierowska in her home about six months before she passed away. We visited the homes of the late Leopolda Kuropieska's daughters-in-law, grandchildren, and great-grandson. Her son Wojtek was abroad on business at the time, and her son Jędrzej was sailing as a navigation officer on a trans-oceanic ship. From Kalisz, we traveled to Kraków where we were guests in Basia Nowak's apartment. I drove in Basia's old

Polish Fiat 126p to Sandomierz. I easily identified the house on Sandy Road, which was now paved and called the Army of Poland Road, a reference to the Army camp built across from our home where the Nazis had interrogated and abused Russian prisoners of war. Part of the adjacent Jewish cemetery remained intact, and it now included a monument and graves for anonymous victims of Nazi murder. A larger part of the old cemetery was now the site of large school. In the Old City near the ghetto, we met with the family of the late Stanisław and Marta Kowalski in their son Marek's home. In Brzesko, we stayed for four days in the home of Irena Nowak, and we slept in the same bedroom where I had slept during the war with her three children. Almost nothing had changed. Even the old Pfaff sewing machine, which my father brought as payment for the cost of hosting me, was still standing there. We spoke endlessly, and Irena prepared wonderful meals for us. During a visit and discussion in the home of Helena Łoza-Skrobotowicz and her husband, amidst plentiful food, drink, and family memorabilia, I was able to glean additional details about the Gestapo's cauldron action against the family, including me. Adam Nowak led me on trails in the thick of the woods, past the train station in Słotwina to the enchanting "three pools" of my childhood. Some members of the Herbert family gathered to see us in the home of the elderly widow Marta. We were warmly welcomed by Julian and Maria Gardziel in the house on what had been then 159 Bocheńska Road. We went down to the basement, where I had lived with my mother under assumed identities. I learned additional details about my family's history during a warm and nostalgic meeting in the home of Janina Gardziel-Irzabek in Niepołomice, in the forested hunting grounds of the ancient kings of Poland. Tadzik, the husband of Bogusia Nowak-Zawistowicz, drove us to Zakopane, where we surprised the deaf couple Geniek and Maria Łoza in their rickety cabin. This was before they moved into a housing project. There was an outpouring of joy in our reunion. As a gift, he gave me a carved shepherd's axe from the Tatra Mountains: He danced masterfully with such axes in a local folklore troupe. We received a heartfelt invitation to visit General Józef Kuropieska and his second wife Teresa at the military rest home in the resort town of Rabka. We arrived by bus from Brzesko. A gulf of nearly fifty years closed as if it never was, together with an outpouring of memories and feelings of affection.

Gathering at the Nowak family's home in Słotwina-Brzesko (1992). Standing (right to left): Yoseph, Azriela, Mrs. Irena Nowak's son Adam, Irena and her daughters Barbara (Basia) and Bogumiła (Bogusia).

Gathering at Eugeniusz (Geniek) Łoza's cabin in Zakopane (1992). From right to left: Mrs. Maria Łoza, Yoseph, Geniek, Azriela and Basia Nowak.

I resolved not to visit any death camps again. However, I broke this resolution after reading in a newspaper about a group of Arabs, Jews, and Druze organizing a trip to Auschwitz-Birkenau. Emile Shoufani, a senior priest of the Melkite Greek Catholic Church, led this initiative. Preparatory seminars were conducted before this trip, which took place in May 2003, and summary meetings followed it. Archimandrite "Abuna" Shoufani, the director of the Al-Mutran high school in Nazareth, a humanist theologian, and expert on the philosophy of Emmanuel Levinas, championed the idea that a human being must take responsibility for "the other." In retrospect, this idea captured the essence of the natural and practical conduct of the Righteous Among the Nations. The visits to Auschwitz-Birkenau and the very human encounters left an indelible impression on all of us. I bid farewell to the group and remained for another week in Poland, for meetings with the families of my benefactors. I traveled to the city of Kielce and spent a night there, trying in vain to stir my memory and summon details from the surroundings. There I was able to verify that an execution had indeed taken place, as I remembered, and I also learned the date when it occurred.

Visiting Helena Łoza-Skrobotowicz at her home in Brzesko (2005).
Standing: Mrs. Helena, Yoseph and his son, Amir.

During the Passover holiday week in 2005, I traveled with my son Amir and his son Gal, my grandson, on a roots trip prior to Gal's bar mitzvah. In Warsaw, we were allowed to visit, with Wojtek, the apartment on 45 Independence Avenue and we saw the hiding place that was discovered. With Wojtek, Jędrzej, and his wife Magda, we laid flowers on the graves of the Kuropieska family in the military section of the Powązki cemetery. I went to tour the woods of Śródborów. In Kalisz, we toured the city and park, and traveled to the small village of Krzyżówki. A visit was arranged for us in the Haft factory, the center of the lace curtain industry in Kalisz. They invited us into the boardroom and I was surprised and emotionally moved when they spoke with appreciation about the contribution my grandfather and his sons made to this industry in Kalisz. They later gave us a tour of the computerized and modern production line. In the curtain design room, I was shown a catalogue of lace curtain patterns from before the war; some of them were apparently designed by my father Moshe. As a gift, they gave me glass photographic plates of two such patterns that were registered as part of the state's heritage. In Brzesko, while on a round of visits to friends and sites, we stopped at the home of Helena Łoza-Skrobotowicz, whose husband had died. She said there were Jewish books in the attic of her husband's family home, where she had moved after her marriage. At my request, she brought down about ten books from "the Jewish bookcase": prayer books and volumes of the Bible bearing the stamp of the Binder family's store in Brzesko. Some of the books included translations to Yiddish or German. The books were printed in cities like Vienna, Vilna, and Lwów, and some of them dated to the beginning of the century. Helena agreed to let me take the books and when we returned to Kraków, Gal gave them to the Moses Isserles – Remu synagogue in Kazimierz. The three of us were very moved by the books and wondered: Were they given to friends for safekeeping by a family that was sent to an unknown destination? Or were they left in the bookcase when a local family moved into their home? In checking the sources, I learned that the house might have been within the bounds of the ghetto, which was liquidated before my mother and I arrived in Brzesko. In any case, anyone keeping Hebrew books in a Polish home during the Nazi occupation risked severe punishment, and letters of appreciation were sent to Helena.

7. The difficulties of acclimation in the new country

Against my request to start learning a profession in a vocational high school, my mother registered me at Ironi Aleph high school in Tel Aviv. The cost of tuition was low, but there was strong competition for achievement. Only a few new immigrants were accepted, and the teachers did not make any accommodations for their difficulties, nor did their classmates. Here I'll describe, without resentment, three ostensibly insignificant incidents that exemplify the difficulties of acclimation.

At the beginning of ninth grade, the well-liked head teacher, who taught Hebrew, and Arabic, offered the choice of two topics for the exam in Hebrew composition, "Friendship" or "My History." The first subject was foreign to me, while contending with the other topic left me in state of shock and mental paralysis. I was barely able to scribble a few convoluted sentences, for which I was mercifully awarded a learned comment in red ink and a grade of "barely satisfactory," which became my grade for the trimester in Hebrew composition. Since then, I have experienced numerous friendships, and have now completed the writing of my history. I would be happy to submit it with sincere appreciation to Ms. Miriam Solel Kimchi, my esteemed teacher.

Meanwhile, I boosted my confidence in school by developing sound mastery of Hebrew grammar, a subject taught by the lauded Bible teacher, a rabbi's daughter. One day, there was a pop quiz. I was doing well on it until the teacher asked us verbally to vowelize the word "two hundred." Under the pressure of the quiz, I got confused about how to spell "two hundred" and asked the pupil behind me. The teacher dashed toward me and immediately marked my quiz with a round zero. Any protest or excuse about being new in the country would have been futile. This lowered my final matriculation score in Hebrew language.

As part of my effort to fit in socially in high school, I joined the chess club led by an upperclassman who was a national youth champion. A competition was held to rank the participants and select the high school team. I studied openings and endgames, and I accumulated a good point total. In the final rounds, I was paired with a successful and ambitious pupil to determine our ranking on the team. The game took place in his home, and his father, who was no less ambitious, watched from the side. In my view, I reached a point of advantage and then my opponent proposed adjourning the game. I agreed, wrote down my next move and sealed it in an envelope. But then I came under heavy pressure from the son and his father to agree to what they argued was "a clear draw." I refused, and when we resumed the game, I won after a few moves. The boy, who indeed went on to great accomplishments, spoke with the coordinator of the club, who presented a radio spot on chess. On his next broadcast, he spoke disparagingly of a young player, an "ignoramus," citing my name, who insisted on continuing to play in hopeless situations. I was deeply hurt by this libelous accusation, which I didn't attribute to the club coordinator personally. Instead, I wondered: Is this the way things work in the Holy Land?

At the end of tenth grade, I registered for the math-science track of studies, which was considered challenging, and also volunteered for a pre-military artillery course, where they taught us how to use firing tables and logarithms. During the summer vacation, we had training exercises at the artillery battalion's base in Sarafand (Zerifin). I fired a 75mm Krupp field gun before I ever fired a rifle (in basic training in the future). In retrospect, the encounter with the camp conditions in the summer, and with the group of enthusiastic campers, was hard for me. My asthma worsened and made it difficult for me to concentrate in class after not sleeping well at night. I think my friends and teacher were determined to lift my spirits: They arranged for me to "win" a lottery for an hour-long flight in a Piper plane flown by my classmate Sambur, who was licensed to fly in a pre-military flight training program. When it came time to take my matriculation exams, I found myself unable to sleep, and I took three of my six exams after sleepless nights. These anxiety-induced sleep disorders continued to plague me for decades: prior to the entry exams for the Technion, before final semester exams, and when facing difficult professional issues and time pressures. I didn't allow nightmares from the past to surface, but I suffered greatly from uncontrolled anxieties about failure. I didn't allow myself to give up on challenges I deemed worthy, and I trace this to the lessons and drives that shaped my identity.

Among the survivors of my generation whose wartime fate was more traumatic than mine, some achieved great things due to their talents, resourcefulness, and drive that grew out of their loss during the years of chaos. Many of those who remained alone, without family, grew up and developed their worldviews in the tough conditions of "the lost generation of learning," and contributed to the heritage of the Jewish people in its land, spiritually, and materially.

9. Developing a personal identity

My wartime experience instilled characteristics of identity in me that I've also noticed in others of my generation who survived and grew up in Israel. "What is permitted for the governor (*voivod*) is forbidden for a little stinker like you" I remember this arrogant and insulting saying from my childhood, spoken by children and adults, in Polish to inconsequential beings like me, a blow I absorbed in silent protest. From such incidents I developed a reserved personality, relying primarily on myself, and finding it difficult to accept authority. I recognized the different mix of good and bad in people, and how this mix can change in different circumstances and, of course, under the influence of the herd mentality. The abundance of human evil and immorality evoked in me a longing for a better world and good deeds, and sometimes I took advantage of opportunities to pursue this longing. However, I never came close to the level of kindness displayed by my benefactors in Poland.

When the liberation came, I naively felt that the war had ended for me and that I would embark on a different type of life, with no fear of death or existential distress. I innocently felt this way each time I faced real trials and tribulations. But this was not to be. It was only decades later that I recognized that my personality, approach to events, and deductive logic had been programmed in that existential situation of my past, and that I was unconsciously compelled to follow this program. My existential experience and knowledge subsequently became absolute criteria, guidelines for action, and an ethical code. Furthermore, they drove me to do the essential and correct things, as if I have no right to invest time in pleasure or enjoyable human relations just for the sake of happiness, without a higher purpose. I slowly grew out of this compulsion.

From the need to pretend, deny, and lie, I developed antibodies that search for the factual truth in every situation and on every subject; I express this truth, even if this sometimes puts me at risk and is against my best interests. In interpersonal relations, I found it difficult to even tell white lies. Sometimes I forced myself to remain silent, despite the embarrassment, and anger this provoked. I chose a profession that I thought offered criteria for truth and falsehood, where success, or failure depends on one's own ability, for better, or worse. When I learned that this situation doesn't exist in reality, I tried to choose and contend with technical problems that depend on engineering knowledge and the laws of nature, and to avoid complex human situations. In selecting the topics of my work, I placed primary emphasis on concern for the resilience of the Jewish state, as a condition for the security of my family. I felt a deep obligation to raise a family, as a response to the devastation, and began fulfilling this obligation even before I was prepared in terms of personal maturity and financial security, while still driven by fixations from the past. I had no doubts about the need to meet all of my commitments and, consequently, tried to carefully weigh each action in advance; I did not abandon my goals or regret past decisions.

I longed for faith in Providence that judges the acts of human beings justly, as defined in Maimonides' thirteen principles of Judaism, and as beseeched in the prayers of believers, "You chose us from among all the nations. You loved us and wanted us." However, from contemplating my own life and the lives of others, and from studying the history of peoples and cultures, I perceived the Western concept of God as a nearly perfect model, as the product of human spirit and aspirations, expressing the desires of individuals and societies, and filling their needs for order and consolation in the face of chaos, distress, and death. In my eyes, the lessons of the Holocaust should have challenged worthy spiritual leaders to revise this ancient model and encourage the voluntary enforcement of its moral teachings. In contrast to the traditional concept of God, there are, in my view, laws of cosmic behavior, secrets of the microcosm, and mysteries of life and creation. We have tried hard to decipher these laws and understand their control over us, but so far we cannot know their transcendental unifying source. I don't know if it's a blessing or a curse to belong to the Jewish people and its ancient culture. The collective creativity of my people and its individuals throughout the generations is challenging and astonishing. However, the foreignness and separateness of the Jewish people (as an essential condition for its existence as a religion and as a people) stirred fatal antagonism among others. Every generation in the history of the Jewish people debated anew: remain in the group or assimilate? So far, the Rock of Israel has been strong enough to avoid disintegrating even after some of its best and brightest leave, preferring the benefits of assimilation. And how could I, a survivor, allow myself to sever the chain of generations and cling to comfortable substitutes instead? I was privileged to learn about the heritage of my people, and I have chosen to be a Jew who loves tradition, and a human being, both at home and in the world. In my view, excellence and a supreme effort are required of every Jew and, of course, from the Jewish state with the goal of making every action an inspiring one. A worthy message would be to promote heartfelt love and to denounce baseless hatred between people and among the community of nations, as Judaism teaches at its best. I still remember all of the kindness involved in saving me during the time of the Holocaust, and I regret that I was not able to thank everyone as I would have liked.

May God grant strength to His people. May God bless His people with peace. (Psalms 29:11)

PART THREE
Moshe – Strength in Silence

Moshe's Memoirs self-recorded

Translated and transcribed from Polish to Hebrew by Yoseph and Itzhak Komem; chronology edited by Yoseph Komem

MOSHE – STRENGTH IN SILENCE

(*From Moshe's remarks during the second stage of the recordings.*)

"I'm now at the home of my older son [Itzhak-Ignaś, in Jerusalem]. He has an apartment on the first floor. Last time, I lived on the ground floor [with my younger son Yoseph-Jurek in Ramat Gan]. The plan was for me to gradually be able to go down the stairs and take a walk. And my apartment [in Tel Aviv] is on the third floor. But I'm still not so healthy and have to continue my convalescence at my son's home in Jerusalem.

This is the continuation of the recording of my wartime experiences, after a break of two weeks. It was quite late when it occurred to me to continue my story, and my son Ignaś placed a tape recorder next to me. It took me two weeks before I was able to continue with everything related to my previous recording. Now I'll continue the story that I told when I was with Yoseph and Azriela, which was interrupted because of my move to Jerusalem. I recorded about seven tapes there, and now I think it will take another seven tapes to reach the end of this recording. I started the story after my second heart attack [about two years ago, the first recording at Jurek's home], and now I'll finish it after my third attack. Today, the 26th of September, 1986. My beloved grandson David bought tapes and put the tape recorder next to the bed so that it will always be ready for me, whenever I wish to talk."

1. In occupied Kalisz

In 1937, on our way home from a vacation in Europe, we stopped in Nuremberg. As we passed near a public park, we noticed a lot of Hitlerites in the streets. We saw them preparing a hotel for Hitler; they hung posters on the walls and marked instructions on the front of the hotel in chalk. We walked around a little and saw a crowd of Hitlerites gathering in a huge square, about four hundred meters from us. We could recognize the speaker from a distance. It was Hitler. When Hitler motioned and waved his fists, the crowd of Hitlerites would suddenly raise their hands in the Nazi salute. Hitler shouted several times and the crowd responded each time "Heil Hitler!" "Heil Hitler!" Later, we were looking for something to do because the train was leaving in a few hours, so we went into a theater. Inside, almost everyone was a uniformed Hitlerite. They stared at us, the civilians. On the stage, all of the actors were English, so we thought they were surely spying in Nuremberg that day. From the theater, we went to the train station in Nuremberg, planning to reach the Polish border via Czechoslovakia. This station served as a transit point. We saw Hitlerites drinking there with the Czechs. We noticed that two people were following our every step until the train arrived. We boarded. The only people in our compartment were soldiers in uniform. They saw that we were foreigners, so they helped us lift the suitcases into the baggage bin. Later, when the train stopped at the next transit point and we wanted to take down the suitcases, they insisted on doing this for us. They took them down and even took them to our platform. At this station, too, Hitlerites followed our every step. When that train started moving, those Hitlerites shouted "Heil Hitler" and raised their hands in the Nazi salute. The train to Poland arrived and we boarded it.

When the Germans entered Sudetenland, our German *Meister* (master craftsman) G. Hänssler disappeared, as if he sensed the impending war. None of us thought the war would erupt so quickly, and we didn't prepare. I faced the problem of how to get along without a Meister, with the factory operating in three shifts. Hänssler had received a government permit to live and work in Kalisz on the condition that he would teach two Poles. One of them, Piekarski, was Hänssler's assistant for several years, but Hänssler taught them in a way that kept them from understanding the core secrets of calibrating the machines and adjusting them for the different knots of the curtain patterns. When he left, I broke into his apartment in the factory and searched in vain for his Meister guidebook, but he had taken it with him. I was furious about this *Szwab* [Kraut], who left us high, and dry. It was a technical manuscript for setting up the lace curtain machines, with knotting instructions for the Meister. I had made the initial payments for the book. Two days later, I received a letter from his friend, by the name of Reinke, protesting the fact that I had broken into the apartment like a thief. He had taken the manual with him as collateral and I had to go pay him the debt. When I came to him, he was lying sick in bed. I explained to him how important it was for us, how we needed it in order to continue to operate the factory. After all, Hänssler could have left a note that the book was with him [Reinke], and that would have been okay. I had no alternative [to breaking into Hänssler's apartment]. Reinke replied that if he were in my situation, he would have surely done the same thing. At that time, there was great demand in the market, and we worked feverishly. I was also able, together with Piekarski, to get along without that Szwab: I explained all of the necessary details to Piekarski and he did the actual calibration of the machines.

The family's factory for curtains, lace and tulle on Fabryczna Street in Kalisz.

The Germans entered Sudetenland and later took all of Czechoslovakia, in the wake of the Austrian matter. Someone I knew from the past was living there, Professor [Heinrich] Neumann [von Héthárs]. I was once his patient and I came especially to Vienna to receive his expert assessment of what could be done about my deafness. Neumann was an observant Jew, but open to ideas, and was held in high esteem. He refused to treat Hitler when the latter came down with the flu. After the Anschluss, they incarcerated him in a hotel. However, the King of England, who did not speak or hear well, and was his patient, sent him a British passport and citizenship. So Hitler could no longer keep him under arrest, and Neumann traveled to England.

Later, there was the Danzig affair. Hitler had long been demanding the return of the Free City of Danzig and its surroundings [also "the corridor" in Poland] to Germany. The marshal of Poland and Piłsudski's successor, Edward Śmigły-Rydz, issued a mobilization order for all of Poland's armed forces. Posters could be seen everywhere in Poland declaring: "We won't return the whole dress, not even a single button," followed by the slogan: "Strong, united, prepared." [Those slogans were attributed to the marshal himself.]

Abram ordered Hersch Ganzweich and me to remain at the factory. Earlier, a large quantity of finished merchandise was sent to Abram's warehouse in Łódź, where Rosenwald was our main representative. The merchandise was sent there thinking that the Germans wouldn't advance so rapidly. Samek Bloch, a second lieutenant in the reserves, was mobilized in mid-August to a battalion of horse-drawn artillery.

When work in the factory came to a halt, my family was on a summer vacation in the village of Krzyżówki. I would join them on the weekends. On my last visit, I wanted to prepare the family for their departure from the vacation village. Hela Lifshitz was also there with her family. It was on a Friday, and Hela asked me to take her father to Kalisz quickly, before the onset of the Jewish Sabbath. I agreed because he was an older man and religiously observant, adorned with a beard. I took him promptly to Kalisz by motorcycle, and as he stepped off the motorcycle he saw a woman in a window lighting Sabbath candles. He was so happy he kissed me on both cheeks and hugged me. I immediately sent the family to Abram in Warsaw, requesting that he find housing for them somewhere in a suburb near the capital. Likewise, Regina, and her family and Ala, and her family traveled to Abram's home in Warsaw.

Second Lieutenant Salomon Bloch with the 25th light artillery battalion of "Kalisz's Lands" before the outbreak of World War II.

On September 1, we crowded around the radio in my apartment: Ganzweich, me, Piekarski, and others. I no longer remember exactly- perhaps also Mietek Kolski. Then we heard Hitler on the radio screaming to the German soldiers, "Go! Kill! Shoot! And plunder!" So, the war broke out. The minister of interior, Felicjan Sławoj Składkowski, issued an order to paint all of the fences along the roads with dark colors and to spread camouflage nets. Chaos ensued; everyone was busy spreading nets and painting, and there was a shortage of paint. There was also a fear of poison gas.

A few days later, Ganzweich told me that he heard the thunder of cannons from afar; there were no aerial attacks yet. The next day, he said he heard the cannon fire coming closer. We prepared to leave and took only a backpack with bread. We later crossed a bridge over a river. We saw they were drilling holes in the bridge and placing dynamite in them. After walking a few kilometers along the road, I could feel the aftershock of a frightening explosion the bridge flew into the air. We continued on foot toward Turek. It began to grow dark. We were very tired from the walk, and we asked soldiers to allow us to climb onto a wagon carrying ammunition. In the end, they gave us permission. These freight wagons were pulled by several horses and moved slowly due to the heavy load. When dawn broke, we all got off, and went to drink from a vat of coffee. But no one wanted to light a fire under the vat, so the black coffee was cold. Everyone was melancholy. We saw no commanders of officer rank; sergeant was the highest rank. It seemed to me that the commanders were abandoning their battalions, and perhaps they were spies or paid agents. [Note: This suggestion perhaps reflects the suspicious nature of Father and of deaf people in general.] When we arrived in Turek, they told everyone to get off. I remember they ordered everyone to load wet leather on the wagons, and they no longer allowed anyone to climb onto them. So, we walked on until we arrived at Kłodawa. We went to the home of Cesia's brother, Zelig Jarecki, who was our factory's agent for this region, and his wife Andzia, who managed a haberdashery there. They fed us lunch. Ganzweich showed us that his shoes were torn from the walk, and Andzia gave him a new pair of shoes. We walked on toward Warsaw. But on the way, there was terrifying sniping from planes at the fleeing refugees who filled the road. Everyone dispersed into the fields. I knew Ganzweich was a big coward, and he ran wildly in the field. I ran and caught him, and we decided to wait until dark and only then continue our journey. When we came to a town - I don't remember its name I noticed that they were transporting dead bodies and injured people in cars from a nearby city that had been bombed by the Germans. Not far from there, we noticed a new Hillman car, whose driver sat in it, completely at a loss. We asked if we could join him in riding toward Warsaw. He readily agreed, conditional upon us finding gasoline to start up the car. So Ganzweich went to look for gasoline, and he would do this later, too. When none could be found, he would usually go to a pharmacy, or any other store where he could buy a little gasoline and pure alcohol. When he couldn't find these, he would even take some kerosene, and the driver was willing to try this. We continued to travel at night. One night, the road was jammed with numerous Army units marching toward the east. Here it was orderly they were apparently elite units. The next morning, we arrived in Śródborów, whose name literally means "in the heart of forests." There, my family lived in a rented home, together with Regina, and Ala and their children. Hersch Ganzweich, who was afraid of the Germans, asked the driver to stay overnight in our house. The driver was traveling eastward to Russia and agreed to take Regina and Hersch Ganzweich and their daughters with him. Only the family of Ala, whose husband was mobilized, remained with us. Our house was off the beaten track, far from the center of Otwock and even from the main street of Śródborów, its wooded suburb. It was hard to find the house. So, I marked every street corner with chalk to help navigate the way home. Refugees from Warsaw were wandering the forests of Śródborów, thirsty, and hungry. They would ask for water and I would bring a kettle of boiled water to every thirsty and tired person. One time, a woman asked for boiled water for her children, and I wanted to bring water to them, but she first took off a ring from her finger and handed it to me. I told her in reply that she did not need to pay for the water with either a ring or with money, everything was free of charge. Before long, we could hear the sounds of shooting and bombing from the air, and we knew that the Germans were bombing Warsaw. Then Abram moved his wife and children to Otwock, but he did not join them yet, and they were helped by Mr. David Domb. Many people who lived in Otwock, or those who arrived there, wandered eastward toward Lublin. Later, we could see them returning. Abram also wandered in that direction and returned.

In the meantime, all of the children fell ill. They looked very frail and we were worried about their condition. I realized that I had to bring a physician from Otwock and went into the city to find and bring a doctor. I found the one and only physician, an elderly man the younger ones had been mobilized into the Army. He rejected my request to come with me, saying that he had to go tend to other patients. I explained that there were four children in danger and liable to die for lack of medical treatment. He thought it over, asked how far it was and whether I had a wagon. I replied that it was impossible to get a wagon and that it was not far. To this he responded that he was an old man and that it was difficult for him to walk a long distance. I told him it was okay. He took a physician's bag with him and we set off on our way. After several hundred meters, he asked, "Where is it?" I answered, "A little more, a little more," until he saw that we had walked for kilometers. He accused me of tricking him. When we arrived at the apartment and he saw the children, he was alarmed, and said that it was scarlet fever, very dangerous, and that I should bring a certain serum from the pharmacy. In fact, Jurek already had scarlet fever and the doctor warned that the other children in the apartment were likely to catch it from him very quickly. He gave me a prescription for the pharmacy. I rushed off toward Otwock. On the way, I saw German tanks and their crews, and there was a Polish cadet showing them the way. As I entered the city, I saw Germans on horses at every corner, ready to open fire. A soldier stood at every corner, stopping the passersby. Groups of soldiers were also constantly patrolling. It was impossible to move.

But I was in a frenzy, because I had to get the injections without delay. So when the soldier was looking the other way, I jumped into a garden and continued on. I just avoided street corners, and kept on a straight and open path. I crossed the street and saw that the pharmacy was closed. I felt it was a fight for life or death, so I went to the private apartment in the back and knocked loudly on the door. When they opened, I saw frightened faces; they thought the Germans were coming to their pharmacy. When they heard me speak, they still thought I was German, because I don't speak well like normal people. They prepared the medicine on the spot, according to the prescription, and even forgot to charge me for it. I went back and asked how much I should pay. I ran back using the same strategy, avoiding the street corners where the Germans were gathered. When I arrived home, Cesia was serving tea to the doctor. The doctor was happy to be able to save the children, and immediately injected the serum. At the same time, German soldiers on motorcycles rode past the front of our villa. The soldiers looked tense and came from all directions, heading straight toward Warsaw. They entered Warsaw after additional days of fighting. Warsaw surrendered. Meanwhile, Russia invaded Poland from the east, stuck a knife in her back. There was nowhere left for the Polish Army to retreat, so they entered Russia. There was no one living across from us except for a deformed boy and the man who took care of him. The man stole my sack of sugar, which I had buried a few days earlier in the ground. We were left with just flour to prepare food to sustain us. It was impossible to even find bread then. I went to the bakery every day; but there were long lines of people, and they were snatching the loaves of bread from each other. I always returned from there empty-handed. The only thing we could make with this flour was water-based dumplings. Ala left us, because people started to return to their homes, including those in Warsaw.

When Jurek had completely recuperated and there was no danger of the illness returning, I prepared myself for a trip back to Kalisz. But there were no means of transportation, so first I had to find a way to get to Warsaw.

I started out on foot, and then caught rides on wagons, one stretch of the journey after another, until I reached the outskirts of Warsaw. The city was partly in ruins: Many houses were destroyed by bombings, burned, and abandoned. Abram was alone in his home. He said he had been arrested by the Germans. There were about two hundred hostages. They chose the wealthiest ones, warning that if there were disturbances in the city, they would be shot to death.

We decided to return to Kalisz in some way or another, in order to see what was happening with the factory. I set out for Kalisz, using various means of transportation. On the way, I came across a bicycle store and stopped there to purchase a bike. But they only had parts. I chose the frame and the best parts and spent about two hours assembling a bicycle, and I continued on the way to distant Kalisz.

I found the city and factory intact, with no damage. Not a single person had remained in Kalisz, so there were no thieves either. A very large inventory of raw materials and merchandise remained unharmed at the factory, and there was plenty of coal in the basement. We had invested a great amount of money in all these, and when the German Army drew close to the city, we only had promissory notes for large sums, as a dividend, and cash in Polish currency that was enough to support the family for a few months. Slowly, the residents who had fled the city began to return. The roads were now flooded with returning refugees. Religious Jews were returning with bandages on their faces because their beards were shaved off en route. In the house next to us, an entire family assembled whose possessions were burned along the way. Ala also came back for a short time. Abram returned in Miller's car and said he wouldn't pay a cent for property that was seized [by the occupiers]. The accountant, Weiss, also arrived, together with his wife, and maid. The Weiss family lived with me. I was happy not to be alone, and we had a woman with us who cooked. Abram returned to his home in Warsaw. The only one who remained with me as a contact with the outside world was Mietek Kolski. He would roam around the city to see what the people were doing. Only with his help and advice was I able to take the necessary action.

We had decided with Ala, before she returned to Warsaw, to hide some cash that we would have for a "black hour." We decided to hide the money in the forest near Kalisz rather than in the apartment, because if they expelled us we wouldn't be able to return to the apartment and take the money. So, we traveled to Winiary in a carriage and told the driver to wait for us because we were going into the village to buy some lard. We entered the forest and looked for a place to dig and hide the money there. On the far side of a small hill, we dug, and placed the banknotes, mine and hers separately, in bundles, wrapped, and spread with grease inside tin cans. Then, to make it easier to find the spot, I carved signs on the trees. Ala also had to remember the place in case I was no longer alive.

This was after the Germans had entered, when the factory was still producing everything under my management. I organized the workers in order to show that I was essential. One time, Germans accompanied by officers came and took valuables from the apartments of the wealthier residents. When some soldiers and an officer came to my apartment, I looked around to see what I was required to give them according to their order. I had two valuables. One was an etching entitled "The Last Drop" I don't remember the name of the artist; and the second was a gold statuette showing Sarah Bernhardt in the role of a young hawk. They took them and also took down beautiful curtains from the windows. Then I asked the officer if they were done, and they wrote on a piece of paper what they were taking. I asked the officer to confirm this. In response, the officer pulled out a pistol and placed it on the table and said, "Here is my signature." I relented, tore up the piece of paper, and I remained in one piece. Another time, officers came to check how much money I had. I opened the safe and showed them. They counted the money and I said the money was needed to pay the workers' wages. They said there must be more money. I said that I had only just restarted the factory and if I sell merchandise there will be money. They left the money and departed.

Now I'll go back to the time when I entered Warsaw for the first time, after Abram was released. I met him at his home after they released him from prison for one day. They chose the more serious and wealthier citizens, and threatened to execute them in the event of a disturbance. They warned them that they would be rounded up if there was another disturbance. The second time I visited Warsaw, Abram was still alone in his home, and he tried to convince me to flee with him via the "green border" to Russia. He feared that the Germans would imprison him again, and it would be the end of him. I asked what about the family, should we flee alone, or take them with us. And he replied that it was too risky to flee with the family, and that we needed to cross [the border] ourselves. He said that he had provided for Bronka materially, and that perhaps Bronka could help another family. I responded by saying that I wouldn't agree to leave the family to its fate; either my entire family would cross, or I would stay with them and fight. He said that from there, from Russia, we could make our way to Palestine, on a circuitous route. The third time I came to Warsaw he was no longer there. On the other hand, his family was already in their apartment in Warsaw [they had returned from Otwock to 38 Nalewki Street]. Later, we received word that he had managed to arrive in Vilna and was waiting there for an opportunity to leave the short-lived state of Lithuania. He was still young, so he grew a beard and dyed it gray and claimed that he was much older so that he could obtain a passport and emigrate. He flew from there to Turkey and then found his way to Palestine. And that's Abram's story so far.

Mr. Reinke, the friend of our former Meister, Hänssler, was appointed chief supervisor of all of the industries in Kalisz and its surroundings. So, I asked him for protection. He agreed to issue me the required permit, stating that I was completely deaf and the only manager of the factory for tulle, curtains, and lace, and that I was the only one who was expert in these matters and should not be mistreated. I exploited this permit one thousand percent, especially since he forgot to note that I was a Jew. From the outset, Jews were forbidden from managing Jewish-owned institutions; they could only do this under the supervision of a German trustee (*Treuhänder*). Thus, we looked for a German expert to manage above us. The only German expert we knew was my acquaintance Mr. Gustav Daub, a Meister, and designer of lace patterns, who used to work at Salomonowicz's lace factory. Mietek brought him to me. We spoke with him, convinced him, and agreed that none of us would reveal that this arrangement was made at our request. He went to Reinke that same morning and proposed that he take upon himself the management of all lace production in Kalisz. Reinke agreed and appointed him to this position. Daub hired two German lawyers who had been expelled by the Russians from the Baltic lands, from

Riga, and so on. Weiss, our accountant, taught one lawyer the ins and outs of bookkeeping at the factory, and I gave the cash box to the second one, and he became a cashier. And so, working together, we managed to keep the factory operating. I was very interested in this arrangement because I knew that I was actually employing Germans who did not want to be sent to the front. And even more, they would take good care of the factory. And so, the factory could continue to operate as long as there were enough raw materials. I served as a translator between the German management and the workers, and I instructed Daub how to manage the factory.

At that time, the Germans were beginning to evacuate the Jews from their apartments and house them in the Szrajer brothers' market hall in the New Market in the city's Jewish Quarter. From there, they were sent to the east, to all sorts of destinations [in the Generalgouvernement]. The Germans started to search homes to check that no Jew had remained in hiding. They even came into the factory, to the second floor apartment where I lived. They asked the Germans in the factory whether any Jew was there, and they answered, "None." This saved me from expulsion, while they were saving their jobs and retaining a valuable expert. I received the same wages as each of those Germans. The Germans in the city also needed some Jews to remain and work, but they were mostly people who were disabled, infirm, elderly, and so on, and they housed them in the ghetto in Kalisz. It was an open ghetto, but it was forbidden to leave its boundaries, and anyone doing so faced severe punishment.

Thus, I was the only Jew who worked, and managed a factory, and lived in the city and not in the ghetto. I was also the only Jew who moved freely in the city without wearing a yellow patch with a Star of David. It was a big advantage that no one was aware that I had met Daub prior to the war, when I visited my best friend Mojszewicz, who was also deaf, at Salomonowicz's large lace factory. Mojszewicz worked there as a Meister, but not as a designer-draftsman of patterns. Daub knew him well, and he liked me. Later, Daub hired a German woman from Riga, and gave her a job in the finished products department in place of Hela Lifshitz, who had already moved to the Kalisz Ghetto with her father and sister. Daub also hired a *Volksdeutsch* [a popular term in occupied Poland for an ethnic German; it is *Volksdeutscher* in German, and is the Nazi term for a person of German ancestry living outside of Germany] for the position of guard and custodian of the building. Daub would open and lock the merchandise warehouse himself. As the only one who lived at the factory, I saw it as a matter of honor to exploit this and remove from the warehouse the finest merchandise, which had already been marked. The German woman had already taken an inventory of the merchandise. I told her that the lace did not belong to this factory, and that someone was supposed to receive it. This was Abram's lace, very expensive. Abram had two lace-knitting machines on the same street in Kalisz, on Fabryczna Street, and two German weavers. So he still had merchandise from the finished material and he transferred it to my warehouse. No one knew that I had copies of the keys, which I made myself since I was trained as a mechanical locksmith. I sent the Volksdeutsch guard on an errand for me in the city to buy groceries and such. The list I gave him was particularly long, so that I would have more time to get the lace out of the warehouse. I had to do this because my wages barely covered my living costs, and I sent some of my earnings to Cesia. I lived one floor above the warehouse, and I prepared a package to send with W., a smuggler. Daub brought a frightening German Shepard to guard the warehouse, but I was able to reach a mutual understanding with the dog and to become friends. When W. arrived, I took him into my apartment and gave him instructions what to do and how to do it. I gave him money and told him I'd pay him more if he was successful. Unluckily, just as he was leaving the courtyard, Daub arrived, asked him what he was doing there, and took the package from him. But I grabbed the package from Daub and asked him why he was not allowing me to send some foodstuffs. The children were suffering from hunger. He blushed and I told W., "Go!" Daub apparently did not want to quarrel with me, since he needed me. This occurred again several times, but I was already more cautious about maintaining secrecy so the Germans wouldn't find out. However, no one imagined that the package contained stolen lace from the warehouse. Of course, I couldn't take the entire inventory of lace, because they would have realized that someone was stealing and would have discovered me. When I told W. that it was the last time, he left; but that package never got to Cesia: He sold the contents and kept the money for himself. This gave him some initial capital to engage in commerce. So, I made a mistake by informing him that our arrangement was ending.

During that time, I received desperate letters from Regina and Ala. They wrote that they had nothing to sustain themselves, and that I should do something for them. Regina had already returned with her two daughters from Vilna or Lwów, from areas of Poland where the Russians initially invaded, annexing Vilna to the state of Lithuania. Hersch Ganzweich disappeared there, and she returned penniless. In any case, only Bronka was secure economically. She had a warehouse full of lace products, and this supported her very well. She helped Regina and Ala to some extent.

There was an attic in the factory where seamstresses once did artistic mending. But due to the war, a directive was issued to cover the floor with a layer of white sand and to place barrels of water on it for use in putting out fires. When Abram came on a short visit to Kalisz, he brought several packages of his lace products and other large packages of unfinished lace for storage in the attic. There was no other place. I planned how to try to remove this merchandise and send it to Regina and Ala. I knew that it was possible to do artistic mending and finishing work on textiles in the Warsaw Ghetto, and that a Jewish dye works operated there. When the night shift began and the Polish guard arrived, I rushed to the attic window via the roof and entered. The windows were well sealed, and it was very stuffy there. I was in such a hurry to load packages of lace into a sack that I lost consciousness, fell on one of the water barrels and was injured. My neck hit the edge of the barrel in a way that plunged my head into the water, which had been standing there since the start of the war and stunk. This dirty water revived me, so I blacked out for only a short time. Otherwise, I would have remained lying on the floor in a state of unconsciousness. I took the sack down the stairs and waited until the guard went to fire up the steam boiler in the laundry. Even so, he noticed that I was carrying a sack, but I went out. I knew that the Pole wouldn't betray me. I went to the city, with the edges of the sack concealing my face. I sneaked along the walls, and at the break of dawn I saw a German policeman from afar, so I hid in the entryway to a house. Then I continued to walk from gate to gate until I reached the ghetto. I don't remember now where I hid the sack so I wouldn't be caught. When the smuggler K. appeared in the ghetto, I gave him the goods. He was an acquaintance of mine from Maccabi boxing practice, and his girlfriend in the ghetto connected us and helped me a lot. He took the merchandise and hid it in a train locomotive and bribed the mechanic. The second time, he took the goods for himself. Before the "green border" was established, I arranged for train porters to bring the merchandise with me to the Warsaw Ghetto. One of them wore a German railroad worker's hat and traveled with me to Bronka. There were several sacks then. I left half with Regina and Ala, and took the other half to Otwock. Bronka was furious and said that it was her lace. I told her in reply that she could go herself and steal from the Germans. She had enough for herself in her own store-room.

I had no experience about how to secure money in the event of war, so I had no gold coins, not even a gram of gold. Some weeks later, my sister Ala sent a young woman to me with a request that I immediately give her the money we had buried in the forest. An order had been issued to promptly exchange the złoty notes of the Polish state for the złoty currency of the Generalgouvernement one for every ten that is, a loss of 90 percent of the monetary value. So, I traveled again in the same way, in a carriage to the village of Winiary, and from there I walked to that forest to fulfill her request. I had a spade hidden in my pants. I panicked when I saw that the Germans had cut down the trees of the forest to send to Germany. I pondered what to do how could I find the place? I had marked the path to it and its location by carving with a pocketknife on tree trunks. I roamed around the forest and it looked the same everywhere, until I happened upon and recognized a small hill next to the place where I had buried the money. I checked the hardness of the earth with the handle of the spade, and when I hit softer earth, I knew I had found the place. I dug and took everything out. I gave all of Ala's money and also all of mine to the young woman whom Ala had sent, so that Ala could exchange it for the new currency. When I arrived in Warsaw, Regina went with me to a family that (illegally) worked as money changers. I exchanged my money for dollars and left them with Cesia, to ensure that she would have enough to live on for a period of time.

Later, another woman came carrying precise and detailed plans from Herman Bloch, Cesia's brother-in-law, and from Mietek Kolski, her nephew, showing the exact location in Mietek's basement where they had buried gold before the war. They noted that deck chairs were positioned on top of the hiding place. When I arrived at the building, on Łazienna Street, I saw that it was opposite an Army base, and that most of the building's occupants were German officers. So, I had to go straight into the lion's den. I spent quite a long time thinking about how to do this. From afar, I watched to see when the officers left in the morning to go to work at the base, and when they returned for lunch. I wrote everything down in an orderly way. I was aware of the fact that I would be in great danger if I were caught. Meanwhile, I decided to meet the people who lived in Mietek Kolski's apartment. About three-quarters of an hour before the officers returned home, I went to the apartment and handed the tenants a letter from Mietek and Helcia, sending their greetings and requesting to give me the deck chairs because they were in a very difficult situation and needed those chairs. The housewife was busy preparing lunch and kneading dough for pastries, but she agreed to show me the basement, and took the keys. I walked behind her in the long and winding hallway of the dark cellar, which had many storage compartments that all looked alike. I traced the path with chalk marks and a hidden cross in front of the door to the storage compartment she opened. The compartment was dark. I carefully examined the objects piled inside, and told her I'd come again with a wagon, maybe in two or three days, and take the deck chairs. She agreed and walked off, and I went out to the street. Now I could plan more precisely how to retrieve the treasure. When the German officials in the factory went to their homes to eat lunch, I remained there by myself. When the guard was not around, I went to the metalworking shop, selected a suitable piece of steel sheet, cut it with a chisel into the shape of a spade, and attached a short wooden handle. When I was in my apartment, I buried the spade in my pants and practiced walking, and ended up shortening the handle twice. I also sewed bags to my belt so that the heavy gold wouldn't rip the pockets and spill out. I continued to monitor the movement of the officers with my wristwatch to calculate the amount of time I would need before their return and to avoid being caught in the act. One day, about an hour before the return of the officers, I went up to that woman and told her that I already had a wagon, and asked her to give me the keys because I could find the door to the storage compartment myself, and that I'd return them to her later. She was busy cooking lunch, and said, "Okay, go." I walked quickly down the hallway and found the door, opened it and locked it from the inside. I quickly pushed the deck chairs aside and began to dig feverishly. The ground was soft because of the flooding of the Prosna River, and here too I tried to find the softest earth with the handle of the spade. I hit two silver candlesticks and presumed they were buried as a diversion, so that strangers wouldn't continue to dig any deeper. I continued digging until I hit bags of gold. I spilled their content into the bags on the belt around my belly. I reburied the candle sticks, covered them, patted down and flattened the earth, and returned the deck chairs to their place. I locked the door to the compartment and went up, limping a bit on the stairs because the spade was again inside my pants, I returned the keys and left, saying, "I already took the deck chairs." Luckily, she didn't know me or know where I lived, so I wasn't worried about her discovering the lie. It was noon on a clear day. I chose the shortest route, through the park. But in the park a German gendarme suddenly began to harass me. He was drunk; he reeked of vodka. I debated what to do: Should I punch him and flee, or should I wait? He began saying something to me in a confused way. I waited and then saw someone I knew who worked at the Drogacz shoe store. He had become a Volksdeutsch he was a Pole who could speak German. I called him over and asked him what this guy wanted from me. So, he told him to leave me alone and let me go. After saying this, he pushed him in the chest and we walked off together. He saved me. We said good-bye and I thanked him warmly and told him that I would come to his store because I needed shoes for Cesia and the children. When I arrived home, there was no one there except for the guard. I went to the apartment. The dog followed me in and I tossed him to the stairs. In the apartment, I got undressed in order to pull out the gold and hide it somewhere. So, this mission was a one thousand percent success so far. Now the problem arose of how to get the gold to Herman Bloch, who lived in Otwock and served there as a Jewish policeman.

Earlier, I mentioned the flooding of the Prosna River, with the entire city flooded with water. The Germans filled one branch of the river with dirt. They ordered the Jews to remove the gravestones from the cemetery, to break them into squares and use them to shore up the banks of the Prosna.

The work was quite difficult, and the Jews went to do it every day, for the whole day. After the gravestones were uprooted, the Germans ordered them to continue digging, because it turned out that under the ground there was another layer of graves. This cemetery was more than two hundred years old. [Note: In fact, Jews already leased the burial grounds in 1287 by a duke's decree.] The Germans again ordered the Jews to prepare rectangles of stone and cover the banks of the river with them. The Hebrew letters carved in the stones had to be facing downward, so that there would be no sign that they were gravestones. And when they had uprooted all of the gravestones from the second layer of the cemetery, they ordered the Jews to dig again. They reached a third cemetery, but there were no slabs of stone. Instead there were gravestones made of round, natural stones, on which the inscriptions were etched. The Germans ordered the Jews to dig out these stones and break them into pieces. They cast these stone fragments in molds with concrete. Some were cut to form granite cobblestones. Yes, and that's how it ended. You could see the banks of the Prosna lined with these stones. If someone wanted to pull out a stone and turn it over, he would see Hebrew letters. That was proof of the source of these stones.

Soon afterward, a registered letter arrived from the mayor of Kalisz, politely demanding that I leave my apartment and move to the ghetto. But I ignored this letter, went to the office of the department that dealt with this and said that I wouldn't leave the apartment, that it was my apartment, that I work in the factory and that I was essential there. Then they asked me several times whether I was a Jew. I replied that I had been a Jew, but was no longer one. They asked me: For how many generations? I said I didn't remember. They said in reply that they would speak with the chairman of the Jewish community, and would ask that a decent apartment be prepared for me.

Meanwhile, Daub hired a designer-draftsman of lace patterns, an expert from Plauen. I figured that he was slated to replace me. I was assigned to teach him how to design patterns in the factory. I led him to an atelier of two rooms in the attic, where I would work and draft new patterns every day before the war. Now, I was busy instructing the Germans, so that they would understand how to manage the factory. One time, as we went upstairs, the German, a huge and stout man, locked the door from the inside, turned to me and asked whether I recognized him. I asked him from where I might know him. He said that he was a friend of my teacher in Plauen, with whom I had lived. Every Saturday he would come, with his wife and daughter, to the home of my teacher and his wife, and they would set off on a daytrip together. In the meantime, I was trying hard to remember him and I recognized him. His name was Staendner. He hadn't changed a bit he was cheerful and loved to joke around. I understood that he wasn't a Nazi, because one time my teacher spoke with him disparagingly about the "Brownshirts" who were conducting propaganda from trucks driving through Plauen. He didn't wear a swastika on the lapel of his jacket like the supervisor and managers in the factory. He said it was good that I hadn't recognized him at first, because Daub might have suspected that we were conspiring about something, and that meanwhile we should act like strangers. He said he would try to arrange matters so that I could stay at the factory as long as possible, and that he would always say that he was not yet proficient - because of the abundance of patterns I had designed, and in regard to all of the technical aspects. He said that he would only be my assistant and that I would be the primary manager of this operation in practice. So, I had a German friend, who could prove to be beneficial. This greatly encouraged me to chart a path of action in which I could take advantage of his generosity. It was very dangerous to transfer the gold I had extracted; the punishment was death by shooting. I knew that I couldn't send the gold with one of the Germans, because they were also afraid. I racked my brains over what to do. I once asked this German whether he could help me send a food package to my wife and children. There would also be a few toys so they would have something to play with. He immediately agreed. It was known that Jews were prohibited from sending packages by mail, so I gave his full name and his factory address as the sender of the package. I brought the package to the post office, I said that the sender was a German, and I sent it by registered mail with a receipt. I thanked my German colleague. Besides foodstuffs, the package contained old dolls. I was afraid that Cesia would toss them in the trash, so I wrote that one of the dolls was pregnant and needed to give birth, and that she should treat it well, like a child of hers. Only a small part of the gold was hidden in the doll's belly, and I debated how to send the rest. I don't want to describe now how I sent the rest of the gold, because it was a big secret that no one would have imagined. I received a share of the gold as a transfer fee. Now Cesia had a means of sustenance for a longer period of time. Herman Bloch and the Kolski family received a larger share, and were now even more secure from a material perspective. The subsequent packages were also sent by the Germans: Daub, the cashier, and the woman in charge of the warehouse. They said that the pattern designer had done this for me and that they didn't want to appear to be worse than him. They were still dependent on me, because without my work the factory would not have produced a thing.

I later received a second letter from the mayor, demanding to know why I had still not moved to the ghetto. I also ignored this letter and didn't respond to it. I sold the furniture in the bedroom to the woman who brought the plans from Mietek so that it wouldn't fall into the hands of the Germans.

Later, the mayor sent an official to me, who asked why I hadn't evacuated the apartment and why I was still there after such a long time. They set evacuation dates two weeks at first, then one week, and then three days. But I did nothing. Then I asked them, "Where am I supposed to go? To the street?" I told them to ask the Germans whether they needed me. After all, they were keeping me. They responded that if there was a suitable place for me in the ghetto, then I would move and could come to the factory when they needed me. This official was very courteous and polite. It seemed very strange to me; he was a civilian who wore a swastika on the lapel of his jacket. He was apparently a decent man. There were, of course, such people among the Germans. Sometime later, the chairman of the Jewish community came to me. He informed me that I would live together with the Weiss family. I would receive a separate room and could have meals with them. I told him that I needed to see the place first, and I went with him. I found my accountant there, Weiss, his blind wife, and a Polish maid, who wore a yellow patch and Star of David so that she would appear to be a Jew and thus could continue to work for them. I moved to the Kalisz Ghetto, to Nowa Street. The Weiss family was very happy for us to be together and the maid was good to me - served me and wanted nothing in return. When I was living in the ghetto, I would walk every day to the factory, and I taught the Germans how to manage it. They were pleased that they were not required to go to the battlefront.

As mentioned, I took advantage of the generosity of Staendner to send packages to Cesia's address in Śródborów, with him as the sender and with his Kalisz residential address. When I had additional money to send to Jews from Warsaw, from Otwock, and others I used a second German. The mail packages weighed two kilograms, and when asked about their contents, I replied, "Toys, dolls for the little children, and a little food". And they believed me. Later, I turned to a third German, and when he hesitated, I boosted his courage by noting that the two other Germans had already sent packages, and I also added shoes to the contents. So, no one refused. There were five Germans there and I did a round of shipments with them, each one in turn. The first, Staendner, had already sent a number of packages for me, at intervals of two weeks. Affluent Jews from Kalisz, who had large warehouses of wood, iron, and construction materials in the past, would send me to three or four wealthy Germans, who took the goods and stored them in their own warehouses. These Jews asked me to collect a small sum for them for these goods, and I went as requested. During the entire period in Kalisz, I didn't wear the Star of David, and the Germans turned a blind eye. Other Jews who sought to act like me were arrested; they were sent somewhere and disappeared. I made contact with smugglers: People would use them as conduits for gold, jewelry, dollars and such. The Jews could not go into the city, so I was an intermediary for them. I bought or sold, and so on. I had to make some money to provide a livelihood for my wife and children. My salary, which was the same as that of the Germans, was not enough to live on. Hela would come to us almost every day, and I also would go to their apartment sometimes. Her mother died in the ghetto. She lived then with her father and younger sister in a house that served as a hospital for Jews, and disabled Jews stayed there.

One day, I came for lunch and met in the apartment a large man wearing a leather jacket and high boots. Weiss introduced him to me and said that he came to see me. The man asked me to come with him. I replied that I couldn't go with him without knowing who he was. To this he responded that if I didn't come, he would have to use force. I replied that I had come for lunch, and asked whether or not I was permitted to eat. To this he responded, "Gladly." Meanwhile, Weiss went to the chairman of the community his name was Landau - who had connections with the Germans. The chairman of the community arrived, and when he saw that man, he stepped back and faced the window, as if looking outside. He stood behind the man's back, signaled to me, and mouthed the words, "Ges-ta-po." I was alarmed and started to wonder what this could mean. I saw there was no point in resisting, finished eating lunch, put on a jacket and we left. The snow was piled high on the path and there wasn't enough room to walk side by side; he walked first and I followed. I took advantage of this and removed all of the pieces of paper I had in my pockets, all of the lists, and tossed them into the snow, without him being able to notice. We arrived at a villa with a small sign on the front: *Geheime Staatspolizei*. He rang, and the door opened without anyone appearing at the entrance. We went inside. He asked me to sit on a bench. The hallway was a bit dark. I sat and checked again that I hadn't left anything in my pockets. Then I noticed a small barred window, and I was curious to know what was there. I walked to the other end of the hallway, and what did I see? Bloodstains on the floor and instruments of torture hanging in perfect order on the walls. I retraced my steps quickly and sat on the bench. I grew increasingly fearful, because I didn't know why they brought me to the Gestapo. I thought to myself, "Let it be," as the popular saying goes, "The goat only dies once." A moment later, a man in civilian dress entered the hallway. He asked the guy I came with, "Who is this man?" He explained to him. He invited me into his office. It was a spacious room, with desks, papers, files and various office machines. The man rummaged through a pile of papers, pulled out a piece of paper, approached me and showed it to me, placing it close to my eyes. I told him that I couldn't see from such a close distance. Then he handed me the paper and I read it. I tried to understand which incriminating things appeared in what was written. The letter was written in a way that made it incomprehensible to anyone except the addressee. It was addressed to a place in Switzerland an address my father had sent me in the past via someone but it was actually a letter to my parents in Palestine. This official moved closer to me and asked whether I was the one who wrote it. I confirmed. "And what is written there?" he asked. I replied, "It's written clearly in the Polish language, no?" To this, he claimed that the letter was not addressed to Switzerland, but was intended to be sent from there to another country, one that was hostile to Germany. I said nothing in reply. Then he went to a typewriter and wrote, "*Briefe nach Aussland senden ist strengstens verboten*" [sending letters abroad is strictly forbidden] and handed the letter to me. So I understood that the matter was settled, and he said I could go. As I was leaving, a fat and tall Gestapo man entered, in uniform with military decorations and swastikas. I smelled schnapps on his breath. He asked who I was. At this point, he could see the Star of David on my back and on my breast, which were previously concealed by my jacket. He called me to come to his desk and tried to communicate with me. When he realized that I can't hear, he began to speak with me by making letters with his fingers. From his sign language, I understood that he was asking me whether there was an upholsterer in the ghetto. He said he needed a good sofa, and winked at me. When I told him that I could inquire, he said, "So tell Landau to let me know." And he said, "You can go." I left. On the way out, there was a guard cell and the guard had a dog. I wanted to leave, but was unable to open the door. I approached the guard cell and he said, "Go, get out!" And I said, "It's closed." He ordered me out again, and I repeated that the door was closed. He pulled out a pistol to hasten my exit. I went to the door and it opened and then I understood that he had opened it with a button. I exited with my heart racing and breathed a sigh of relief. I knew that people who entered there didn't get out alive. I walked straight to the ghetto, almost running, but I again hid the Stars of David under my jacket so I wouldn't be stopped on the way. When I arrived at the house in the ghetto, Jews were standing there, having gathered to discuss what happened to me. When they saw I was alive, they said to me, "What a rare miracle." Some of them wanted to unravel threads from my jacket and keep them as a good luck charm.

A few days later, I found a letter of dismissal on my desk at the factory, giving me three weeks' notice. It was written and signed by Daub. An order had come from Berlin, but I didn't believe this and I ignored it. I didn't even go to him to find out what happened. Daub saw that I was continuing to work and remained silent. Some time passed and a second letter of dismissal arrived. Again, I ignored it. When a third letter arrived, I went to Daub and said that I couldn't travel from Kalisz to the Generalgouvernement because Jews were prohibited from traveling on the train or in other means of transportation. "So what should I do?" I asked. Could he help me? He said I should try to speak with the draftsman and to go with him, that he should declare that I was teaching him, and perhaps it would be possible to receive a travel permit. Later, I learned that an order had indeed come from Berlin, asking why that Jew had not left the management and demanding that if the supervisor, Daub, did not fire that Jew immediately, then the supervisor himself would be fired.

I went with Staendner to the police headquarters without wearing the Star of David. Staendner whispered in the official's ear, telling him what I had been doing the whole time, and that I wished to go to my wife and children in the Generalgouvernement. The official said that this was beyond his authority, and referred me to the chief commander of the police. So I went on my own to the police headquarters in Kalisz. I saw that the commander was a real Hitlerite, with a swastika on his arm, but he looked like an intelligent man. I went without wearing a Star of David. This demanded a lot of courage, but I took this risk because I knew that travel permits were not issued to Jews. I said that I was requesting a permit that would enable me to travel to the Generalgouvernement by train. I saw astonishment on his face, but he referred me to the secretary and instructed her to issue me the permit. The secretary sat about twenty meters away, in a quiet place. She asked me to show her an identity card, and began to type on a typewriter. She suddenly froze, went to the police commander and whispered something in his ear. He began to look me over, from tip to toe, and he smiled a bit. He signaled with his finger for me to approach and asked in a gentle whisper, "*Du bist Jude?*" ["Are you a Jew?"] I told him that I had been a Jew but now had no religion. To this he responded that the identity card lists me as "Jude" and that there was nothing he could do, it was not within his authority; he said I had to submit the request to Berlin. He searched and found a special form for such matters, but I hesitated. He said he would help me fill in the form, and he did this, and even signed it and said he would send it to Berlin. I was surprised. I asked him when the answer might arrive, and he responded, "To be on the safe side, within six weeks". I returned six weeks later and he immediately told me there was no answer. I told him that if there was no answer after six weeks, this meant that they had tossed the form in the wastebasket there in Berlin. When he heard this, he got very angry, stood up, struck his desk and shouted, "*Warten!*" ["Wait!"]. His faced turned red and looked menacing. Then I asked softly when I should come again. He said, "In three more weeks." I was a bit frightened. I wondered what would happen if there was no answer the next time. After three weeks had passed with no sign of an answer, I went one Sunday to the apartment of that secretary. She was surprised that I was so brazen. She introduced me to her husband, who had recently been expelled from Riga by the Russians. He said they were able to take the piano with them, but were not permitted to take everything. This secretary was very courteous toward me, even offered coffee. What she was going to tell me, she said, must remain top secret. In fact, a negative response had arrived, rejecting my request. The police commander took personal affront at this and so he wrote in anger to Berlin: They must give me a permit or he would quit. I asked her why he was being so good to me, even threatening to resign. Then she told me that she wanted to share a secret with me. He had a deaf-mute sister, so he could better understand me, and he wanted to do everything in his power to help me. I asked her what I should do - whether I should come again to police headquarters. She replied that it was better not to. If there was a positive answer, it would come to my address, and if not, it would come to the police headquarters. In the latter case, she would secretly warn me.

I didn't receive severance pay from work, as required by law, except for one additional week's salary. But the supervisor, Daub, tried to satisfy me. He expressed his willingness to purchase from me the manual of diagrams for producing curtains. He handed me a sum of money, though it didn't cover even ten percent of what I had paid Hänssler for it. The supervisor explained this by saying that the book still belonged to me, even though I was handing it over to him, because it was impossible to know how the war would end. And if the Germans lost, he would leave it in an agreed-upon place, which he indicated. This satisfied me.

While living in the ghetto, I continued to engage in this commerce that is, in sending money to hungry people in the Warsaw area with Cesia's help. This was via an address through which Jews could send messages to the ghetto to make contact with me. Jews in the ghetto learned that they could use me to transfer money and would give me money to send. In this way, I earned a commission of ten to twenty percent, depending on the sum of the transfer. In the Kalisz Ghetto, there was a shop where Jews made various products, including boots with wooden soles. I really liked the craft of cutting and producing shoes from wood, and I wanted to learn this. I spent a lot of time in that basement shop. [Note: It was apparently there that Moniek learned how to hide gold coins and such inside wood products, such as clogs and brushes, and then to glue, sand, and cover the opening with lacquer.] Out of the blue, an envelope arrived with a registered letter from Berlin, approving my request for a travel permit. It instructed me to report to the police, to that man, for the issuance of an official permit. I went to him with this letter, and he suddenly became happy and cheerful, and showed the letter to all of the officials, as if to say that he had won. The secretary typed the permit, and the commander signed it and wished me well.

I couldn't take furniture or other things with me. The chairman of the community asked me to give him the rug, so I was happy to leave it with him. I left the furnishings for Weiss, so that he could sell them and have some money to live on. As an accountant in the ghetto, he earned very little, and now he was losing the rent income from my residence in his basement.

So, I traveled to Otwock. In the meantime, my family moved into the ghetto there, renting a wooden cabin from a Jewish blacksmith.[13]

2. Sandomierz

The apartment in Sandomierz was completely empty at first, without even a single piece of furniture. I couldn't allow myself to purchase furniture, so I bought boards and made myself beds, benches, a table and a chest of drawers.

In those days, I had a smoking habit and couldn't function without cigarettes. In Sandomierz, I went to a wholesale store, but they sold me only

---

13 The order to form a ghetto in Otwock was issued on September 26, 1940. Otwock was captured by the Germans on September 29, 1939. Thus, Father stayed in occupied Kalisz for slightly over a year.

a few cigarettes. A man named Stanisław Kowalski worked there, and he took great interest in me; I was the only deaf person he knew in the whole city. I really took a liking to him. We started to converse and he gave me a few more cigarettes under the table. I would go to him from time to time, and he would always give me a double amount of cigarettes, and so we became friends. Later, I saw that he was my neighbor. He had his own house and yard just two houses away from our apartment. I invited him and his wife to my place. When they entered the apartment and saw Cesia and the children, with their Jewish facial features, they looked completely stunned and surprised. He didn't expect this, because he was sure I was Polish. Later, he called me into the other room, sat on the bed with his wife beside him, and said with a strained expression, but with a slight smile, "Despite everything, we'll remain friends." And indeed, I could see that our friendship didn't suffer at all from this. On the contrary, it became warmer and deeper. I went to him again at the store and met my relative there, Pakuła, and other Jews who helped him. Pakuła was surprised that the man had started to help Jews, giving them work. In the past, he had been known as one of the worst anti-Semites in Sandomierz. I visited him at his house nearby, but he no longer came to us. He started to ask how I was coping in life, what work I did, and he sometimes helped me to sell shirts I received from the Warsaw Ghetto.

The food was cheaper in Sandomierz. So, I mailed packages of peas, butter whatever I could get to Warsaw, and I made a profit on the price differential. Millet grits were an excellent nutritional item for the residents of Warsaw, so I sent millet grits. It was an expensive item! When we were in Sandomierz, I would go out to the villages to sell soap in exchange for flour, buckwheat, and so on.

One time, my best friend, Meir Mojszewicz, came to visit me. He had moved with his wife and little boy to Radom. He came to Sandomierz to sell women's brooches, produced in the ghetto there, and said he made his living from peddling them. When he came to us, he brought a goose and told us to cook it for all of us. He slept with us on a hard wooden bench there was no other place for him. He gave me addresses in the ghetto, and then I also started to sell brooches that I would buy in the ghetto. This gave me a bigger supply of goods and provided us with about half of our livelihood. I even gave some to an acquaintance who sold them on commission. I also gave brooches to the Hirszbergs [the family of Genia, Mother's sister] to sell, but they never returned any money to me. They were apparently suffering from hunger.

Meanwhile, I received an anonymous letter from Kalisz, warning me to flee. It was a second letter from Hela. I wasn't prepared for this, since I was living in Sandomierz incognito, without registering, and I didn't believe that Poles or Jews would turn me in if by chance the Germans came after me. In any case, I left the family as they were and fled from Sandomierz. I traveled to a village in the boonies, where I knew there were deaf people, and I asked about them in the village. The villagers directed me to a deaf shoemaker, who had a hearing wife and children, and I asked him where I could find a place to spend the night. He invited me to stay with him, and his wife said she would also cook for me. He said they were poor, but would find a way. If there was not enough food, it was always possible to water down the soup. Another deaf person came to visit them. He had a flour mill, the only one in the area. You could see that he had once been wealthy. He took me to a family he knew; the daughter there was in love with him. He was very young and handsome, impressive and charming. Some time passed and I received a letter from Cesia that nothing had happened, and I returned home feeling the joy of relief.

However, soon afterward, Cesia's sister Frania suddenly came running one morning and collapsed in a faint on the floor. She screamed that they had killed her husband, Benek Wartsky. At dawn, several Germans from the special services units – Sonderdienst (SD) arrived at the house of the farmer where Frania and Benek lived, and found Frania and her husband in bed. They claimed he had fled from the Warsaw Ghetto and immediately shot him in the head in Frania's presence. This stirred great commotion and apprehension throughout the city. On the same street, behind our house, there was a Jewish cemetery, and the Jewish residents of Sandomierz buried him there. Frania came to live with us, and seemed to be barely conscious, until one time she got seriously ill. If I remember correctly, I think she was pregnant, and we sent her to a doctor we knew outside of the city. He may have performed an abortion, but I'm not one hundred percent sure. Sometime later, she left us and moved to the center of the city. She lived in one small room with another woman, who sewed custom-fitted bras. I visited Frania from time to time to make sure she was healthy and that she had enough to eat.

I met an old acquaintance of mine, David Lieberman, who lived with his father, brother, and sister in the center of the city, on the ground floor, and engaged in commerce. He was a very courageous and energetic guy, whom I had known for a long time. Lieberman was an apprentice in Kalisz at Bieżuński's metal workshop, where I delivered metalwork from the factory. When he came to me at the factory, he was still a redheaded boy. I saw that he was a resourceful youngster with a promising future. I appreciated and liked him. Now, when I came to the center of town, I would go to him to hear the news, and we discussed all of the issues of the day. His father, brother, and sister stayed at home all the time, and he alone worked to provide for the entire family.

After a while, an edict was issued to black out windows at night, so that Russian or other aircraft wouldn't be able to see the electric lights. Then a good business idea popped into my head: to install blackout blinds for windows that could be easily rolled down at night and rolled up in the morning instead of needing to attach and remove blackout paper, or, alternatively, [leave the paper on and] use lights or open blacked-out windows during the day. That's what people did in the city. I built a small model of the device, concealing the mechanism well so that it couldn't be easily copied. I went with this model from apartment to apartment and from store to store. I received an order from Bata, a shoe store in Sandomierz. Here another idea occurred to me: In the store's large window display, I cut out the letters of the stylish Czech brand "Bata" from the blackout paper and attached transparent red cellophane behind it, which was illuminated by a lamp. In this way, the store could be seen when it was open after dark and people could see its familiar name. I needed a partner in order to do the installations quickly and take advantage of the idea. As a partner for distributing the invention, I had two options my deaf friend Oskar Wassermann, or my acquaintance David Lieberman. In my view, Wassermann was too gentle and was not a good salesman, while Lieberman was bolder, resourceful and quick-witted, so I chose him. I offered him a fifty-fifty partnership. Lieberman's apartment, unlike my distant apartment, was well located for storing the tools and materials. He would do the talking and install, and I served as a mobile ladder; when there were several windows to black out, he would stand on my shoulders, and nail the device to the windows above, and I walked with him standing on my shoulders from one window to the next. In this way, we could black out a number of windows at a rapid pace and profit. The post office, which had very high windows, invited us to submit a bid, and we asked for a good price. The manager, a German, agreed to everything we asked. Germans worked there: telephone and telegraph operators, professionals who wired electric boards, and others. The post office manager was a German officer, but he didn't act harshly: He allowed Jews to send food packages, even to the Warsaw Ghetto. Next, we went to the police headquarters. It was on the second floor of a building in the market square. The police chief was a middle-aged German. A large photograph of his wife and children stood on his desk. We figured that he was a moderate man, not like those in the SS. He was a regular officer in the Wehrmacht. We counted many windows there, and we made a calculation. When the officer asked about the price, we showed him the calculation and he wrote it down himself. We didn't have enough blackout paper, and also couldn't buy the amount required. In the store, they gave everyone only a limited amount. We had already taken a lot, and they refused to sell us more. We asked the police chief to issue an order to sell us blackout paper for the police's needs. As a result, we could buy extra - for future customers too - and at a discounted price. We worked very quickly in order to finish the installation in one day. We went to the chief and said, "It's ready!" We gave him the bill, based on the starting price we had offered. He was surprised that we had earned so much. Lieberman responded with a very wise reply: If he thought it was too much, he could pay less, whatever he deemed to be fair. Then he hesitated, calculated, and paid what we had asked. Naturally, he thought we were Poles. Lieberman could speak broken German, so they didn't suspect we could be Jews. When we couldn't find any more work in the city, we looked for work outside of Sandomierz. We found work at a flour mill and received flour and grits as payment. In the peasants' huts, the windows were usually so small that there was no place to install the device.

You could say that throughout the war period I lived from hand to mouth. As long as I was healthy, I did whatever I could do to provide for the family. But when I was sick, large losses occurred.

One day, I was outside of Sandomierz doing business in a village. The owners of one of the huts invited me for dinner. It was evening, and snow was falling. It was getting dark when I left the warm hut, stepping out into the cold winter. I saw that the snow was piled high, covering the road leading home. I couldn't see where the road was. I pondered how I could find the way when it was impossible to see the roads, and then it occurred to me that there were telephone poles along the road. It was dark, but I could see them. I followed those poles and could already feel the concrete under my feet, but I had to wade through snow up to my hips. I walked slowly until I managed to get home. The next day, I went to the village again, but there was a terrible wind and ice on the roads. I felt pains in my shoulders, lower back and spine, so I had to stop work and return home.

From that point in time, my health began to deteriorate, and there was ice on the walls in the apartment. They would come from the hospital and give me strong injections, but the relief only lasted for a short time. I had to use injections all the time. The pain became more severe, and continued to get worse. It was a nerve infection, and on top of this I had sciatica. I would scream at night. Cesia would have to get up in that cold, get dressed, and prepare food for me. I had to eat at night because I lost strength. I was barely able to walk to the doctor. His name was Radwa. He gave me various injections. Finally, when I could no longer walk, they brought me to him in a wagon. I screamed, so they let me in without an appointment. He said he had three more milk injections for pain relief. One of them would last me two days. He told me to stand up. I couldn't. He said, "Get up, get up." Finally, I stood on my feet. The same thing happened a few days later. My condition got worse; I couldn't walk. He took another milk injection from the safe and said he was saving the last injection for a case of life or death. I could walk again, but only home. I was lying down all the time. My muscles hurt. I could even feel the fibers of the sheet in my nerves. The illness continued until the first days of sunshine arrived. The pain decreased and I gradually recuperated. But from an economic perspective, I lost half a year. The expenses were very large. At first, before I went to the doctor, I asked for sleeping pills at night. When this medication was finished, and I told the doctor, he was alarmed. He said that if I had used two more pills, I would have died.

In Sandomierz in the spring, after regaining my strength, I would go to the villages to sell dry goods I purchased in the Warsaw Ghetto, where the prices were lower. One wintery day before Christmas, I went into the Warsaw Ghetto and bought lace to sell. When I wanted to leave the ghetto, the Polish guard I always bribed (while the German guard was patrolling) wasn't at the gate. This time, there were Germans gendarmes or SS personnel. A German guard ordered me to show him a transit permit, but I wasn't prepared for the Polish guard's absence, so I showed him some document, but it wasn't a transit permit. He locked me in the guard booth and went to look into the matter. I wondered how to get out of the booth and decided I would pretend to be German. I started to write on a piece of paper in Gothic letters, thinking that he was young and had surely learned Latin letters in school and not Gothic ones. I wrote that he should let me go because I was German, from the city of Plauen, had come to Poland to marry a Polish woman, and had children with her. I explained that I had only entered the ghetto to buy some lace, and planned to give it to my wife as a Christmas gift. The guard came close to the small window. He was very tall and bent over so he could read it through the windowpane. I held the paper against the window; he read it but didn't open the door. He resumed walking back and forth, and appeared to be thinking what to do. Later, there was a change of guards, and he briefed the new guard. The new guard read what I had written. But he was also young, and perhaps didn't fully understand. However, he saw that it was authentic German Gothic writing, and that I must be from the old generation of Germans, and certainly had been in Germany. They huddled about what to do with me. The first one opened the door and ordered me to come out. He asked me whether I wanted to enter or exit the ghetto. I said to exit. The first guard accompanied me, and after some tens of meters I told him I'd be turning to the right. He said that he was continuing straight ahead, and he allowed me to set off on my way. It was sheer luck that he didn't arrest me and take me with him - that he just walked out with me. The price of the goods I bought in the ghetto that day was three times higher on the outside, so it was a good deal. But I could have paid with my life if they had taken me for interrogation. The whole time, I completely depended on being inventive and resourceful; I was risking my life. I had no other choice.

Commerce, moneychanging, and smuggling flourished in Warsaw. People bought products at low prices in the ghetto, smuggled them out, and sold them at higher prices on the other side. The profits were average, depending on the circumstances in both parts of the city. There was great hunger in the ghetto. People died of hunger like flies in the street. Usually, they weren't thin instead, they became swollen from hunger. Those with money could eat at a first-rate restaurant and order anything they wanted. And there were those who had nothing to put in their mouth. The bread in the ghetto was not well-baked; it looked like clay. But people had to eat it because they had no choice. They even produced American coins of pure gold in the ghetto, which they sold outside the ghetto as real dollars. Later, people were already aware of this, but still bought and sold these coins at a different price. I was usually a contact person in smuggling and trading between the ghetto and the other side. The profits were so-so. I knew a goldsmith in the ghetto, a deaf-mute who made artistic gold bracelets. I sold them outside the ghetto or kept them for myself in case of emergency. The Jews sold whatever they had: jewelry, rings, silver candlesticks, watches, etc. - in order to avoid starving to death, and sometimes it was their last possession.

3. Sandomierz – the ghetto

Moshe's remark during the second stage of the recordings:

"The following is recorded in the apartment of my son Yoseph's family while recuperating after my third heart attack (1986). The previous chapter was recorded about two years earlier, at the same place, after my second heart attack."

Today I will talk about our move from the outskirts of Sandomierz, to the ghetto formed in the Old City. We lived outside the city without registering, with the help of friends. We didn't want our address known, because the Gestapo had already searched for me in Kalisz I wasn't sure why. The Jews were ordered to move to the ghetto within three days. Do you know that Sandomierz was the last city where they forgot to form a ghetto? Therefore, it wasn't a closed ghetto at all, even after the transfer there. The move to the ghetto made my blood pressure soar, as I needed to find lodging, even temporary, within three days. Luckily, Stanisław Kowalski, the Polish friend who lived near us, agreed to take our things in storage, so we could move to the ghetto without our belongings. The boys found a single bed at the home of an old widow. During the first day or two, our beds were crammed one against the other. The next day, I went to look for better accommodations, where we could think more quietly about the future. We moved in with a family, where we received a place in exchange for payment. Here I could no longer get up every day at five o'clock in the morning, leave the ghetto for the village, and sell soap and goods, and barter for foodstuffs.

One evening, the police chief came unexpectedly to the ghetto square with an order for those living around the square to gather in it. He himself began to go from apartment to apartment, searching for Jews who were hiding. Meanwhile, I placed the family in the attic and lay in bed in pajamas, pretending to be ill. The police chief arrived, led by a wealthy Jew from Sandomierz, G., holding a kerosene lantern in his hand. When they approached me, that Jew pointed at me and said I was deaf. The police chief looked me over and recognized me, remembering that I had once done blackout work at the police station, together with Lieberman, for a high price. He motioned for me to go downstairs. He was surprised that I was Jew. The expression on his face suggested that he was impressed by my daring. They left, but on the way out he again signaled to me to go downstairs. This time I refused, however, shaking my head from side to side to say that I wouldn't go. Moving aside the curtain, I looked toward the square. I saw that the chief was looking at my window and waiting for me. Below, he indicated that I was deaf, took a look at his watch, and decided to continue with the *Aktion*. He ordered his personnel to beat the assembled Jews with sticks and metal poles. They injured them. I expected him to send people to take me downstairs. But this didn't happen. When the beaten Jews returned to the apartments, they were very badly bruised. I coughed as much as I could to justify my refusal to go down. They complained about me, afraid of being arrested. I moved with the family to another apartment, in a quieter place. The owners of that apartment were a couple with one daughter.

One fine morning, Gestapo personnel came to the quarter in a car and asked for the location of the Jewish community council. They entered and met with the chairman of the community, Dr. Goldberg. They shot him to death on the spot, and several others, too. That was the start of a pogrom. I decided to leave the city, to flee Sandomierz and find another place to live. I knew the city was surrounded by the Army. Meanwhile, the owners of the apartment asked me if I could take their daughter with me. She had Aryan papers hidden under the cupboard. They asked that I take care of her when leaving the city. We pretended to be lovers, holding hands as we left the city. After leaving the city, soldiers with bayoneted rifles surrounded us and came straight at us. I ignored them. But she suddenly panicked and wanted to flee. I held her tightly by the arm and pressed strongly to prevent her from doing so. The soldiers walked past us with bayonets in their hands. It was a large group of soldiers. We continued on in the direction of the village, to the field, and we hid in a pile of hay. A peasant came out of her hut; she knew me from selling soap there. She didn't say a word and went back to the hut. Night fell. Meanwhile, the girl couldn't restrain herself and lit a cigarette. I asked her not to do that, because a lit cigarette was very visible in the dark, and they would find our hiding place. We lay all night without closing our eyes, so we wouldn't fall asleep. We waited for dawn to break. Then we walked on, not on the main road, but on side paths. We darted into a train station and there we said farewell. She preferred to travel to Warsaw alone, and she showed me a forged Aryan certificate, similar to the one I had.

On the way, I entered Częstochowa, where the ghetto was still open. You know, it was a big city. I went into the ghetto and visited cousins and the Friedensohn family. I stayed in a hotel near the ghetto, using forged documents to register. The Friedensohns implored me to stay with them, but I refused, thinking, "Why should I take a chance at night when I have a hotel nearby?" At that time, many uniformed soldiers from special services units (Sonderdienst, or SD) roamed the city. The Jews started to be afraid. When I returned to the hotel to rest, I felt that someone was moving about near the door. I opened the door and caught the doorman peeking through the keyhole. I asked him what he was doing, and he replied that he had knocked and knocked at the door, and didn't know that I couldn't hear. He wanted permission to put another sofa in my room. Many Germans had arrived. There were already lots of beds in the hallway, and he asked if I would agree to bring in a sofa for one of the Lithuanians. I firmly responded, "No!" And he retreated, cowering. I locked the door and lay in bed. When I woke up the next morning, I noticed what was happening in the street: The streetlights were still on, even though it was broad daylight. I looked out the window toward the ghetto and I shuddered. I thanked God I hadn't stayed with the Friedensohns, because I would have been caught. Lithuanians armed with long, thin rifles surrounded the ghetto, standing a few steps apart from each other, as I had once seen by the Warsaw Ghetto. I came to Częstochowa with the goal of producing forged identity cards (*Kennkarten*) in collaboration with Minelman, from Kalisz. Minelman was looking for someone to bring identity cards from Warsaw, which he would sell. Of course, after the ghetto was surrounded by the Army, this enterprise was scrapped. I had to discuss this entire matter in Częstochowa with someone I knew. I went to visit a woman from Kalisz named Melamed. I brought her to the hotel. She told me she had parents in the ghetto and didn't know how to save them. I ordered some beer, and she drank all of the bottles and lay on the bed. She didn't know what to do. I also didn't know what she should do or what I myself should do. I felt bad. I wished her well and set off. On the way to Sandomierz, I stopped at a city where Oskar Wassermann lived with his family. His wife studied with me in the same class in Vienna, and I met him through her. I felt sick, so I lay there in bed. Oskar gave me the address of his friend, [Roman] Jaworski, a deaf Pole in Kraków, and a letter of recommendation to help me. I had no time to stay overnight there because the events were developing so rapidly and I needed to act to find and reach a place where we could survive. When I arrived at my family in Sandomierz, I immediately went to bed, burning with a high fever.

Not long before this, I met my cousin, Torończykowa, and she gave me as a gift an identity card with her picture, so that I could give it to someone else to use with their picture. After removing the picture, and replacing it with a picture of Frania, I saw that three-quarters of the stamp was missing.

I traveled to Kraków and looked for an engraver to make a matching stamp with a swastika, and to complete the missing traces of the picture. The stamp makers refused to make this type of stamp, even for a hefty price. They demanded approvals and a written order from the Germans, which I couldn't provide. So I returned empty-handed. Of course, I couldn't give up such a valuable document. So I had to make a stamp myself with the help of blotting paper and a roller, while drawing by hand. When the document came out well, I gave it as a present to Frania.

Oscar and Paula Wassermann in prewar Kraków.

Frania herself suggested taking Ignaś with her because of his "bad appearance," while she had a "good appearance" (Aryan typical Polish). In the Sandomierz Ghetto, there was already a constant atmosphere of an impending pogrom, so there was no point in remaining sick in bed. I got dressed in order to help prepare Frania and Ignaś for their trip to Kraków. I knew that the SD was guarding the train station in Sandomierz, so I wanted to devise a plan for Frania and Ignaś to arrive in a closed horse-drawn carriage at another train station, where the express train to Kraków was scheduled to stop for half a minute. I had a schedule for this train, and I knew exactly when it was supposed to stop at the station. So the carriage arrived just on time, enabling me to immediately get them onto the train.

The home of Roman Jaworski and his wife Julia served as a transit station where we could meet. Hotels didn't accept guests for more than one night, so Frania moved from one hotel to another until I arrived. I started to prepare my wife and second son to flee. The second station where the express train stopped for half a minute was called Tarnobrzeg, and from there the three of us headed to Kraków so that Frania and Ignaś wouldn't be left alone for a long time. We went to the Jaworski family, because we didn't have anywhere else to stay because of the [Jewish] appearance of my wife and son. We had to immediately find another place where we could stay on a regular basis. We had no acquaintances or friends in all of Kraków, so we could only ask Jaworski for advice. I received the address of a guesthouse outside the city, and the three of us traveled there in a tram to the final station, and then continued by foot. Suddenly a Polish policeman appeared. Cesia had a "bad appearance," and so she dyed her hair then, and it made the situation even worse. The policeman was apparently waiting in ambush for such victims. He took us to the field and declared that she was a Jew. I said that wasn't true, and that he should let us go. He spoke for a long time with Cesia. But since I was so emphatic, he also accused me of being a Jew. He then threatened to turn us in. It was blackmail, and I didn't know what to do. He demanded that we pay a ransom. I had a few gold dollars in my pocket, so I took out a few coins and placed them in his hand. I figured that if he turned us in, he would receive fifteen thousand złoty from the Germans for the three of us, so I offered him twice as much. I was ready to explode with anger, and I regretted not having a weapon, because I would have shot him in that field. Actually, I never imagined such an incident might occur, or I would have prepared myself accordingly. After the policeman left us, we walked on angry and irritable, to the guesthouse which Jaworski and his wife Julia had told us about. I knew that we wouldn't be able to stay there long because of the frequent inspections there.

Roman and Julia Jaworski in prewar Kraków.

Jaworski, who worked at a government printing house as a bookbinder, gave me the address of his friend, Antoni Herbert, a deaf bookbinder in Brzesko. He gave me a letter to give to Herbert, with a few words asking him to help me, without noting that I was Jew. So, we traveled to Brzesko and stayed in a hotel, the only one in the city. There was an *Aktion* then, liquidating the ghetto in Brzesko. I went to Herbert's apartment. Herbert was the son of an Austrian general in World War I, married to Marta, a Polish woman who could hear. He introduced me to his father-in-law and mother-in-law, his wife and children. I saw that they were poor. His brother-in-law was a shoemaker. But they were all nice people. I brought him to the hotel so he could see Cesia and Jurek. I saw something in his face, a sort of expression of hesitation; but he promised to look for lodgings for us, and he returned after a short while. We looked out the hotel window and saw him walking in the street. He didn't look at our window at all, to give us any sign. He walked by. I went downstairs and ran to catch up with him. We walked together to his home. He said there was an apartment in the basement of the home of Mrs. Gardzielowa, a widow who seethed with hatred for the occupier because the Germans had murdered her husband. Her husband had been a music professor and died in Auschwitz. Herbert took me to Mrs. Gardzielowa, who lived in a raised ground floor apartment. He introduced me, saying I was from Warsaw and was looking for an apartment, and asked whether she would rent the basement apartment to us. She said she would be glad to rent to us, but that before we moved in, there were things that had to be cleared from there. I quickly moved Cesia and Jurek into that basement apartment. Herbert helped a lot to move our possessions, and we needed to also clear potatoes, coal, and wood for heating before we could live in one of the two rooms in the cellar. The owner came down with a tray of steaming cups of tea, which had the aroma of steeped linden blossoms (*lipa*). She looked at Cesia and Jurek and didn't say a word. She was poker-faced. Later, she introduced us to her daughter, who was almost a grown-up, and to her son, who was still a young teenager. If they harbored suspicions, it was impossible to detect. As far as we could see, they were pleased that someone else was coming to live in their home.

4. Between Brzesko and Warsaw

I cannot recall how Frania came to live near Brzesko, in a village called Słotwina-Brzesko. She rented a room from someone and lived with Ignaś. I visited her and saw that she was doing okay.

Herbert brought a friend to us; his name was Geniek Łoza, a deaf-mute. He was a nice fellow, and was happy that another deaf-mute friend had come to Brzesko. He was a tailor, very talented. Later, he brought me to his house and altered my long jacket into a short one, and sewed a hat for me with the leftover material, so my attire became more urbane. He introduced me to his mother, his young sister Helena, and his sister Irena Nowakowa and her children. Nowakowa was a widow. I could tell they were decent and good people. Geniek was the only man in the family at home, so he was very helpful in all matters. One day, I went to their home to say good-bye before departing for Warsaw. I had to make a living somehow and look for work. At five o'clock tea, when we were all sitting at the table, Geniek's mother and his sister Irena turned to me, and the mother asked whether I'd be willing to take her young daughter Helena to Warsaw with me. They couldn't send her by herself, because she was too young and beautiful, they explained. I said, "Yes, gladly," and I bit my tongue. At the moment I agreed, I had forgotten that I was a Jew. I came to my senses and realized I couldn't put her at risk if they caught me en route, since there were many German detectives roaming around the train station in Kraków. I thought for a moment and then said that I would invite my friend Kowalski to accompany us to Kraków. I said that I would rent a room in a hotel across from the train station for two and a half hours, until the departure of the train to Warsaw, because the Germans check everyone at the station. They check the lists of wanted persons and sometimes send people on the spot to forced labor in Germany, and they could also just detain and extort us. When Kowalski arrived, we went to the Łoza and Nowak family, and this is how they met him. The three of us traveled by train to Kraków We parted in Kraków from Kowalski, who remained at the hotel, and the two of us, Helena and I, went to the station about ten minutes before the train was scheduled to depart for Warsaw. A Pole, with a detective's badge under his jacket lapel, approached and stopped us on the platform, and asked us for identification. I slowly reached into the pocket of my jacket and handed him a document. I don't remember whether it was an identity card or another forged document. He looked at it, returned it to me, and dismissed us with a "Heil."

In Warsaw, we took a taxi and traveled to the apartment of her brother, a physician, Dr. Emil Łoza. The brother's family was very happy that we arrived and thanked me. His wife set the table and served hard-to-find delicacies: ham, bacon and more. We sat with their two little children at breakfast. Everyone spoke and understood each other well, because Dr. Łoza had a deaf brother; Dr. Łoza understood me and could also speak in sign language. After breakfast, he invited me to his clinic in the same apartment. He climbed a ladder, reached the top shelf to bring down and pour me a drink from an expensive bottle he had received from a patient from Italy. He was a gynecologist. [Note: I later learned from Helena that he was also a specialist in skin diseases and lectured at Łódz University after the war.] When I left, he implored me to come and visit from time to time, and to turn to him if any problem arose.

Events were happening now in Warsaw at a very rapid pace. I rented a room on a side street near Napoleon Square, in the home of an elderly widow. I told her I would only use the room for sleeping and would leave early in the morning. Lots of *szmalcownicy* (extortionists) roamed around outside, as well as other agents, detectives, and informers for the Germans. It was essential to watch out and exercise caution, each and every step of the way. Before arriving home, I had to check carefully that no one was following me. Meanwhile, I wanted to obtain a real identity card, because I only had a forged document, produced and given to me as a gift by the dentist Szejnfeld, who was a relative of Mietek and was actually my *sandak* (godfather) at the ritual circumcision. I focused all my thoughts on the problem of how to obtain an original *Kennkarte*. In order to issue one, a birth certificate was required. A man from Kalisz, Karo, was engaged in this field [of forged documents] and was willing to help me obtain the birth certificate I wanted in exchange for payment, of course. I gave him all of the information, and specified as my place of birth Stołpce, which was held at the time by the Russians, so the Germans couldn't easily call there to confirm that it was indeed an authentic certificate. It was the copy of a certificate from the parish church in Stołpce. But the paper was fresh, white. I folded the paper in quarters, and kept it in my breast pocket so it would get a bit worn out. I later placed it on the toilet tank in the bathroom to give it a yellowish color. It separated into four quarters, and then I cut a piece of cloth and pasted the pieces onto it, to my satisfaction. The birth certificate looked like an original, and with this document in hand I went to the German office to ask them to issue an identity card. They took the certificate and told me to come back in six weeks. When I came, the identity card was already waiting, with swastika stamps, signed by the German commander, and all the rest. They checked that the details matched those written in the birth certificate, asked that I sign my (new) name, Mateusz Filipowski. They took fingerprints of my two index fingers. As my prewar address, I gave the address of a home that was burned down, where there was surely no list of tenants to check. There were Jews in hiding who never went outside because they had no identity card; there were some who asked me to arrange this for them, because I had certain connections.

[*Note: Here there is a missing section in the Jerusalem recording, the picture can be filled in by the testimony of Marysia Silberstein in Part Four, Chapter B. Stasia: Marysia told me how she once turned to Mateusz to prepare a forged identity card for her cousin, Leon Szeinfeld-Walicki. Mateusz asked for the personal information for the document, and a half-profile photograph. The nose in the photograph looked too "hooked," so Mateusz straightened it with a new razor blade, retouched the picture and re-photographed it in a laboratory.*] The man in the laboratory did as I requested. When everything was done, I saw that it was excellent work. I asked him, "How much do I pay?" He responded, "As much as you want." I gave him a decent sum and asked that he give me the negative. I wanted to be sure that no traces of the photograph would remain with him. When the identity card was ready [in Walicki's name], I went to his apartment and placed the document on the table. After studying it, he said it wasn't his face. I replied that they didn't want to do a document with that photograph, so I had no choice. And since I wanted to help him, I fabricated his face myself. He asked, "What am I supposed to do with this bulge?" I answered, "If you know a plastic surgeon, he'll fix your face." And indeed, a physician shaped his face to match my photograph. I didn't want any payment. I told him this was a gesture of appreciation for his previous gift. He didn't agree, saying that he hadn't spent any money and it must have cost me a large sum. Finally, I agreed to take only enough to cover my expenses, without any monetary profit for my efforts. A few months later, I visited him. I was astonished to see that his face had completely changed. However, I recognized him because his face was similar to the photograph I had fabricated. He said that he had found a plastic surgeon who shaped his face according to the photograph and also changed his penis from circumcised to uncircumcised, like a non-Jew. And he was still bandaged. He said it was really painful and that when it healed, he would show me how it was done. But I didn't see him again after that visit.

ID card of Mateusz Filipowski, a deaf mechanic born in Stołpce, issued on January 23, 1943, including address changes in Warsaw and in Gorzkowice.

During my stay in Warsaw, I didn't really have a place to sleep. So I had no choice but to sleep in Mietek's bachelor's room. He lived in an apartment with a family. Upon his advice, I looked for a place to sleep in the newspaper advertisements, but I couldn't stay for more than one night in any place. This search continued for weeks. One day, I saw a group of prisoners being led somewhere. I envied them, because I didn't have a roof over my head or means of subsistence. It was a very difficult period for me, because I also had to look for work.

I lived in Warsaw at first in an outlying neighborhood, Powiśle, near the Vistula River, on 13 Furmańska Street. The houses were in ruin on the street, and I chose No. 13, thinking that Jews searching for a hiding place would skip over a house with a number associated with "bad luck." I lived with a married couple and their small children. The rent was low. I received a large room, which was unfurnished except for a bed. There was a bowl in the room for washing, and I had to bring a heater so I wouldn't freeze from the cold. I bought a heater. The owner of the apartment was a barber in the neighborhood, and he suffered from a stomach ailment, apparently an ulcer. He and his wife were decent people. I would bring a pound of sugar each time for the children; it seemed to me they were suffering from a lack of vitamins and food. So, they thought of me as a good man. I had quiet there, without any fears. The owner set up the heater and didn't ask for any additional payment. But then a major mishap occurred. Mietek's father, Moritz, still had no place to sleep. So Mietek brought him to me, so he could sleep with me in my bed for just one night. Afterward, Mietek found a place for him. But the owner of the apartment came to me and said that unfortunately he had to ask me to leave the apartment because he suspected that the man who slept with me was a Jew. He said he has a wife and two children and could not take chances. Moritz's Polish accent was bad and his Polish was awful. I had to keep quiet. I couldn't deny it, because then I would fall under suspicion! He said we would part amicably, and helped me dismantle the heater and pack it. He even cleaned the exhaust pipes. As I left, he put his hands together and prayed. I kissed the children on their cheeks and wished everyone well. He said he would give me some time to find new lodgings, and again apologized that they could not take a chance, because of the children, and he wished me, "Be well." I felt relieved, because I realized these poor people wouldn't turn me in to the Germans in exchange for payment, despite their severe poverty.

I would leave my place of residence early in the morning and return late at night, so they wouldn't know which home I was entering. One night, I noticed that someone was following me. I didn't turn my head to look. In the light of the tall street lamps, I could see the shadow of someone plodding along behind me. To check whether he was following me, I suddenly bent down, as if to tie my shoelaces. Watching his shadow, I saw that he stopped, too, and I understood that he was indeed following me. When I reached my home, I didn't enter the gate. Instead, I continued down the street and entered another building, where I knew there was an exit to the parallel street through a long courtyard. I went up the stairs to check whether he would also enter the gate. When I saw him enter, I realized that I'd have to go down the same stairs to get to the parallel street. I did this when he was leaving the gate, apparently in order to signal to someone or make a telephone call to the Germans, telling them to come. From the other street, I circled the house to return to the previous street in order to watch and see whether the Germans came to the place I had fled. And this is what happened: Germans arrived in a car and entered the gate. I waited for them to enter. When none of them remained in the street, I went to my house. This was one of the precautionary measures, to avoid getting caught. Besides Mietek and Stasia, no one knew where I lived. I felt safe that way.

In the past, when Mietek was still living on Łódzka Street in his bachelor's apartment, and also when he got married and continued to live there with his wife, I would go to the workshops in the area and bring them turning and other metalworking tasks. Once I noticed they had introduced a process that was new for me: arc welding. I marveled at the work and observed. I was not careful to avoid looking at the welding arc, even after the owner of the workshop told me I would ruin and burn my eyes if I looked. The next morning my eyes were swollen and I couldn't open them. I couldn't see anything. I had no choice but to stay in bed. Stasia, who was worried by my absence, came to visit me. She brought me lunch and took care of me. Luckily, she had my address. Otherwise, who knows what would have happened to me. She led me like a blind person to her house and bandaged my eyes. Many days passed before I was able to see and go out with swollen eyes to my work.

[*A break in recording*] … He suddenly informed me that Frania had abruptly fled from her room in Słotwina and was waiting for me in a hotel by the train station. This occurred in regard to the [Jewish] appearance of Ignaś and not Frania's. He was harassed by szmalcownicy [extortionists], and she pulled out her remaining money for a ransom. For me, this came out of the blue, as a complete surprise, and I had nowhere to send them.

Another difficulty for the entire family was that Mietek had recently married, in a church wedding in October 1942, to Stasia, a Catholic Polish woman. Stasia turned out to be an angel from heaven, but she didn't know before or after the wedding that Mietek was a Jew. The only place where I could try to put Frania and Ignaś was in the apartment of Mietek and Stasia on Grzybowska Street, an apartment he had recently rented. However, Frania was not idle. She managed to meet with a Polish friend from Kalisz, Mr. Krzyczkowski. He was now living in Warsaw, divorced from his wife, and worked as a driver in the city's tram network. So, we met with him at some place in the city. He had worked for me in the past. I extended my hand to him to show there were no hard feelings from the past, even though we hadn't rehired him after a shutdown at the factory in Kalisz. That was because the family didn't want Frania to continue to go out with him; he was courting her at the time. Instead, I hired a deaf Jewish worker and taught him the same work that Krzyczkowski had done. But Krzyczkowski was a decent fellow, made a serious effort to help, and was able to find a residence and guardian for Ignaś. Frania was rewarded for the great success, thanks to Krzyczkowski's help and recommendation.

Ignaś was lucky to have an outstanding caretaker, Mrs. Leopolda Kuropieska, a very nice and impressive woman. I introduced myself as a friend of Ignaś' father, and Frania as his aunt. Mrs. Kuropieska agreed that Frania could live with her as a nanny of Ignaś. Her children Barbara, about twelve, and Wojtek, about eleven were good companions for Ignaś, and played with him. Her husband was a captain in Poland's regular Army and was in Germany in a POW camp for officers. The apartment was elegant, well-ordered, comfortable, and very clean. Her husband's library was full of interesting books that thrilled Ignaś. When we came to meet her, she was just leaving with a sled to bring coal, and we accompanied her on the way. I promised to visit every Sunday, and she invited me to lunch so we could eat together. So, I moved Ignaś from Mietek's apartment to their home. It was far; the apartment was almost at the edge of the city. I took Ignaś inside openly so the neighbors would see him. One day, I made a special trip to register him with the building custodian. He didn't ask anything and handed me the registration book. So Ignaś was registered according to the forged birth certificate (*metryka*) I had purchased for him with the assumed name of Marian Dąbrowski. Kuropieska said she would calculate payment in exchange for food, and not charge anything for housing him. So, Ignaś could play freely with other children in the neighborhood in the backyard and in front of the house. She also asked Frania to move out and find other lodgings. She was willing to take full care of Ignaś on her own. He no longer needed a nanny. I had to adapt myself to her requests in order to avoid endangering Ignaś. Now I could turn my attention to Cesia's situation in Brzesko, and also focus on looking for work and earning income. I was left almost penniless. I ate lunch every day at Stasia's, and stayed with her for several free hours. She thought I was Polish, Mietek's best friend from childhood.

My brother-in-law, Second Lieutenant Salomon Bloch, was in the Woldenberg POW camp for officers (Oflag) in Germany. I spent a lot of money on him. I sent him food packages each month; he sent me stickers from the camp that served as authorization for the packages. I stayed in contact with him the whole time I was roaming around Poland. I always sent him my new address, where he could send stickers for the packages. He was a devoted partner in the factory in Kalisz for many years before the outbreak of war. He was one of my best friends; we fully understood each other in every way. Leopolda's husband, Józef Kuropieska, a captain in the Polish Army, was in the same camp, and he knew Samek Bloch, who was in a separate barrack for Jewish officers, and even became friendly with him. What a fortunate coincidence! When Leopolda sent him a family photograph in which Ignaś also appeared, he showed Bloch the photograph and asked him whether he knew the Jewish boy in the picture. Bloch recognized Ignaś and told Kuropieska whose son it was. Leopolda wrote to her husband that she was afraid to keep that Jewish boy with her. Of course, she didn't write "Jewish," but let him understand this in a different way. Captain Józef asked for Bloch's advice, after telling him about his wife's letter. Bloch told him it was very dangerous and that he would have to decide himself, with his wife. When they met the next time, Captain Józef said that he had decided to write to his wife and tell her to protect that boy as if he were her own child. That would reinforce her decision - the fact that her husband is of the same mind. [Father becomes very emotional.] I have great admiration and appreciation for this noble couple. I saw them as true heroes; there were few like them in those horrible conditions. If the Germans found a single Jew with a Polish family, they would shoot everyone. I had great respect for Leopolda and appreciated her as a person who devoted and risked her life.

As Easter approached, I went to visit Cesia and Jurek. I arrived in Kraków after the ghetto there was liquidated. During the layover before switching trains, I wanted to visit my cousin Torończyk. I had arranged a place for her to live near the city, upon the request of her husband, who was my most beloved cousin. I traveled to the edge of the city in a tram, and then continued by foot. The snowy weather was very beautiful. I walked. In that village, I suddenly saw a member of the SS in a black uniform. He was walking with a dog in the same direction as I was, but on the other side of the road. I was wearing two coats and looked like someone fleeing from the liquidated ghetto. He drew closer. I didn't want to look like I was trying to dodge him, so I crossed to his side, straight at him. He ordered me to stop and show an ID card (*Ausweis*). I slowly pulled the document from my pocket and handed it to him. I saw that he didn't look at it because he held the document upside down. Instead, he watched the dog, who circled me several times. The dog sniffed and sat down; he didn't find anything from the ghetto, as he was trained to do. Only then did he look at the document. It was written there "deaf-mute." He told me to go, and then called me again. He wanted to know what I had in the box under my armpit. I gave him the box with a feeling of relief. I knew that he'd find something there that would rule out the possibility that I was a Jew. The box contained a lamb made of sugar, which I brought as an Easter present for the Herbert family. Then I opened my bag and there were regular things there a notebook, a toothbrush, soap, and a screwdriver I used as a weapon. He returned the ID card to me and let me go. I continued on until I reached the house where my cousin Torończyk lived with her son. It turned out there had been a fire there. Many of her possessions were burned, as well as cash and foreign currency. She didn't know what to do. She talked about returning to Piotrków, to her husband. I couldn't stay any longer, because we were invited for a holiday dinner at the Herbert family. So I set off for Cesia and Jurek. I told them and explained about the meetings with Kuropieska.

I killed a rabbit, skinned it, and Cesia prepared a casserole. She made a sort of torte cake from the casserole and brought it to the Herbert family. The entire Herbert family had gathered, including his father-in-law, his brothers-in-law (his wife's brothers), and quite a few guests, including us. Herbert prepared wonderful appetizers, and everyone ate heartily and drank vodka. It turned out that the meal was prepared from what was collected in nature, and mainly from frogs' legs. When he revealed this to us, people vomited. A few days later, Herbert, who lived in poverty, was summoned to the offices of the Germans. They demanded that he sign a document testifying that he was a *Volksdeutscher* because his father was an Austrian general. He explained that he was afraid that his wife, a Pole, would leave him if he signed, and that he wanted to continue to be Polish. He refused to sign. They closed him in a room for several hours. Left with no alternative, he signed. A few days later, I met him in the street. He gave me a small package of butter and said it was for Marek [Jurek's assumed name]. I told him that his children didn't look well, so they needed it more. He replied that he would be angry with me if I didn't accept the gift. Since I didn't want matters to come to this, I accepted the package. A week or two later, we met again, and again, I had to accept a similar gift.

I traveled to my wife Cesia and my son Jurek only on the Catholic holidays. I also tried to think and plan how to obtain an identity card for Cesia, because it was impossible to move in Poland then without one. The old temporary IDs had already expired. Cesia didn't want to show herself for the purpose of obtaining an ID, and pretended to be ill. So, I had to carry out this task on my own. Luckily, I knew the mayor and the authorized official at the municipality. I would meet them on Sundays at a restaurant, where everyone drank beer and vodka, and I would go up to them and raise a glass in toast. So, they already knew me; I was the third deaf-mute in Brzesko, and it was easy to recognize me. Cesia introduced herself to people as my cousin and Jurek as her son. I went to the official at the municipality and asked for his help, because my cousin Krystyna was very sick and could not come in person. I asked that he give a directive to issue an identity card, based on my personal guarantee. Upon his directive, I handed Krystyna's documents to a female clerk. I told her that Krystyna could not come at the moment and I asked her to give me the ID, which already contained all of the details, so that Krystyna could sign it herself at home. Cesia signed the ID at home, and I immediately returned to the municipality so they could certify it with stamps and signatures. It was winter and the clerk was warming her hands by the heater. She asked me in curiosity what Krystyna looked like, what color hair and what color eyes she had. I said she was quite good-looking, that it wasn't important, and it was enough that I was a guarantor. Then she got goose bumps, warmed herself by the tiled heater facing me, and shivered.

Once Cesia had her identity card in hand, she was emboldened and walked around the city, so that people would see her. She soon entered into a partnership with her landlady, Mrs. Gardzielowa, in order to make a living. Cesia's job was to sell rolls in the city, very delicious rolls, which the owner of the house baked in her home oven. Cesia went from home to home, selling the rolls. But soon afterward, some people asked Gardzielowa whether she had a tenant who looked Jewish. Gardzielowa replied, "Look, she has an identity card, she's Polish, and I'm not interested in what's inside her." So people accepted this, and they continued to purchase the rolls every day, fresh and delicious. But they wondered what the profits were relative to the expenses. I advised Cesia to stop dying her hair, in order to return to her natural shade of black. In Galicia, you would see more women with black hair than blond. It was close to Romania, and the same was true there. Most of the women there have black hair, and they told me jokes about this in Warsaw.

And now, more on the extortionists in Warsaw who hunted Jews.

I knew Oskar Wassermann from before the war, when he was chairman of the deaf club in Kraków. He married a very wealthy deaf-mute, Paula Dar, whose father owned a large shoe factory. She was my classmate when I studied in Vienna. She had weak eyesight from birth. During the war, I was in contact with Oskar from time to time. We helped each other. Thanks to him, I had the address of Jaworski in Kraków, and through Jaworski I received Herbert's address. This really helped me in times of crisis.

One time, he asked me to sell some things he had: a gold cigarette box that was painted another color and gold watch covers. He needed money. I agreed, and I took everything with me to Warsaw. When I left the store of the goldsmith where I wanted to sell the covers and gold chains, two people cornered me and said that someone told them I was a Jew. I denied it, said it was not true. They asked me to come with them to a gate and show them that I wasn't a Jew. I told them it was rude, that I didn't agree. They told me, "Okay, we'll go to the Gestapo." I said, "Okay, let's go." I figured they wouldn't dare to enter the Gestapo. Meanwhile, as we approached the Gestapo building, I saw through the glass door that it really was the Gestapo. When I opened the door, they said to me, "After you." I saw that they actually wanted to turn me over to the Gestapo. I knew that the payment per head was five thousand złoty. So I turned back. I went down the stairs and told them I didn't want to [report to the Gestapo]. "Have a heart," I said. "They even kill Poles." We walked in the street, and on the way back we entered the gate of the same house. I told them I didn't want to [do it] there, so we entered a side wing of an empty house and went down wooden stairs by the first window facing the yard. They asked what I had with me. I showed them the watch covers and the chains. So they took that. Then I took out the money I had with me. They counted; it was a measly sum. They said they would leave me money for the tram and take all the rest. I took out everything I had in my pockets. There was a pocketknife, handkerchief, and several trivial items. I put them back into my pocket. Then they left. I saw through the window that they exited to the street via a second gate. I was angry at myself for not putting up a fight. I regretted that I didn't have the screwdriver this time. I would have murdered them in cold blood. I stood there for so long that it got completely dark. Meanwhile, I saw through the window that they were returning. They came up to me and told me to give them the pocketknife. I asked why. They said that I hadn't come out of the building for so long, that they were afraid I would slash my wrists.

This chapter is devoted in large part to the memory of Mietek Kolski. Mietek and I were born in the same year and suckled milk from the same wet nurse. He was the nephew of Cesia, my future wife. Fate brought us together in common battles during the German occupation. He offered me great assistance and I can't imagine achieving what I did without it. He was my advisor and carried out all of my instructions. He knew my entire family, because he worked in my factory delivering merchandise, together with Hela, Cesia's best friend. He was a friend of my childhood buddy Wartski, who went to *heder* with me until age six, when I could still hear.

Wartski emigrated to Australia before the war because he saw it would be very bad for Jews when Hitler takes over Poland. Mietek was my most loyal friend since the time I was in the ghetto, and outside the ghetto, and during the uprising and even after the war in Poland and in America. He was the first one to begin living on the Aryan side. He was still a bachelor then. After I left Kalisz and was staying with Cesia and the children in the Otwock Ghetto, in the home of a Jewish blacksmith, it was Mietek who brought me an anonymous letter to that ghetto, warning me to leave the residence with my wife and children because the Gestapo was hunting me.

The beginning of his career on the Aryan side was very interesting. He became a smuggler, to and from the ghetto. Mietek completely believed in my family's luck, so he asked my brother Abram, who lived in Warsaw, to give him his widest pants so he could use them to smuggle out children's clothing made in the ghetto and sell the clothing in Kercelak [a large market for goods in Warsaw]. And indeed, when he smuggled merchandise in those pants, the ghetto guards never caught him. He had a type of transit permit for the ghetto, a forged document he purchased. He had a license in exchange for a monthly payment, and continually expanded his business until he jokingly referred to himself as a wholesaler that is, he smuggled with the help of trucks. He had someone on the Aryan side who received his merchandise, stored, and sold it.

He loved his mother very much, and his father and sister. First of all, he saved his mother and rented a room for her with a married couple from the intelligentsia, because his mother had very good command of the Polish language. He even arranged a husband for his sister: They married and lived separately. His mother, Helcia, was always the apple of his eye, and he spoke with her on the telephone every day, even several times a day. I visited her from time to time in her apartment. We had interesting conversations.

He also brought sewing machines from the ghetto of course, only their heads. He kept a few heads of overlock sewing machines in his home, and sold the rest to Mrs. Pinkus, I think. It occurred to me that, as a good mechanic, I could try to work in the field of sewing machines. He placed an overlock machine on the table and asked me to study its mechanism. In the factory in Kalisz, I had many overlocks for sewing curtain hems. But I never thought of getting involved in repairing these machines. We would take them for repair at the Singer branch in Łódz. Now, when Mietek went off on his business, I had time to learn the structure of the overlock. It was quite a complicated machine. Since I had observed overlocks for many years, and since I had also engaged in sewing, I had an idea how to take care of them, and I started to take an interest in the overlocks. He also put me in contact with mechanics who repaired special machines, and I observed their work.

He was still a bachelor then, and one time he brought me a boy and said he had no experience taking care of children, and asked me to bathe him. The boy was circumcised and I didn't know who he was. Later, Mietek brought me to a couple who survived on the Aryan side, thanks to an engineer who worked in their factory and his young wife. The couple was Max and Marysia Silberstein and the name of their child, whom I bathed, was Alek. They were from the Kolski family, and I didn't know them. Since Max usually lay in bed dressed in pajamas, I guessed that Mietek introduced me as a person who could be trusted to connect them with people on the outside, as they never left the house. Earlier, Max had asked me to sell his gold dollar coins, and said I could profit from this. I knew a café where there were traders of this type of foreign currency. I approached someone who looked decent and showed him the coins. He placed a coin on his fingernail, hit it with a pencil, brought it close to his ear, and apparently heard a sound that proved the coin was authentic and wasn't produced in the ghetto. Accordingly, he offered me a better price. R. from Kalisz, the son of the owner of the Oasis cinema there, approached and greeted me, and then went to the telephone and spoke freely. I was very surprised. He told me to come again and that he would tell me something then. But after seeing him speak freely on the telephone, I lost faith in him and didn't go back there. Later, I learned that the Poles shot him when he was in bed with his wife. I learned that he had been an undercover agent for the Gestapo.

Max [Silberstein] asked me to visit him, that he had a business proposal for me. When I came, he told me about his problems, that he was very scared of the SS, which was going around the city at night and searching for Jews who were hiding in the apartments of Poles. He begged that I do something for him. Max wanted a place where he could immediately hide when they knocked on the door at night, and he asked that I build a hiding place for him. I thoroughly examined the apartment and came to the conclusion that there was no suitable place to hide. I told him I would seriously think about what we could do, and would return the next day. I came back the next day and took measurements in the room and in the apartment, especially the thickness of the walls. I saw that the depth of the wall under the window was fifty-six centimeters. It was good that the apartment was on the ground floor, because the walls were narrower on the higher floors. I realized that the best place to hide was under the windowsill because there was no need to build a ceiling there. I sketched a drawing of a small cabinet under the window with precise measurements. I went to a carpenter to order a cupboard according to the drawing and the dimensions. I gave him the sketch of the cabinet. A few days later, I returned to the carpenter, asked him to disassemble the cabinet, which he had made with precision, so that I could take its parts and assemble them myself at the site. I asked the owner of the apartment, the engineer's wife, to remove the bricks and debris from the wall in a covered garbage pail and to empty it at night in the trash bin in the cellar, without anyone witnessing this. I started removing the bricks from the wall, slowly and without a sound. To prevent anyone from hearing the blows of the hammer, I wrapped it in rags when I hit the chisel. After I assembled the cabinet, I inserted it in the niche and then sealed it with cement all around so that it wouldn't budge. When everything was assembled and covered with cement, I asked Max to place a pillow and a thin blanket on the floor of the hiding place and to lie on it in the (closed) hideout for two hours in order to check whether the flow of air was sufficient via the two small holes I made. The test was successful. I told him to repeat this drill for two hours every day, and to let me know if he found any problem. Later, I told Max that I would give him some work to do, because he wasn't doing anything all day. He was excited to work. I told him that I would bring him wallpaper that he should paste on all of the walls in the room, but that I would do this myself on the hiding place and cabinet, so that there would be no trace of a concealed cabinet there. During the entire time, Marysia sat in the other room and didn't interfere with my work. I left them and forgot the whole matter. I was busy with work. A few weeks later, when passing through the neighborhood, I remembered them and went to visit. Silberstein embraced me, and kissed my face and hands. He said that the SS came at night with dogs, and found nothing. We were all happy. Then I forgot about them again.

Mietek took me to the workshop of Mrs. Pinkus. She managed a sewing workshop for women's undergarments, and he sold them. The workshop in her apartment was almost at the edge of Warsaw, and I had to get there by tram. The trip took about three-quarters of an hour. She had old, special sewing machines that Mietek had sold her for a lot of money. Mietek advised her on commercial matters and brought me there to maintain the machines so that there would be no halt in production. I came to her whenever a machine needed to be repaired. I earned very little, so I had to look for additional work. It was very difficult. I would buy sewing machine heads that were slated to be melted down; I brought them to my room and took them apart. I took whole parts to be coated with lacquer so they would look like new ones. Then I would precisely reassemble the machines after cleaning. Sometimes I bought parts I needed as replacements. There was a shortage of sewing machines, since they were not imported at all. So there was great demand for my supply. Sewing machine mechanics would give me the heads of special machines they didn't know how to fix, and I would fix them at home. This work became a source of some income for me. When they asked me for my address, I always answered that I don't give out my address because I have merchandise "on the left side" (illegal), and that I deliver the goods to the customer myself. Over time, I became a well-known deaf mechanic. [Note: In the second part of the tape recordings, Father finds it harder to talk and becomes emotional more often. Some physical weakness can be detected, and sometimes the chronology is out of sequence.]

One day, I went into a store on Nowy Świat Street. I went up to the first floor to select a manual spinning-wheel for Mrs. Pinkus, so she would have thread for the sewing machines. I left with the device in hand (it wasn't packaged) and I stood at the nearby tram stop. Mrs. Pinkus' apartment and workshop were at the edge of the city. I saw that a group of people had gathered. I didn't know why they had gathered; I thought they were waiting for the tram, but the trams passed and no one boarded them. Then, a person approached me, looked at me, and looked up. I also looked up and I saw a radio. The people who were ostensibly waiting for a tram were standing in the street in order to listen to a radio. Then a second person approached and looked at me, and then a third approached and looked at me. I thought to myself that I was being surrounded. When my tram arrived, I didn't board it right away I waited for it to start moving, and then I caught it on the run and jumped aboard. I entered the first car, which was reserved for Germans, and I sat in the first row of seats. I looked straight ahead at the windshield, as if looking at a mirror, to see whether they also had jumped onto the tram. I assumed they wouldn't dare to enter the Germans' car. But the tram had three cars. I sat motionless. The trip lasted for twenty [to] thirty minutes. When I got off, and was walking in the snowy street, someone suddenly approached me, a short man, and said something to me. I signaled to him that I couldn't hear what he was saying. He motioned with his hands that I must show him an identity card (Kennkarte). I replied scornfully, also with my hands, that he show me his ID. He took it from his pocket, showed me, but clutched it tightly. I grabbed the ID from him forcefully and took off. I saw that he worked at the airport, and that he wasn't a policeman. I put his ID in my pocket. I deliberately did the opposite of what Jews did when the extortionists asked them to identify themselves and then took their IDs from them. He came up to me and said, "Give the ID back to me." I asked, "You want the ID?" and I tossed it into the snow. He ran and pulled it out, and I went on my way with the device. Then I saw two men on the other side of the street. They wore long leather jackets, boots, like Gestapo personnel. It was clear to me that they were extortionists. The short man suddenly blocked my way. I went around him, and then threatened him with the device I was carrying, but I didn't hit him. He signaled to the other two. He apparently figured that a Jew could not behave as I did. I continued on my way. He didn't follow me. The two men also went on their way. I turned into a side street where Mrs. Pinkus lived. I didn't hurry. And they stood at the corner of the street and watched which house I would enter. I went to Mrs. Pinkus, placed the device on the floor, said I wasn't feeling well and would return the next day [to explain how to operate the device]. I didn't tell her what was happening. She commented that I looked very pale. "Yes," I said, "I don't feel well."

I went downstairs, but exited to the street through a different entrance to the house. I saw that one of them stood in front of the house. I continued to walk, [and] turned into another street. The street was completely empty, with tall buildings on both sides. One of them was set further back than the other houses. I thought it would be a good place, where they wouldn't notice me. I stood there, took the screwdriver from my bag and placed it in my belt. I put the bag on the ground and I waited. The two tall men in leather jackets and boots passed by, saw me, hesitated, talked among themselves, and walked very slowly. I laughed. I stood with my arms crossed against my chest. They saw that I was provoking them, hesitated, and continued walking at a slow pace. This time, I walked after them in the street. It was already dark. When they disappeared, I reached the tram station, and traveled to Stasia for lunch. Stasia asked why I was so pale. I told her I didn't feel well, that I had brought the spooling device to Mrs. Pinkus and had told her that I'd return to her the next day.

After these days of relative quiet, a great storm erupted. A telegram arrived from Cesia, urging me to come immediately to Brzesko. But this incident occurred later. Now I'll tell about something else that happened before those events. The Germans announced that they were willing to send the Jews who were hiding and wished to be released from their distress to Vichy, a French health resort. Many Jews who were hiding outside of the ghetto came to Hotel Polski and registered for the trip to Vichy. Two or three weeks before this German affair at Hotel Polski, I met Bronka at someone's home, and she gave me two packages of dark blue lace as a gift. I was very lucky to receive this gift, because I had no money left to pay Kuropieska for the month. Lace was very expensive then, and it was almost impossible to obtain. It gave me enough to pay for several months. Bronka apparently already knew about the affair, but didn't tell me anything. I learned about it from others and went alone to Hotel Polski to see for myself what was happening there. Many people were in the hotel's courtyard and rooms, many Jews. In one of the rooms, I found Bronka with a friend I knew named Berger. He registered people for departure and collected a payment from them. So Bronka and her children, Rysiek and Berta, were also there, and Domb, too. Bronka turned to me and offered to pay the ransom price for me if I was unable to pay. Though I didn't trust the Germans, I gave my consent to this because I was already exhausted and depressed, and was looking for a way out of this maze of hiding and the struggle to provide sustenance for the family. I viewed the trip to Vichy as lifesaving. So Bronka paid for me, for Cesia, and for Jurek and Ignaś, and I was told to go immediately and bring the family, because only a few days remained before the departure. I traveled urgently, straight to Kraków. I had to wait for two and a half hours for the connecting train to Tarnów, to Brzesko. In Kraków, I went to visit Kowalski, who was living temporarily with a German woman. I told him about everything that was happening, and that I was traveling to take my wife and son, with the intention of bringing them to the hotel in Warsaw, and from there to travel to Vichy. Kowalski was eating breakfast, which the German woman had prepared. I politely declined. He said that I could speak openly, that she didn't understand a word in Polish. So I told him everything in detail. Kowalski listened attentively and with great concentration. When I finished, he told me that he didn't trust the Germans one bit, that it was all a German ploy. When I told him that I planned to send only half of the family, he couldn't understand this. I told him this was like insurance that the second half would remain. To this, Kowalski replied that two basic things must be considered: A. traveling to Vichy meant certain death; B. remaining as Poles on the Aryan side meant either life or death, one of the two. In the end he got up, seeing that I was about to leave, stood tall and declared in forceful voice, "I won't permit it! Don't go!" I traveled to Brzesko and told Cesia everything, in detail, even everything that Kowalski said. I told Cesia to decide whether she would travel with one son, while I stayed with the other son, and that she should decide about herself, because I couldn't decide for her. It was a question of life and death. Cesia listened quietly to the whole story, and asked me in the end, "And what does your heart say about this?" Then I said that my heart told me that Kowalski was right. "So, if that's the case, let's stay," Cesia said. Okay, but meanwhile we had to inform Bronka to go without us. However, we had no way of doing this, because we didn't know a telephone number where we could reach her. Later, when I was in Warsaw with the Puchalski family, who rented a room with an older couple, Puchalski told me that Bronka had called her to say that she was waiting for us, and asked why we hadn't arrived. Puchalski replied that she didn't know anything, that she didn't even know anything about the Vichy business. And it ended with that.

Several weeks after that group traveled to Vichy, I received a postcard from Bronka with a picture of Vichy's beautiful scenery. She wrote that everything was fine, their lives were good and comfortable, they had a lot of food and were satisfied, and that it was a shame we weren't with them. That postcard made me think a lot. Kowalski insisted it was dictated by the Germans, with the sole aim of earning more ransom money in the same way. He claimed that the Jews were gullible, and would be "sucked in" by these promises. Afterward, no word came for several months from either the first or the second transports, and then this ploy largely faded from memory.

I forgot to say that before Ignaś came to Kuropieska, he was placed with the Markiewicz family. Markiewicz was a weaver who had worked longer than anyone else for me, and for my father; he was then living in a place far from Warsaw, in a workers' colony. He lived together with his wife, daughter, and son. The son belonged to the Polish underground and worked; I don't know whether he was already an adult. He became friendly with Ignaś, and then one day disappeared. I later learned that he was caught with other Poles and placed behind bars. [Note: This was an enigmatic relevation for me. Itzhak did not remember details of this period, and Father was no longer among us to be asked. It can be assumed that some-how a connection had been established between Markiewicz, Krzyczkowski, Mila (Frania), and Father.]

Now I'll move on to the subject of the telegram I received from Cesia and my ensuing trip to Brzesko. It turned out that Cesia received an anonymous letter from someone from Kalisz, who was always watching the Słotwina-Brzesko train station [and keeping track of] each train that arrived at the station. Several times he saw me exiting the train and walking to the city. Apparently, he followed me in order to discover where I lived with Cesia. He wrote in the letter that he knew who we were and that he wanted a payoff. He demanded that Cesia come to a certain place at a certain time with a diamond ring and that he would take it. I immediately suspected who the author of the unsigned letter was, and I knew what I had to do. Only someone from Kalisz could have known about us. I knew his brother, who became wealthy there in the flour milling business.

I also knew where he lived in Słotwina. I called Kowalski to accompany me, posing as a German. He responded to my call immediately; he was always ready to help. The previous day, I peeked into the office of the mayor of the village. The office was situated opposite the home of that wealthy man. That man noticed me, and I walked away, without speaking, as if nothing happened. I just wanted to confirm that the miller was alone and didn't have other people at his home. The next day, I came to the mayor with Kowalski. He was very alarmed. I asked him authoritatively where P. lives, and he pointed to the house across the street. We walked a short distance away, and I said to Kowalski that now the mayor would go and urgently warn P. that Germans had come and that he should flee from the house. When we approached P.'s house, we saw him suddenly emerge from the house with a new and shiny pair of shoes in his hand. When I greeted him and said I was coming to see him, he said that he was bringing shoes to the shoemaker and would be back right away. We went to his house and waited on the stairs. It was the ground floor of a villa built of wood. I joked with Kowalski, "You see, everyone who flees first of all thinks about shoes." He had new shoes in his hand, and it was just an excuse to say he was going to the shoemaker. At some point, he returned and invited us inside. His wife and I knew each other quite superficially from Kalisz. I introduced Kowalski as a friend who protects me. We had decided in advance that he wouldn't say a word, and then they would think from his appearance that he was a German who didn't speak Polish. I told P. that I wanted to lay everything on the table, straight and to the point. I asked, "Here's the letter. Do you recognize it?" After he read it, he confirmed that the letter was from his brother. Then his wife set the table and served good food: cold cuts, ham, bread, vodka, liquor. We finished the dinner and Kowalski didn't say a word. P. said to me that he would tell his brother not to do this. He said that his brother was a bit psychologically disturbed, so he wasn't working. For him it was just a game. He said he would keep an eye on him to prevent him from pursuing this foolishness, or engaging in similar acts of stupidity. In the end, I told P. that if anything happened to my wife and son as a result of his brother's actions, it would not only be bad for his brother, but also for him personally. I told him he should keep close watch over his brother and make sure that nothing bad happens, and that I lived in Warsaw and had friends working on my behalf. He asked that I bring my wife in the evening, and said he wanted to speak with her privately. To avoid alarming my wife, I could remain outside and wait for her. I agreed and we parted in customary fashion. We left. In the evening, I took my wife to P. and stood in front of the house. After a short time, Cesia came out and we walked home. And I learned what he said. He told Cesia that she could live quietly in Brzesko until I found a place in Warsaw where I could move her. He could vouch for his brother only for a limited period of time and no more, since his brother was not entirely normal. He might tell someone else who could use this against her. But meanwhile he would protect her, until I found a place in Warsaw for Cesia and the son. In short, getting out of this new complication was beyond my power. If my memory doesn't deceive me, first I took Jurek to Warsaw, and left Cesia for another period of time in Brzesko.[14]

With Jurek, it was a very difficult matter. I told Kuropieska that there was a mishap with Ignaś' brother and asked if she would be willing to take him. Kuropieska replied, "Okay," she would take him in. I had to think carefully how to bring Jurek into the apartment in a way that no one would take notice of him. This was when Ignaś was no longer free, but had been in hiding in her home for some time. She came up with a very clever stratagem for bringing Jurek into the apartment. So, Wojtek put on a short winter coat with fur and hid his face from the cold with his hat. Jurek waited in a park not far from there. Wojtek came to Jurek, dressed him in his coat and hat, put on Jurek's coat and remained in the park. Then I walked up with Jurek, as if he were Wojtek, and called to him, "Wojtek! Wojtek!" and entered the apartment. Then, I packed Wojtek's coat and hat in a package and brought it to the park, and Wojtek wore them and returned home alone. I packed Jurek's coat into the package; about an hour later, I came to the apartment with the package.

---

14   Father did not mention, and perhaps did not remember at the time of the recording, the period that Marek (Yoseph or Jurek) spent in Kielce and the period following his return from there to Brzesko. He referred only to a later period, about the time when the snow melted after the winter of 1943-44, and Marek traveled with Mateusz to Warsaw, while Krystyna (Cesia) remained alone in Brzesko until May or June of 1944.

5. Warsaw

So, the two brothers were together now. Pleased with this situation, I hurried to bring Cesia and the luggage to Warsaw. In the layover between switching from the Warsaw train to the Tarnów train, I would go to the Jaworskis' home to avoid being out in the city. I fervently hoped that after bringing Cesia to Warsaw, the train rides from Warsaw to Kraków, and Brzesko, and back would finally be over. The journey was about seven hundred kilometers. This demanded considerable effort and entailed a lot of anxiety. Passengers boarded and disembarked. There were Polish refugees everywhere. Some could be from Kalisz, so I needed to be very careful to avoid being recognized by someone. When I feared that someone was following me, I would enter the compartment of German soldiers, who were returning from France en route to the Russian front. I wore a yellow ribbon on my arm with the inscription **Taubstumm** (deaf-mute) in Gothic letters, which the Germans found difficult to decipher. But no one asked about this, not even the Germans. The soldiers shared cognac with me that they had brought from France. These were special cars for the German Army; it was strictly prohibited for Poles to enter them, so I had some quiet there. I can't exactly remember the details of Cesia's trip with me from Brzesko. I told the Herberts and the Gardziels that I had found a job in Warsaw, and that I could take members of the family with me so they could live together there in better conditions. I can't remember where I brought Cesia at first. In any case, Cesia stayed with Mietek and Stasia for a while. [According to the Gardziels' testimony, Mother might have left for Warsaw on her own in May or June 1944.]

Now, I need to go back several months in time, when a huge tragedy occurred in the Jewish ghetto in Warsaw. I don't remember whether I already described this after my second heart attack several years ago. Now I'll tell about the ghetto a few months before the uprising, when they sent the Jews to the Umschlagplatz, together with Janusz Korczak and his orphans. I would enter the ghetto as a Pole. The gate was guarded by a German and a Polish policeman. The armed German walked back and forth, and the Polish policeman was unarmed and only checked the documents of those entering the ghetto. I would give him the document with some money inside it. He would discreetly pull out the bill and return the document to me. At first when the ghetto was formed, I would enter the ghetto to visit my two sisters and their children, and my sister-in-law Bronka and her children; Bronka lived in her apartment without her husband, who fled to Russia when Warsaw was captured. In the summer, I worked in the factory in Kalisz. I stole merchandise, smuggled it across the border, and gave it to my sisters so they would have something to sustain themselves. At the end of this period, Cesia and the children lived together in the ghetto in Otwock.

Now, during the days of the the mass extermination of Jews in the Warsaw Ghetto [The "*Grossaktion Warschau*"], they were ostensibly sending Jews to work in the East, but in reality, people didn't actually know where they were being sent. Previously, the two parts of the ghetto were connected by a bridge above Chłodna Street. This time, only one part of the ghetto remained, the larger one, and the smaller one was liquidated. Cesia's older sister Bala (Balcia) Bloch and her daughter Esther (Lalusia) were sent from Otwock to Poniatów. Her husband, Herman Bloch, was a policeman in Otwock and he was hiding somewhere. The ghetto in Otwock was liquidated. Later, the Jews in the Warsaw Ghetto had to leave the apartments and search for workshops in which to live and survive. But my sister Regina, who wore a necklace with a small bottle of poison, could not stand to suffer any longer, and gave the poison to her children to drink and drank it herself. That was the end. My sister Ala remained in her apartment as a house manager for the Germans, who set up a factory there to produce steel helmets. She hid the children to keep them from being murdered. I came to visit her then, this time pretending to be a sewage worker. The ghetto was already closed then; there were no guards. So I entered and mixed in among workers. They gave me a hat so that I would look like a sewage worker. I went to Ala, my sister, and told her that Mietek had found someone from Kalisz who was willing to take in Ninka, her daughter. But her son could not join her because a boy would be conspicuous. I came especially to take Ninka with me. But Ala asked what would happen with her son, Marek, and with her. I immediately responded that it was impossible to find them a place on the Aryan side, and that we had to take care of each person, one at a time. Ala replied that she wouldn't hand over Ninka I would have to take all of them or no one. So I realized nothing could be done. She was adamant. Then an SS man came he was missing one arm. He saw me and asked who I was. Ala gave some explanation and told me to go. I had to disappear; otherwise, they would have shot me. I left the ghetto with the same workers. In the streets, I saw feather and woolen blankets, and discarded chairs, and I realized it was already the end of the ghetto. There were just a few people left. The streets became empty of people and full of garbage.

Soon afterward, a horrible tragedy occurred in the ghetto. It was Passover and a German effort to conduct a "final *Aktion*" sparked a Jewish uprising in the Warsaw Ghetto. I had intended to visit Ala again, because I assumed she had changed her mind. I found the ghetto surrounded by Lithuanians with long, thin rifles. They stood about seven to eight meters apart from one another. There was no possible way to enter. That same day, a few hours later, the Germans were already firing at the homes, and there was shooting from the homes at the Germans. There were German casualties. Later, a German tank entered and fired in all directions, setting the houses ablaze. I saw one plane dive from the sky and drop incendiary bombs on buildings and then disappear. I circled around the ghetto; I saw women covering themselves to protect their modesty and jumping from top floors, from windows, and from balconies with children in their arms. I saw grenades exploding that killed Germans. More and more houses went up in flame, tall city buildings; the red flames rose high into the sky. I saw Poles watching the battles in the ghetto. Some were saddened, and some rejoiced, rubbing their hands in glee and joking that they were burning the lice-infected. For them it was a theater performance. During the battles between the Jews and the Germans, the ghetto was clearly lit up at night, and you could see Germans evacuating the dead bodies of their comrades. The defenders had prepared for this battle, which continued for weeks. They prepared bunkers for themselves in advance, which the Germans were unable to destroy so quickly. I went to Kuropieska's apartment; from the window, I could see the ghetto burning. I wanted to be with my son. I cradled Ignaś to my breast, so he would know who was lost there. He knew everyone from before the beginning of the expulsion from Kalisz to Otwock. [Father can be heard sobbing. Father was very emotional when speaking about the loss of his sisters and the destruction of the ghetto.] I told him there was an uprising in the ghetto. At that moment, Kuropieska arrived. Turning to me, she pointed at the fire in the ghetto and said, "Look what the Germans did." And I remained silent. I was still in shock from standing close to the ghetto. And so the ghetto burned for several weeks. No one could extinguish that fire. The houses were destroyed by cannon fire in order to bury those hiding in the basements, the insurgents who fought courageously, without any help from the Poles. The Poles just did good business from this: They sold the Jews weapons, even old ones, for a lot of money. The partisan organizations AK and AL "fell asleep" and didn't lift a finger to help.

My story, as I see it today, cannot be in exact chronological order, because over forty years have passed since this momentous occurrence. Sometimes it's hard for me to decide which occurrences to place in context with each other.

Mrs. Kuropieska firmly demanded that I take Jurek with me and place him somewhere else. She was unable to handle him because he was being too loud. When he played, he sometimes jumped, and sometimes moved chairs on the floor, and the neighbors from the floor below asked her who that stranger was who was making so much noise. Later, there was a huge mishap with Jurek. Basia came to Mietek to inform me that extortionists had discovered Jurek in the hiding place her grandfather had built. A "blue" Polish policeman and another man dressed in civilian clothes entered the apartment and demanded to conduct a search. They went straight to the hiding place; they knew where it was. Jurek and two women who were hiding there were pulled out. Ignaś sat quietly on the top shelf and was not discovered. Kuropieska was so shocked she almost fainted. In order to get rid of the uninvited guests, she took off her diamond ring and gave it to them so they would leave. After this, all of the people hiding there had to evacuate the apartment, except for Ignaś the only one Mrs. Kuropieska was willing to continue to hide in her apartment.

I can no longer remember how I made contact with Geniek Łoza to ask him to come to the train station in Warsaw, to take Jurek with him to his family, and to place him in the hands of his sister, Mrs. Irena Nowak, in Słotwina-Brzesko. I also gave him a sewing machine head to keep with him in case I didn't have money to pay for his upkeep on time. Mrs. Nowak received Jurek with great kindness and treated him like her fourth child.

Soon afterward, another extortionist visited Kuropieska's apartment, again searching for Jews. Even though Ignaś was not discovered he hid under a down blanket that Leopolda sat on we decided to move him out of the apartment. Frania brought him to the apartment of Stasia and Mietek. Leopolda became so ill that she immediately traveled to her sister in Częstochowa. Basia was helpless and didn't know what to do. Basia and Wojtek remained at home alone, without their mother. I had an opportunity to go there and take care of them.

We occasionally traveled to Krzyczkowski, who lived in an area of fields outside the city. He had recently remarried, and the couple lived temporarily with the wife's parents. They didn't have an apartment. His first wife left him, leaving him with four bare walls. I asked Krzyczkowski to rent an apartment and live together with Cesia and Ignaś. This would give them the protection of a trustworthy man. He said he would try. A few days later, I met him in the city and he told me that he had found a residence in a good area, but that it cost a lot of money, and he couldn't afford to rent an apartment in a new building. One apartment remained for sale, and not for rent. It was apparently the only building that was constructed during the war. I was happy about what he had found. I told him to register the apartment in his name. He would receive ownership of the apartment if he kept Cesia and Ignaś with him in one of the two rooms in the apartment, and the other room would be for his use. We shook hands to signify our mutual agreement and satisfaction.

[Ignaś moves from Mietek and Stasia to Mr. Krzyczkowski.] I went to the Powiśle quarter to buy a pair of new shoes for Ignaś in the black market, without [ration] coupons. He had grown and could no longer wear his old shoes. I helped him put on the new shoes, and in the evening I told him to leave the house and walk until he saw me about one hundred meters behind him, and to keep walking at this distance ahead of me until we boarded a tram. But I already saw from the window that he was slipping a lot in those new shoes. Perhaps he forgot how to walk, or the soles were simply too slick. So I went up to him and roughened the soles with a stone to make it easier for him to walk. He walked, and I followed him. I had a long, thin screwdriver in my pocket that I always kept in my bag and used as a work tool. It was a very sharp screwdriver and it was easy to stab with it. His hair had grown; it was a long time since he had a haircut, and he had sort of side curls. So it was easy to recognize that he was a Jewish boy. At the tram station, he stood a distance from me. I gave him money for a ticket and told him to board the tram and stand at the other end of it, and to watch me carefully. When we got off the tram, he walked about fifty steps behind me until we arrived.

Every Sunday morning, I visited Jews in hiding in order to deliver the monthly payments to the owners who kept them in exchange for payment - good money. In one particular case, I didn't see the Jew who was hiding. I didn't worry, I was busy; I think I was in Brzesko. When I came to pay the next time, I again didn't see this Jew in hiding. I asked the owner of the house (he was a single man) where that Jew was. He replied in sign language, his hands shaking, that the person had left. I asked him if he had turned him over to the Germans. He answered in a vague manner, and from this I deduced that this indeed had occurred. I said to him, "We'll meet again." He trembled from head to toe. I left and went to the man who gave me the money to pay the owner, returned the money, and demanded that they shoot him, because he had it coming to him. They should send people from the underground to do this. The next time I met with him, he told me when those people would come to shoot that informer, and that I should wait in the courtyard and give them a signal. That's what I did. They arrived in a car. I was surprised to see them dressed in Nazi uniforms and carrying weapons. They asked me his name and where he lived. I gave them his name and said that he lived on the bottom floor, and where. A moment later, there was shooting and they immediately emerged. A jeep stood in the courtyard; they got in and drove off.

Meanwhile, I got a new job in the munitions company of the German Army, totally by chance. An advertisement for a sewing machine mechanic appeared in a Polish newspaper. I went to the address that appeared in the advertisement, I opened the gate, and I saw German guards standing there. I figured I was at the wrong address, but it was indeed the address that appeared in the advertisement. The guards approached me and asked why I had come. I showed them the advertisement and they directed me to the office. I entered the office and saw a tall, fat German with a swastika on the lapel of his jacket, and a Polish secretary who knew German. He spoke German to me, and I pretended I didn't understand the language. He called the secretary to help translate. I said that the advertisement didn't mention the type of company, and that it was my mistake, because deaf people were not subject to compulsory labor for the Germans, which paid just five złoty per day. The manager told the secretary to tell me that he would pay from his own pocket the difference between my wage and the standard pay for laborers. He asked me what I thought. I looked at him and figured there was no room for bargaining. But I saw by the expression on his face that he was apparently a decent man and that he urgently needed a mechanic. It was a large factory and they had no sewing machine mechanics.

I asked if I could have a tour of the factory to observe its work processes. He told the secretary to call the foreman, who arrived immediately and spoke in German with the manager. Then the foreman led me to the first floor of another building, introduced the workers, and showed me the factory, including machines waiting to be repaired. But I paid no attention to the machines. Instead I studied the faces of the people to see if anyone might know me and would be able to turn me in. While scanning the faces of strangers, I encountered a familiar face that of Alexander Wasserman from Kalisz. He was the son of a factory owner and had completed a degree in chemistry at the Sorbonne. He was blond and blue-eyed, very handsome, a beautiful young man, but now he looked bad. He also recognized me, but we pretended that we didn't know each other. Now the foreman asked me to take a close look at the machines that were waiting for repair. For the first time in my life, I saw sewing machines for fur - big ones. I felt frightened, but I told my escort that it would be child's play for me. Everything would be fine if I took on this work. It was a big sewing workshop that sewed fur coats for the German Army for the front. I thought to myself that if Wasserman could work in this factory, it would certainly be suitable for me, too, and there was no special fear of being discovered. I went to the office downstairs, and the manager was no longer there. The secretary asked me, "So, what did you decide?" I told her it was a beautiful factory, but that I would need a few days to think before deciding. She asked, "And if another mechanic comes, should we hire him or not?" I told her that I could work on a trial basis and if I continued, I would stay and take the job permanently. So I stayed. It was one of the factories owned by the German industrialist Walther C. Többens in Warsaw.

Mateusz Filipowski's work permit at the factory of Walther C. Többens, renewed every two weeks. The factory was first located in Warsaw and later in Piotrków.

The work certificate I received proved to be excellent for protection and cover. It was a certificate from the Ministry of Armament, with a swastika and SS stamps, and with a date that was renewed every two weeks. The next day, I came to work and was assigned to fix the machines that awaited repair. I had no idea how the machines operated. In order to become thoroughly familiar with them, I started to disassemble all of the parts of one machine. The foreman came, his eyes gaping wide in astonishment, and asked angrily about this major overhaul. I replied that I was familiar with other types of machines, and needed to study these closely in order to know how to fix them. He was silent, because he had no other mechanic. We went on to the sewing workshop. Very young and beautiful women worked sewing the furs, girls from Warsaw. They came to work here to avoid being sent to forced labor in Germany. I carefully studied the sewing work of these women in order to get an idea of how these machines operated. When I finished putting together the first disassembled machine, the fur seamstresses started to suddenly come to me with requests to repair their machines when they ostensibly malfunctioned. I didn't have time for everything. I repaired machines in a random order and argued that I could not satisfy all of them at once. I could just take care of one machine at a time. The skilled furriers cut the furs and gave them to the girls to sew. I saw that they hid entire furs under their work tables. Later, the furriers smuggled them out of the factory with the help of these girls, who were not inspected by the Army. The guards were fully aware that theft was occurring and they joked about it. They would turn to women and tell them that when they entered they were light afoot, and when exiting they looked pregnant. Each furrier had a seamstress who smuggled fur for him. They absconded with scraps of fur, as well as complete fur vests. Officially, they received a meager wage of five złoty per day. They had to steal in order to survive.

Wasserman supplied furs for the work and transported the finished fur jackets to warehouses. One time, while I was fixing a machine, he came over to me and introduced himself by a different name (a Polish one, of course), and I introduced myself so that he would also know me by my assumed name, Mateusz Filipowski. We shook hands as new acquaintances, as if meeting for the first time. Since no one was nearby, we could speak relatively freely. I asked him, "Why do you look so bad? You were so handsome and now you're so thin, your ears stick out, your nose has become long and prominent, and so on. You're the only one who looks like someone who fled from the ghetto, and here everyone looks plump as a pig." He replied that everyone was stealing, and that he was the only one who didn't steal. He was afraid of getting caught and being discovered as a Jew. I responded, "You're wrong. I order you to do the same as everyone else and steal. Otherwise, you'll come to a bad end. You'll stand out and they'll discover you." He said that every furrier who stole had a woman, who smuggled for him. If he wanted to do this, he wouldn't be able to find a young woman. So I told him, "Okay, I'll try to find a woman who will take furs out for you. You must eat! Pork, lard, ham until you become ruddy like everyone. The back of your neck should be thick like a pig's. I don't want you to meet with me at work the way you look now." When a new candidate for work arrived, I brought her to Wasserman and introduced them. She was a dancer in a nightclub, young and gorgeous. Afterward, Wasserman glowed when he saw me. Some time passed, and I noticed that he didn't look bad at all, and his appearance continued to improve. His mother lived in the apartment with him, and he had to earn money. She was the only person close to him. His brother, a physician in the Jewish hospital Szpital Starozakonnych na Czystem in Warsaw, was shot to death by the Germans.

In regard to my work at this factory, I went to the manager's office and told him via the interpreter that I didn't want to be paid from his own pocket. Instead, I asked to take a number of sewing machine heads that were missing key parts. I saw that he was writing in a notepad which parts were disassembled from the machines. I knew that Jews in Poniatów dismantled important parts from the machines and threw them away so that the Germans wouldn't be able to use them (after sending the Jews to their death). I told him that these machines were not very valuable and that I would have to wait a long time to receive the missing parts from Germany. I told him I wanted ten heads. His eyes opened wide, as if to say: So many? So I told him it was not a lot and that my work during one month was worth more. He agreed, and told me I could choose. Of course, I chose the heads that were in greatest demand in the market. They were heads of special machines, which could be sold for a high price, even though the missing parts were ordered in Germany and I had to wait for them to arrive. I selected and gathered ten heads in one place so they could be quickly and easily loaded onto a wagon surface. I noticed a platform tied to a pair of horses, and asked the manager to issue me a transit permit so that the guards would allow me to transport them. The document stated, *Der Mechaniker Mateusz Filipowski nimmt heute zehn Maschinenköpfe für Reperatur für drei Wochen lang, bitte, lassen Ihm passen.* (The mechanic Mateusz Filipowski today is taking ten machine heads for repair for three weeks, please, let him pass.)

I sat on the platform to make sure nothing happened on the way that no head or part of it fell from the wagon or was stolen. We rode in front of the house where I lived, also on Grzybowska Street. I got off, struggled to carry the ten heads, one at a time, up to the third floor apartment, and I arranged them in the kitchen. I told Michał, my roommate, that they were heads I had taken to repair for the Germans, and that I would wait until I received the missing parts from Germany and gradually return them to the factory. Soon afterward, the manager came and asked me to install a machine for sewing gloves in another production hall, behind the office. Through a mechanic I knew, I obtained a special sewing machine for this, complete, and installed it in a way that suited the required products. The manager hired an expert in producing gloves from before the war, and he expressed satisfaction. I told him that the money I earned was not enough, and that instead I would take more heads the next month. Meanwhile, the commander of the guards came to me and said that three weeks had passed already and I still hadn't returned any repaired heads, and that it was time for me to return them. He asked what was happening. I told him I was still waiting for parts from Germany that had yet to arrive, and that when they arrived, I'd bring back [the repaired heads]. In any case, it was almost time for the next payment. I was fearful that the guards would ask me again when I planned to return them. On the day when I was supposed to return them, I went to the manager and said that the guards were asking me all the time, and that I didn't feel comfortable with this. How could I take machine heads a second time? He thought for a moment and then turned to me and said I could relax, everything would be okay. When I arrived the next day and opened the gate of the factory, I saw that the entire contingent of guards had been replaced. New faces. I wanted to ask the manager how he did this, but I figured he must have sent his group of guards to the Russian front. The next time, I received a transit permit for fifteen heads. The kitchen in the apartment filled with heads, which stood against the wall.

Earlier, Mietek had brought Michał to me. He was a former Polish policeman who had committed some crime and had to hide from the Germans. He was the husband of Stasia's cousin. I didn't know what type of person he was, but I couldn't refuse to take him in, because Mietek and Stasia had done so many favors for me. He slept with me in the same bed and prayed before going to sleep.

Soon afterward, Mietek bought an apartment with his money and registered it in my name, on the condition that I would take in Michał and his wife, Hela; he would hide under my name. It was a third floor apartment with one room and a kitchen, and my name was supposed to be on the door. The three of us slept in a single room on two beds. Michał cleaned the machine heads, just as he cleaned the floors. He served lunch and dinner to all of us. He walked around in stocking feet and wouldn't open the door to anyone when someone rang. He never left the house except for when it was dark at night. When I returned from work, he would listen to my explanations about what was happening from a German newspaper. Soon afterward, I installed an overlock, a special sewing machine, in the room. I taught him to sew women's underpants and tricot shirts. Mietek would bring the cloth and take the finished products, and sell them to stands in the Kercelak market. In this way, Michał had a full day of employment, and even made a good living.

One morning, an incident occurred in the courtyard of the Többens factory. Large trucks came and unloaded clothes and shoes from the death camps, some of them stained and covered with blood, including even shoes and clothes of little children. It was a huge pile. When I looked at it, I was disgusted to see how the Poles quickly scooped up these shoes and clothes. It pained and weighed upon my heart. [Father becomes emotional, almost weeping.] I was surprised the Poles had sunk to such a low level, to be humiliated by the Germans to the point of taking the clothing of murdered people, even of children, with blood stains on them. After two or three days, there was no trace of the huge pile of clothes. I asked myself why the Germans brought this clothing to the Poles instead of burning it and concealing what took place.

One morning, the Army, the SS, and other Nazi organizations conducted a hunt in the streets. They arrested me, too, but when I showed them the document from Többens, they released me immediately, and I went to work. About a half an hour or an hour later, everyone was watching out the factory windows at the yard where a group of Poles were being led. The Germans sent them one by one and stood them with their face against the wall with hands raised. About twenty people stood like this by the wall. Then shots were heard, and they fell one after another. The Germans left, leaving the bodies in the square. Poles came and took these executed people away, placed flowers, and lit candles. The work document from Többens saved my life more than once. There was even a case when Jewish acquaintances asked me for help in getting an apartment for them after having been refused everywhere. When I arrived and showed the owner the document, the people were immediately accepted into the residence.

When I took the machines from Többens, none of the workers noticed this. Therefore, I was about the only worker who wasn't thought to be a thief like the others. They feared me, suspecting that I was a planted informer. One day, while I was repairing a machine in the workshop, I noticed a man, sent by the furriers, hovering around me. He circled me several times, and then approached me by surprise and asked me how I supported myself without stealing. After all, it was impossible to exist on the meager wages. I felt threatened, without knowing exactly why, but I plucked up my courage and was quick-witted: I told him that I didn't steal small things, only big things. Then he asked me, "What?" So, as an explanation, I said, "This machine, whose serial number is such and such, you see it standing here? When you come to work tomorrow, it will no longer be here." He looked at me and it appeared that I had won his respect, which no one else had won. He walked away, satisfied. I don't remember which trick I used to make sure the machine would indeed be missing the next day. Instead of that machine, a different one stood there for repair. After that, I felt at ease; I wasn't afraid of him. A long time afterward, I was quite alarmed when the manager walked around me several times, while I was repairing a machine in the workshop. He gave me a strange look and smiled under his moustache. I was sure that he suspected I was a Jew. In general, the main topic of conversation in Warsaw was: Jews, Jews and again Jews. I called Wasserman aside and asked to speak with him in the street where no one was watching. In a written message, I explained my fears. He calmed me and said that the manager himself was a Jew. Every day, he organized soccer competitions during the work breaks so that the Poles would stop chattering about Jews, and so that he himself would feel better concealed. He also disclosed to me that he knew of another Jew, an expert furrier. During the breaks in the afternoon, we all gathered in the dining hall and had soup with a slice of bread. Now I could look people straight in the eyes without my previous fears.

I don't remember how I managed to collect such large sums of money that enabled me to buy an apartment in cash. I gave the money to Krzyczkowski without a receipt and without any control. Later, I deeply regretted giving the Többens' address, where I worked, because after some time, he came to the Többens factory and complained to me that the apartment was empty, without a single piece of furniture. How could he live in it? I thought this was a bit of chutzpah on his part, and it looked to me like extortion. I was in his hands. I explained to him that I had given him all of the money for purchasing the apartment, and that he should wait patiently for additional payments. I would pay him in monthly installments so that he could slowly buy the furniture he needed most. In any case, I had to give an address to him and to Cesia, an address where they could contact me. I didn't give the address of my apartment to anyone, not even to Cesia. Only Mietek and Stasia knew my address.

When Jurek was in the care of Nowakowa, and Cesia and Ignaś were being cared for by Krzyczkowski, I was finally at ease to focus on working and making money in order to provide for all of us. I continued to come to Kuropieska after she returned from Częstochowa. I offered to continue to pay her as I did when Ignaś was with her, but she refused. When I secretly put this money into a drawer in the living room, she asked me the next time why I did this, because she didn't want the money, and she put the envelope back in my pocket. When Cesia and Jurek still lived in Brzesko, she made her living as an elite seamstress of women's clothing, and she had regular customers.

I traveled to Słotwina-Brzesko to visit Jurek. At Mrs. Nowakowa's home, I met Kowalski, who shared an apartment in her home with Jurek. When I gave money to Mrs. Nowak, she refused and said that I should keep it for myself. [He becomes emotional.] She said that I needed it more than her. I had left a sewing machine head with her, which her brother Geniek brought from Warsaw when he took Jurek from Warsaw back to Brzesko. I told her she should keep the head with her for "a black hour" and that in the meantime, I would pay her all of the money she deserved and another month in advance. I found Jurek in good condition; he was cheerful, satisfied, played with Mrs. Nowakowa's children, and felt free. Kowalski shampooed his hair, which had previously been bleached so he would have blond hair. He asked about his brother Ignaś and about his mother. Kowalski cooked meals for himself and for Jurek. He loved potatoes and said there could be no lunch without them.

Kowalski was cut off from Sandomierz when that city was captured by the Russians. Fortunately, he brought money with him for conducting commerce. He engaged in trade in cigarettes and other products that were under the Generalgouvernement's monopoly, but he didn't buy merchandise to trade because of the cutoff from Sandomierz. Kowalski told me that he wanted to use the money he had to make a profit from trading, and that he also wanted to give me a chance to profit. He put me in contact with an acquaintance of his, Z., who became my business partner. He had an idea of buying gold dollar coins near Warsaw, because people were selling them cheaply there. We would sell them here and split the differential in purchase-selling price fifty-fifty.

I set off with the money that Z. gave me. Near Warsaw that is, in a suburb where there were few people, I looked for a place where there was trade in foreign currency. I met a few people and bought several twenty-dollar coins. I went immediately to Brzesko, gave the coins to Z., and told him how much they cost. He went into the city, and immediately sold them, and he fairly divided the profit between us. I was pleased.

The same thing occurred on the second visit. I set out again, this time with a larger sum. I returned with gold coins in a belt. But at the Piotrków station I saw that the Germans were surrounding the entire train. The passengers realized what was happening. They ordered everyone to disembark and to go to the station hall. There was a big crowd, and I saw the Germans finding dollars on the women, and how they loaded the women onto a truck. Meanwhile, the men waited for their turn to be searched. The Germans set up tables and placed typewriters on them, and they checked each person's documents in turn. There were about four people conducting the searches and several officials typing on the machines. I thought to myself that I needed to get rid of the gold, because if they found it, they would send me off on a truck.

But I calmed down after a moment. I watched how the Germans were searching: running their hands over the whole body, from top to bottom. I saw there was a fat German with a protruding belly, who could not bend down to shoe level, only to the knees. So, I went in his direction. I took the coins from the belt and when I was still far back and no one could see, I bent down as if to fix my shoelace and I slipped the coins under my sock.

The coins stuck to the soles of my feet and I stood on gold.

I went up to that fat guy. He started the search with my bag, then my sleeves by the shoulders, my underarms, stomach, knees ... and stop! I breathed a sigh of relief that I hadn't gotten rid of the gold. He instructed me to proceed to a second hall at the station, which was already full of people. I went there. There was no snack bar, no water and no bathroom. Everyone became irritated. As it was growing dark, I looked at the clock and knew that the police curfew would soon go into effect and that I wouldn't be able to go into the city during the night. I didn't know what they wanted to do with us. I thought to myself, *They took the women in trucks, and when the trucks return they'll take us in them, too.* I was very worried. I thought I should flee. But there was nowhere to flee. I decided on an act of desperation. I knocked loudly on a door. I was wearing my armband with "deaf-mute" written on it in German Gothic letters. I banged on the door and kicked with my feet until someone opened and asked what I wanted. I handed him a piece of paper requesting the return of the ID of someone with the family name so and so, because I was in a hurry. So, they looked for the ID and gave it to me. Then I headed for the exit. The same soldier followed me. I figured he was going to shoot me for sure, so I decided to take a risk. What could I do? I walked toward the exit. Meanwhile, he pulled out the pistol from his holster and shoved me so I'd continue walking there. Then I walked very close to wall so that he'd miss if he fired. I suddenly broke into a sprint. I turned my head and saw that he was surprised, but was still holding the pistol in his hand. I ran and went into the city, ten minutes before the start of the curfew. I walked and ran alternately until I reached the home of a deaf-mute shoemaker, an acquaintance of mine, who lived in the basement.

After sleeping at night, I hurried to the train station early in the morning, but I was afraid of entering that station because I wasn't sure whether the people who had been detained were still there or perhaps Germans. So I walked to the next station where the train stopped. I didn't encounter anyone there, so I boarded the train. When I arrived at my base, I didn't mention a word about this adventure to Z., Kowalski's acquaintance. He asked me whether I wanted to try again. I replied, "I'm exhausted, I want to rest a bit. When I come again to visit, we can do a lot of business."

6. The uprising in Warsaw

And now I'll tell about the uprising by the Poles in Warsaw in the summer.

The Russians that is, the Red Army advanced rapidly toward Praga, the eastern neighborhood of Warsaw, across the Vistula (Wisła) River. There was tension in the air. They didn't issue stamps for the next two weeks of work at the Többens factory. The guards abandoned their posts at the factory. Of course, they closed it. The Kierbedź and Poniatowski bridges were packed with pedestrians who wanted to cross to Praga. I also debated whether to cross to Praga in order to be liberated from the Germans sooner. But it was already too late. The uprising appeared to be imminent. I went to Krzyczkowski's apartment, where my wife Cesia and son Ignaś were hiding. On the way, I saw garages where they were installing armor on cars and making other preparations for the revolt. The Germans began to retreat, but encountered resistance from the Poles, and many Germans were captured by the insurgents.

When I arrived at the apartment, I found my wife and son in good health. The uprising immediately erupted in full force. They called upon citizens to dig anti-tank trenches. They recruited me, too, and I dug and dug until I became exhausted. Krzyczkowski was not in the apartment. Apparently he went to his unit in the Armia Ludowa (AL), the socialist underground. His wife didn't appear either not then, and not later. She apparently rode or walked to her parents somewhere in the suburb. I was grateful for my fate that the family was united, and that Jurek was in a safe place in Słotwina. This meant that the whole family was alive. [Father's voice quivers with emotion here.]

The trenches were dug wide and long, and we were sure the German tanks would be unable to cross to Warsaw. We lived almost at the edge of the city, and we saw that preparations for warfare had begun. The small children were the most active. For them, it was an adventure they prepared lots of Molotov cocktails to toss at the tanks. Gunfire and explosions of distant fighting could be heard. The suburb was in flames. The tanks fired at the houses and destroyed them one after another. The buildings collapsed and buried their inhabitants under the rubble. The Germans manned the tanks with Ukrainians, because they knew how the Ukrainians hated the Poles.

The tanks advanced slowly, firing at the houses and demolishing them, and they drew closer to our home. We saw how the children climbed onto the tanks, opened the turret hatch, and tossed the Molotov cocktails inside. Tanks burned. Those little ones were insanely courageous.

We couldn't sleep at night. They broke the door to the apartment, and there was no privacy. We gathered in the shelter below, and this was the first time we saw the residents of this new building. It turned out that there were Jews among them! The Poles fired at the tanks. The Germans, or perhaps they were Ukrainians, caught pregnant women and placed them in front of the tanks because they were certain the Poles wouldn't shoot at their pregnant women. They advanced toward the trenches. The pregnant women screamed, "Shoot, shoot!" But the Poles didn't fire because they didn't want to harm the pregnant women. The suburb was in flames. The houses became ruins, one after another. We had no choice but to abandon the house and prepare to wander toward the center of the city.

It got crowded and there were narrow transit corridors. We wandered for a long time before reaching my apartment, where I lived on the third floor on Grzybowska Street. Meanwhile, the planes bombed the houses in the center of the city with incendiary and explosive bombs. Immediately after entering the apartment, an alarm sounded. As quickly as possible, we found refuge in the shelter of a neighboring building, because there was no shelter in our house. Our home was immediately bombed and totally demolished. The house where we found the shelter was also destroyed, and we couldn't get out. We all tried to dig an opening through our wall to the neighboring house. The walls were thick and everyone had to help in the effort to carve an opening. Finally, we managed to create an opening and climbed through it to the shelter of the neighboring building - which was not destroyed, or was only partly destroyed - and we could get out.

We went into the street and looked at our house. It was a heap of rubble. We saw women tossing flowers on the ruins, certain that many of the residents were buried underneath, unable to reach the shelter in time. Not a single one of the more than twenty sewing machine heads I had earned from my work at the Többens factory remained. I had planned to sell them and this was a great loss for me. I had also hidden two brand new overlock machines in the basement, packed in crates. I had purchased them with my last remaining funds because I thought it would be the best financial investment. When I went to take them out, they weren't there. Now I was left penniless.

We went to Mietek's apartment, but there too the apartment was a heap of ruins, and we could only find shelter in the basement. [Michał, Hela and their infant Wiesio also gathered there with Mietek and Stasia.] Later, all of us, together with Mietek [and his parents and sister], Stasia [and Michał's family], and Basia [Rena Kolska], wandered to Łódzka Street, where Mietek had previously lived, and where we could rest in the apartment of people who were still living in it. Of course, we had no food with us, so we wanted to leave the city at night and look for food.

But when we walked in some destroyed neighborhoods, there was such strong bombing that we had to stop each time. In one abandoned military garage, we found a basement where we could take shelter. It was full of coats, and we rested on them. We lay down but couldn't fall asleep because we didn't feel safe enough as they could catch us any moment. So, we left, and we fearfully checked whether anyone was following us. The ground shook from the thunder of explosions. We had to find better shelter as fast as possible.

We came to a big building, in ruins. We decided to look for a shelter in the basement, because they certainly wouldn't bomb it again after all, it was demolished. We looked for a shelter in basements. We noticed a narrow hole in the ground. I crawled through it until I saw human excrement. I thought there were many people hiding there. The tunnel we crawled through became larger until we could stand up and walk upright. We came to a large hall containing boilers. It turned out that the hall was a power plant for the tram cars. A door from the hall led to a tunnel with large pipes; the pipes were apparently used as casing for electric cables. We walked on until we came to another hall, where people sat, tram workers. They didn't expect us to discover them, but they also couldn't expel us - they would be endangering themselves. They looked at us distrustfully, with hostility. Consequently, we didn't join them in the hall, but settled down a distance away from them, along the big pipe. There was still electric light there, powered by giant batteries. We lay on the ground and we were all hungry. Those tram workers had food; we didn't know where it came from.

The next day, I checked the tunnels and corridors around us. I saw a great many people, all tram employees. They had apparently planned in advance to enter this shelter, and certainly had prepared food. Otherwise, how did they think to survive? There were certainly hundreds of tram workers. They had even prepared places to go to the bathroom.

Meanwhile, Michał roamed around and sniffed out a food pantry not far from us. We didn't have drinking water and we were thirsty, so I searched with Mietek until we got to the boiler room, where there was water that condensed from the engines. We emptied the water and filtered it through cloth. We could drink. The tram employees had stockpiles of water. They didn't give us any, and we didn't ask them because we knew they would refuse. They could see for themselves that we had nothing, yet they didn't offer us anything.

At night, I managed to get out of this structure and searched for food in the bombed houses. At one point, I came to an abandoned carpentry workshop. I found hard crusts of bread on the windowsills. Apparently the toothless carpenters placed them there. There were quite a few of them and I took them all. I first thought of Ignaś, because he was still a boy who needed to eat. I offered him several crusts, but he refused. He said he wasn't hungry and that I should eat them. I moistened the crusts in water and gave them to him, "Eat!" He said he wasn't hungry, and just drank a little water. I marveled at his resilience after not eating for several days. I gave a few crusts to everyone, so they would have something to nibble. The only one who didn't experience hunger was the Michał and Hela's baby, because his mother nursed him.

Michał was distressed that his wife might become weak from hunger. He showed me the food pantry. A small window at the top was open. The pantry itself was closed. We decided that he would lift me up and I would enter through that window. I would fill my pockets with whatever I found. Of course, I agreed to this, though it was risky. There was no one around; we had to act very quickly. He lifted me. I entered. I saw that sausages were hanging from the ceiling, so I tore them off and held them under my shirt. I jumped to the small window. Michał was already on the other side and he helped me down. I gave him one sausage to hide. I had the second one, under my shirt. "We have to eat them quickly," I said. If they noticed that they were missing in the pantry and started to search, it would be best if they didn't find anything, no trace of our theft. We cut the sausage into equal slices, and gave everyone [a slice]. Then Ignaś ate something for the first time.

We could already hear movement above, the sounds of tanks. That is, the Germans had captured the area above us, and we were ostensibly their captives, in their hands. They certainly were unaware of the tunnel beneath them.

The next day, we saw the tram employees looking at us suspiciously, especially at Michał, and they insulted him for involving himself with Jews. Indeed, you could see we were Jews. There was Helcia, Cesia, Basia, and so on there, a complete family group, and Michał felt ashamed. They cast aspersions on him, and he got angry. He became even more irritable when he saw me embrace Cesia and kiss her. So he called me over to an empty area in the tunnel and turned on a light that is, he screwed in a light bulb until it turned on. He grabbed a pickaxe, brandished it at me, and said, "You dirty Jew." I saw another pickaxe on the ground, snatched it in a flash and raised it toward him, and said, "You dirty Pole, you hid under the protection of a Jew." Then he threw the pickaxe to the ground, and so did I.

Later on, Michał ran quickly to the pantry storekeeper, holding a lit kerosene lantern in his hand that was missing a protective glass pane, and he asked for kerosene for lighting. The storekeeper became angry and said, "Okay, I'll give you kerosene." They walked to the pantry. That tram worker, instead of taking a can of kerosene, took a can of benzene, a volatile and toxic kerosene distillate, and poured it on Michał. He immediately caught on fire because of the missing pane of glass in his lantern. Michał grabbed a can of benzene and splashed the storekeeper with the liquid. He also caught on fire from the lantern and both of them were in flames. Hearing the sound of their screams, people ran toward and put out the fire that engulfed them. Michał came to us, his skin glowing red. He lay down on the floor. We could not move him. He writhed in pain. Meanwhile, the storekeeper could no longer stand it. He climbed to the exit opening above and lifted the cover. The Germans had thought it was a sewer cover. When they saw a demon, a blazing ghost, emerge from there, they fled in panic.

When they realized that it was a human being on fire, and he showed them there were people below, they pushed him aside and tossed grenades inside. They climbed down and fired in all directions, without seeing anything.

In the meantime, darkness prevailed. All of the lights were out. I didn't know what was happening. Later, I realized that there was no one near me. I clutched my handbag and tried to get out. Meanwhile, the glowing bullets slid along the tunnel walls in the darkness. I walked forward, but they didn't hit me. Near the door, Moritz pulled me by the hand and wanted to hide together. But it wasn't a good hiding place, so I freed myself from his hand and hurried in the direction of the exit. It turned out to be a large hall of a power plant with a boiler in the middle, apparently for generating steam. Burning wooden beams were falling from the ceiling. It was dangerous; those beams could have killed someone. So, I quickly crawled under the boiler; there was enough room there to lie down. The beams struck the boiler; I could feel the vibrations. Meanwhile, night had fallen. I looked around me. The burning beams that fell illuminated the hall. So I was able to get my bearings and see what was happening in that hall. From afar, I saw a gate, and through the gate a small tank and Germans who had undressed to sleep on the ground. I remained underneath the boiler and decided to stay there until dawn, when I could better orient myself and decide what to do. I fell asleep. I woke up. I fell asleep again, until dawn broke, actually before dawn. I saw that the gate through which I had seen the Germans undressing to go to sleep was now closed. The only exit was a long and broad corridor, about three meters wide. I took off my shoes, placed them in my bag, and walked in stocking feet along the wall to avoid waking anyone.

From afar, I saw a soldier next to the exit gate. He slept, with his chin resting on the barrel of his rifle. I hesitated whether to walk past him. I had to take a chance. I walked on my tiptoes in order not to wake him, held my breath, walked past him and reached the gate, which was open. I went out, but had to walk on corpses in order to reach the street.

Across from me was the same garage we had left, with the basement. I went upstairs. The foreman's apartment was there. Beds were set up there with down blankets. There was water in the bathtub. I looked for something to eat; I was famished. I found two cans of sardines and put them in my pocket. I wanted to wash up and went toward the bathroom. Suddenly I saw a person whose hair stood on end, with a black face, unshaven. Then I realized I was looking in a mirror, and that was how I looked. I found soap, took water from the bathtub, and washed up. I wanted to shave, but found only razor blades and no razor. I soaped my face several times so there would be a lot of lather, and then carefully shaved my beard, slowly, using only a razor blade, until I was shaven. There was a can there with alcohol and I washed my face with it.

I went down to the garage because I saw two soldiers with rifles on their backs carrying pails of water, and I was afraid they would want to go up. I wanted to eat the sardines. There was no bread or anything else. I found a stone to use to open the can, but I was afraid of the noise of the stone hitting my knife. So I waited until there was cannon fire that drowned out the sound. I hit. I waited. And again I hit. The cannons fired every other moment. I ate all of the sardines, I drank the oil and I was satiated. Then it occurred to me that it was dangerous to stay there. They could surprise me. There were lots of garages and there was nowhere to hide.

I went out into the street when it grew dark. I found a coat and put it on to stay warm. It was autumn. I walked slowly along the walls of houses to leave the city, to be free of hunger and thirst. Suddenly a spotlight shone. It was a tank. There were concrete pipes in the street that were intended for use as sewage pipes. So I hid inside a pipe and crawled. I saw that I wouldn't get out of the city this way, because at some point the pipes ended. So, I went back through the pipes and returned to the garage. I debated whether to return to the same garage that had a basement, where we rested before discovering the tunnel.

I saw that the basement windows were broken, as if someone had tried to get in there. I took a candle I had in my pocket, and matches, and lit the candle and went slowly down the stairs. I could feel the smell of human breathing. I tore the screen from the entrance and saw, lo and behold everyone was there. They had fled from the tunnel Cesia, Ignaś, the charred Michał who lay on the floor, and Hela with the baby. Everyone was there. The basement was full of coats.

Cesia said, "We don't have any food. We need boiled water so that we don't get upset stomachs." I said there was water upstairs, not fresh water.

It needed to be filtered through cloth, and then boiled. There was alcohol upstairs that I could use to light a fire to boil the water. I went quietly upstairs and brought a can of alcohol, a can of water and a sheet to filter the water, as well as boxes of shoe polish, a pot, cups, and matches. Whatever I could, I brought. I poured alcohol into the box of shoe polish, lit it and placed the pot on it. Now, for the first time, we could drink boiled water.

Ignaś dripped boiled water into Michał's mouth with a teaspoon. I rubbed his feet. I saw they were cold and that he would die that way, so I started to massage his feet. They warmed up, the blood began to flow in them, and then I turned to his hands. They were also cold. I rubbed them with alcohol until they also warmed up. Michał's mouth was burned and swollen. He could barely talk. He asked to be forgiven, said that he was very sorry for his actions, and asked how I could forgive him. I told him I wanted him to return to life, that he had a wife and child, though I was angry at him.

When I went up to bring Michał's dose of water, I found two bottles of red liqueur. I put them on the shelf.

Two days later, planes dropped leaflets calling for the insurgents to surrender. If they didn't surrender by a particular time, the soldiers would toss grenades into the shelters. We didn't go out. First, we didn't trust the Germans. Secondly, we wouldn't have been able to manage with Michał in his burnt condition. We didn't want to leave him alone in the basement because that would have meant certain death for him.

A few days later, they called from the yard and asked whether anyone was in the basement. We didn't answer. I told everyone to sit on the floor, and if they entered, to put their hands up. And that's what happened. Soldiers entered, tore the screen, came into the basement and aimed their weapons at us. When they saw that we all had our hands up, they asked why we hadn't come out as instructed in the leaflets. We said we hadn't seen them, that we knew nothing about them. They asked who was lying on the floor there. We said he was burned, injured. I offered them the liqueur. They ordered me to drink it first. I drank, and then they drank the two bottles. It turned out there wasn't even one real German among them: They were Czechs, French, Yugoslavs, and so on. One of them spoke Polish; he must have been Serbian or Czech. They helped us to go outside, and told us to wear warm clothing. They said they would bring the person who was lying there to the hospital. They had to report to their commander. They led us to him. The commander was from the SS. He sat behind a desk, with loaves of bread on it. He called to Hela with the baby and gave her one loaf of bread. He didn't give one to anyone else. The soldiers told him about the one who was lying there. He gave them directives, which we didn't hear, and ordered them to take us to the church through the streets of the city.

The church was far, almost at the edge of the city. There we met Mietek, Stasia, Helcia and Basia. We all sat on stools and waited to see what they would do with us. No one gave us food and there weren't many people there. Hela wept that she had left behind a backpack with a Leica camera, and first of all needed diapers for the baby. It was very dangerous to return to that basement and first we needed the Germans to accompany us.

Mietek went up to two German noncommissioned officers and asked them to accompany us to the basement because there was a backpack there with things we needed for the baby. In return, one of them would receive the camera we had left there, and the other would receive a wrist watch; they would decide between them who receives what. They agreed to these terms and accompanied us (Mietek and me) back to the basement via the city. On our way, we met Ukrainians who wore several wristwatches on their forearms. They stood the two of us against a wall, said we were insurgents, and wanted to shoot us. The Germans protected us with their bodies and yelled, *Freund, Freund!* ["They're friends!"] So the Ukrainians backed off.

We arrived at the entrance to the basement of the garage. The Germans said they wouldn't go into the basement with us - that they would wait for us in the yard, and that we should enter alone. We had candles and matches, and we entered the basement. We saw that Michał was shot in the forehead and lay dead. Mietek covered him so the Germans wouldn't see him if they entered the basement. We frantically searched for the backpack. We didn't find it. We went out to the yard. The Germans asked where the camera and watch were. We said we would search a little more until we found them. They started to lose patience. We went down again and searched among the coats. We were afraid of what the Germans would say if they didn't receive the gifts we promised. They would want to take revenge against us and would refuse to accompany us to the church again, or perhaps they would shoot us. We were already in despair because we couldn't find anything and we were about to leave when suddenly I detected a tiny glimmer below. I went there and saw the camera; the glimmer came from the buckle on its strap. Next to it was the backpack with the diapers. We were happy to be saved thanks to that tiny glimmer. This backpack was previously next to Michał, where Hela had left it. But Michał apparently didn't want the Germans to take it, and threw it to the wall with his last exertion of willpower in order to put it at a distance from him. So, we found the backpack there, near the wall.

The way back to the church was like the Via Dolorosa. Gangs of Ukrainians had bunkered down, ready to shoot every passerby as a suspected rebel. The Germans worked hard to protect us. We were dressed as civilians, and they couldn't communicate with the Ukrainians, who didn't understand German. They yelled, "*Freund, Freund!*" to lead us forward and protect us. This happened several times until we finally reached the church. We breathed a sigh of relief. It was not worth endangering ourselves on such a perilous outing for the sake of diapers. But we never imagined that the Germans would encounter such difficulty from the Ukrainian bandits.

That same day, they put us on a train to the Pruszków camp. They separated us there, sending Ignaś to one camp and Cesia and me to a camp for the elderly, infirm and deaf. There were long lines for hot soup, but we didn't have anything to put it in until we found an empty can, and so we had hot food for the first time.

The next day, we racked our brains over how to bring Ignaś, who was in the other camp. We decided to take immediate action. I walked toward that other camp, which was bigger. Suddenly I noticed people around me looking at me in fear. I turned my head and saw a soldier who was about to stab me with the bayonet attached to his rifle. He must have called me and I didn't hear him. I signaled to him that I couldn't hear. I saw a nurse nearby. The soldier still stood there with the bayonet jutting toward me. She slipped her arm under my arm and asked where I was going. I told her that my small son was in the other camp and that I wanted to bring him to me and my wife. She led me arm-in-arm to the other camp, a distance of about five hundred meters. She approached the two SS men standing at the entrance of the camp. They asked her why I was coming there with her. She told them that I was looking for my son, who got lost in that camp and that I wanted to bring him back to me and to his mother in my camp. So they allowed us to enter, to search for the boy. I asked people who had seen me and Cesia earlier with Ignaś, and they said he was there. Meanwhile, I met Helcia, Herman Bloch, and who else? I don't remember. They asked me to take them, too, and I said no, I would only take Ignaś with me. That was the only reason they led me there. Otherwise, if they saw me with such a big group of people, I wouldn't be able to take him.

I led Ignaś in the direction of the camp exit and instructed him to sit on a box on a pile of rocks and to look the other way, so that the SS men wouldn't look him in the eyes. Meanwhile, the nurse spoke with the SS men and asked them to allow us to leave. They agreed. The three of us left, feeling happy [Father becomes emotional], with Ignaś between us. Cesia waited in front of the camp, happy. She took off the only ring she had, her wedding ring, and gave it as a gift to the nurse. [He becomes emotional.] But the nurse refused to accept it. We thanked her, and she left to attend to her duties. We were happy to be together, and we thought we'd remain that way.

The next day, the detainees were separated again. One train was destined for Germany, and the second would head to the rural areas in Poland. We debated what to do. An SS man decided on the assignment of groups and individuals, to the right and to the left. The three of us stood before him. As a deaf person, I was not considered suitable for work in Germany, unlike Cesia. They asked us who would take Ignaś. We decided that he would join me. I gave Cesia my shoes that were in my bag, because she wore only light shoes. Yes.

7. Living as refugees with Ignaś in the village of Gorzkowice

They took us in a train car designed to convey coal. They loaded people into it for transport. The transports to Germany were loaded on trains traveling westward. All I had was one large woolen kerchief, which I used to cover Ignaś. We sat on the iron floor of the car.

It was late at night and dark when the train stopped at a small station.

We disembarked. There were people waiting on the platform who took the neediest with them. One man took Hela with the baby, as well as the two of us, Ignaś and me. We walked behind this man until we reached a farmhouse. The farmer who owned the house was a carpenter who made coffins. It turned out that he was a good man. He took us to his barn so we could sleep in the hay. We also covered ourselves with hay and slept.

We woke up early in the morning. The farmer, the owner of the house, came and said that it wasn't healthy for my boy to sleep in the barn, that his wife was preparing a place for Hela and the baby, and also for the two of us, in a room of a separate bakery building, and that she would set up two beds there. He invited us to his home for breakfast and served us dry bread and milk. His wife was a middle-aged woman. His married daughter, the mother of a small child, sat with us. The two women scrubbed the floor of the room that would be ours, cleaned and prepared it for us. After the meal, we went out to the yard by the well and washed with cold water. The farmer's young granddaughter was very happy to have a friend to play with, and she said she'd only eat breakfast if Ignaś ate with her. This was very fortunate, because he was fed good meals, the same food the girl received. Every morning, he ate an egg, bread with butter, and so on. The farmer's son-in-law was a nice man, and played the organ at church.

Every day, I went to the committee for assisting refugees, which provided hot soup in jugs, for free. That was our only food for the morning hours. Later, I took Ignaś with me and taught him how to take the soup himself. No one harassed him, despite his Jewish appearance, because they were all refugees from the uprising in Warsaw. The baby fell ill and we desperately searched for a doctor. Miraculously, we found one, also a refugee from Warsaw, who had no instruments, not even a thermometer. But he felt the baby's body and determined that the baby, Wiesio, was not ill, but was adversely affected by the changes.

We didn't have a penny to buy anything to eat. So, I hung advertisements on telegraph poles saying that I was a sewing machine technician from Warsaw, ready to repair, and so on. This reached someone from a nearby estate. There was a broken sewing machine and there were women, refugees from Warsaw, who sewed for the owner of the estate. I didn't want payment in cash, only groceries. The housekeeper caught a duck in the yard for us. It was the first time we ate meat. In this way, I became the breadwinner for the three of us. Hela proved to be a good housekeeper and good caretaker for Ignaś. She would bathe him every day and wash all of our clothes, which she would hang to dry while the two of us were naked, because we didn't have a change of clothes. I didn't even have a pair of underwear because my last one was completely torn. I had abscesses on my chest and went to a clinic where they could be treated with cream and bandaged. The doctors were unable to heal them, so I continued to visit there. I asked the doctor where it came from, and he said from hunger, cold, sadness … and dirt. The abscesses grew, the pus accumulated, and I suffered a lot. The farmer's wife saw this and said she would help me. I asked her how she would do this, but she didn't want to say, and said I'd see for myself. One morning, she said she had prepared something for me, would bring it and put it on my chest, and that I should prepare myself. She brought something that was very hot, put it on my chest, bandaged it and said that everything would pop the next day, and that would be the end of the abscesses. She said the doctors didn't know anything, and that she had learned this treatment from her grandmother and great-grandmother, from generation to generation. The next day, I indeed felt that the abscesses suddenly had popped, and they didn't appear any more. [Note: Here there is a break in the story, perhaps due to a malfunction of the tape recorder.]

I met a deaf-mute tailor, and I invited him to visit us. When he saw Ignaś, he gave him money and became very friendly. When he visited us the next time, he again gave him money. I guessed that he must have recognized Jewish facial features. I thought that perhaps he also once had a family, a wife and children, and that he had lost them. Now he latched onto whatever work he could find. He was not only deaf, but didn't speak at all, and also didn't know how to write properly. The farmers fought over who would host him, because he was a first-rate tailor, with hands of gold. But that man told me that he wasn't suited for the village, and that he preferred to work in the city with a first-rate tailor.

About a dozen or more kilometers from the city of Piotrków was a larger city, Piotrków Trybunalski. When the trains began to operate again, I took the train to Piotrków. I wanted to have a look around, to find work. I had no connections. I saw an excellent tailors' shop and went in. The owner of the firm had several assistants, but he needed an outstanding tailor to sew sleeves. I told him about the deaf-mute. He asked me to bring him there. He wanted to see him, and if he was suitable, he could sleep in the workshop and even eat there. We came, and when the owner saw the hands of my tailor friend, he immediately realized that he was a skilled professional. I asked if he wanted to hire him on a trial basis. No, he replied, he already saw that he would be good.

In our small and distant village, we felt cut off from the world. No news reached us. We didn't know about the changes in the war map how far the Russians had advanced, where the Germans were digging in. So I decided to look for Jurek and traveled to Kraków, to the Jaworskis. Julia Jaworski and her friend M. were living there. Julia told me that she understood that I had left Warsaw empty-handed, with only the clothes on my back. She told me that her husband, Roman Jaworski, had died in Kraków during the time of the Warsaw Uprising, and fortunately for me, I could take some underwear and other clothes he had left behind. For the first time in a long time, I had a change of underpants and undershirts. I met Oskar Wassermann at her house; he complained that during the time of the uprising I had stopped sending the monthly payment [Note: Probably from Żegota; see Part Four below] to him. I was angry that he came to me with complaints. After all, he would have been dead a long time ago if it weren't for my help. I had no money at all to pay for Jurek, who lived with Mrs. Nowak under her protection. I went to the Aid Committee for Refugees from Warsaw and told them about this. They gave me a substantial sum so I could pay the debt for the care of my son, and for the cost of traveling to and from Brzesko. In light of this, I boarded the Tarnów train and got off at Brzesko. In Słotwina, I saw huge trenches, and I learned that the Russian-German front was getting closer. [Note: The previous section in the recording is enigmatic. Father did not come to Słotwina from the outbreak of the Warsaw Uprising until the liberation of Brzesko by the Red Army. This was his testimony to Yad Vashem in 1983 on behalf of the Łoza-Nowak family, and this is what Yoseph clearly remembers. Perhaps Father made an unsuccessful effort to go there, or perhaps part of this section, which was recorded in Itzhak's home in Jerusalem, was a mistake in Father's chronological memory, and the timing of the described trip should be attributed to the first trip to

Słotwina after Brzesko was already liberated.]

Meanwhile, a new major crisis occurred. Hela wanted to leave the house and search for Michał in the hospitals. I asked her where she planned to search, and said it would be best to wait until we received some word on where he was. She said, "No, I'm going. I'll search for him in the hospitals, I'll ask about him," and so on. She was planning to leave with the baby. When she was already in the yard, walking toward the street, I caught up with her. I said to her that she shouldn't search for him, because he was already gone. She began screaming and crying, and returned to the room. She was angry at me for not telling her sooner. I told her that Mietek and I had decided not to tell her anything so that she wouldn't become ill and miserable from sadness. Wasn't it better that I told her now? Otherwise, she would have broken her legs searching in vain. She was very tense, hysterical, and the owner and the neighbors complained to me that I shouldn't have told her. I explained my view to them, and what could I do? She might have become even more miserable after searching and not finding her husband.

The farmer's son-in-law, an organ player in the church, organized a memorial Mass for Michał and announced its date. All of us contributed money to purchase the candles. I taught Ignaś when to kneel and told him to learn the liturgies from the others. Yes, I taught Ignaś how he should kneel, make the sign of the cross, and listen and watch what the others do and say during the prayer.

Later, I don't know in what miraculous way, Mietek found where I was living in Gorzkowice. He sent me his address so that I would come to him. It was a very complicated address, a far-flung village that was not accessible by any means of transportation. I wandered as if through a jungle until I luckily found them: Mietek, Stasia and Basia were there. They slept in a barn. Stasia brought gold coins from Warsaw that I had skillfully hidden for them in boxes, brushes, and other items. Mietek lent me several coins on condition that I would return them to him after the war. Stasia gave me a coin to give to Hela so that she would feel more secure.

From this point, the events began to unfold at a dizzying pace. One time, a gendarme came to our room and said he was taking me for one day to work on fortifications. I pointed to Hela, the baby, and Ignaś, and said I couldn't abandon them. He said, "For half a day." When he suggested that

I take a blanket with me, I understood that it wouldn't be for half a day or for a full day, but for a long period. And I refused to go. He brought two soldiers to take me. They were middle-aged or even older. You could see that their uniforms were shabby. When they led me in the road of the village, the women shouted to them that they were taking a man who couldn't hear, and who had children at home. The soldiers were embarrassed, but carried out their duty and continued to lead me to the square in front of the church. There was a big crowd of people, and SS men, too. The soldiers reported that the women had shouted that they were taking a deaf-mute. Yes. They asked me if I knew how to write. I said yes. They gave me a piece of paper and a pen. I wrote that I was a German from Plauen, had married a Polish woman and that I had seven children at home to feed, and therefore could not leave them. I wrote it in the Gothic alphabet, so that whoever read it passed it on to an older person, who understood the letters. They saw that it was proper German, and believed that I was German. They let me go home. In the square, there were quite a few trucks on which they loaded various people. But I didn't see any of the neighbors. Later, I asked them where they had hidden. They said, "In piles of hay, in the field."

I couldn't find work in Gorzkowice, so I traveled by train to Piotrków and roamed the streets of the city. I came across a man who was unloading machine heads from a car. They looked familiar to me. They were burnt heads from the uprising in Warsaw. I knew that man, and he also recognized me. He was happy and said, "I have so much work." He told me that Többens had relocated to Piotrków. I should go to the manager, he said, he'd be glad to see me. And indeed, the Többens factory was situated in that wing of the building. The manager welcomed me. It was the same manager as before, in Warsaw; there were some others, too. Even Wasserman was there. I asked the manager to give me some cloth so that I could sew a shirt and underwear: [one each] for myself, my son, the widow, and her baby. In the storeroom, he gave me cloth that I could wrap around my body and make sure no one could see what was being done with that cloth. He told me that two mechanics worked for him, but they weren't good enough. He asked me to work there and be their supervisor. He said I would earn well, because he had no mechanics for special machines.

The factory's supervisor was an SS man. He was hated. In Warsaw, he used to shoot people who smuggled goods via the wall, and he injured people. In the yard, someone drew my attention to the fact that the cloth I had stuffed into my pants was protruding, and he helped me fix my pants. I returned home pleased that I would be able to lift myself up and would no longer be a beggar. I gave all of the cloth to Hela, who immediately hid it under the pillow. I told her to sew something for Ignaś and for me - whatever was needed - but she didn't sew anything because she thought all of the cloth should be hers. A few days later, I traveled to the factory and started to work seriously there. My workplace was in the hall in the wing of the building where there were many heads from various machines. The SS man apparently knew I was coming, perhaps having learned this from the manager, and he came to the workshop in the wing of the building to watch me. His eyes sparkled when he saw me. I pretended that I didn't see him because I was so focused on repairing the machine. When he came closer, he extended his hand to greet me, but I felt such revulsion toward him that I didn't extend my hand to him; I pretended that my hand was busy at work. He left insulted and angry. The mechanics became pale with fright. They said he would come to shoot me now. They left the workshop in fear. I told them not to be afraid; he really needed me. It would be a shame for him to shoot me dead because he would lose a good mechanic. When nothing happened to me, this greatly boosted my prestige, and they started to respect and help me.

A few days later, a special machine for making small holes broke down. A mechanic went and tried to fix it, and when he didn't succeed, the SS man, who stood on the steps and watched him, told him to call that deaf guy. The mechanic told me the SS man wanted me to do the repair. It was the only machine of its type in the factory. If they didn't manage to fix it, everything would come to a halt, because without holes, it's impossible to sew underwear or uniforms for the Army on the front. I told the other mechanic that I didn't want that man watching me do the repair, and that if I was successful in fixing the machine, he would go to the SS man and tell him. Ten minutes later, when the machine was already repaired and operating, the mechanic went to the SS man, who had waited up high on the stairs and watched everything, and claimed that he personally had done the repair. Later I went out. [Father laughs.] He had seen everything, so he knew that the mechanic was lying. But I was pleased that I didn't have to speak with him.

Meanwhile, I miraculously learned that Marysia [Silberstein] and her boy were living in Piotrków with a couple who were both engineers. So I immediately went to see her. I embraced them. It was also an excellent opportunity I would have somewhere to sleep and not have to return home every day. It was winter and snow was falling outside. The Red Army was drawing closer to Piotrków and soldiers on horseback could already be seen retreating from the city, and that SS man also disappeared.

I told the mechanics that they should take for themselves all of the machine heads that needed repair and leave for me the special ones, which they didn't know to repair, but that we should only do this when the Russians entered. The manager convened the workers to hear their views on how to divide the merchandise and the machines. He asked me what would happen if we took the machines home and the Germans returned, as occurred in Warsaw. I replied that each worker should take home the machine he works on, and if the Germans returned, they would have machines ready to operate. They voted in favor of my proposal.

Meanwhile, the Russian Air Force appeared on the horizon. They flew at high altitude; the planes looked small, but dove rapidly and sniped from machine guns, and then soared again into the clouds. It lasted for seconds. Horse carcasses lay in the streets. The Germans retreated, riding on horses or by foot if their horses had been killed. There were also dead German bodies in the streets.

We learned that the Russians had conducted a large raid on the factory during the night; they broke into it and found a lot of vodka bottles. They drank and dropped dead because the Germans had injected poison in the bottles via the bottle caps, without leaving any trace.

We divided up the merchandise from the storeroom. Russian soldiers broke into the storeroom. They wanted to take merchandise. So we locked the storeroom to get rid of them.

I chose fabrics, brought them to the engineers' home, and gave them to Marysia. I told her landlady to split them fifty-fifty. The landlady offered to give us a sled so that we could take more merchandise from the storeroom. I gladly agreed and we went to the factory in the snow. I loaded only heavy materials on the sled. I thanked her and told her to take half for herself in exchange for her help, and the other half would go to Marysia. Yes, and that's what happened. Later, I loaded machine heads on the sled and placed them on the floor in Marysia's apartment. There was a considerable number of special heads of great value, though they were in need of repair. It was impossible to return to Gorzkowice because the Germans fought fierce battles against the Russians. So, I had to wait a few days until everything calmed down. I was worried about what was happening, whether they remained safe in the farmhouse. When the battles died down, I set out, on foot, because there were no means of transportation.

I saw many corpses on peasants' wagons, which sometimes fell onto the road - naked corpses. Then the peasant would lift them again onto the wagon. All of them were naked. Signs were stuck in the ground with the names of the fallen, by units. When I entered the forest, I saw decapitated heads in the snow, with their blue eyes looking right at me. I saw hands and other organs scattered around me. I looked up. Entire body parts were hanging from the trees. I didn't get particularly upset by this. I thought to myself, "They wanted war, they got war."

I found Ignaś in good condition, and Hela and her baby, too. I was very happy that everything was okay. The Russians entered Gorzkowice on January 15, 1945, the anniversary of our wedding and also Ignaś' birthday. It was winter and snow fell. A single young man with a rifle led a whole group of German prisoners. They were starved, and they hobbled along in small steps and scanned the ground for cigarette butts. They were completely lost, lifeless. There were several hundred prisoners. Trucks arrived with Russian soldiers. They unloaded machine guns from the trucks and ordered the captives to stand at the bottom of a hill, facing its slope. And they shot them to death, one after another. Yes. The captives fell to the snow, one after another. Then the Russian soldiers left, just as they had come. Fifteen minutes later, the snow covered all of the dead. There was no trace.

The war continued on, and it seemed that it might continue for a long time. But the Russians were undoubtedly advancing. I already thought about wandering westward with them in order to reach Kalisz, but I had to ensure the children's welfare before I could set off on my own, without them. It suddenly occurred to me that I could place Ignaś with Władysław, who had sheltered two Jews in a basement for several years. I had almost nothing to take with me. The cloth I had smuggled earlier from the factory provided a living for Hela. I gave the large woolen kerchief to the owner of the home as a gift, because she had asked for it previously.

I took Ignaś with me on the trip and placed him with Władysław, together with the pair of Jews who still lived there, so they could take care of him. Then, I returned satisfied to Piotrków. I took the fabric I had left there. I contacted Wassermann, who also had collected fabric. We returned together by foot. I asked Wassermann to stay close to me all the time, because the roads were full of Polish gendarmes who stopped people, checked documents, and arrested Germans. They could call to me from behind and I wouldn't hear them, so I needed a travel companion who could hear.

We joined a group of young people, women and men, and we stopped in a hut. They fed us there because there was some festive anniversary. We filled our bellies. We slept on the floor. In the morning, we continued on. But at some point, I bid farewell to Wassermann and continued on alone. I don't remember what happened. Yes. I joined another group to avoid walking alone and being shot in the back. Later, the group separated because they could not go on walking. I remained alone. I was starving after not eating for several days. I saw a hut with an adjutant standing in front of it; an officer sat behind a table inside. I entered without saying a word, and cried out, "Bread, bread, give some bread." That officer stood up and froze, didn't move. On the table was about a quarter of a bread loaf. I pointed at it. He didn't move, he didn't tell me to take the bread; he didn't move at all. I reached my hand toward the bread. He stood like stone. I took it, thanked him and left. His adjutant waited for an order to stop me, and when he didn't receive this order, he let me go. I walked away. I walked and turned my head and I saw the officer and the adjutant standing and watching me.

Somewhere along the way I met Wassermann, and again we continued on and even boarded a train that was just about to leave for Łódz. He met a couple he knew who were heading to a villa in Łódz. They apparently had some standing with the communists. We slept comfortably in the villa. We left our fabric with them for safekeeping so we could reach Kalisz without baggage. Where the Russian Army had completed its expansion of the railway lines, there were trains that traveled short distances. Using various means of transportation, we arrived in Kalisz.

7. In Kalisz after the liberation

On the Prosna Stone Bridge (*Kamienny*), I met one of my workers, who had been guarding it with a rifle. I approached him and told him I was hungry. He led me to his wife, who prepared soup. I slept there under a down blanket. The next morning, that worker brought me to Piekarski. Yes, he was a Meister, and expert in his craft, a good guy. He brought me to the factory.

That's not correct. I came to the factory alone. I knocked at the gate. An unfamiliar doorman opened and asked who I was. I told him I was the owner of the factory. He looked at me like I was nuts. I wore clothes made of paper, but they looked quite elegant. I asked if there were workers. He replied that they were playing cards. I told him to go tell them that the owner of the factory had arrived. He went. The workers came, lifted me in their arms and tossed me in the air. They were happy. [Father's voice is very emotional.] They told me that they were taking care of the factory. The Russians came to steal coal, merchandise, whatever they could find. They didn't allow the Russians to enter. They were so happy that I arrived. They said that now we could operate the factory and they would have bread. [Father is again emotional.]

I told them I would do my best to arrange everything and to ensure they would have something to eat. They said that as the owner of the factory, I could demand that it be returned to me, and that they would even come with me to the court to support me. One could see that there was not even a single communist there. They suggested that a worker named Zegarek put me up in his home because he had no children, and he had a stock of food. He readily agreed, and I lived with him.

The next time I came to the factory, I saw a red flag on the roof with a hammer and sickle. Yes, I understood from this that the factory had been nationalized, and that I wouldn't have the right to express an opinion. But I trusted my workers to be very devoted to me and satisfied. Before the war, after forming a strong union, their salary was the highest in all of Poland. Each weaver earned like a government minister. In Poland, there were only two factories of this type, for curtains and for tulle. Therefore, I could count on these workers.

As I was preparing to organize and operate the factory, suddenly, out of the blue, Samek Bloch appeared, back from captivity. He was very sad and depressed. I was very happy to have him back because it was difficult for me to manage everything on my own; I had no contacts with the government and the shortage of raw materials made it difficult for us. So, we worked hard to operate the factory, and even started to allocate food to the workers. We brought pigs and distributed them to the workers. But this occurred later, because first the workers, who were dissatisfied with the meager wages they received before I arrived, decided to travel to Germany and conduct a "*szaber*" (that is, to loot and steal property from the Germans). Entire trains would return from Germany with lots of people, full of doors, windows and boards stripped from homes, and so on, and even roof tiles. I told the workers that I didn't allow them to go off on forays of plunder. I would make sure they had food.

Yes. Samek arranged for us to receive an allocation of lard, meat, and so on. That saved us. Meanwhile, what they earned was not enough for them. They wanted to receive the same level of wages they had received from us before the war. They wanted to drink vodka, to revel in nightclubs and such, and to compensate themselves for their suffering under the German occupation.

Markiewicz, the oldest worker, returned. He began working in the factory with my father when he was fourteen. He was too short then to reach the worktable, and Father placed wooden beams under his feet so he could reach. He worked there for about fifty years. He became a weaver and didn't advance further. In Warsaw, he helped me when he took Ignaś into his home for a short period, but he returned disabled and could not do physical work because he was injured while taking part in the war. He was a weaver, but I kept him in the factory by assigning him responsibility for the workers' welfare. He distributed portions of food and salary bonuses. A workers' council was formed at the factory, and Markiewicz was its chairman.

The worker Lis, who was guarding the bridge when I arrived in Kalisz and was the first one to see me, tried to acquire the apartment the factory's supervisor had left. He was waiting for an answer. Meanwhile, Samek tried to acquire the same apartment via the municipality. They told Samek that they would allocate it to him if I lived there with him and if Lis would withdraw his request. Lis said that he would yield to me, that I deserved it. It was a beautiful apartment. Valuable pictures hung on the walls, and we had to sign a declaration that they were state property. The previous owner of the apartment, Daub, was a German who worked before the war as a lace pattern designer in Salomonowicz's large factory in the city, and had artistic tendencies, so he had good taste when he appropriated these pictures for himself.

For a long time after the end of the war in Poland, there was still no sign from Cesia. So I assumed that perhaps she was no longer alive. In the meantime, I brought Jurek. I don't remember if Łoza brought him or whether I traveled to him myself. I absolutely cannot remember now. I'll ask Jurek.

In Samek's absence, the workers' council approached me with a proposal that I arrange a second salary for them. In exchange, they would give me a free hand in management and a certain percentage of all of the factory's profits, after expenses. I immediately rejected their proposal the percentages they offered were too much for one person. I proposed taking half of what they offered. They immediately agreed and were pleased. Samek would travel to Łódz to the Ministry of Industry in an effort to obtain raw materials and money, and I remained in the factory to manage it properly. The Russian cotton was not suitable for our production because of its thick fibers, and we needed to adapt them in order to be able to wrap them on the weft disks [bobbins]. But the length of the string on the disk was too short, and this led to wasted time in production. The same production assistants were employed as before the war.

I assigned Piekarski to tend the garden in front of the factory, and he turned it into a beautiful garden, with fruit trees, vegetables, and flowers. He was proud of his work. But others envied him, and he had enemies because they suspected him of being a Volksdeutscher. He explained to me that only his mother had German roots. Her name was Laufer. They envied him, he said, because he earned more than them, but it was natural that he earned more because he had better knowledge and skills, and worked long hours. I protected him from the workers' attacks.

There was another Meister, a Frenchman whose name I don't recall. He came to me and complained that the workers were accusing him of being planted by the Germans and of collaborating with them. I had to calm him and tell him that he shouldn't pay attention to their insults. He had worked for us for a very long time, and he also worked for our competitors in a tulle factory. After the Germans seized that factory, he discarded our outdated machines for [making] tulle and installed the competitor's new machines. In this way, our factory improved. But now the heirs of those competitors came to us and demanded "rent" for those machines that were now operating in our factory. But it was no longer my factory, so I referred them to the government.

I racked my brains how to organize merchandise to enable me to pay a second salary to the workers and to secure profits for myself. This was possible by over-reporting the loss of thread during production. I also bought cotton thread in the black market, some of which might have been spun in cotton mills that operated in Kalisz - how was I to know how much of their production was stolen and sold illicitly by workers and managers?! They also wanted to survive.

From time to time, an oversight committee would come from the government ministry. One of its members was Mr. Rosen, a friend of Alexander Fuks [Note: Father's future in-law]. They weighed and listed the merchandise and the stock of thread in order to prepare a report on how much was missing. But in my factory, everything was always listed as satisfactory.

Of course, Samek had no clue what I was doing at the factory or how much I was paying the workers. I also had to organize a mechanism for selling surplus merchandise throughout Poland. I needed very reliable people for this, and I thought of turning to some people who had helped me during difficult times; now I would help them make some earnings. When I had more merchandise, I'd call Władysław, and then that carpenter from Gorzkowice. I didn't set any price limit for their sales. They would make their profit from this. All of them returned with the money they collected from the buyers and would set out again. Everything went as smooth as butter. None of them disclosed where their merchandise came from.

Samek still wore an officer's uniform, without ranks. He had no money to buy fabric and sew a civilian suit for himself. I gave him a handsome sum of money and told him he deserved it, about a half of my profits. He didn't want to accept it. He asked, "Where did it come from?" I told him that I managed various businesses. He didn't agree, saying that it was dangerous. I told him that if he didn't want to, okay, but didn't he need this? He replied that if he had a pistol, he would shoot me. He said he didn't want to do any dirty business. I told him that this was not dirty business, just independent business, which we deserve. But I didn't want to tell him which business I was conducting. From that time on, he felt better. He started to smoke the best cigarettes, to buy clothes, essential things, and I gave him money gradually. I told him, "Don't ask anything. Take the money because it would be a shame if you later regret not taking it."

I think it was the month of May, in the year 1945, when suddenly Markiewicz came with Cesia to the apartment. I was happy. We strongly embraced, together with Jurek. When she saw that Ignaś wasn't there, she assumed he hadn't survived. I told her this wasn't true, that he was alive, at Władysław's, and that we would bring him.

Cesia looked very well. I was surprised. Her face was round and ruddy. I couldn't understand how this could be when she was at the concentration camp in Stutthof, a camp for Poles. She explained that she was so late in returning because she had been roaming through eastern Prussia. She was hungry, so she worked on farms. Ate and ate, and lost her way on roads she didn't know. She helped with the farm work in exchange for food. She told about her life in the Stutthof camp. When the camp was evacuated as the Russians approached, she fled with a friend during their [death] march across the land.

Hela [Lifshitz] came from Gdańsk to visit us; she was the one who saved my life by sending me an anonymous letter via Mietek, warning me to immediately disappear and to leave Otwock. At first, a small group of Jews who had survived the camps or had survived thanks to Aryan documents gathered in Kalisz. Other family members who arrived were Mietek, Stasia, Basia and Frania, no one else. Everyone would meet at the community council, which organized a kitchen, and we could receive lunch there for pennies that is, just soup. Mrs. Skowrońska (née Bauman) arrived with her daughter and relatives, the Znamirowski brothers and attorney Danziger. Skowrońska moved into a well-kept home that she received. There was a large store there, which the Germans had organized very well. We formed a partnership with Skowrońska, Mrs. Pinkus and Stasia to sell our products.

In fact, I needed a company name, so we called it Partnership (*Wspólnota*). I was able to use the store as a façade for the company.

Józef Kowalski came to visit us and I invited him to lunch. [He was a friend of Samek from prewar Kalisz. They were together at Oflag Woldenberg; he had the rank of second lieutenant in the reserves.] We discussed business. He held me in high regard. He was appointed to manage Kalisz's textile industry and said he would try to obtain a license from the Ministry of Industry for the purchase of merchandise, because now we already had a company. Later, I started to travel on my own to the Ministry of Industry in order to get to know the officials who issued the licenses. One of the managers at the ministry was Halina, whose husband was killed during the war. I knew him since childhood. He was a physician.

I made Mietek my contact person for obtaining the merchandise licenses. I asked in stores which merchandise they need, because there was a shortage then and people went around dressed in rags after the war. After a while, I realized that there was no need to bring lots of merchandise when you didn't know whether it would be easy to sell, and I would visit wholesale stores with Mietek to learn which merchandise was in highest demand. My income grew significantly. The wholesalers also profited and were pleased.

However, one clear day, there was a tremendous shock. Everyone felt depressed after the pogrom in Kielce and began to think about leaving Poland.

Leopolda's husband was appointed as Poland's military attaché in Moscow, and later as military attaché in London. She came to us from London and was now ready to take Ignaś with her to England as a family relation. She would add him to her passport and bring him by plane to England, with the Polish government paying the expense. But she set a condition: Ignaś would be her son until age 21 and study together with her son, and later complete diplomatic studies, all at the expense of the government of Poland. After considering this briefly, I accepted her conditions and was even grateful to her for relieving us of one of our many worries after the pogrom in Kielce.

I later obtained a passport to Sweden for myself, Cesia and Jurek. Later, when Ignaś was already in London with her son Wojtek, Leopolda returned and expressed readiness to take Jurek with her as a family relation. I told her it was very nice that she was willing to bring the two brothers together, but that I would need to first speak with Jurek, who wasn't at home, and then I would give her an answer. She returned to Warsaw. I spoke with Jurek, who was about ten. He was very sad when he heard the proposal to join his brother in London. His response seemed strange to me and I couldn't understand him. Jurek simply refused to travel to London. When I told him that we have a passport and would travel to Sweden, he shook his head to indicate that he didn't agree. I understood him even less. Then I asked him, "In Sweden, we'll wait for an affidavit for America. It's only temporary. Helcia and [her daughter] Cesia, with her husband [Jonas Virshup they got married in Sweden] are already there, and Mietek will also go there." He still didn't agree. I asked him again, "So, where do you want to go? There have been pogroms and no one wants to remain in Poland." He didn't respond. I asked, "Where do you want to go? to the moon?" He said he wanted to be a Jew. I told him that there were Jews everywhere in the world, and that it was possible to be a Jew among other peoples, too. He said this wasn't true, that there was anti-Semitism everywhere and that what happened with Hitler would occur again in the future. Yes. I asked him, "So, where do you want to go?" Only to Palestine, he replied, because he wanted to be a Jew among Jews. Jurek was so adamant that I had no way of persuading him. After a conversation with Cesia, I tore up the passports to Sweden. I said we'd go to Palestine, as my mother had requested. [Father's parents lived in Tel Aviv.] Cesia said that she didn't believe in Palestine, and that I would have no work among Jews only. Meanwhile, Samek Bloch married Halina and obtained a passport to Sweden for himself.

Samek brought as his replacement in the factory a person who had been with him in the camp, and had served as the director of the Ministry of Finance in Kalisz before the war. I worked in cooperation with him. Meanwhile, Samek left Poland. He wrote a letter thanking me very much for the fact that he was not penniless, because there was a great need for money there [Sweden]. His successor was, unexpectedly, a very pleasant man, and we understood each other well. When he found money in the drawer of his desk, he asked what it was. I disclosed the secret that Samek had been receiving this, and now that Samek was gone, it would go to him.

He said that he couldn't accept it, because he didn't want to be responsible. He asked me to stop this. I explained to him that this would be impossible, because otherwise the workers would rebel. I asked him to be patient and that gradually this would vanish.

Only one problem remained: how to leave Poland. At that time, exit permits from Poland were not granted to anyone, Jews or Poles. I didn't leave the apartment. I rested. I rested and my mind worked intensively on how to find a way out of this situation.

It occurred to me to visit Leopolda and consult with her about what I needed to do to receive a passport and visa. My considerations proved to be correct. I set off to visit her and told her everything that I needed to leave Poland with the family. After listening to me, she picked up the phone and called someone. A few minutes later, she told me that she had called the director in the Foreign Ministry who deals with military personnel, a friend of her husband, and that he would come immediately to meet with me.

Remembering Moshe

As we can learn from his memories, our father Moshe was endowed with creative powers and a talent for action, as well as the energy to fulfill them - sometimes without the inhibitions that characterize people who can hear. With the help of his brother Abram, he started a workshop in Ramat Gan for woolen fabrics. Moshe assembled used Crompton machines that came dismantled in boxes, and brought their production quality to the level required for exporting to England, the land of quality textiles. At its peak, the factory worked in three shifts, with a single weaver operating as many as twelve automatic looms; Moshe maintained the machines and the production. Cesia, his wife, worked alongside him until her death, and served as an important connection to the outside world. Hearing and deaf people were trained and employed at the factory. Moshe also put his heart and soul into public activity and was one of the leaders in establishing the Association of the Deaf in Israel and its branches throughout the country. He proposed the idea of building the Helen Keller House in Yad Eliyahu and led its implementation. He also initiated and lobbied for establishing a memorial corner at the Helen Keller House for the deaf people who were murdered in Europe. This section was built only after his death, following the work of a committee chaired by Haim Apter, his young protégé, who served as chairman and secretary of the association for many years. Moshe's son Yoseph was also a member of this committee. The corner includes a sign on which Moshe expressed his spiritual legacy, translated from the Polish language:

> In eternal memory of the six thousand deaf people who were among the Nazis' first victims during the Holocaust period. This house bustles with life and is a memorial to them. I miraculously survived that inferno. I saw it as my duty to make every effort to memorialize my dead brethren and to build, with the help of deaf friends, this center for the benefit of the living. Moshe F.

This memorial corner also includes a sign in memory of Eugeniusz (Geniek) Łoza, the deaf Righteous Among the Nations. The sign-hanging ceremony was attended by many of the association's members, family and friends, as well as Poland's ambassador to Israel, Dr. Maciej Kozłowski, and Kamila Cronberg-Kuropieska, the daughter of Wojtek and granddaughter of Józef and Leopolda Kuropieska.

PART FOUR

The Kalisz 'Underground' in Warsaw

Recordings, translation from Polish to Hebrew and
transcription: Yoseph Komem

A. ACTIONS TAKEN BY MIETEK KOLSKI AND HIS FAMILY TO CONFRONT THE TERROR

Memories recounted by Cesia Kolski-Virshup

1. The families of our mother Cesia - Jarecki and Jaffe, a partial reconstruction

Cesia Kolski-Virshup: I didn't know our great-grandfather Jarecki. He was from Kutno. They had land in the villages there. My mother [Helena Kolski, née Jarecki] would travel there with her parents on vacations. I knew some of his descendants from wonderful pictures that Mother had, including pictures of rabbis. Nothing remains now. Our great-grandfather Jarecki had three wives in his lifetime. During the period when they worked in agriculture, the first mother gave birth to Behr (who lived in Warsaw), Shaje, our grandfather Itzhak Leib Jarecki in Kalisz, Yankele Jarecki in Częstochowa, and Regina Głowińska in Warsaw. All three of Grandfather Itzhak Leib's brothers were very devout. The second wife gave birth to numerous children there; I knew some of them. They included Grünwasser, Estusia (Esther), Frenklowa, and there was Mietek. Actually, I knew them all, but I can't remember any more. He also had a third wife, who was killed by the maid. The children were no longer at home then; they had all left Kutno. Aunt Regina married a man who owned land. I knew Estusia, Hela, and Mietek, and they were quite assimilated into the Polish surroundings. Ignaś was the first child named after Grandfather Itzhak Leib Jarecki. In regard to Grandfather Itzhak Leib's marriages, Cyrel Jaffe, his first wife, was my mother's mother, the daughter of Shime Jaffe. I have pictures of him that I received from Moishe, who is now in Israel and known as Michael Jaffe, the son of David Jaffe, who was the last *kashrut* inspector on the Polish passenger ship *Stefan Batory*. In 1939, David was in the US and local émigrés from Kalisz implored him to stay, but he returned to Danzig and died in the Warsaw Ghetto of natural causes. The Germans took his wife Roza Chana and his son Zalman from the ghetto, and they perished. David Jaffe's two brothers had jobs as rabbis. He also had received rabbinical ordination, but didn't serve as a rabbi. He always wandered.

When our grandfather Itzhak Leib Jarecki died, rabbis came to Kalisz for his funeral. He was a scholar and was always studying. Grandmother from the Jaffe side was a merchant. At that time, the women worked and earned money, and the men were *belfers* (assistant teachers). Our grandfather, Itche (Itzhak) Leib Jarecki, was a Hasid. He had a long beard. I assume that Great-grandfather Jaffe was also a Hasid, but I'm not sure. Great-grandfather Shime (Shimon) Jaffe was an ordained rabbi.

Yoseph: How many children did my great-grandfather Shime have?
Cesia: From what I remember, there was my grandmother, Cyrel; there were two boys, David and Zelig Jaffe; then there was your grandmother, Esther, and Dorcia (Dora) Goldberg in Warsaw [the mother of Avraham-Adek in the Land of Israel and of young Tusia at home]. There were more [Sender, Bela and Shaya-Yona, according to Elias Jaffe]. Our grandmothers were the daughters of Shime Jaffe. Dorcia was the prettiest and youngest. Shime Jaffe's wife was Freide Daum; there was a large family there. The son of David Jaffe, the kashrut inspector on the *Stefan Batory* ship, was Yosef Haim Jaffe, the father of Elias and Sabina, who was murdered in Stutthof in [June] 1940. Yosef Haim's wife was Hendel-Hela (née Kott) from Kalisz, and they lived in Danzig. Hela Kott, the mother of Elias and Sabina, survived and reached the shores of the Land of Israel with her daughter, but they were deported [to Mauritius]. Meanwhile, Hela's son wound up in England, enlisted, and fought. My mother, Helcia, traveled to Danzig for the wedding of Yosef Haim Jaffe and Hela Kott.

Great-grandfather Shime Jaffe and the children of his son David and David's wife Roza Chana. Standing (right to left): Zalman, Bela and Hela. Sitting (right to left): David with his grandson Elias, Shimon (Shime), Roza Chana and Michael (standing).

2. Fragments from our grandparents' home

Cesia: Do you know who the children of Itche Leib Jarecki were?
Yoseph: Yes, Aunt Pola told me.
Cesia and **Yoseph** [reconstructing together]: Helcia (Helena), Yaakov, and Zelig - from the first mother, Cyrel; and from the second mother, Esther - Balcia, Genia, Yosek, Roza, Pola, Shmuel (who died as a young boy from tuberculosis), Cesia, and Frania.
Cesia: My mother Helcia functioned as a mother to everyone. The second mother, Esther, also died young at the age of thirty-eight, and the children were raised alone. And there was the father. The father, a relatively young man, never married again. There was a maid and there was the business and there was everything they needed. After the father died, when only Frania and your mother Cesia remained, they received a small apartment for the two of them. Cesia ate with us, and Frania ate with Bala. When

Cesia married, Frania started to work in Cesia's father-in-law's factory, and she lived with Bala. In our house, when everyone sat together at the table, Roza sat with a book in her hand; she didn't speak, she only read. I remember the tree in the park where she sat and read, devouring books. She didn't get married. Genia also read a lot, but not as much. Everyone studied. Frania studied the least. Cesia, your mother, went to the religious school Havatzelet and then to [the bilingual Jewish] high school. My mother [Helcia] attended a private school. It was a Russian high school. There was a problem of schooling. Grandmother Jaffe operated a haberdashery. Grandfather studied and the women worked. There was a private girls' school run by Mrs. Sieradzki in Kalisz, Pensja Sieradzki. Grandmother Jaffe wanted my mother and Dorcia to go to school. And one time she said, "I have daughters and grand-daughters, I would like all of them to go study." But there was a problem of writing on the Sabbath. And then the women teachers told Grandmother, "Mrs. Jaffe, we trust you, we can accept your daughters and your grand-daughters at the school, because we learn Polish here, which is against the law" [under the Russian occupation]. Mother and Dorcia went to the high school. Mother knew Russian, the language of instruction, and she knew German, from her studies; and she also studied French. Grandmother Jaffe had eight girls at home, and they all had to keep a secret. Mother went to high school: They studied in Russian until 1:00 p.m. and then the girls did handicraft and learned Polish. They had Polish books at home, but they wouldn't bring them to school. How did I happen to study at the government high school in Kalisz? There were thirty-five Jewish girls. Mother's friends were teachers in the government Polish high school. When they asked Mother where she wanted me to study, she told her friends, "At the Jewish high school." Then they asked, "Why not at ours?" [Their school was the government Polish school.] She said I was Jewish and they wouldn't accept me. Then they told Mother, "Send her to the entrance exam," and I was accepted at the government high school. In the first year, there were thirty-five to forty Jewish girls among five hundred girls studying there. I was able to enroll thanks to two of my mother's friends: a dentist, Pilcowa, and a nature teacher. That's how I was accepted. Dorcia started to study at the same high school where I learned in Kalisz, and then they moved to Łódz and she continued to study there.

The young Jarecki sisters. From right to left: Pola, Cesia and Frania, in Kalisz.

3. The flight and the story of the buried treasure

Yoseph: Now tell me about the war period. I want to know everything in precise detail.
Cesia: For that, we'll need to sit an entire night.
Yoseph: So we'll split it up.
Cesia: When we left Kalisz, your parents, Balcia (Bala Bloch) and her daughter Esther (Lalusia) had already left Kalisz and traveled to Otwock. I don't know about her husband, Herman Bloch. There were three Cesias: your mother, big Cesia; me, little Cesia; and Yaakov Jarecki's daughter, who was called Cesinka. I don't remember exactly when your mother traveled to Otwock. I was in Kłodawa with my father and with Mietek; beyond that, I don't know.
Yoseph: We traveled via Kłodawa.

Cesia: You couldn't have traveled to Otwock via Kłodawa.
Yoseph: I remember that we were in Kłodawa.
Cesia: Perhaps earlier.
When the war broke out, Mother [Helcia] traveled from Kalisz to Tomaszów, and she took undergarments and money to her brother, Yosef (Yosek) Jarecki. We traveled from Kalisz to Warsaw in December 1939. Yaakov, his wife Karola, and their daughter Cesinka traveled with us.

Karola, Yaakov's wife, was a Bloch, the sister of Herman Bloch, who was the husband of Balcia, Yaakov's sister. Weiss, who worked as an accountant for your grandfather, and his blind wife also traveled with us. We traveled to Warsaw by train, and an order was issued at that time prohibiting Jews from riding on the trains. I remember one fact: Before the train left Kalisz, a German entered the car, approached Cesinka, Yaakov's daughter, and asked, "*Jüdin?*" ("Jewish?") And she answered, "*Nein, eine Schülerin.*" ("No, a student.") And then he shouted, "*Jüdin, Rauss!*" ("Jew, get out!"); and threw her out of the car. Then Karola and Yaakov also ran out of the car. But Mietek ran from the other side and pushed Cesinka, Karola, and Yaakov back into the car, and the train immediately began to move. Mietek was always courageous. And that's how we got to Warsaw. It was in December 1939.

In September 1939, the Germans expelled everyone, including Poles, from their apartments on the main streets of Kalisz. They also evacuated Balcia and Genia, who lived on those main streets. They were replaced by Baltic Germans refugees of German origin who were expelled from places that fell into the hands of the Russians. Balcia and Genia came with everyone in October to our apartment on Łazienna Street in the city. Together with Father – Moritz - I entered the basement, and we dug into the ground and buried all of the silverware, silver candlesticks, and gold dollars. Only Balcia had gold dollars. My mother had a diamond and also a gold chain belonging to my father.

One day, your father Moniek sent a package to us in Warsaw with old things. It was preceded by a letter in which he wrote, "A friend of Jurek, who is blind in one eye and needs a tonsillectomy, visited me." The package included a teddy bear that was missing an eye. We unraveled it and Mother's diamond was inside. Your father had ideas. [She laughs.].

Yoseph: Wasn't there a risk that you'd toss it into the trash?

Cesia: In those times, when people sent something, we would search its contents. When he sent the teddy bear, we understood that it had some significance. So we wouldn't have thrown it away. Moniek would send things. As I told you, my father and I went down to the basement and buried things in the ground. Balcia had gold dollars; there was jewelry of Mother's the diamond, the chain. What else was there? All the silverware, silver candlesticks, so much tableware, silver kitchenware, also Genia's. And Father and I buried all this in the ground in the basement. We covered it with deck chairs. And your father was later in Kalisz for a long time - he worked. And Balcia had nothing to live on. So we sent him a sketch of that basement, marking the place where it was buried. So Moniek went to our landlady to get the keys; we had friendly relations with her. He told the landlady how difficult our lives were and that he wanted to take those deck chairs because we had nothing to sleep on. So she gave him keys to the basement and he dug up everything. He took only the jewelry and the contents of the jar of gold dollars. After the war, Mietek went to retrieve the silver items, but couldn't find them. Those silver items might still be buried there.

Yoseph: Should Father have taken out the candlesticks and the silver items? But that would have been too much.

Cesia: We didn't speak about this after the war; they didn't mention this. Only now I think about this. There was silverware for table setting of three types: for meat meals, for dairy meals, and for Passover. Complete sets of silver. Balcia's, Genia's, and ours. Ritual objects for holidays: My father had elegant Hanukkah menorahs and candlesticks, items my father received as a newlywed. There was a five-branched menorah, a tall and beautiful one. Everything was buried, but when your father dug, the important thing was that he took out what he did and sent it to Balcia, hidden in all sorts of ways. He had ideas: Several hundred dollars in twenty-dollar coins were hidden inside wooden brush handles. Your father received a share, I don't know how much. He sent the diamond and Father's chain to Mother. And don't forget that letter and all sorts of rags. He wrote that Jurek's friend, who has one eye, needs a tonsillectomy. And when we received the package, there was that teddy bear with the missing eye; we opened it and it was right there inside. In this sense, your father was a genius.

4. In occupied Warsaw

Cesia: So, we were in Warsaw, in the area of the future ghetto. Most of the family came to Warsaw. Mietek never wore the armband. He immediately went to trade in the giant Kercelak market, at the stalls with the vendors. When he had things to bring from the ghetto, he would sell there a shirt one time, something else another time. But he never wore the armband. Mietek was called Nafcio. He had two names: Naftali Mendel. In Kalisz, he was registered as Naftali Kolski. He himself told me that when registering in Warsaw he said his family name was Kolski and was later asked, "And what is your first name?" He thought quickly, like a flash of lightning: Naftali? Mendel? And immediately came up with the name: Mieczysław, and he responded, "Mieczysław." And that's how it remained until he arranged forged papers for himself. In the family, his pet name was "Mietek." When they closed the ghetto, he would enter freely because he arranged official transit papers for himself.

We arrived at the home of the Hauswirth couple, the parents of Marysia Silberstein. Her mother was a Kolski from Kalisz who married Hauswirth. We lived with them and wore yellow armbands. I don't remember where Yaakov went in Warsaw. Marysia and her husband Max lived with his parents at the time. Her husband's parents, the Silbersteins, had a factory where they produced undergarments, shirts, and so on. They lived on 14 Nalewki Street. From the start, Mietek went out without an armband. When they stopped him and asked, "What's your name?" He would respond, "Mieczysław Kolski." A mass of people arrived in Warsaw, and you couldn't buy yourself a slice of bread if you were a foreigner. The Joint [Distribution Committee] arranged kitchens for the refugees. And we went to receive lunches. I don't know how the money arrived to set up the kitchens for the refugees. There was some sort of Jewish organization in Warsaw. In any case, we could buy lunch. It was impossible to buy food because the Warsaw merchants didn't want to sell. They were afraid to sell to strangers. Mietek would go out and sell. Later, we moved. We rented an apartment nearby, on a small street, Lubeckiego. The apartment was between Pawia and Gęsia streets. On one side, you could see the Pawiak prison. And on the other side, on Gęsia Street, I don't know what was there before the war, but later they built a prison for Jews. Jews caught without an armband were incarcerated there, and gypsies too. They called it Gęsiówka, and that was even before the ghetto was formed.

Yoseph: How did Mietek learn the trade of selling knitted underwear, and where did he get his merchandise pants, etc.?

Cesia: Listen, he arrived in Warsaw without a profession. He engaged in trade, purchased merchandise in Kercelak it was a huge market in the Wola neighborhood, and he sold.

5. In the Warsaw Ghetto

Cesia: The edict to close the ghetto in Warsaw was issued on Yom Kippur in 1940, when we were living on Lubeckiego Street. You were all in Otwock the whole time. When the edict to form the ghetto was issued, Walicki, from the Szeinfeld family, who was the son of my father's sister and who previously served as a dentist in the Polish Army, became friends with a village leader (*sołtys*) from the eastern territories. The village leader had all sorts of "passports" certificates of birth, baptism and such, and original stamps. Walicki allowed him, as they say, "to make a profit." Mietek acquired a "passport" through this Szeinfeld-Walicki, and it looked completely original, all from some place in Wołyń. Then he arranged for himself, in a documented way, the name "Mieczysław Kolski." If his birthdate was April 13, 1912, he made it April 13, 1910. He listed his mother's maiden name as Helena Jabłońska, instead of Jarecki. I don't remember what he put as his father's name. He lived on the Aryan side and needed access to the ghetto because he would buy merchandise there, usually sweaters. At that time, a tram line ran through the ghetto. No one was allowed to disembark from the tram in the ghetto. Mietek would ride the tram, and pass through the ghetto. A redheaded Polish policeman stood there - Michał was his name. His wife Hela was Stasia's first cousin. Mietek explained to him that he couldn't disembark in the ghetto, and then gave him an address and money to buy sweaters somewhere in the ghetto. I don't know if it was at our place, because "Kolski" was written on the door to our apartment. I suppose it was the address of a merchant who had sweaters.

Yoseph: Did Michał know that Mietek was a Jew?

Cesia: Of course not. Mietek didn't tell him. He no longer appeared as a Jew. Before he left the ghetto, he already had an identity card. Walicki arranged it for him in one day. In one day, it was done. So, Michał would go to the ghetto and Mietek, you understand, was alone, a young man, among Poles. He wanted to have acquaintances, because it was also suspicious for a young man not to have a home. On Saturdays, he was afraid to walk alone in the street. There were plenty of Poles from Kalisz in Warsaw. Suffice it to say that he became friends with Michał. That Michał, the policeman, invited him to his home, and there he met Stasia. This was all in late 1940, after the ghetto was formed. Mietek gave Michał addresses of merchants in the ghetto, in the Nalewki area, and there Michał would purchase merchandise for him - sweaters and such. Mietek paid him for this, but the most important thing for Mietek was to have an Aryan home in Warsaw where he could go. Later, it was perhaps in January 1941, I don't know how, he was also in contact with the German employment bureau (*Arbeitsamt*), and there he obtained a transit permit for the ghetto, because all of the factories in the ghetto were still operating, sewing undergarments. Max Silberstein had a factory on Bonifraterska Street in the ghetto for high-quality fabrics for linings, for women's tricot undergarments, and so on. In response to the edicts, Silberstein later moved the factory and registered it under the name of a Polish engineer he knew, Bandurski. Mietek would come and take merchandise from there. In the ghetto, everyone lived by improvising like this. Some people in the ghetto mistakenly thought that Mietek was that Bandurski, who became the owner of Silberstein's factory, and they called him "Mr. Engineer." In December 1940 or in the following January, Mietek received a transit permit from the Arbeitsamt and could enter and leave the ghetto on a daily basis. Mietek was unable to eat any form of meat from a pig. When he came to the ghetto, they would make him a home-cooked lunch that he liked, and I would buy merchandise for him, according to his preferences. He would take a wad of bills from his pocket, all of the money from his sales in Kercelak. Father would arrange them by types of bills, and I would go to pay the suppliers. The "hottest" items then were warm undergarments, particularly for winter. They sewed those in the ghetto.

At Christmas [December 1940], Mietek was invited to Michał's family. And so, during the entire year of 1941, he would enter the ghetto every day and buy. He already told us then that he went out with Stasia, but didn't think he would marry her. He spent time with her, and she would even visit him. He would always buy her a nice gift in the ghetto. Mietek conducted himself in an elegant way. He had a light-colored jacket, green hat and a pipe. On 14 Nalewki Street, there were stores that sold gifts that were appropriate for Stasia. When he visited, they would shutter up the stores because they thought Mietek was a German. Then Silberstein said, "Don't be afraid, don't close the shutters. He's a decent Pole, he's not a German, and you have nothing to fear." Then they thought on Nalewki that I was that Pole's sweetheart. Our father didn't show himself in the street because Mietek was very similar to him physically in certain aspects, and he didn't want the secret to be revealed.

Yoseph: Already then, in the ghetto, Mietek made sure to change his identity completely?

Cesia: From the beginning, they didn't know in the ghetto that he was a Jew. Mietek didn't comply with the order to wear an armband even in Kalisz, and never wore it at all. He said, "I won't wear that armband!" It was his way of providing a livelihood for the family. He was very responsible for supporting the family. We had no other previous resources of money. I even wanted, at the beginning, because of the hardship, to travel to Russia, because my friends went there. Then Mietek said, "No, Cesia. You must stay with the parents, and I'll take care of income, right away!" And that's how it was. We didn't lack anything. Yaakov didn't have an apartment. He came to the ghetto and for some months lived in someone's private apartment with Karola and Cesinka. He had no money and had to leave the apartment because he couldn't pay. Housing centers were later formed to provide shelter for the homeless in schools inside the ghetto. Karola's elderly mother was still alive and was staying with Basia at the home of Balcia and Herman Bloch in Otwock. We didn't lack a thing because Mietek took care of everything. He would come to the ghetto, buy supplies, take merchandise and say, "Miss Czesława will come to pay." As I told you, the money was all mixed up, and Father sorted it and I went to pay. Mietek laughed and said it was dark when he put the sales revenues in his pocket, mixing all of the different bills.

Throughout that year, Mietek told us he was dating Stasia. I was always busy, and I was nervous when Mietek left or entered the ghetto. I was young, but this weighed upon my nerves. After all, he was my brother; the blood of family isn't water, and it was dangerous. And every month he paid on the Aryan side, at the Arbeitsamt, to renew his transit permit for the ghetto. The clerk who worked at the Arbeitsamt said that Mietek must be a Volksdeutsch because he spoke Polish well. The clerk at the Arbeitsamt would say to Mietek, "Mr. Mieczysław, come on Monday and I'll give you the transit document." And Mietek would pay him the fee and add a tip. Mietek ate bread with cold cuts, but without butter. Stasia never noticed this. She didn't even pay attention to the fact that he was circumcised. But immediately upon crossing to the Aryan side, Mietek obtained for himself a certificate from a doctor stating that he had to be circumcised because he had contracted a sexually transmitted disease. I don't know who the doctor was. Once, when he went to the Arbeitsamt, that man served breakfast. Mietek ate bread and meat without butter, and the guy said, "You eat like a Jew." Mietek asked him, "How do you know?" The man from the main Arbeitsamt was also a Jew with an assumed identity, and told Mietek, "We're the same thing." Mietek would also deliver various things to other people, and they paid him a commission. Once, he had a mishap. There was a man who produced colors for juices and he asked, because of some constraint, for Mietek to deliver the raw materials for him. But Mietek had transit documents for transporting textiles and not for juices or chemicals. The man pressured him. Mietek hesitated, but then agreed, because that man paid well. At the crossing, they stopped him and asked, "What kind of juices are these?" Somehow, he paid extra and passed. When he passed through the crossings, he would give various gifts to the different Germans on guard duty: a shirt, sweater, women's undershirt, and so on. He gave. That's what saved him when a problem arose.

Later, in 1942, it was very important for Mietek that I get married. But I didn't care. I would run from here to there, and it wasn't on my mind. We didn't lack for anything. Every Sabbath, Karola would come to us with Yaakov. They would stay with us and we also gave them food to take home. Father's young brother Władek, who was in the ghetto, would also come. Mietek would come to us in the ghetto and leave in a three-wheeled rickshaw. The gate was on Nalewki Street. There were many beggars in the ghetto; you can see pictures at Yad Vashem. And Father would say to me, "Go down and give a gift to all of the beggars in the area." His heart ached to see all of the poverty, the hardship of children and all that.

The Gestapo had many Jewish agents. Mietek was more wary of the Jews in the Gestapo than of the Poles who worked there. For example, the husband of R. from Kalisz was F., from a good family. He studied in Warsaw and was manager of the Jewish Academics House. He was in the Gestapo. In Kalisz, there was the Oaza cinema owned by T. R., who was also an agent in the Gestapo. There were many Jewish agents in the Gestapo, and Poles, too. These people in the Gestapo were not clerks they were agents, who gave information and turned in people! Informers (*szpicle*) without uniforms. Mietek feared them. On the eve of Tisha B'Av in 1942, an edict was issued for a transfer of the population (*wysiedlenie*). They chose to impose all of the decrees on important dates in the Hebrew calendar. The ghetto was also formed on Yom Kippur in 1940.

Now I'll tell something about myself. On Sundays, I would go out a little. I would go out to tend to Mietek's business affairs. By chance, I met a young man by the name of Arnold Walfisz. We met one day in 1942. He was from one of the more distinguished families in Warsaw - *yiches iber yiches* (Yiddish: an outstanding pedigree). His father and grandfather were also there. I made his acquaintance, but didn't get myself all worked up about it. I said I had no intention of getting married, but we would get together. He liked me. His father was much older than most. When Arnold Walfisz, my friend, asked if I had a family, I told him I had a married brother in the provinces, and he didn't inquire further. We met once a week and I didn't tell him anything. He lived on Muranowska Street, and a Gelbfeld family from Kalisz lived in the building there. So he told them he had a friend, Cesia Kolska. They said to him, "What? Do you know that her brother is a Gestapo man, an agent? Go to Nalewki Street, on the border of the ghetto, and see him go in and out every day." Everyone who knew him from before thought he was a Gestapo agent. But by chance, in the same building there lived a man named Skowron, a good friend of Father from Kalisz, a member of Hamizrahi, and Father confidentially shared his concerns about his children with him. His second wife was the daughter of Rabbi Rappaport from Belz, a great distinction. Once during the hours of curfew, when they met in the home for *mincha* prayers, Walfisz's father told Skowron, "My son is going out with the young Kolska woman. What type of family is it?" And he responded, "Oh, they are very good people from Kalisz, from the Kolski, Jarecki, and Jaffe families." He asked, "Is Kolski's son in the Gestapo?" He replied, "That son goes out every day and brings food not only to his parents, but to his entire family, and also to others." It was very important to Mietek that I get married. Suffice it to say that Skowron came to Father, without my knowledge. And Father arranged a meeting with Walfisz's father, and then they set the "terms." In the ghetto, this became known as an exceptional story. We were engaged around April 1942, and it was an engagement according to Jewish law. Everything was written down. I even received a diamond from him, and later I was able to save Mother thanks to it. My parents also planned to buy him a gift. So, we got engaged. I said that it was just some nonsense. But my father said, "I'll make sure that you get married in this home in September, and then you'll live as a young married couple."

6. The Grossaktion Warschau

Cesia: In July, on the eve of Tisha B'Av, an evacuation order was issued. That very day, my fiancé's parents came to visit my parents, and we took a walk in the ghetto. On that day, Sunday evening, they hung posters proclaiming that the transfer from the ghetto would begin that day. My fiancé, Noldek, was at work. Between Dzielna Street and Gęsia Street, there was a military worksite (*placówka*). Before the war, there was a military warehouse there for blankets, sheets, and other emergency supplies for the Polish Army in case of war. These warehouses were captured by the German Army and my fiancé worked in them. His group would travel from there every day to work outside the ghetto. Then, when the expulsion order was issued, they transferred the entire group to Praga, to Pelcowizna, where there were large warehouses of the Polish Army from before the war. They housed them in barracks there. Here in the ghetto there was the Többens factory, and other factories, too. Anyone who had a job clung to it. When Noldek moved to Praga, I started working at the worksite where he had previously worked, in the ghetto. Father and Mother also started working there. We wanted his parents to also come work there, but they were disinclined to do so. His father had a good Aryan appearance, and he spoke Polish well. His mother also had a good appearance and her Polish was mixed with German she was from Danzig. We worked there during the day, and in the evening we'd return to our apartment on Lubeckiego Street. Thanks to my work there, I had documents from the Wehrmacht. I felt safe because the worksite was under the purview of the German Army. Meanwhile, the Germans evacuated one street after another. They hadn't come to Lubeckiego Street yet. They had already sent people to the gas chambers, and to Poniatów, to all sorts of places and in all sorts of ways. From Kalisz, many were sent to Chełmno, because Chełmno was close to Kalisz, and from Chełmno they sent them to Treblinka, to Majdanek. They would distribute bread and say they were sending the people to work, and that they would receive plenty of bread there. Every day, they would come and evacuate complete buildings for transfer [The *Grossaktion Warschau*]. My uncle and aunt, Yaakov and Karola, fled to the factory on Bonifraterska Street. Władek-Wolf, Father's brother, didn't have papers, and I got him some papers from Többens. He lived on Leszno Street. Then I said to myself, *I'll ride the tram that stops in the ghetto (and from which you could disembark), and I'll bring him the papers I obtained for him for work at Többens*. Imagine, the tram was on Gęsia Street, and suddenly they shouted, "Rauss!" I showed my Wehrmacht papers, but they again shouted, "Rauss!" They moved us to other tram cars and squeezed us into them. On the corner of Gęsia Street, there was a Jewish police station, and they let us out there. One of the Jewish policemen was our neighbor, Jaskar. He told me there was nothing he could do, but immediately left his post and ran home and told my parents that I was caught at the Umschlagplatz, and that's it, *shoyn*. There was nothing anyone could do now; everyone was going to the cars. I didn't know what was happening, and they took me to the Umschlagplatz. Father quickly caught a rickshaw and rode to my fiancé on Muranowski Street, because he had returned from work in Praga, and he told him. They immediately rode in the same rickshaw to my worksite, and together with the German from the worksite, they rode in the rickshaw to the Umschlagplatz. Meanwhile, when I entered the Umschlagplatz in Stawki, I saw that they were leading groups, thousands of people. Suddenly I saw a Jewish policeman from Kalisz named Hershkowitz. I approached him and said, "Look! I have papers from the Wehrmacht." He said, "Do you see that German over there? Go to him and maybe you can be released." Meanwhile, people were being pushed forward toward the cars, while I tried to retreat by pushing backward. I don't know, perhaps ten thousand people went. They were transported from the ghetto in the train cars.

Yoseph: To Treblinka?

Cesia: [We thought] it was almost certainly to Majdanek, straight to the gas chambers. We didn't know yet where they were headed, we knew they were murdering in Chełmno. But at the time, we didn't know exactly what was going to happen to those transports. I pushed backward and wanted to reach that German. Sometimes I fell, and people kicked me and stepped on me. The Germans pushed everyone toward the cars and shouted. The people complained that they would shoot everyone because of me. And I wanted to get to that German and I held that document. In the end, four or five hundred people remained, because the cars were already filled with about ten thousand people. Later, when I was standing, a senior Jewish policeman came. I recognized him because he would come to the Proporcow family in the building where I lived. So, I said to him, "I'm Proporcow's neighbor. I have papers!" He looked at me and said, "Shut up!" and walked on. What happened? When the Jewish policemen had already filled the first quota, they were allowed to enter the Umschlagplatz, and when they met someone from their family, they would try to get him out. Later, that policeman returned. Perhaps he went to look for someone from his family, and when he didn't find anyone, he came back and asked me, "Did you call me?" I said, "Yes." He said, "Keep quiet and follow me." I walked behind him and showed him my papers from the Wehrmacht. He accompanied me to the gate of the Umschlagplatz and instructed a Jewish policeman there to lead me outside of the gate of the outer fence. I went out, took a rickshaw, and said, "Lubeckiego Street!" The neighbors there stood on the balconies lamenting ("*gevalt*") because everyone knew I'd been caught. Mother was also there. When she heard they'd taken me, she suffered a spasm. Father had not yet arrived, because he went with that German again to the Umschlagplatz to look for me. But, of course, they didn't find me. He was the German who managed the worksite (*placówka*). They allowed

him to enter the Umschlagplatz.
Yoseph: Why was he interested in releasing you?
Cesia: I worked there and he knew my fiancé. I didn't ask why he was interested in pulling me out. It's a fact. And thanks to that, he met another young woman who worked for them and got her out. And she was rescued for the time being. You should know, not many were rescued from the Umschlagplatz. That German, the manager of the worksite, had the authority to remove people from the transports. He was a Volksdeutscher and a Polish speaker. The Umschlagplatz was a train station; there was also a Polish train station there before the war. The people would stay there for a day or two, and also sleep there at night. Suffice it to say that I got out that Sunday. Very few escaped from there. The next day, they caught people from another street they cleaned. Those who remained at the Umschlagplatz waited for the next transfer. They removed about ten thousand Jews from the ghetto every day. It was horrible. They also collected [Jews] from all of the towns. And this continued for about two months. People worked in shops and there weren't enough working hands. When we saw that the *Aktions* were getting close to Lubeckiego Street, we went to my worksite and spent the night there. Perhaps Noldek was the one who arranged this for us. Mother, Father and I were at that worksite and didn't go home to sleep. Now they took transports from Lubeckiego Street, too, from our building, but we were no longer there. We worked at the site in all sorts of jobs: We cleaned machines, laundered sheets; Mother also did something. Suddenly, a rumor circulated – it was July or August of 1942 – that these worksites in the ghetto were going to be eliminated. The worksites inside the ghetto were on Gęsia Street and other facilities were outside the ghetto. My fiancé was there. As I mentioned, he initially was employed at this worksite in the ghetto, and was later moved outside the ghetto. He would travel there and back. Later, about two hundred Jewish men were housed there in barracks in Pelcowizna in Praga. And here [inside the ghetto], there was a mixed group of men and women. We worked here and even slept here at night.

I want to tell you about an incident that happened, and it's a very important testimony. [Cesia was very emotional and the testimony was difficult to decipher and edit.] Our chief commander, Lahman, was a Jew from

Poznań. He managed that site. There were two managers. Lahman had a beautiful sister, Luba, eighteen years old, and she worked and boarded with us. A pretty girl, a beauty. She wore makeup and painted her lips. My mother asked her, "Why?" Two Germans would come there, senior officers. In general, every morning in the ghetto we saw dead bodies by the walls. The Germans caught young Jewish women, raped them, and then killed them, because it was against German law to engage in intimate relations with Jews. Anyone caught with a Jewess would be sent to a concentration camp. Later, I met German prisoners in a concentration camp who had relations, even random, with French women. There was another Jewish commander, I forgot his name, who had a girlfriend. One day at dusk, the two senior Germans came looking for Jewish women. This time, our top commander, Lahman, Luba's brother, was on the other side, in Praga. They came and ordered us to stand in formation. Everyone came out of the huts and stood in formation. And the first of those Germans called, "Luba! Inside!" and the second called for the second young woman (the other manager's girlfriend), who was under Lahman's command. We stood in formation. When he approached Luba, the beautiful eighteen-year-old, she had her period. There was also a doctor in our group, a Jewish doctor. The German called that doctor and asked him where he should shoot a bullet at her so that she wouldn't suffer. The doctor told him, and he shot her in a frenzy because she had her period. We stood there, and she had a father and an aunt there, and no one reacted. We saw that the father was shaking all over. Then they told us all to form one group and go into a barrack. They called several Jews to take her and I still today remember where she was buried. The Germans ordered her buried immediately because they were afraid. Because with a Jewess ... We came out of the barrack and saw that Luba's body was gone. There was fear, and the father ... Luba was gone. And the group ... They dug a grave for her on Gęsia Street. The German called three Jews and ordered them to dig. The Germans warned us not to say anything to anyone who came. They were afraid. The second woman he raped her and sent her away. The next day, we worked there near the bushes and we saw signs of digging near those bushes. No Luba. We realized immediately that they shot her to death. Perhaps she's still buried there today.

Soon afterward, they started preparing to liquidate our worksite. Mietek couldn't enter the ghetto then. But there was a Jewish smuggler on Bonifraterska Street who would go outside the ghetto. Every day they would send out a group to work. This smuggler was the same one who spread the rumor on Nalewki Street about me being the sweetheart of that Pole [actually her brother Mietek]. When I heard about the liquidation, I went to Lahman. There were about two hundred men at that worksite where Noldek worked, outside the ghetto. So they arranged something with the Germans, telling them that those workers had twelve or fifteen women, and that I was one of them, and the Germans allowed them to bring the women to that worksite outside the ghetto. They sent Father to the coal worksite, *Kohlenlager*, outside the ghetto, but we worried about Mother and the older women. When I heard of the danger, I approached Lahman and said to him, "Mr. Lahman, tomorrow you must contact Mr. Mieczysław via the Jewish smuggler." Mietek knew him. I wrote a note to my brother saying only, "SOS, Helena is in danger." Later, the manager came to me and said, "He'll give your mother a ride? He'll take you, Miss Cesia!" He didn't know that Mietek was a Jew and he thought I was his sweetheart. I told him, "Mr. Lahman, the smuggler shouldn't worry, he should just deliver the note so it gets to Mr. Mieczysław." The next day, when the smuggler returned at six o'clock in the evening from work, he came to me right away and said, "Tomorrow morning, Mrs. Helena should be here and I'll take her." Mother left with a group for work outside and Mietek waited on the other side and went with her. And that's how Mother crossed over to the Aryan side. That's Mietek! Mietek, you know, was not a person who believed in God. He had, from what he traded, perhaps twenty to thirty thousand złoty and nothing more. With this sum, he couldn't forge papers for her overnight. So he purchased the original papers of an old unmarried woman by the name of Maria Tomaszewska, perhaps she had died, and he paid twenty thousand złoty for them. I later asked him how he managed to do this, when all he had was twenty-five or at the most thirty thousand złoty, and he replied, "That's how much I had that day. Tomorrow God will provide for me. Today, first of all I got Mother out." That was Mietek. He was one of a kind, I can tell you that. He got his mother out and took her to his place; he lived in a rented room with a Polish family on Łódzka Street. And that wasn't natural at all. When Mietek would enter the ghetto, he wanted those Poles to make a better profit. We lived in the ghetto with the Perkowicz family. They were two brothers and one of them previously worked for Abram, your uncle, in Warsaw. Mietek arranged for both of them to make a better profit - both his landlord and our landlord. I would buy extra merchandise, I don't remember what, via that Perkowicz, or via his brother, and Mietek would take it and give it to the owner of the apartment where he rented a room. That landlord worked in the post office and didn't earn much, and thanks to this he could occasionally go to sell at Kercelak, and supplement his earnings. In this way, Perkowicz also made some money in the ghetto.

7. Two weddings and a battle on the Aryan side

Cesia: So, Mietek lived on Łódzka Street and took Mother to his room, and she stayed with him for many days. I don't know if he revealed to the Polish landlords that Maria was a Jew. I assume he didn't. He introduced his mother to Stasia before they were married. Stasia would come to him. He introduced her as a Jewish woman from the Poznań area who had registered a lot of property in his name that he would receive it if she survived the war. Mietek felt and concluded earlier that Stasia was a good-hearted person. She had sensitivity and empathy for the Jews in the ghetto. He started going out with her in December 1940. He was happy with their relationship, and it was now already 1942. Later, he rented a room for Mother, for the first time on her own with a Polish Aryan identity. He rented it from someone called Nina. Well, that woman was a real whore. Each time, a policeman came to her, and others, too. Stasia also came to visit Mother and said to Mietek, "Look, it is dangerous there for Mrs. Maria." So he found her another apartment on Świętojerska Street. It was an apartment very near the ghetto walls. The landlady had an apartment of her own somewhere in Otwock, and so she had rooms to let in Warsaw. She became friendly with my mother and told her, "Mrs. Maria, perhaps you know someone who would like to rent a room. I'd be happy if you rent it out for me." Mother herself rented a room from her, and she also rented out another room for her. On Sundays, Mother would go to church. Stasia would come quite often to visit Mother in her room. I was staying during that period at the worksite in Pelcowizna, outside of the ghetto, where my fiancé was employed and lived. And Father stayed and worked at the coal depot. Our group of Jews worked and also spent the night at the place, while the Poles who worked there would come for the beginning of their shift and go home when it ended. It was an important military supply depot and large dispatch center for personal equipment for the German Army, which was being sent to the eastern front: woolen Army blankets, sheets, soap, and so on. Noldek, my fiancé, was sometimes taken into the city of Warsaw for various types of work. Once, Noldek paid a bribe to a German, rode to Świętojerska Street, and burst into Mother's apartment. He knew where Mother lived, and he told her where he was working, and this and that. He also gave her the address of a reliable Pole so that in the event of danger, heaven forbid, she could pass a written message to him.

Of course, Mother and Mietek were in contact, and he would come to Mother. Mietek knew where Noldek worked, and he would come visit us in Pelcowizna. Since he roamed freely in different places, he sometimes went to that Polish guy, too. We lacked for nothing; Mietek would bring us bread, cold cuts and so on. Mother would buy bacon as camouflage for her, and also sent some for us with him. Mietek himself never ate pork at Stasia's. Later, Mietek told Noldek that he must bribe Germans in order to get his father out of the coal depot, where he was working so hard. In fact, Father didn't have it so bad because he was assigned responsibility for the hall where the group slept, and his job was to sweep. One time, when Noldek traveled from our worksite to the coal depot, he took Father and brought him to us. So, the three of us were there together. The food would arrive from Mietek, so we didn't lack a thing. My father remained religious, despite everything. We gave him food without pork. It bothered Father that we were living together out of wedlock. That Pole brought us packages and also letters from Mother, and we sent letters to her with him. Father, I don't know how, apparently wrote to mother that he was upset by the fact that we were together without being married and without any institutionalized status, and Mietek responded. Imagine, a Jewish wedding was conducted at that worksite, without the presence of a rabbi, which isn't required [according to Jewish law]. We got married. They put up a *chuppa* of blankets and such; there were Jews, there were two rings, which Noldek brought from Mietek and placed on my finger. About two hundred people were present. Mietek sent refreshments; vodka was served and some people stood outside on guard. They made a Jewish wedding for me at a worksite!! [She laughs and chuckles.] Before, at home, Mietek had told me, "Cesia, I won't get married before you." We told him, "Don't pay attention." But he said, "No, you'll get married first!" Even earlier, when he got engaged with Stasia, he wanted me to also get engaged. And we got engaged: Mietek went into the ghetto then, and you know, there were cakes and Władek was also there, and Karola, too, perhaps. You know, it was enough that now we were wed. Two weeks later, another letter arrived from Mother, and Father took the letter from that Pole and read it. In this letter, Mother wrote that Mietek had married Stasia. There was a wedding. Mietek was still living on Łódzka Street then. They still lived in his bachelor's room. Stasia made a party. Mietek didn't want to get married on a Sunday, only on a weekday. He didn't even know the daily prayers, nothing. I said at the time to Mietek, "Learn the prayers!" Mietek claimed that it wouldn't help if he didn't pay a ransom. So there was no reason for him to learn the prayers, because if they caught him, they would check whether he was a Jew. Mother wrote that they married in a church and that she had stayed home. Stasia prepared a wonderful lunch, and she wrote, "I grated horseradish for the party, I stood and wept." So, two weeks after my wedding, Mietek married Stasia. He had to go to confession, so he confessed a bit. [It was apparently not a proper confession, with all of the rites.] He looked for an intelligent priest. In one church or another, I'm not sure which, he found a priest. He went to that priest and told him he wanted to get married at his church. They talked and the priest took a liking to him. So Mietek said, "I beg your forgiveness, Father, I'm a Catholic from birth and was baptized, but I don't follow a Catholic lifestyle. I can come to confession, but what value would that have?" And he put five hundred or a thousand złoty on the table and didn't go to confession. In Polish they say, "For money, the priest prays." So, the marriage was held in a Catholic church in a regular Catholic wedding ceremony, but without confession beforehand. Mietek knew Latin and learned the prayers for the Mass before the wedding. Hela and Michał came to the church, and also the Lewandowski family, with whom they were living. Michał and Hela prepared a party at home, and the Lewandowski family participated. There was a group of acquaintances who were in contact with them, and perhaps they also invited the priest. And Mother "Maria Tomaszewska" was also there. Stasia would visit her and Mother would also visit Stasia. Mother continued to live there, in Świętojerska. Stasia lived with Mietek; they started looking for an apartment, and they rented one on Grzybowska Street, number 22. It was just about opposite the former Jewish community building and the first Judenrat, number 26 on the street.

Yoseph: Why did they live so close to the ghetto?

Cesia: Don't ask me. They had to live somewhere, and I understand that it was easy to find a vacant apartment in that area. Polish refugees also arrived there. There were two rooms in the apartment, with a kitchen and a hallway.

Yoseph: Did they do sewing work there, like at Kuropieska?

Cesia: No, no! Mietek didn't have a sewing workshop.

Yoseph: So where do I remember seeing a sewing workshop? And I remember the concept of overlock from there. [Note: When Father accompanied me to the train station for my trip to Brzesko, perhaps we stopped on the way at Mrs. Pinkus' workshop in Warsaw.]

Cesia: There was a sewing workshop on Bonifraterska Street. Silberstein's factory was there. My manager, Lahman, lived there on Bonifraterska. Yaakov and Karola were also taken from there [apparently to the Umschlagplatz for transport to a death camp]. Mietek wasn't an industrialist, and he didn't employ workers. He engaged in trade.

We lived in barracks in Pelcowizna, and Mietek lived on Grzybowska Street. Stasia would bring Mother to her all the time; she loved Mother very much. Mietek wasn't pleased by this, but what could he do? She would bring her every Saturday. Mietek "didn't know" why. Later, Mother told what she heard from Stasia, "I don't know how his mother educated him; he eats this and he doesn't eat that." Stasia would make fish for Friday night dinner. Mietek didn't eat fish, only stuffed fish. Stasia would complain to Mother that she had nothing to feed him on Fridays because he didn't eat fish. Mother said, "You know, Mrs. Stasia, perhaps I'll make Jewish-style fish for him," and Stasia watched how Mother prepared gefilte fish, and Mietek loved it. Stasia told me this later, in the United States. Since then, Stasia would prepare gefilte fish. She was wonderful! There is no one in the world like Stasia!

Yoseph: Didn't this lead her to suspect that Mietek was a Jew?
Cesia: No, he liked the way it tasted, so he ate it. There were so many Poles who ate Jewish food before the war. Mother saw that Stasia didn't have meat on Fridays because Catholics don't eat meat on that day, and she prepared gefilte fish. In Kalisz, and certainly in Warsaw, too, Poles went to eat "Jewish fish" gefilte fish and other types.

Suddenly in 1943, rumors started. Stasia knew that Mrs. Maria had a daughter and a son-in-law at a work camp. But she knew nothing about Father. Then, in early 1943, Noldek heard that they planned to liquidate the Jewish worksites, and he passed on the rumor to Mietek. Consequently, Mietek immediately, already in February, arranged papers for Father. During that period, the production of forged papers via the Jewish underground didn't cost much. In January 1943, there was again the danger of expulsion and transfer to the gas chambers. Father no longer left the worksite, and worked only inside. I don't know what kind of work he was assigned at the beginning. They brought sewing machines for us - the fifteen women transferred from the ghetto to Pelcowizna - and we worked mending old and torn sheets and such. Suffice it to say, Mietek met with Noldek and arranged papers for Father. One day, I don't know how Noldek did it, Father rode in a rickshaw from our worksite to the real Aryan side and remained there. [Note: "Mateusz", my father, explains in his memoirs the repercussions of that day for him and the loss of his housing!] And the Germans indeed began to liquidate the worksites, the *placówki*, and sent the workers to death in the gas chambers. Perhaps Mietek got wind of this from that Polish guy. Mietek took care of forging papers - first for Father - and he took him. Father also lived as a Pole, lodging at first in the apartment of a Polish woman. He had a good appearance, good papers, and spoke Polish well. About a month later, Mietek arranged papers for me and for Noldek, and, I remember, for a friend, too. Noldek really knew how to get by. So, I left the *placówka* in a work group, the only woman among a group of men. Noldek bribed a German with money so I could sit in the front of the car between two Germans while he sat in the back. The German stopped at a street Mietek had given Noldek an address where an apartment was waiting for us, and had explained how we were to get there. I don't know where they stopped. I don't know whether it was the place where all of the people in the group were going to work. Noldek was from Warsaw and he knew the place. The Germans let us out of the vehicle and we walked secretly to that address. Noldek arranged this. The things he was able to do, you couldn't imagine! In the end, he got caught because he dared too much. At the apartment we received, the landlady was apparently of Ukrainian descent, and I lived with Noldek in her apartment in a rented room for a short period of time. She had a lover. I don't know whether she knew or sensed that I was a Jew. Noldek looked like a thousand Poles: blond hair, blue eyes, six feet tall, thin, handsome, gold-framed eyeglasses; he was a high school graduate who spoke excellent Polish with a local accent.

Father also lived with a Catholic woman and she also had a lover. Once, by chance, Mietek came there and that lover was also staying there. And he asked her, "Is that an acquaintance of the engineer [Mietek]?" He knew that Mietek came to visit there. That lover began to say something like: Here comes the engineer, he's so similar to Father. As I mentioned, that was why I went to take merchandise at Nalewki and not Father. Mietek was very similar to Father: blue eyes and bald, chubby, just like Father, exactly! He was a typical Kolski. I want to tell you something: Mietek, you know, kept the name Kolski, as he was known in Kalisz, and one time, at the Kercelak market, a Pole said to Mietek, "You know, I knew a Kolski in Łódź, so similar to you." He was referring to Roman Kolski, Father's brother, the father of Rena (Basia Smarzyńska). Roman was murdered, together with his wife, after someone informed on them in Rembertów, in early May 1943. It was then that Stasia discovered that Mietek was a Jew. It happened that one evening the landlady's lover arrived, got drunk, and provoked a fight. He turned to Father and said to him, "You're a Jew!" and then the Polish police arrived. That man said something, and Father said something. Then the Polish policemen, they were decent, said to Father … (mumbling). Father and I always had cash, one thousand or two thousand złoty in case something happened. A loaf of bread cost fifteen or twenty złoty. Father gave money to the Polish policemen. That man made a fuss and they told Father, "If the Germans come, it will be worse. Sir, come with us and spend the night in jail, and we'll release you in the morning." Father gave them one thousand złoty, or a similar sum, and said he would bring them more money. They took him, and Father stayed in jail overnight.

They were decent Polish policemen. Then Father was released. Mietek didn't have a phone at home then, but there was a barber downstairs or some sort of shop, and Father called there and asked them to contact Mr. Mieczysław Kolski and tell him, "Mr. Michael called and he is with Mrs. Czesława." Father came to us then. I was with Noldek, we were together then Father, me, and Noldek. No one thought they were Jews; only I was suspected of being a Jew. So it happened that we were sitting, the three of us, and someone approached and addressed me as "Mrs. Jewess." Not Father, and not Noldek. I squirmed and handed over some money. There was no choice; it was pure extortion. Mietek already knew that Father's cover was blown. It happened at the same time, the same day. He called Rena (Basia Smarzyńska) Kolska's mother that day, and she told him, "There's a woman in the same building where I live who might take in Cesia."

Mietek searched and found another apartment for Father, as a Pole. He also found an apartment for Noldek on 11 Grzybowska Street. All this searching went on for a week or two. There was a paper warehouse in the building on 11 Grzybowska Street and Noldek also got a job there and worked in his place of residence as an ethnic Pole. When Mietek went with Noldek to see the prospective apartment, by chance a woman named W. was living there at the time, a Jewish woman from Kalisz who had converted to Christianity and was married to a Pole. She was also living on the Aryan side now. She and her Polish husband had children and they were with him. When she saw Mietek, she was alarmed she recognized him from the ghetto and he also recognized her. They looked at each other as if they had never made acquaintance. Noldek rented an apartment there under the name Roman Woźniak. According to the forged papers, Father was Michael Krajewski and I was Czesława Kowalska. That woman left the apartment right away. She was a Jew who became a Christian, but they put even the third generation of Jews in the ghetto. The Germans must have had her documents in Warsaw, because the documents in the city's population registry were not burned during the occupation, and the municipal offices operated as usual. There was a church in the ghetto on Leszno Street, and on Sundays it was packed with people. The Jews who had converted to Christianity were required to live in the ghetto, but still went to church there. Noldek worked in that building, lived in it, and even came to Stasia from time to time. She knew that he was the son-in-law of Mrs. Maria.

Mietek arranged lodgings for me with Mrs. Zofja Kałuszko on 19 Ciepła Street. She knew that I was a Jew in hiding. Mietek paid her, and if she took me in, she apparently wasn't afraid. She was a midwife and knew how to do abortions, and she told me, "All my life, I've been afraid of my side business, fearful that the police would come to check what I was doing. So, for me to keep Jews, it's the same thing." However, it was considered a crime that was immeasurably more severe. So I lived with Mrs. Kałuszko. Stasia also knew I was a Jew, and that I was the daughter of Mrs. Maria Tomaszewska. For some reason, she would come to me often. Meanwhile, soon after I entered there, Father again had a problem in his apartment. Mrs. Kałuszko knew that Noldek was my husband and would even come to visit. She knew that all of Noldek's property was registered under the name of Mr. Engineer (Mietek), and that's why the engineer paid for us. And Stasia was Mrs. Engineer. Mietek didn't want Stasia to come to Mrs. Kałuszko at all. And this is what happened: Not far from there was the Hale Mirowskie market. Stasia would suddenly arrive and bring groceries. For example, Stasia would come and say, "Such beautiful raspberries and blueberries, I must bring to my Mrs. Cesia." Or she would bake something and come and say, "I have a cake." That was Stasia. She would come all the time and bring me good things. And she would invite Mother to her. Mietek and none of us wanted her to do this. Why take the risk? But it was impossible to dissuade her. The Easter holiday came [1943] and Father joined me, and there was a problem, because Father looked like Mietek. But Stasia was told earlier that Mr. "Michael" (Moritz, my father) was the uncle of "Roman" (Noldek), my husband. We lived in the annex of the building, on the second floor. When someone was approaching, Father would warn the landlady, "Someone is coming."

Zofia and Jan Kałuszko

Yoseph: I remember that Father would watch the path to the entrance.
Cesia [confirming, and continuing]: Prior to the uprising in the Warsaw Ghetto, we were already on the Aryan side, and Father hid together with us. I was only alone for a short time. Because father's cover was blown again his identity began to be exposed. Father sat all day hidden next to the window in order to announce to Mrs. Kałuszko who was coming. There was another Polish woman who hid Jews, Mrs. Przyborowska, who would come from Krochmalna Street. Her son's friend also came and would exchange books in the library. The young son, Jan, had graduated from high school [he assisted his mother] and kept his mouth shut. She had another son, an older one, who was already an engineer. He had a communist worldview and had a girlfriend. When the older son, Adam, saw that his mother was keeping Jews, he got married and left the house. The risk was unacceptable to him. The neighbors didn't know a thing and didn't suspect that she was harboring Jews. And she kept us, two Jews. Later, there was the uprising in the Warsaw Ghetto. I remember it like it happened today. At seven o'clock in the morning, Mrs. Zofja would go down to buy bread and milk. The Hale Mirowskie market was close to the ghetto walls, and two or three blocks from Ciepła Street was Leszno Street, at the edge of the ghetto. That day she returned and said, "What is going on there? What is happening there?

There are so many Germans along the wall, so much army." It was the eve of Passover and then it started. And my mother lived on Świętojerska Street and saw from her window that feathers were flying. She saw tanks enter. There were exchanges of gunfire from the ghetto. Stasia immediately ran and took Mother to her, and didn't ask Mietek.

Even my husband would come to Stasia. He had a good appearance. Here's what happened in the building where he lived and worked. Below, there was a paper warehouse. Many Poles in the building belonged to the Home Army (AK) underground movement. So, one time they said, "Let's make a sort of aerial defense in case there's a bombing, so that we'll be organized" [for the Polish uprising], and Noldek also joined this committee. When he went from one apartment to the next at that building on 11 Grzybowska Street, he came to one apartment and met a group of three friends from the shop. He pretended that he didn't know who they were and then went inside the apartment. What did he discover? It was a group of people who had left the ghetto. There was a wall full of weapons. They were from the Jewish underground [the Jewish Military Union – ŻZW]. Those who left the ghetto split into several groups. They made a headquarters at 11 Grzybowska Street, and some were centered nearby on Ogrodowa Street nearby, in the Mokotów quarter, and elsewhere.

In the meantime, while I was hiding with Father at our host's apartment, she took in a third Jew. It was Dr. Józef Sack.[15] He was active in the ghetto

---

15   Dr. Józef Sack was a member of the Jewish Fighting Organization (ŻOB). According to Prof. Israel Gutman, he was one of the founders of the Anti-Fascist Bloc in the Warsaw Ghetto in March 1942, as a representative of the Poalei Zion socialist movement, together with M. Anielewicz, P. Kartin, M. Tenenbaum, and A. Fishelson, in cooperation with the communist Polish Workers' Party (PPR). The ŻOB was established on these foundations. Józef Sack was a literature teacher in Częstochowa and organized the Dror underground high school in the Warsaw Ghetto, where he taught together with the poet Itzhak Katznelson. The son, Jan Kałuszko, also found a hiding place for Dr. Sack's wife and daughter, Janina – the future writer Yonat Sand - with the Filiszczak family. According to additional sources, the mother and her son also hid and saved other Jews, besides those mentioned in Cesia's testimony. Yad Vashem recognized Mrs. Zofja and Jan Kałuszko as Righteous Among the Nations in 1983.

underground, one of the leaders of the socialist Poalei Zion, who managed to escape to the Aryan side. I don't know how he had our address, but he arrived there. He lived on the money they distributed to Jews, apparently by Żegota, the Polish-Jewish aid organization. We were divided like this: In one room was a niche in which her husband slept. Then, Sack slept on the sofa. In the second room there was a sofa bed, and I slept with her on it, and Father slept on the bed. After the uprising in the ghetto, there were very dangerous times and we built the double walls then. For Sack alone, they made a double wall in the bathroom. In the room where Father and I slept, there was a niche in the wall below, so they made it flush with wall and made a brick door that turned on its hinges, so that if something happened, Father and I would be able to hide. If something happened, we would crouch and enter, and she would close the door behind us, move the sofa or the bed, remove the sheets and throw them in the laundry basket.

Yoseph: I remember that the sofa was on the other side.

Cesia: Well, that sofa folded up. I slept with her on the sofa, and Father slept in the bed. When the bed stood there, the doors to the hideouts had already been built.

That Dr. Sack was in the underground and he received news all day from Ogrodowa Street. They had a radio there. They heard news that the Russian Army was approaching. He would say, "Mrs. Zofja, go buy and serve some *bimber* (moonshine vodka); we'll drink bimber because the Russians are drawing near." Every day, there was news about what was happening. I knew everything. We even knew about Katyń. We heard about Katyń from Antek - Antek Cukierman from Kibbutz Lohamei Hagetaot, I knew him. Antek would come to our place, to Sack; he would enter as a Pole. He looked one hundred percent Polish, but when he said "please" (*"proszę"*), you could immediately identify him as a Jew. He was from Vilna. He would come and Mrs. Kałuszko would ask, "Who's there?" Because Father was on the lookout and Father would say, "That Antek gentleman is entering." And only then she opened because she feared it might be a German. So I knew Antek, and I also met with him after the war, in 1975 at Kibbutz Lohamei Hagetaot. Sack survived, but I didn't see him after the war at Lohamei Hagetaot. He had already died. Before the ghetto closed, Mrs. Kałuszko would go there and smuggle in foodstuffs and merchandise. My landlady was in business with smugglers. One of them - Leon, I forgot his last name - was a briber-smuggler in the ghetto. He had a daughter, a young girl, and they planned to come to Mrs. Kałuszko to hide, but they didn't come in time, because then there was an expulsion transport (*wysiedlenie*). He wanted to send the girl with a smuggler, but didn't manage to do so. So, we hid: me, Father, and Dr. Sack under his assumed name. One day, Leon came - he had fled from Poniatów. That's where they took Jews who were caught, and they shot them, simply murdered them. But they caught him earlier and assigned him to work sorting clothes and items of the murdered people, and he managed to flee to Warsaw. He knew the address of Mrs. Kałuszko, came to her and said, "I wanted to live. I didn't know what to do on my own." And he said to her, "Mrs. Kałuszko, you have to help me, I fled from a *Lager* (camp)." Then Sack said, "Let him in." He slept in Sack's bed. He had no money. Kałuszko had (she counts): one, two, three rooms. As I told you, money came from America, via England. They parachuted from planes; there were Jews in the woods.

Yoseph: And Żegota?

Cesia: There was the AK, but not in the woods. The Jews were in the woods. [Note: Really? Is that what she thought?]. Sack, Antek, and also a Jew from Kalisz - from the Bund, who was on the committee, dealt with the distribution [of money collected by Żegota and the Joint Distribution Committee for Jews in hiding]. They distributed the money based on word of honor. I also gave them names for distribution. I referred thirty-six thousand złoty per month. There was the deaf man from Kraków, Oskar Wassermann. Wassermann, a deaf friend of your father, had a wife and two children.[16] I received three thousand złoty each month for Wassermann. Our cousin Madzia Munwes was on the Aryan side, and she received,

---

16   The Wassermann family lived in hiding in the village of Radziszów, south of Kraków, at the home of Franciszek and Adriana Tomek (recognized by Yad Vashem in year 2012 as Righteous Among the Nations). Mateusz Filipowski served as a messenger and delivered the allowance from Żegota to them.

together with her son Gabriel, fifteen hundred złoty per month.[17] There was the Rolider family from Kalisz - her maiden name was Dunkelman. There were eleven people; I received eight thousand złoty a month for them. There was Dr. Rapaport, the uncle of Madzia Munwes and his mistress Janka, who received fifteen hundred złoty per month, and there were others. So the money got through. My husband, Noldek, transferred the money. This was after the Jewish uprising in the Warsaw Ghetto in 1943.

I'll return to what happened later at 11 Grzybowska Street. As mentioned, they saw Noldek, saw that Noldek entered the apartment, and they recruited him for the underground [the remnants of the ŻZW in Warsaw]. He worked there, but also served as a messenger-runner (*goniec*), delivering news from the underground at Grzybowska to Mokotów and other places, taking advantage of his good Aryan appearance. Mietek didn't know about this. Mietek begged us not to do this. I also wanted to enlist in this activity; I underwent military training for women at the school. "I ask you not to get involved in this," Mietek repeated and demanded. But Noldek became involved in their activity; he worked with them, and served as a messenger. One day, imagine, I don't know how, there might have been an informant; in any case, Germans came there. They shot at each other. Four Germans fell. They defended themselves, they had nothing to lose. Four

---

17   The husband and the father, Dr. Jakub Munwes, was a physician in the na Czystem Hospital and later in the hospital on Gęsia Street in the ghetto. According to the journals of Dr. Emanuel Ringelblum, he also directed a vital public activity there. Faithful to his medical and public commitments, he remained in the ghetto on his own volition, despite opportunities to flee, and he was murdered by the Nazis during the uprising. His son who survived is the writer and editor Prof. Gabriel Moked.

Germans fell.[18] He was working in the same building, on the ground floor, in the warehouse. He even told Mother that he helped carry a German on a stretcher. He fled and came to Mother on Świętojerska Street. He told her what happened there. Then Mother called Mietek. That night, Noldek stayed with Mother, and they met at her place. Mietek said that Noldek should not "play" any longer, and should stay there. When this happened, Mietek quickly started preparing new papers for him and looked for another apartment. He stayed the night with Mother. The next morning, he said to Mother, "I saw my father in a dream, and he threatened me with his finger." Mother said to him, "Wait until Mietek comes," and he replied, "No, I must go to Mokotów to warn the group there, so they'll know what happened, that the place there is 'burned,' that they shot each other and took the others with them." Mother said, "But come back!" So he left and went there. And Mother said, "After all, I couldn't hold on to him by force." Imagine, he didn't return to Mother. Meanwhile, Mietek had new papers ready for him. Now, *à propos* Stasia: As evening fell on the day after that battle, Stasia went downstairs before the curfew hour. Basia was already living in Stasia's home. [That is, Stasia already knew that Mietek was a Jew.] And here she saw that there, on 11 Grzybowska Street, there was a Gestapo vehicle and they were pushing a young man inside. When the car drove off, she approached and asked what happened there. Then people told her, "You know that blond man with the gold eyeglasses, he's apparently a Jew, we don't know. They took him." You can imagine how terrified Mietek and Stasia were. It was almost the hour of curfew, but they had an alternative second apartment as a backup. Apparently, it was at the place where

---

18   A group of fighters from the Jewish Military Union (ŻZW) of the Revisionist Beitar movement lived in hiding at 11 Grzybowska Street. They had participated in the Warsaw Ghetto Uprising and escaped from the ghetto at the end of the uprising. The battle on Grzybowska Street occurred on June 19, 1943. Four Germans and seven underground fighters were killed, including Paweł Frenkel, the commander of the ŻZW. Three underground fighters were captured alive and lost. In her testimony, Cesia Kolska did not differentiate between the different movements in the Jewish underground. According to Cesia, Arnold Walfisz collaborated with ŻZW members as well as members of the Jewish Fighting Organization (ŻOB) in Aryan Warsaw.

Moniek, your father, lived later. Suffice it to say that the next morning Stasia and Mietek left the building and went there, and they left Basia in their apartment. They told her, "Basia, go to the church," because they were afraid that Noldek would reveal something. He wouldn't have necessarily had any written addresses, but the Gestapo men would beat and torture prisoners in such a way - like executioners - that they would get everything out of them. But I told Mietek that Noldek had cyanide. Each underground member had cyanide. I did too. If I had remained alone, then I wouldn't have remained alive. I would have swallowed it. My mother didn't want any for herself. My Polish landlady also had cyanide (*cyankali*), and she told me, "If I fall into the hands of the Germans, I'll take cyanide. He [Noldek] had [cyanide] so I said, "Mietek, don't be afraid." Because everyone in the underground army knew that if they were caught, they would be brutally tortured, and they had cyanide and swallowed it. The Germans wouldn't suspect at first, and they didn't search for poison when they caught them, and meanwhile they would take out and swallow [the poison] in the hour of need. Never mind. The fact is that every underground activist had cyanide. And in particular, he carried two pistols. How do I know? Because Basia said that he would come to them and tell her, "Basia, feel me here." So she felt uncomfortable that a man was asking this of a young woman, and feared that this was a sexual provocation, and it made her blush. And he repeated, "Basia, touch me here," and she felt the weapon. He wanted to check whether someone could feel the pistols from the outside. He had two pistols: One in the back here, and one on the other side. He had high boots. And my landlady said that he had a pistol in his boot. He didn't admit it to me, but she indeed knew this. He told my landlady that he was in the underground, and her sons were also in the AK. That was the end of Noldek. You understand what happened. Mietek wasn't at home. They didn't inquire further about what happened with him because they were afraid. Later, it was quiet. So I said to Mietek, "He's already gone."

Yoseph: When did Stasia learn that Mietek was a Jew? Did she already know then?

Cesia: She already knew then that Mietek was a Jew because Basia already came to her three days after the ninth of May 1943 [Three days after she learned that her parents were murdered in Rembertów, as per details in chapter B. Stasia, below]. Never mind, Noldek would come to them at 22 Grzybowska; Stasia did as she pleased. He would come to them often, would eat something at her place; he would also come to me. It was, forgive me, in May or June of 1943, I don't remember. After the liquidation of the ghetto, all of them were on the Aryan side in 1943.

Yoseph: Was he also involved in the Polish underground?

Cesia: The Jewish underground! Those who remained on the Aryan side in Warsaw. He lived on Grzybowska and worked there. He knew those people there, and he was their messenger-runner (*goniec*). Mietek didn't know about it and I didn't know.

Yoseph: He was an extraordinary man, a devoted man.

Cesia: Yes! He was. And he was a great optimist. He would say to me, "Cesia, I was born in June, I'm the last fighter. I'll survive! And when I survive, we'll travel to Palestine and the money will come from America." Because his grandfather, Rothewald, wrote a Torah scroll [a sign of wealth, and he lived in America]. It was a very well-known family. When I was in Israel, Madzia Munwes, who was from Warsaw, said, "Do you know what kind of husband you had?" He was so handsome and from what a family, one of the largest - *yiches* (distinguished pedigree), as the Jews say. The year 1943 ended and in 1944, when you arrived, Noldek was no longer alive. Suffice to say that in 1943 Noldek was with me, I was pregnant … (mumbles). He would come to me, stay for an hour or two, and leave. In 1943, during the days of Easter, my landlady felt really sorry that we were young and not together. She would say to him, "Roman, spend a night here with your wife." We did as she said, and I got pregnant. The landlady offered to perform an abortion; she was a midwife and had a unique method for doing this. So he said to me, "Cesia, the war will be over by the end of January. Don't feel distressed, don't do an abortion." Then I said, "No! I won't have a baby now." Father wasn't living with me yet - we lived apart then, or perhaps he did already live here. Meanwhile, there was that mishap with those Germans who arrested him. I was pregnant then. When I did the abortion, Noldek was no longer alive. Then Father came to me, in 1943, and we lived at her place, both of us, and we lived there, as they say, in fear. And Dr. Sack from the Jewish Fighting Organization (ŻOB) lived there, and we would hear what was happening with the Russians, and that Russia was already drawing near.

8. The Warsaw Uprising

Cesia: It was on August 1, 1944. The first bomb landed right in front of our building. At the time, Father and Dr. Sack were still there, as well as a woman who arrived that day.
Yoseph: What do you know about my parents at the time?
Cesia: Your parents, I don't know where they were then. I know that your mother and father were in Warsaw, that they had to take Ignaś from Kuropieska, and that you were in Brzesko. That, I know. Later, when the uprising erupted, we met.

My landlady Mrs. Kałuszko and her son went down to the basement while the bombing was still going on. Dr. Sack went right away to Ogrodowa Street. He was carrying a large sum of money, and he took it with him. He would distribute the funds, and he took them. At first, we didn't go, because we were afraid. We were in the apartment. There was a sort of niche and we stood inside it. In front, that bomb landed. Afterward, I ran with Father, and we even took that Jewish woman with us. We went to Mietek on 22 Grzybowska Street. The bombing was terrifying. The Germans bombed from the air, Ignaś remembers that. And we were with Stasia. Your mother and father arrived at Stasia's with Ignaś. Hela, with her husband Michał and the baby, also came to Stasia. I remember there was a Polish woman there who recognized me as a Jew and said, "If you emerged from one inferno in the ghetto, then you'll escape the second one, too." Then there was another bombing. My landlady also came there. She had a small dog that barked in a very annoying way. The people asked her to set the dog free. So she went out with the dog; she didn't want to stay any longer. Then there was again a terrible bombing.
Yoseph: Did Mrs. Kałuszko survive?
Cesia: I don't know. It wasn't nice of me that I didn't inquire.
Yoseph: She deserves recognition as one of the Righteous Among the Nations.
Cesia: We walked amidst the bombing and fire until we reached Wolska Street, where there was a power station of the city tram system. I was even barefoot; I lost my shoes. Stasia didn't object to anything. After all, we were all Jews, and we looked like Jews. We arrived there, on Wolska Street, and we hid inside the tunnels of the power station. There was a network of

tunnels across Warsaw for the electric cables; you could see the manhole covers in the streets of the city. Two people could stand up in the tunnels side by side. In general, many Poles worked there, and besides us there were a lot of power station employees there. There was even a small room that served as a kitchen, and it was stocked with food and vodka, as much as you wanted. Father, Mother, Mietek, Basia, and I were there, Cesia, Moniek and Ignaś, all Jews, and Stasia. Marysia, Max, and their little son Eli were not with us. Meanwhile, we stayed there maybe a week or two. We ate and we drank. But Hela had that baby, Wiesio, and the baby cried. So the Poles told her husband, the policeman Michał, to kill that baby so they wouldn't be discovered. And he replied, "I will not kill the baby!" In the end - I wasn't present at the time - one day they poured kerosene on Michał and he caught on fire. Mietek was alert enough to remove Michał's pants. Another Polish man was also badly burned in this incident and ran, on fire, out of the station. And up above the uprising was raging, with the sounds of bombs and gunfire. He ran into Germans, and during his interrogation, he revealed that there were people down below. One day, or one night, while we sat there in the dark - we were eating and Stasia was making tea - the Germans opened the manhole covers in order to go down to the tunnels. We dispersed and fled in panic. Mother, Basia and I stayed together, and we found shelter from the bombings above in a basement where there were barrels of lubricating oil. We didn't know what happened to the rest of the people. In the morning, the Germans started searching for us in the tunnels. They asked, "Who's there?" We came out, raised our hands, and Mother replied in German, *"Hier sind drei Frauen"* ("There are three women here"). They asked, *"Allein?"* ("Alone?"), and she responded in the affirmative. We were smeared with grease. They ordered us to come out. They took and led us to a church at the corner of Wolska Street [Kościół Św. Stanisława]. The three of us arrived there, the first ones from our group. I was barefoot. We met many Poles, and I also recognized several Jews among them, too. As they say, "A Jew can smell a Jew." One of them asked, "Are you one of us?" I replied, "Yes." He asked, "By yourself?" I replied, "No, I'm here with my mother and a relative." He said, "Come, when they take us to work with German peasants, we'll present ourselves as a married couple." After a day or two, Stasia entered with Mietek. They also went out and were caught somewhere else. Meanwhile, Stasia was lugging a variety of things she had a coat and fur gloves, and she gave me a pair of shoes. After a day, or perhaps five days, I don't remember, your father arrived with your mother and Ignaś, together with Hela and the baby. They had hidden for several days in the nearby Philips light bulb factory, and Michał lay there with burns. And your father told me for the first time, when he was in the United States, that he was the one who went out at night and brought water for everyone. He told us what an anti-Semite Michał was. Michał didn't know that your father was Jewish. Your father said that when they were together in that Philips factory, "It was bad. We didn't know whether or not we'd survive, so I hugged Cesia." Then Michał grabbed something, because he knew that Mietek had contact with Jews, and said to Moniek (Mateusz), "You too are a mangy Jew!" [Note: According to Father's recordings, such an incident occurred at the power station, before Michał was burned]. And your father said that he was the only one who made an effort to bring Michał whatever food he could find: a carrot, potatoes and water, and then, in that situation, Michał could still curse him as "a mangy Jew?" So until the Germans came there. We asked, "Where's Michał?" They claimed that the Germans said they would take him to a hospital. A few days later, Mietek was curious and went into the Philips factory to check, and he saw Michał lying, shot.

Yoseph: My father said that other Poles, tram employees, also acted in an anti-Semitic way toward the group.

Cesia: Everyone faced the same danger; I don't know about that. They identified us as Jews because I was there. Then we were in that church. It was a church and the Germans turned it into a military transit station. They needed someone to cook. So Stasia offered to be a cook, and she cooked for them; she prepared tasty food with vodka, minced dishes, and they stuffed themselves. Stasia also brought food for us, because she was working as a cook, and they knew that Mietek was her husband, and we didn't lack anything. And so, a number of days passed. Mietek whispered that your father told him that before they went out of the tunnel, he saw that the manhole cover was open and a bomb had killed my father. We thought that Father was dead. Mietek whispered to me, "I'm going there to see. If I find Father, I'll bury him and I'll tell you where I buried him, and

if one of us survives, we'll bring him for burial in a cemetery." Then Mietek told a German that he was going to bring him vodka, and he left. He did indeed return with vodka, but Mietek walked along the entire length of that tunnel and didn't find any trace of Father's body. Father didn't arrive at the church. It turns out that they caught him in a different place, and he was sent and spent time in Auschwitz. Then they started to evacuate the Poles from there and send them to Pruszków. Stasia, Mietek, and Basia stayed longer in the church, because Stasia was a cook for the Germans. Mother and I, and your parents and Ignaś, arrived in Pruszków. The Germans transported the people there in regular passenger trains. I was with Mother in line at the church, and they took everyone to Pruszków.
Yoseph: And my parents?
Cesia: They were no longer there. So, I said to Mother, "Come, let's go with the group and be on our way." Suffice it to say that we traveled to Pruszków. The trains to Pruszków passed via Ursus. Then Mietek, Stasia, and Basia got off at the brief stop there - they took a risk and didn't return to the train. We arrived in Pruszków and Cesia, Moniek, and Ignaś were there. And there was Herman Bloch, Bala's husband. Bloch lived with Leopolda Kuropieska's father, and Mietek paid for his upkeep.
Yoseph: Did he earn so much that he could support him?
Cesia: *Freg nischt!* (Don't ask!) They tell you "morning," so it's morning. He earned money, and he helped as best he could. I also received money for Bloch's upkeep [from Żegota] and we added the rest.

In regard to Bloch, don't ask. I'll tell you! Imagine, when the uprising began, Kuropieska's mother told him to go. He could have remained in Praga, and then he would have survived. But he left Praga, came to Warsaw for the uprising, and arrived in Pruszków. Later, we also met your mother. We were in Pruszków for a number of days. It was a train station, and from there they took the people in train cars. You've seen those cars, as they say for animals. First the Jews were transported in those cars, and now it was for the Poles. We were transported in those cars to Stutthof.

9. At the Stutthof concentration camp

We remained in Pruszków for several days. I thought I was traveling to work among the *Bauern* (German peasants). We didn't expect to be sent from there to a concentration camp. Then Herman even said to my mother, "You know, Helcia, you'll appear as my wife and Cesia as our daughter, and we'll be together as a family." It was only later, in Stutthof, that I met your mother, Cesia. Then they loaded us into those railroad cars. We were together: Herman [Bloch], Mother, and I. The people being transported knew nothing about wearing striped clothing. I already knew from the underground that people in the concentration and death camps wore striped clothing. I received news every day, because while in hiding I was in contact with Dr. Sack. The people lay one on top of another. There were cracks in the wooden walls of the train cars, and I looked through them and my eyes beheld: striped clothing! Then I said out loud, "Oy! We're not going to peasants, but to concentration camps." Then the Poles said, "You, stupid woman, you better shut up!" I shut up, because I was always afraid of being discovered. I was the first one in the train car to notice this. I saw camps outside of Stutthof that appeared to be quite orderly. Perhaps they sent them out from there to work; there were also subcamps of Stutthof. Suffice it to say that they brought us to Stutthof. We spent about a week outside before they transferred us to the *Lager* (camp). It was good that Mother had a jacket, so she covered herself well. We were still with Herman Bloch men and women. We were all considered insurgents (*powstańcy*). There was a whole group of young people there, even female Jewish insurgents who had escaped from the ghetto and later fought in the uprising in Warsaw, in the Old City. There was a whole group of Jewish women who pretended to be Poles. Later, they separated us from the men and from Bloch, and they took us to the Lager. They took Herman to the men's camp, and they stripped us, gave us a dressing gown, and then that lice-infested clothing. The lice bit us and drank our blood. Later - I don't know how - I received a note from Herman saying, "I'm like a newborn baby." So my mother understood that they had taken everything from him. After all, a newborn has nothing.

They took the women to those camps. I knew from the underground that even in the camps, if you had a piece of gold, you might have a chance of surviving. So I had a two-carat diamond that I received from my husband at Mrs. Kałuszko's home; the diamond ring I'm wearing now; Mother's wedding ring; and a gold Cyma watch with a gold chain. I hid them in female private parts. Mother did the same thing. Your mother had a beautiful three-colored gold bracelet, and she also had other things, and she did the same thing. My mother even had a gold watch, and she threw it to me! We were afraid, because they would conduct examinations of the women. In the end, they didn't cut our hair or examine us. The Polish women tossed out handfuls of gold. Mother whispered fearfully "Cesia!" because she was afraid they would conduct examinations. Cesia, your mother, didn't say a thing. She also kept the bracelet with her, and I don't know what else she had. In any case, we made it through and I still have Mother's ring and this inlaid ring, but I lost the watch.

They took us to the concentration camp. I pretended to be Polish. I had one bit of luck: I was with the Polish intelligentsia. They were all from Mokotów, and that was an expensive section of Warsaw. The riffraff didn't live there. Doctors, engineers, and the like lived there. There were also some doormen and prostitutes, but the majority were from the elite, and I became very friendly with them. They put us in barracks with one bunk for every three women, and there were four or five women per bed. There was one woman who lay on the bed with me, and another woman who was a prostitute. And she said, "Oh! We have a Jew among us." And I remember that one of the women said, "There are none here! We're all Poles!" Another time, when one woman just blurted out something, two women responded - one was an engineer's wife and the other one a doctor's wife - "We're all Poles!" And that was lucky. Cesia, your mother, right away told stories and tales: that her husband was in a POW camp or labor camp, it doesn't matter. After they took us, no barracks remained on that side, where there were Polish women. No room remained. There were Christians there from all over Europe: French people and others from every country. There was no room. A bit earlier, they also brought a group of Christian women from Vilna. Then they cleared out a barrack that was among the Jewish barracks, because in Stutthof some of the prisoners were Jews who were kept separate, and the others were not Jews. And there, among the Jewish women [barracks], they housed the women from Vilna in such a way that each had a separate bunk. When our transport from Warsaw arrived, there were about six hundred people I think, including the men. About three hundred were women - so they said. Well, they brought us to that barrack with the women from Vilna. We were defined, immediately upon arrival, as political prisoners, marked with badges of red triangles (*czerwone winkle*). Not Poles, not Jews, but "political." We all received the red triangles. I was with Mother and we immediately became friends with one woman, Mrs. Lamańska. This woman took a special liking to me. She was from a small town near Warsaw, the wife of a blacksmith. She apparently had contact with Jews, and this stirred her affection. We became very friendly. She didn't know I was a Jew, but they suspected me. And there were other Polish women with whom I got along very well. Even the chief inspector in our block (*blokowa*) didn't treat me differently. There was just one woman from Vilna, a young girl, who was so obnoxious. Among those women from Vilna, there was a group of Poles, and it's known that most of the Catholics there before the war were not anti-Semites. It's known that there was not much anti-Semitism in Polish Vilna. When they brought our group to the barrack of the Vilna group, they divided us into those who go out to work and those who remain in the camp. At first, I placed myself on the side of those going out to work, and I took Mother with me. I felt that since I was young, I would be taken for work. They only left the older people and the infirm behind. A roll call (*Appell*) was conducted in the morning, and we stood in rows by the entrance of the barrack. The Vilna women were there, and among them was Maria Pjeret, a Polish woman, an actress in the Polish theater. She came up to me and said, "What are you? What's wrong with you? Your mother won't last a single day there." I said, "But they'll take me to work!" Then she said, "Tomorrow, stand on that side, the one that stays in the Stutthof camp." So, thanks to her, I remained inside the Stuffhof camp. I'll never forget what she did for me. The women from Vilna always helped me. I don't know whether it would have been safer to go to work; I don't have an answer for that. They said they were going to dig trenches. She said, "It's not suitable for your mother, it's not work in a factory, stay here." Later, there was also a nun I'll never forget what she did for me.

Your mother also remained in the Stutthof camp. I don't know how; I don't remember. She didn't offer herself for that work. The people decided which path to choose. Cesia, your mother, stayed, and there were other young Jewish women who remained. We could feel who the Jews were. There were two young women, seventeen and nineteen years old, with their aunt - undoubtedly Jews. And there were also two sisters from a rural estate. Your mother even met them after the war. Well, and there was the group of insurgents who were captured in Warsaw, and Jewish women among them. The insurgents comprised quite a large group, and they were assigned a separate room. The Poles would bring them extra food out of admiration, as if to say, "*Powstanki!* (Insurgents!) They fought for Warsaw!" The Jewish women had no problems there. I also had no problem, because those Polish women didn't let anyone taunt us or inform on us. There was one young woman with us who never spoke, not a word. Her aunt was also with her. Mother and I decided that she was a Jew. The aunt never left the barrack, while Mother and I always went out for inspection. They allowed the older women to stay in the barrack. Even the Russian, Mariuszka, who was responsible for our barrack, allowed them to do this. But there was one young woman, Jadwiga, supposedly a nurse, who helped when someone was sick or something like that. She sent me one time to call my mother to come stand in the inspection. The Polish women said to her, "Miss Jadwiga, Mrs. Maria stays here! She's an older woman." Then she kept her mouth shut. I was afraid of her; she made faces at me. I'll tell later about a nun who was also a nurse, Julia ... [who apparently had greater professional authority]. They put us in one room, and your mother was in another room. Anyway, the conditions were very tough. Before, the Vilna women had a separate room and each of them slept in a separate bed. Suddenly, an order was issued that the Vilna women would have to put more people in the room because there was a shortage of rooms. So the nurse-nun Julia lived with us. And Mrs. Lewandowska was also with me, sharing the same bed, and the wife of Piłsudski's aide-de-camp was also with me, and the lover of Prince Radziwiłł. That's how we held ourselves together. We slept five or six women in one bed.

Yoseph: Did you see my mother every day? Which barrack was she in?

Cesia: I would see her at the roll calls. She was in the same barrack with us, but in a different hall. We saw her every day; sometimes also when we peeled potatoes. Your mother received a package at the camp. She came and gave us something from the package. They told us we could write letters, and they distributed letter forms. But it was only permitted to write in German, once a month. My mother was the only one who knew German well. They stood in line for her to write for them. Mother even filled in the forms for them. We wrote to Kalisz; we even wrote to Mietek, who was in Ursus. Our letters didn't arrive. But Samek Bloch received a letter from your mother, and she received a package. Now, after my mother filled in the forms, the people would give her a small onion here, a potato there, you know. Mother wrote. I was in good relations with all of the women there. There was just that Jadwiga who treated me rudely. The prostitutes didn't say anything anymore. And in the end, Jadwiga, the nurse's aide from the Poznań area, stopped harassing me. How was I able to improve relations with her? I'll tell you later, it happened a few days before Christmas.

After a few days in Stutthof, we heard people saying that some people were hiding gold items or something like that. I stood without responding. Your mother secretly took out a gold bracelet and buried it in the sandy ground at the camp. Later, when they brought us back, she couldn't find it. Then she took a rake and started to rake. A German woman came and said to her, "*Du wirst hier Ordnung machen!*" ("You will make everything orderly here!") And so, she became a groundskeeper (*Hofcowa*), who received two portions of bread and two portions of soup. She didn't find the bracelet, but it gave her this privilege - light work. I went to dig potatoes (*Kartoffelkommando*), and Mother would stay in the barrack. I also received extra soup when I returned from work. Everyone who went to work received extra portions. I was strong and I went out to work. I kept my valuables with me. Later, I moved them from place to place - gave them to Mother, and so on. Later, an order was issued to thoroughly clean the barracks. Everyone was removed from the barrack. It was very cold outside; it was already winter. They took us to shower. Your mother had some Russian gold coins. (Now, Cesia asked me if I knew this. I replied that I didn't, but that Mother had told me about the bracelet and the raking. However, I had already forgotten this.)

Cesia: [continues the recording]: Your mother hid the coins inside soap, two or three bars, I don't remember. The water in the shower was very hot, and they took us in groups. Then she said to me, "I'll go first and you and mother will go later." And she gave me that soap, "Hold on to it!" Meanwhile, they didn't return and they took our group and I was with that stuffed soap. What can I tell you? What could I have done? I said to Mother, "Whatever will be, will be." Everyone took one piece of soap. I held it in my hand, I don't remember exactly. I think there were two pieces of soap. Afterward, they didn't take us to the barrack, but to a big hall instead, because they said they needed to disinfect our barracks. Perhaps from typhus, or maybe they were searching for something. I have no idea. We were there for quite a few days, in terrible conditions. One person piled onto another. Later, we went back to the barrack again. They told the young women to bring mattresses into the barrack. I immediately volunteered in order to get a good bed. I did that immediately. I took two mattresses and saved two bunks: for my friends and for Mother. Cesia was in the other barrack [or perhaps in another part of the barrack].

Yoseph: Did you intentionally try not to be with Mother?

Cesia: No. That's the way it turned out. She was in another room. In the barracks, there were these types of rooms - haven't you seen pictures? Yes, there were bunks. When there were three levels, I was always in in the middle bunk. Three people to a bunk. The Jewish women in Stutthof also had bunks like these. They lay one on top of another, that's the way we were there. I went to the group that dug potatoes *Kartoffelkommando*. [Note: In 1992, three years after the meetings with Cesia, I went to the Stutthof camp, which was mostly preserved, and in the prison barracks there were indeed subdivisions into large rooms, called "sleeping halls," with wooden beds with three levels of bunks.]

Cesia: Afterward, in January 1945, an order was issued that anyone who was healthy had to move to a different place. Your mother went with that transport. They took most of the healthy ones and sent them out of Stutthof.

Yoseph: Where did they go?

Cesia: Back to Poland in January.

Yoseph: In the death march!

Cesia: No, we didn't know. They said they were taking them to work. I don't know. Many people fell because it was a harsh winter. Many from that group returned to Stutthof. Your mother went to Kalisz.

Yoseph: Mother came to Kalisz only in June 1945.

Cesia: In any case, many died en route. Your mother told us. I don't remember the details. They left us in Stutthof. Imagine, afterward a typhus epidemic broke out. It was after your mother had already left. They left the hospital - they didn't take anyone from the hospital. The hospital remained, and among the healthy ones, there was only one room left. I remember twelve people in all. The others were taken to the march, where your mother went. I was the youngest one, and there was the nurse Julia, that beautiful nun. Then, meanwhile, before the march, I was struck by a terrible cough. So she went and brought suction cups and she placed them on my back. That nun was wonderful. You could get everything at the camp: gold, medicine, anything you wanted, from friends or in exchange for valuables. Yes, suction cups were very popular and people brought suction cups with them.

Yoseph (chuckling and laughing): But it doesn't help!

Cesia (shouting): It most certainly does help! It's better than penicillin! If it weren't for the suction cups, I wouldn't be alive today. I was coughing terribly, Mother told me. Afterward, my back was black from the cups. Perhaps thanks to that, I'm alive. And there was typhus. Suffice it to say, there was typhus. I don't remember with certainty whether the typhus was before your mother left or afterward. I think it was after they left. So I knew that for gold, it was possible .... (mumbles). Then, that nurse Jadwiga remained. Now, when we were sick, there was also a doctor there, a Polish woman from Częstochowa. After that transport, we were so lice-ridden, so she sent someone to bring sabadilla to the room, saying, "Wash your hair with this, because the lice are drinking your blood and spreading typhus." And Mother contracted typhus. Then she, that doctor, said to that Janina, Mrs. Jadwiga, "Madam, after all, you can arrange something, find a way, find a solution." That Janina-Jadwiga was a practical nurse - actually a nursing assistant in the hospital, if I'm not mistaken - and that one was a real physician, a lady doctor. So she told her, "Mrs. Jadwiga, you have friends on the other side [she had "lovers-admirers"]; you can get medicine." That's what she said in regard to my mother, because my mother had a high fever. When I heard this, I went to her and said, "Mrs. Janina, I'll give you something if you do something for my mother." And I gave her this diamond. This was before your mother left. [Here Cesia corrected her previous statement.] But your mother didn't have typhus. At that time, there were still many insurgents in the camp who knew how to give injections. They would come and give Mother those injections. Afterward, she gave glucose, and they didn't know how to do this; they didn't have ampoules for this. So my mother would swallow these medications and she recuperated, in exchange for that diamond. What did she do with that diamond? It's not my business. She must have surely kept it with her. What gave it away?! She survived. I saw her after everything. She was able to get the medication from the men. Because they stripped everyone who arrived there, and they would collect everything they had with them. There were storerooms full of medications, whatever your heart desired. And when she had a sweetheart on the other side, then she obtained the medicines. Doctors and others arrived at the camp and the things that were taken were arranged orderly in the storeroom. If you had someone on the other side ... she had a "lover-admirer." She had a man. Suffice it to say that I gave her, and Mother received ... (mumbles – the name of a medication). I think with this help, she regained her health.

After her, I became ill with typhus. Mother thought I was going to die. But think how fully aware I was: I had that small package. We had one woman there from Riga, Mrs. Eva. She spoke German, and Mother thought she was Jewish, but she wasn't a Jew. Mother told me this, because I didn't remember, I was burning from fever, like fire. But Mother still couldn't get out of bed, she was sick, lying down. Then she called Mrs. Eva to help and she wanted to give her something so she would take care of me, and she said, "I have something here for you." She said, "My daughter is surely going to die!" And I said to Mother: "Don't give her anything, because I'm going to live." My mother told me this, because I don't remember. (She laughs.) But I was so cognizant that I said to Mother, "Don't give anything, because I'm going to live." And Eva, who didn't understand what this was all about, also told Mother that I was still young, that I would overcome and survive. Mother told me, "You were so feverish; someone could get a burn [from touching you]. But your mind was working." And I survived.

I went to the *Kartoffelkommando*. Even before I became ill, Janina wanted Mother to send her "to bring things." And I wanted to get on her good side. And it so happened that before Christmas she wanted to give a present to her friend on the other side of the fence. She brought four pieces of cloth, thread, and a knitting needle, and asked who could knit lace for her. I said, "I'll knit lace for you." She was not a *kapo* – she helped the sick and was with us in the barrack. I always knitted, mittens and such, before the war, too. In history class in high school, when they would catch me knitting, they would write a note, "Kolska is not paying attention." So, I knitted for her, and won her heart, but I kept the knitting needle. One time, I was sitting in the lavatory when our chief inspector was also sitting there that creep Mariushka, the *blokowa*. She barely knew what a silk stocking was, but she had silk stockings she had received from the things women had brought from Warsaw. In Russia, they didn't have such things. She wore beautiful silk stockings, but a stitch unraveled in one of the stockings. She screamed, "*Oy! Czoszki, czoszki!* ["Oy! stockings, stockings!" in broken Polish.] Then I said to her, "Mariushka, give it to me, I'll fix the run." In Poland, there were special needles for fixing runs, but I thought I could fix the stocking even with the needle I had. So I fixed the stocking and gave the mended stockings to her. In exchange, I received a whole loaf of bread, a cup of jam, and margarine. It was worth more than a million dollars to me today. I shared those gifts with a few of my friends. Later, she realized that my mother understood Russian. She entered the room, and I was peeling potatoes, and then she asked, "Where is the "*Dievushka co robi czoszki*" ["the girl who fixes stockings" - broken Polish mixed with Russian]?" My mother called me, "Come here." So I approached and she said that I was her daughter, "*moya dochka*." Since then, she spoke Russian with my mother and I could disregard Janina, because the chief creep, the head of the block, was now on my side. She continued to bring me stockings to mend, and each time I received a chunk of bread in return. And if I was out peeling potatoes, she would give bread to Mother, and I didn't have to worry about Mother's food. These are snapshots of events.

Yoseph: Do you know details about my mother?

Cesia: Wait a bit.

Yoseph: The tape is about to run out.

Cesia: About your mother, I only know that she could have remained with Ignaś, because [at the selection in Piotrków] they stood together. Your father, as a deaf-mute, they wouldn't send. And they would have kept Cesia as a mother of a child. And how that would have actually turned out, it's impossible to know. But because they stood together, they placed Ignaś with his father and sent his mother to the camp. That's what I know about your mother. More than that, I don't know, except what she told me afterward herself.

Yoseph: How do you know that your father was in Auschwitz?

Cesia: I only learned this recently. In the 1960s, a woman from Kalisz came to the United States, and she had a Polish husband. She was also in Auschwitz and she thought at first that my father was also a Pole. When she arrived in New York, she heard that there was a Kolski there. There was an acquaintance, Rakowski, and he telephoned Mietek. I was then with Mother, with Jonas and with Meikel [her husband, Jonas Virshup, whom she married in Sweden, and their son Moshe – Mosch Virshup] on a visit to a summer camp. She told Mietek that my father was in Auschwitz. So, when Mietek went to that basement and didn't find Father, he came to me and said, "Cesia, the last time we saw Father was August 22, 1944, and whoever of us survives, this date will be set as the day he died." When we arrived in Sweden and registered in the community, we gave that date, the third day of Av, as the day of his death - that was the date in 1944. Later, when the woman from Kalisz came and heard the name Kolski, she contacted us. She was with the Jewish women in Auschwitz, and the Polish prisoners were the ones who brought them muddy coffee (*lura*) in the morning, in a vat for distribution. Our father was the man who would bring the coffee in the morning, posing as a Pole. He would come every day and quietly ask, "Is there someone here from Kalisz by chance?" and she said, "I'm from Kalisz."

Yoseph: And he wasn't afraid?

Cesia (angrily): Listen to the facts, there was no question of fear. If you wanted to help, you had to take a risk! Mietek didn't endanger himself? Your father took risks! So they whispered together. I knew that woman from back in Kalisz, and he said to her quietly, "I'm Kolski from Kalisz, my daughter is Cesia, and my son is Mietek-Nafcio. They have Aryan papers." He told her, "Your father won't survive. You are young and will stay alive. Cesia will survive, my son will survive, my wife won't survive and I won't survive. When you survive the war, you must look for them and tell them

I was here." He left her a will. She looked for us back in Poland. When she arrived in New York, the first question she asked was, "Is there someone here from the Kolski family?" We thought he died in 1944, in the month of Av, and she saw him in early 1945. They sent all of the Poles in the camp to the gas chambers.

Kolski family reunion in the United States. Standing (from right to left): Rena-Basia, Mietek and Cesia. Sitting: Stasia and Helcia Kolski.

[Note: I didn't record Cesia telling her story and the story of Helcia, her mother, during the maritime death march on the death rafts, in late April 1945. Cesia told me that they were loaded onto four motorless river rafts, without food or water. After a nightmarish voyage, during which they were bombed from the air, the sea current took their raft to the coast of Malmö in Sweden. Two rafts capsized, and many on their raft died of typhus, hunger, and exhaustion.]

Cesia: Mietek wrote to us [in Sweden] that we should come to Poland, but I didn't want to travel to Poland. I had no sentiment. I told him we'd come another time. Then, after the pogrom in Kielce, Stasia wanted to leave Poland. It wasn't Mietek who suggested this. I wrote to Mietek, "Come, and

we'll travel to America." Then Mietek wrote to America, asking that they send papers for us. Duell handled this over there. He also was in Israel.
Yoseph: Stasia had an exceptional personality.
Cesia: She has outbursts of irritability. At first she can get irritated and then she cries. Mietek suffered a lot from this, but she's remorseful after her outbursts. She's good in a way that you can't find, even today. Most of her tenants [in the cabins she rents out in Florida] are Jews. Even the ultra-Orthodox Jews leave kosher kitchenware with her, for her to keep in her home. Esther [Esther Doron, the daughter of Aunt Pola in Israel] knows this. She was once in the US and then Stasia took her to a synagogue for the first time in her life. And Basia, that was Rena Kolski, Mietek didn't want her in the house, but Stasia didn't let her go. For Stasia, she was like an older daughter. After the war, Basia was together with them in Kalisz, and they sent her to study at a high school. When she traveled to Israel and married [Kuba Rzeszewski], she received an entire dowry from them, and cloth for a wedding dress. When Mietek came to the US, his name was changed to Martin Kolski.

10. Bad news for Adek Goldberg and details about Arnold Walfisz

On October 18, 1945, Cesia Kolski wrote a letter to our cousin, Abraham (Adek) Goldberg, in Mandatory Palestine. At his request, she reported to him in this letter what she knew about the fate of his parents, Meir and Devorah-Dorcia, and his only sister, Esther-Tusia Goldberg, who perished after they were sent, from the Warsaw Ghetto to the death camps, as Cesia witnessed. The letter was sent from Sweden. Abraham Goldberg arrived alone in Jerusalem in 1938 with a student's visa, completed a master's degree at Hebrew University in Jerusalem, and would later complete a doctorate in geology. In this letter, she "consoles" him by telling about her own tragedy, writing:

> Now it's the fourth year since we married. Unfortunately, for two years and four months I don't know anything about my husband. We were in Warsaw on the 'Aryan' side with forged papers. My husband went around the city freely and even worked at a

company. He had a real 'Aryan' appearance. He volunteered for the [Jewish] underground political party. There was an incident, you know, as sometimes happens in such underground work, and he was arrested. That occurred on June 22, 1943. I haven't heard any word from him since. Maybe you know him: He was born in 1918 in Warsaw, his name is Arnold Walfisz. He studied at the Hinuch high school and lived on 18 Świętojerska Street. I myself didn't believe I would survive. I experienced horrible moments and today it's hard for me to believe that it occurred in reality.

We can deduce from the letter, first of all, that Arnold Walfisz joined the Revisionist underground on the Aryan side, perhaps even previously, in the Warsaw Ghetto. Secondly, Cesia Kolski cites the date of his capture by the Gestapo, according to what she knew at the time she wrote the letter. Was he really caught the day after the battle? We know today that the battle on 11 Grzybowska Street took place on June 19, 1943. Cesia didn't provide any further details about Arnold's affiliation, apparently because she was fearful of the British Mandate's censor.

B. STASIA

Memories recounted by Stanisława Kolski

Stasia: I was born in Kolno on November 13, 1912, and was named Stanisława Rogińska.[19] I came to Warsaw in 1930. I worked with my uncle and aunt, who ran a wholesale meat store. My uncle worked in political investigations, and fell ill and died in service at the age of thirty-two. When the war broke out, my aunt lost everything, but continued to run the store with me. Mietek (Mieczysław) Kolski arrived in Warsaw at the end of 1939, when the Germans started to concentrate the Jews in Kalisz. Mietek, his parents, and his sister Cesia lived in Warsaw in the area of the future ghetto. Mietek would purchase merchandise in the ghetto and sell it to stands and stores in Warsaw. He needed a policeman for his business. He would travel on the trams and observe the faces to see which policeman would be suitable for his business, and the connection was made. When he boarded the tram from Żoliborz to Nalewki Street in order to deliver merchandise, Michał, my cousin Hela's husband, was the right policeman. And they worked in collaboration for a number of months. On Christmas 1940, Michał invited Mietek to come and stay at his home in Warsaw. I also came there, and then we met. We also met on New Year's Eve and continued to see each other afterward. Michał knew that Mietek was bringing merchandise from Jews. Sometimes the merchandise was at the home of Mietek's parents. When Michał came to take merchandise from their apartment, Mietek would tell him to wait and would remove the sign from his parents' door with the name "Kolski" so that he wouldn't know there was a family connection between them. In terms of his language, accent, appearance, and behavior, there was no shadow of a doubt that he was a Catholic Pole from birth, and I had met many Jews long before, from living in close

---

19   This chapter is based on excerpts of testimony during a meeting between Yoseph Komem and Stasia (Stella) Kolski in the US, at her home in North Port / Mineral Warm Springs, Florida, on October 4-5, 2002, and on other testimony, as cited.

proximity and from business contacts. Our marriage was held on October 28, 1942, at my Roman Catholic parish church. Mietek rented a room until March 1943. Then we rented a small apartment on 22 Grzybowska Street. Our relationship during the German occupation was very good.

One morning in May 1943, just as someone was about to arrive to buy merchandise, a girl about sixteen years old knocked at the door and introduced herself as Barbara Alicja Smarzyńska. She was in a state of shock. She asked for Mr. Kolski. I answered, "He's not here right now, what can I do for you?"

Basia: I'm his cousin.[20]
Stasia: A cousin. Please, come in and sit down. What kind of cousin are you? He never told me that he has such a young cousin here.
Basia: Of course, my father and his father are brothers. [Basia started to cry, and her eyes were swollen even before.]
Stasia: Why and what are you crying about?
Basia: Why? Because the Germans killed my parents three days ago.
Stasia: Jesus Christ. Why did they kill them?
Basia: Why? Because they're Jews.
Stasia: Her mother had sewn our address and that of Maria Tomaszewska in the lining of her coat, and she came to us after wandering for three days, after already considering the possibility of surrendering herself to a German soldier and putting an end to everything. I was furious about the web of lies. I left the room, slamming the door. I returned a few minutes later and told her to get out immediately and to never come back. She left. I was also nervous, because the customer was expected to arrive any minute. But immediately after she left, I felt remorseful and I took pity on the girl, who was orphaned in those circumstances. I telephoned Maria Tomaszewska at Mrs. Krajewska's home, and told her that a sixteen-year-old girl came, whose parents were murdered by the Germans. Maria replied that the girl must be Basia Smarzyńska. Now I realized that it was Mietek who had arranged the papers for both of them.

---

20   The following dialogue is taken from a copy of the testimony of Basia (Rena Kolski or Rzeszewski) for Yad Vashem, in Montreal, in April 1989.

Basia had come to Maria already. After the telephone call from Stasia, she stayed with her. Later, Stasia asked Basia, "Where are you staying?" Basia replied, "At the musician's, and I look after the children." This was near the residence of Stasia and Mietek. Stasia told her, "Don't tell them anything, because then they'll tell you to leave, but if this happens for any reason, come live with us."

Stasia: The fathers of Mietek and of Rena, Moritz, and Roman Kolski were brothers. At first Basia lived with her parents in the city of Rembertów near Warsaw, all of them with an assumed Aryan identity. Later, only Rena's father remained in Rembertów, with his sister and her husband. The mother lived in Warsaw and gave music lessons. Basia lived in Warsaw with a musician whose wife had tuberculosis, and she took care of their children. Before her mother traveled one weekend to visit the father, she sewed the addresses of Mietek and Stasia and of Maria into the lining of Basia's coat. When the mother didn't return after two or three days, Basia traveled to Rembertów. The neighbors told her that the Gestapo had murdered her mother and father, along with his sister and her husband, and that the neighbors had buried them. The neighbors asked Basia what she was looking for, and she said that the mother was supposed to sell her shoes, and she departed. There was an informer.

Earlier, Mietek had taken his mother, Helcia (Helena Kolski) from the ghetto under a Polish identity. Papers were prepared for her in the name of Maria Tomaszewska. Helcia didn't have typical Jewish facial features, though her eyes were brown. But her gray hair gave her the look of an ordinary Polish elderly woman. Luckily, she spoke the Polish language very well. She lived in a rented room in the apartment of Mrs. Krajewska.

Stasia firmly decided to join Mietek in his rescue efforts. Basia moved in with Maria for a while, and then went to live permanently in the apartment of Mietek and Stasia. Stasia bought Basia clothes and fed her well, since she was in a state of starvation. Maria asserted that Basia should look for work. Stasia replied that Basia must not go to work because she didn't have the strength for it. Stasia was also certain that, if Basia went to work, she would be discovered, and there were indeed some incidents that illustrated such danger. On Sundays and holidays, Stasia would take Basia with her to the church where she prayed.

After rescuing his mother, Mietek also smuggled his father and sister, Moritz and Cesia Kolski, out of the ghetto. They had a more pronounced Jewish appearance. Cesia had already been taken to the Umschlagplatz once, but a Jewish policeman ordered her to leave. They caught her when she was out tending to affairs related to Mietek's merchandise. The policeman apparently knew her. Cesia was engaged then. She got engaged in the ghetto and later married, already in the Aryan part. Her husband's assumed name was Roman Woźniak. He was from Warsaw, and many people in the city knew him. He was the son of an engineer, and his mother had died and his father remarried. Both of his parents were murdered in Treblinka. Roman escaped from the ghetto before Cesia and lived near Mietek and Stasia. One time, he approached Stasia in the street to help her carry baskets, and she told him not to come near her in the street. In the building where Roman lived, there was an apartment in which about eleven to fifteen Jews were hiding. And here's what happened: The Germans discovered the group and opened fire, and then the Jews started to defend themselves and tossed grenades and hit the Nazi soldiers and their helpers. She was told that same day that they had killed one German and injured several others. But in the end, the Germans defeated them they took everyone who remained in a truck and finished them off. Roman emerged from the storeroom and helped carry the injured Germans on stretchers, and later he came to Maria Tomaszewska. Stasia said, "I sent him a message that he must not return to his room, not for any sum in the world, and that he should hide like Cesia." The next day, when Stasia went out to Grzybowska Street to wait for a delivery of coal from young coal peddlers, she suddenly saw Gestapo personnel standing and pushing someone into their closed vehicle (buda). Stasia recognized Roman from behind, by his leather jacket and high boots.

Stasia: Cesia and her father, Moritz Kolski, hid on Ciepła Street in the apartment of Mrs. Zofja Kałuszko. There was a hiding place there. There was also a dog that barked whenever someone approached the apartment entrance. Two other Jews hid in that apartment: Teitelbaum and Parucki [Dr. Józef Sack]. Parucki survived, and his wife and daughter, who hid somewhere else, also survived.

Stasia: So it happened that I became connected with the family of my Jewish husband: On his father's side, the Kolski and Silberstein families, and on his mother's side, the family of Cesia and Frania Jarecki, all from Kalisz and with forged documents and an assumed identity in occupied Warsaw. I believed that my religion and the way I regard others obligated me to save people who were in mortal danger. Now I felt a personal responsibility to save the lives of all the members of this new family of mine. It also became my personal war against the Hitlerite occupier, and I was prepared, fully conscious, to sacrifice my life, and in so doing perhaps endanger my Christian family members. The people there knew me. I was well versed in the vernacular of the Warsaw streets. I maintained my village look and habits, and I felt very sure of myself.

Stasia: One time, people in civilian clothes, who were actually policemen, came and asked about Mietek's father. Maybe he was registered at that address. Basia who was sleeping on the couch, turned pale, and Stasia sent her to the bedroom to get dressed. Mietek asked if he could offer them vodka, and then Stasia shouted at Mietek in street slang, "Drunkard, you already found some drinking buddies?" They summoned Stasia and Mietek to report to the police station, and there they found a way out.

Stasia met the deaf man Mateusz Filipowski (Moshe-Moniek) right after she and Mietek married. After their wedding, he came to visit Mietek, who wasn't home. Mateusz told her, "So, I'll wait." At the time, she didn't know yet that Mietek was a Jew. It was when they still lived in the rented room.

Another time, Mietek went out of the apartment and at the gate of the building encountered a gang of about five punks who demanded to see his identity card, the *Kennkarte*. Under pressure, he handed it to them, and they refused to return it. Mietek went back home, gave them a sum of money in exchange for the document, and told them he'd give them the rest the next day at a different address. Stasia decided that she would be the one to deliver it. She went to that address, and Mateusz and Krzyczkowski - a Christian friend from Kalisz of Frania, my mother's sister, who lived in Warsaw and was in contact with them walked behind her as backup to see what would happen. Stasia met them and started to loudly yell at them, "How dare you? I'm the wife of the man you're waiting for." They asked her, "How do you know us?" Stasia replied, "Not only do I know you, there are other people who know you well." They got onto a carriage and left. Mateusz and Krzyczkowski rented another carriage and followed them to see where they lived.

Stasia also recounted that Maria had stayed for a while at Leopolda Kuropieska's home, with Ignaś and another Jew. One time, Stasia went to a window in Mrs. Kuropieska's house to look outside, and Ignaś told her, "Please don't go to the window, because they'll see you."

Stasia also thought that I, Marek-Jurek, and my brother, Marian-Ignaś, passed through their apartment on 22 Grzybowska Street. After I was discovered at Mrs. Kuropieska's home, she moved me to the hideout of Moritz and Cesia Kolski in Mrs. Zofja Kałuszko's apartment. Later, she transferred me from the hideout apartment to their apartment and from there to Krzyczkowski. Stasia remembers a tall and handsome man from Brzesko perhaps it was Eugeniusz Łoza who came to bring me to the destination, near Bochnia in Galicia. She thinks that Ignaś stayed with them in the apartment for a longer period of time (about two to three weeks) after a second search was conducted in Leopolda Kuropieska's apartment, when Ignaś again miraculously went undiscovered.

Stasia also said that during most of the period of Nazi occupation, Mietek (and later she, too) was in personal contact with his cousin, Marysia, and her husband Max Silberstein. Max owned a textile factory in Warsaw, which they handed over to Mr. Jan Kubicki with promises for the future. Mietek would come to Mr. Kubicki, pay, and take products for his trade. Marysia Silberstein, the daughter of Moritz Kolski's sister from Kalisz, lived with her husband Max and infant Eli in the Warsaw Ghetto, and they also had assets outside of the ghetto.

Marysia told me that she and her husband worked in a factory outside of the ghetto.[21] When the situation in the ghetto became worse, she smuggled her son out of the ghetto one day when she went out to work. The child, Eli, who was born in the ghetto on April 11, 1941, had a Polish identity, and they called him Wojciech-Wojtuś. He was taken to the home of Stasia

---

21   This is a transcription of an interview with Marysia Silberstein at an assisted living facility in New Jersey, conducted by Yoseph Komem, on September 29, 2002 in the presence of her second son, Avi, and Myron Kolski, the only child of Stasia and Mietek.

and Mietek Kolski for a few days, until a more permanent place could be found for him. My father, Mateusz, also helped take care of him there, because "he already had experience with little children." Mietek and Stasia gave the boy to a woman they trusted, who found a place for him to stay on a farm with a friend whose husband served in the Polish Army in exile in London. The friend knew that the child was a Jew, but loved him very much. He lived with her for about nine months, until one day the friend's mother, in a moment of anger, blurted in front of neighbors that the child was a Jew. This was after the child was given milk and none remained for her. So the child had to leave, and he was taken to Marysia.

This was soon after young Marysia had left the ghetto in Warsaw under an assumed identity, as Janina Majdowska. She exited through the gate, accompanied by a Pole or a bribed Polish policeman, who took her outside of the ghetto "to work." The guards at the gate of the ghetto didn't check her thoroughly. Marysia told me that she turned to my father, Mateusz Filipowski, who collaborated with the couple Stasia and Mietek Kolski in many areas, and visited their home often. She said that Mateusz had a friend who forged documents essential for living on the Aryan side. Marysia told me that one time she asked Mateusz to prepare a forged identity card for her cousin, Leon Walicki, who was a member of the "good" AK. Mateusz asked for personal information for the document, and a half-profile photograph. The nose in the photograph looked too hooked, so Mateusz straightened it with a new razor blade, retouched the picture, and re-photographed it in a laboratory. When the man saw the new document, he shouted, "But that's not how I look!" Mateusz said there was no alternative, and that he should go to a plastic surgeon to operate on his nose in order to match the picture. And he was able to do that successfully. Mateusz also knew how to exchange gold dollars, which they had in the ghetto, for paper money. Marysia, who spoke and looked like a Pole, rented a room in Warsaw. A bit later, just before the uprising in the Warsaw Ghetto, Stasia and Mietek Kolski also helped Max Silberstein, Marysia's husband, escape from the ghetto to the Aryan side. Max, who looked suspiciously Jewish, lived in their apartment until they brought him to the Grodziński family. So Marysia took the infant Wojtuś and joined her husband at the home of the Grodziński family, who presented them to their Polish neighbors as cousins. Mietek and Stasia Kolski brought my father, Mateusz, and he built a hiding place with his own hands for Max Silberstein under the windowsill in their home, from boards and matching wallpaper to camouflage it. They watched the gate of the house, and when someone approached, Max would go into the hiding place.

Stasia, told about the uprising in August 1944 in Warsaw, "During the uprising, which erupted in Warsaw on August 1, we came to the underground power station for the trams. Thirty-eight tram personnel and twelve members of our family gathered there." The family members included: Marian Dąbrowski (Ignaś); my parents, Krystyna Łągiewska (Cesia) and Mateusz Filipowski (Moniek); Maria Tomaszewska (Helcia), Michael (Moritz) Krajewski, and their daughter Czesława (Cesia) Kowalska; Stasia and Mietek Kolski and Basia (Rena) Smarzyńska; and Stasia's cousin, Hela, her husband Michał (the policeman), and their infant Wiesio, four or five weeks old. The baby developed inside the tunnel, nursed, and when they only had water, Hela gave him just water to drink.

She told how the electricity went out later, and they walked in the dark tunnels to bring kerosene. Mietek walked behind Michał, and Stasia followed Mietek. Michał started to quarrel with Sobczyk, one of the tram workers. The kerosene spilled and Michał caught on fire and screamed in pain. Stasia thought the Germans had tossed grenades. Mietek began to put out the fire that caught hold of Michał's body, and Stasia removed his pants. Krystyna Łągiewska, my mother, took care of Michał.

According to what my father Mateusz told me, and recounted afterward, his feeling was that this quarrel arose from anti-Semitic complaints by Sobczyk and his colleagues about the presence of my mother, Ignaś, and Cesia and Mietek's parents, whom they suspected of being Jewish. This occurred in an atmosphere of severe tension, deprivation, and crowdedness. These events revisited my father as recurring nightmares. Michał was not told that Mietek and his family were Jewish, and he kept whatever he surmised to himself.

Stasia said, "Then they started to burn the coal coke in the power station – the Germans set it on fire. We wondered which way to flee: to Łódzka Street or to Grzybowska Street." Stasia decided to flee to Grzybowska Street, because she used to live there. Stasia had a few gold dollars. Mietek told her to get rid of them, because he was fearful of what the Germans would do if they found she had gold. Stasia lied to him, "I already tossed it." They reached a fence. The Germans shouted, "*Halt!*" Stasia said in Polish, "*Niech Pan nie strzela!*" ("Don't shoot, sir!") Mietek answered in German. The SS soldier commanded that they be taken out to the street. The Germans asked, "Do you know there were Romanians who shot at the insurgents, and shot well?" Four men went out - tram workers - and the Germans apparently killed them. They didn't shoot Mietek and Stasia. They ordered Mietek to inflate the tires on a car.

Earlier, Moritz said to Mietek and Stasia, "Go and save yourselves!" and they went. Cesia Kolska, Helcia, and Basia found another basement, but the Germans discovered them right away and sent them to the St. Stanisława Church.

They were now Hela, the baby and Michał (who was burned), Mateusz, Krystyna and Marian. Michał told everyone they should leave him alone. Moritz started to run in one direction and got lost. A woman said after the war that she had met him in Auschwitz, while waiting in line for coffee, and that he perished.

Hela and the infant did what Michał said and left. The Germans killed the burnt Michał. Mateusz and Krystyna wanted to take Michał out on a blanket, but the Germans told them that an ambulance would come and take him to a hospital. They didn't want to say that they would shoot him, but they later killed him. Ignaś was shoeless, and a big pair of shoes was found for him. They wrapped his feet in rags so that the feet would fit.

They assigned a soldier to guard Stasia and Mietek, and they changed the guard every hour. Later, an elderly, Polish-speaking soldier was the guard. He stood with his back to them and said, "You must have a good explanation if they take you to a court martial." At the trial, they stood alone in front of older German officers. They wanted to send Mietek to work abroad, in Germany. The court issued a ruling that the woman (Stasia) was ill and needed to be with her husband there, in Poland. Stasia was then in the early stage of pregnancy with Maryś (Myron); perhaps she didn't know yet. They were led to the court by four SS men, with bayonets drawn. A Romanian officer entered and said to Mietek, "If you were alone, they would have killed you long ago. It's only thanks to the woman that they didn't harm you."

After the trial, they sent them to the St. Karola Boromeusza Church, and they walked about four kilometers from the court to the church. There were lots of women's wallets and cards hanging on the walls, which people wrote in hope of finding relatives. The soldiers drank alcohol. Stasia asked for and received a little liqueur from them, and she drank it as food. She asked for Mietek, too, and then they gave her a little bread, canned food, and coffee. Stasia said they shouldn't eat meat, because they might get sick since they hadn't tasted meat for a long time. Afterward, they moved to the St. Stanisława Church, where they met Mietek's family: Maria (Helcia), Cesia, and Basia (Rena).

Maria, Cesia and Basia, who were together, were sent to Pruszków. A selection was conducted in Pruszków. They didn't want to take Maria Tomaszewska, but Maria volunteered to travel with her daughter Cesia to Stutthof. Basia was assigned to forced labor. At the St. Stanisława Church, Mietek and Stasia also met Cesia, Moniek, and Ignaś, as well as Hela and the baby, who were all gathered there. Later, they were sent to Pruszków; all of them were ordered to go through Pruszków. They had to travel there by tram. Mietek, Basia, and Stasia got off the tram at the Ursus station and didn't return. The stop was only for one minute, but they didn't shoot those who got off the train. Their liberation came in January 1945 in the village of Walka Kosowska (the Battle of Kosovo).

During the Polish uprising in Warsaw, Marysia and Max were separated and lost each other, and also lost contact with Stasia and Mietek. Later, Max Silberstein was found, and the Kolski couple sent him to where Marysia and Wojtuś (Eli, their son) were staying. Mateusz (Moniek) lived with them in the home of an anti-Semitic Polish policeman in a village, all under assumed Polish identities. [Stasia was not precise about this – the "village" was Gorzkowice, where Ignaś, Mateusz and Hela were staying with the baby. Later, when Mateusz returned to work at the Többens factory, he stayed with Marysia and Max in Piotrków.]

Stasia and Mietek returned to the home of Mietek's parents in Kalisz, at 11 Łazienna Street. The parents' apartment and store were occupied. Maryś was born in Kalisz on May 3, 1945, on Constitution Day, not long before the Germans signed the surrender agreement. They immediately moved to Łódz.

Stasia claimed, in regard to my mother, "Cesia returned to Kalisz from the Stutthof death camp prior to Easter 1945." According to my estimate, Mother only arrived in May or June, after Germany's surrender that is, shortly after the birth of Maryś. But Stasia might be correct in regard to what she remembered about Maryś' date of birth and her return. I remember traveling with my parents to visit Stasia, Mietek and the baby Maryś in Łódź, not long after that 'historic birth'. Then, in the clinic in Łódź, an operation was conducted to remove an inflammatory polyp in my troublesome nose, which had been responsible for revealing our hiding place in Mrs. Kuropieska's apartment.

Stasia said that in the death march from Stutthof, Helcia and Cesia Kolska were loaded onto motorless rafts, and there were no sea vessels to pull them. There were Poles, Russians, and Norwegians on the rafts, and they ripped off boards to row in the sea. The rafts were bombed by the English or Americans. When they reached the coast of Sweden, after the nightmarish sea voyage, a narrow board or beam was lowered from the raft to the shore, and Helcia walked along the beam to the shore "like a circus acrobat" (*"byłam cyrkówką"*). Stasia said that my mother had left the camp earlier on the land death march.

Of the family from Kalisz, for whom Stasia and Mietek served as a hub, everyone survived through courage and grace, except for Moritz Kolski. Stasia served as an active contact person for them, taking initiative and providing strong Aryan-Catholic cover vis-à-vis the neighbors. From her family, she lost Michał the husband of her cousin Hela and the father of the baby Wiesio.

In a telephone conversation with Stasia on May 23, 2004, after submitting a request and testimony to Yad Vashem to renew processing of Stasia Kolski's recognition as Righteous Among the Nations, I asked her about other members of our family with whom she was in contact on the Aryan side in Warsaw. She mentioned Herman Bloch, the husband of Bala Bloch, my mother's sister, who was apparently dead already. He hid in Bródno, a neighborhood in Warsaw. Stasia said that people saw him in Stutthof after the Polish uprising. He apparently died there or during the death march. Józef Jabłoński is the one who built the hideout in the apartment of his daughter, Leopolda Kuropieska.

Stasia died about four months after receiving the recognition. According to her request, she was brought for burial to a section for Polish immigrants near Philadelphia, Pennsylvania. A priest conducted the burial ceremony in Polish, and her son Myron (Maryś), who had converted to Judaism, recited the *kaddish* prayer. Two representatives of the Israeli consulate in Miami also participated in the funeral. Stasia had arranged for Helcia, Mietek, and Cesia to be buried in a Jewish cemetery in New Jersey, and she visited there many times.

Excerpts from this interview were presented to Yad Vashem as part of the process of receiving recognition as Righteous Among the Nations, an honor awarded to Stanisława Kolski in December 2005.

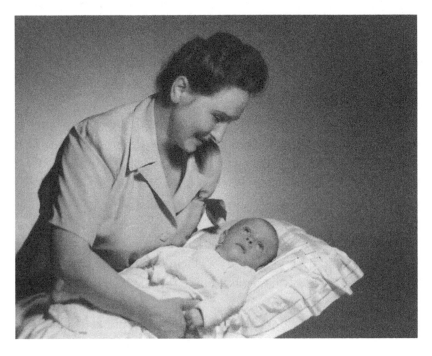

Stanisława-Stasia Kolska and Maryś, Kalisz, May 1945.

FAMILY MEMBERS AND OTHERS MENTIONED IN THE BOOK

Abram (1901-1957). Son of Shmuel and Devorah. Husband of Bronka and father of Rysiek, and of Berta, older brother of Moshe. Entrepreneur and manufacturer in Kalisz, Warsaw, Łódz, and Tel Aviv. Held hostage by the Germans in Warsaw. Arrived in Palestine during the war.

Ala. See Bloch, Sheindel-Shlomit.

Berta (born in 1939). Daughter of Abram and Bronka, sister of Rysiek, niece of Moshe, and cousin of Itzhak and Yoseph.

Bloch, Marek (1934-1943). Son of Ala and Salomon Bloch, nephew of Moshe, and cousin of Itzhak and Yoseph. Perished in the Warsaw Ghetto during the uprising in the ghetto.

Bloch, Ninka-Yocheved (1931-1943). Daughter of Ala and Salomon Bloch, niece of Moshe, and cousin of Itzhak and Yoseph. Perished in the Warsaw Ghetto during the uprising in the ghetto. Composed a poem of testimony.

Bloch, Salomon (Samek) (1905-1987). Husband of Ala, sister of Moshe, and father of Ninka-Yocheved and Marek, who were imprisoned in the Warsaw Ghetto while he was a captive in the Oflag Woldenberg in Germany. A source of testimonies and family letters from the Warsaw Ghetto, from pre-state Israel, and more.

Bloch, Sheindel-Shlomit (Ala) (1907-1943). Daughter of Shmuel and Devorah, wife of Salomon and mother of Ninka-Yocheved and Marek, and sister of Moshe. The book includes excerpts from her letters from the Warsaw Ghetto to her husband in Oflag Woldenberg in Germany. She perished in the Warsaw Ghetto during the time of the uprising.

Bronka. Abram's wife. She remained in the Warsaw Ghetto with her children and hosted in their apartment Ala Bloch and Regina Ganzweich and their children. She arrived with her children from the Hotel Polski to Bergen-Belsen after fleeing the ghetto to the Aryan side. She later immigrated to the Land of Israel with her children. She died in 1973.

Cesia-Cyrel, "Krystyna Łągiewska" (1911-1975). Daughter of Itzhak Leib and Esther Jarecki, wife of Moshe, mother of Itzhak and Yoseph Komem.

Key figure in the saga of the nuclear family's survival.

Cukierman, Icchak ('Antek') (1915-1981). One of the top commanders of the ŻOB in the Warsaw Ghetto uprising. Also active in distributing money to Jews hiding on the Aryan side.

Daub, Gustav (born 1902). German master craftsman (*Meister*) and lace pattern designer in Kalisz. Assigned responsibility (*Treuhänder*) for the lace industry during the occupation of the city.

Fryde Jakub-Jan (Janek) (1918-1992). Lieutenant in the Red Army, second husband of Frania Jarecki; they married after the war in Kalisz. They lived in Poland, and later in Israel.

Fuks, Alexander (1910-1973). The in-law of Moshe (Moniek) and Cesia, and father of Azriela Komem; a knitting machine expert and technical manager of Aryeh Shenkar's Lodzia factory in Tel Aviv and later in Holon.

Fuks, Esther (1908-1992), née Synaiko. Wife of Alexander, fled with her small daughters, Ora and Azriela, from occupied Łódz to the Land of Israel.

Ganzweich, Hersch. Husband of Moshe's sister Regina, father of Janka and Rutka (Ruth). All traces of him were lost at the beginning of the war, after he fled with his family to the east.

Ganzweich, Janka and Rutka. Daughters of Regina and Hersch Ganzweich, nieces of Moshe, cousins of Itzhak and Yoseph Komem, perished in the Warsaw Ghetto with their mother in 1942.

Ganzweich, Rivka-Regina (perished in 1942). Daughter of Shmuel and Devorah and sister of Moshe. Wife of Hersch Ganzweich and mother of Janka and Rutka. The mother and her daughters died in an act of desperation in the Warsaw Ghetto.

Gardziel, Feliksa. Wife of Jan Bolesław. Landlady of Cesia-"Krystyna" and Yoseph-"Marek" in Brzesko.

Gardziel-Irzabek, Janina (1924-2006). Daughter of Jan Bolesław and Feliksa Gardziel from Brzesko. She gave her account in an interview.

Gardziel, Jan Bolesław (1891-1942). Teacher and choir conductor in the Brzesko high school. Murdered in Auschwitz.

Gardziel, Julian (born 1931). Son of Jan Bolesław and Feliksa. He gave his account in an interview.

Helena (Helcia) Jarecki-Kolski. See Kolski, Helena.

Herbert, Antoni and Marta. Deaf bookbinder and his hearing wife. Became friends with Moshe in Brzesko and helped his family. The connection was made upon the recommendation of Mr. Roman Jaworski, the deaf bookbinder from Kraków.

Jaffe, Elias (1924-2008). Grandson of David Jaffe, brother of Sabina Jaffe-Lavidor. Fought as a bomber pilot in the RAF. Gave testimony.

Jaffe-Kott, Hendel-Hela (1899-1966). Wife of Yosef-Haim (son of David) Jaffe, mother of Elias and Sabina. Deported to Mauritius.

Jaffe-Lavidor, Sabina (Born 1930). Sister of Elias Jaffe. Clandestinely immigrated to Palestine on the *Atlantic* ship and was imprisoned with her mother, Hendel-Hela, on the island of Mauritius. Interviewed.

Jarecki-Jaffe, Cyrel. Daughter of Shime Jaffe and Freide (née Daum), the first wife of Itzhak Leib Jarecki. Mother of Helena (Helcia) Kolski and her siblings.

Jarecki-Jaffe, Esther (born 1877). Daughter of Shime Jaffe and Freide (née Daum), the second wife of Itzhak Leib Jarecki. Mother of Cesia (mother of Itzhak and Yoseph Komem) and of Cesia's siblings.

Jarecki-Fryde, Frania-Frańciszka, "Mila" (1913-1997). Daughter of Itzhak Leib and Esther Jarecki. Cesia's younger sister. A key figure in the story of the family survival. Benek Wartski, Frania's first husband, was murdered in Sandomierz. Frania married Jan Fryde after the war.

Jarecki, Itzhak Leib (1866-1924). Son of Meir and Ita Chana. Husband of Cyrel and, after her death, husband of her sister Esther; both were daughters of Shimon (Shime) and Freide Jaffe. Father of Cesia (mother of Itzhak and Yoseph Komem). Lived in Kalisz.

Jaworski, Roman. Husband of Julia. Deaf bookbinder from Kraków, helped after the two escapes from the Sandomierz Ghetto, a friend of Antoni Herbert in Brzesko.

Kałuszko, Jan. Righteous Among the Nations (1983). Son of Zofja Kałuszko, and partner in her actions.

Kałuszko, Zofja. Righteous Among the Nations (1983). She hid Moritz and Cesia Kolski, Dr. J. Sack, and other Jews in her apartment in Warsaw at 19 Ciepła Street.

Kerszner, Bela. Wife of Leon Kerszner. Cousin of our mother Cesia. Emigrated to France prior to 1939.

Kerszner, Leon (1906-1976). Emigrated from Poland to France, husband of Bela, saved his family thanks to his activity in the Resistance in Paris.

Kerszner, Marcel (born 1940). Son of Leon and Bela Kerszner from France. Gave testimony in an interview.

Kolski, Helena (Helcia) "Maria Tomaszewska" (1889-1972). Daughter of Itzhak Leib and Cyrel Jarecki from Kalisz, mother of Mietek and Cesia, older sister of our mother Cesia. Survived in Warsaw and in Stutthof.

Kolski, Moritz "Michael Krajewski." From Kalisz. Father of Mietek and Cesia, husband of Helena-Helcia. Murdered in early 1945 at Auschwitz.

Kolski, Naftali (Nafcio) Mendel "Mieczysław (Mietek) Kolski" (1912-1976). Son of Moritz and Helena-Helcia. Key figure in the family 'underground' in Warsaw. See testimony of his sister Cesia Kolski-Virshup and the memoirs of Moshe (Moniek).

Kolski, Roman. From the city of Łódz, father of Rena ("Basia Smarzyńska"), brother of Moritz Kolski. Murdered with his wife in Rembertów in May 1943.

Kolski-Rzeszewski, Rena "Basia Smarzyńska" (1927-2008). Daughter of Roman Kolski, lived with Mietek and Stasia in their apartment after the murder of her parents.

Kolski Stanisława (Stasia), née Rogińska (1912-2005). Wife of Naftali -"Mieczysław" (Mietek). Righteous Among the Nations (2005). Primary interviewee – appears in chapter of memories.

Kolski-Virshup, Cesia "Czesława Kowalski" (1917-1995). Daughter of Moritz and Helena (Helcia) Kolski, sister of Naftali (Mietek). Primary testimony in the chapters of her memories from Kalisz, Warsaw, and the Stutthof camp.

Komem, Azriela (born 1939). Daughter of Alexander and Esther Fuks, wife of Yoseph Komem. Smuggled in her mother's arms from occupied Łódz to Mandatory Palestine.

Komem, Itzhak (Ignaś) "Marian (Maryś) Dąbrowski" (1935-2014). Son of Moshe and Cesia; author of primary chapters of testimony, which were summarized in this book.

Komem, Sharona (born 1937). Daughter of David and Pnina Igra, wife of Itzhak Komem, survived with her parents in Lwów and in the Bergen-Belsen camp.

Komem, Yoseph (Jurek) "Marek Łągiewski" (born 1936). Son of Moshe and Cesia; editor of primary chapters of testimony and author of the book.

Kowalski, Marta (1910-1988). Wife of Stanisław Kowalski, active in the AK underground in Sandomierz.

Kowalski, Stanisław (Staszek) (1912-1969). Resident of Sandomierz, helped our father Moshe, mother Cesia and Yoseph-"Marek" in Sandomierz, in Brzesko and in Kraków at critical junctions and fateful situations, without any recompense. Member of the AK underground.

Kowalski-Kamys, Ryszarda (born 1937). Oldest daughter of Stanisław and Marta Kowalski. Interviewee in Sandomierz.

Krzyczkowski. A Polish acquaintance from Kalisz. Helped Frania and Itzhak on the Aryan side in Warsaw. Itzhak and Cesia lived with him in his apartment there.

Küchler-Silberman, Lena-Leah (1910-1987). Educator, writer ("My Hundred Children" and more), and a renowned educational psychologist. Founded and managed an orphanage for children survivors in Zakopane (Poland) and later in Bellevue (France), and was active in Israel.

Kuropieska, General Józef (1904-1998). Husband of Leopolda. Professional officer, statesman and writer. POW in Oflag Woldenberg, socialist Poland's military attaché in Britain, sentenced to death for "treason" during the Stalin's purges, commander of the Warsaw Military District.

Kuropieska, Leopolda, née Jabłoński (1906-1980). Righteous Among the Nations (1967). Hid Itzhak and Yoseph Komem, as well as other Jews, in her apartment in Warsaw, under particularly difficult conditions. In 1946, she brought Itzhak to live with her family in London.

Kuropieska-Kuczmierowski, Barbara (1932-1993). Daughter of Józef and Leopolda, Full partner in her mother's actions. Interviewee.

Kuropieska, Wojciech (Wojtek) (born 1934). Son of Józef and Leopolda. Full partner in his mother's actions. Interviewee.

Lieberman, David. Acquaintance from Kalisz. Appears in the interview section about the partnership with Moshe installing blackout blinds in Sandomierz.

Lifshitz-Schönbach, Hela (1912-2004). Friend of our mother Cesia. A senior employee in the family factory in Kalisz. Played a key role in rescue actions. The book includes excerpts of three interviews.

Łoza, Eugeniusz (Geniek) (1921-2001). Son of Stefania and Bazyli. The deaf man who put Moshe ("Mateusz") in contact with the Łoza family. Righteous Among the Nations (1983). Resident of Słotwina-Brzesko and Zakopane.

Łoza-Nowak, Irena (1915-1999). Daughter of Stefania and Bazyli. Righteous Among the Nations (1983). Resident of Brzesko. She and her family took care of Yoseph ("Marek") Komem, posing as a Catholic Pole, in Słotwina-Brzesko, until after liberation.

Łoza-Skrobotowicz, Helena (1925-2010). Daughter of Stefania and Bazyli Łoza. Resident of Brzesko. Righteous Among the Nations (2000). Primary interviewee.

Łoza, Stefania (1890-1987). Righteous Among the Nations (1983). Resident of Słotwina-Brzesko. Mother of Irena, Eugeniusz and Helena.

Markiewicz. Veteran weaver in the family factory in Kalisz. Hid "Marian" – Itzhak (Ignaś) Komem near Warsaw.

Michał. A Polish policeman, husband of Hela, cousin of Stasia Kolski, and father of the infant Wiesio. Burned and shot during the Polish uprising in Warsaw.

Mietek. See Kolski, Naftali-Mendel.

Moked (Munwes), Prof. Gabriel. Son of Dr. Jakub and Madzia Munwes.

Moshe (Moniek) "Mateusz Filipowski" (1911-1987). Son of Shmuel and Devorah. Deaf. Husband of Cesia and father of Itzhak and Yoseph Komem. Recorded primary memoirs-testimony.

Munwes, Madzia. Widow of Dr. Jakub Munwes (a doctor at the "na Czystem Jewish Hospital" and later in the hospital on Gęsia Street in the Warsaw Ghetto) and the mother of Prof. Gabriel Moked. Our mother Cesia's cousin from Warsaw, from the Jarecki family. Hid with her son on the Aryan side of Warsaw.

Rysiek, son of Abram and Bronka (born 1935). Nephew of Moshe and cousin of Itzhak and Yoseph. Submitted information about his family in the Warsaw Ghetto, Aryan Warsaw, Otwock, and the Bergen-Belsen camp.

Sack, Dr. Józef. Member of Jewish Fighting Organization (ŻOB). One of the founders of the Anti-Fascist Bloc in the Warsaw Ghetto in March 1942 as a representative of the Poalei Zion socialist movement. Hid together with Moritz and Cesia Kolski in the apartment of Zofja and Jan Kałuszko in Aryan Warsaw.

Salomonowicz, Pola. Daughter of Itzhak Leib Jarecki, Cesia's older sister, who lived in the Land of Israel.

Shem-Shmuel, Devorah (1879-1971) née Rosenwald. Wife of Shmuel, mother of Moshe, Abram, and their sisters, grandmother of Itzhak and Yoseph Komem.

Shem-Shmuel, Shmuel Hacohen (1882-1959). Father of Moshe (Moniek), Abram, and their sisters, grandfather of Itzhak and Yoseph Komem. Well-known entrepreneur and manufacturer in Kalisz; built Bauhaus homes in Tel Aviv and the Tova lace curtain factory in Bnei Brak. The book includes excerpts from his typewritten memoirs.

Silberstein, Marysia "Janina Majdowska" (1915-2005). Mother of the infant Eli (born in 1941). A niece of Max Kolski. Interviewed in New Jersey in September 2002.

Silberstein, Max (died in 1993). Husband of Marysia and father of the infant Eli. He hid in Aryan Warsaw. Moshe built a hiding place for him.

Staendner. A German designer of lace patterns, from Plauen. Supported the employment of Moshe at the family factory in Kalisz during the Nazi occupation, and helped Moshe.

Walfisz, Arnold (Noldek) "Roman Woźniak" (1918-1943). The first husband of Cesia Kolski-Virshup; they married at the worksite in Warsaw in Pelcowizna. He was recruited or volunteered for ŻOB and ŻZW activity in Aryan Warsaw. He fell into the hands of the Gestapo (and apparently committed suicide with poison) the day after the battle at 11 Grzybowska Street, where four Germans were killed and where the ŻZW commander Pawel Frankel and his comrades fell; others were captured there and later executed.

Wartski, Benjamin (Benek). First husband of Frania Jarecki, they married in Kalisz. He was murdered in Sandomierz on March 31, 1942.

Wasserman, Alexander. A Jewish worker posing as a Pole in the Többens factory in Warsaw and in Piotrków. He apparently was expelled from Kalisz to Warsaw.

Wassermann, Oscar (1903-1983). Deaf friend of Moshe and of Roman Jaworski in Kraków. His wife, Paula, studied with Moshe at a Jewish school for the deaf in Vienna.

MORE FROM THIS SERIES

I Only Wanted to Live *by Arie Tamir*

For 6 long torturous years the only thing that kept Leosz safe in the whirlwind of the Holocaust was his unwavering will to live. This is the incredible and inspiring story of a 6-year-old boy who managed to survive all possible levels of hell by clinging on to life.

Lalechka *by Amira Keidar*

A little girl, smuggled out of a Ghetto by her parents. Two brave women, willing to risk their lives. An inspirational story of survival based on the unique journal written by the girl's mother during the annihilation of the ghetto.

The Strange Ways of Providence in My Life *by Krystyna Carmi*

Krystyna Carmi's childhood in 1930's Poland was full of happy moments. But her happy childhood did not last long. The second world war brought disasters upon her and the Jewish community. The death of her parents and sisters, hiding, hunger, thirst and fear for life. It might be easier to part with the world, but the strange ways of providence of her life have chosen for her to live. A remarkable true story of survival against all odds.

Raking Light from Ashes *by Relli Robinson*

When Relli was just a baby, the Nazis occupied Poland and she, together with her parents, was imprisoned in the Warsaw Ghetto, a final station before death. This is the amazing story of a young Jewish girl holding a false identity, who was able to overcome the most difficult times in the history of humankind thanks to kindhearted, courageous people and a tenacious capacity for survival.

YOU MIGHT ALSO BE INTERESTED IN :
Best selling World War II Historical Novels

Surviving the Forest *by Adiva Geffen*

Shurka, her husband and their two children lived a fairytale life in their idyllic village in Poland. Or so they thought… When WWII breaks out, they are forced to flee their home and escape into the dark forest. There, surrounded by animals, they know that this is their only hope of hiding from the real beasts. They have no idea what awaits them, but they know that doing nothing is not an option if they want to survive.

Escaping on the Danube River *by Shmuel David*

Europe, 1939: As the Nazi threat becomes a terrifying reality, Hanne and Inge know that their only option to survive is a daring escape down the Danube river. But their journey becomes increasingly perilous as time goes by. On board a ship, they fall in love, but their desire to build a new life together is in serious danger…

My Name is Vittoria *by Dafna Vitale Ben Bassat*

Vittoria is a noble Jewish woman living in northern Italy. When the Nazis invade her quiet town, She and her family are forced to flee and cross the border under fake identities. But not everything goes according to plan. One of her children is not allowed to cross the border with the rest of the family and must be left behind. Now, Vittoria must make a critical decision that could scar her and her family forever.

The Jewish Spy *by Hayuta Katzenelson*

Poland 1938. Rivka sends her husband and three beloved children to the United States, where they will find safe shelter from the war. She tells everyone that she is staying behind to care for her aging parents, but in reality her motive for remaining in Poland is entirely different. Beyond her work as librarian, Rivka serves as a spy for the Jewish underground. Rivka's brave choice may come at a painful price - losing her own family.

A Hungarian Portrait *by Orly Krauss-Winer*

Hungary, 1944. Yoshke's life is thrown into disarray. His wife Martha's friend, a Nazi recruit, makes a split-second decision to send him to Mauthausen Concentration Camp, a decision that may seal his fate. Martha, stunned and hurt, refuses to forget. Israel, present. The sudden illness of her sister Noa forces Daria to attain a significant sum of money for an urgent operation, and she is at a loss. However, their family's past during the WWII Holocaust holds an old secret that could be the answer to her problem. What will she be willing risk to save her little sister's life?

Made in United States
North Haven, CT
07 April 2022